SELECT

EARLY AMEl ....

1607-1800

EDITED BY

WILLIAM B. CAIRNS

ASSISTANT PROFESSOR OF AMERICAN LITERATURE
IN THE UNIVERSITY OF WISCONSIN

New York

THE MACMILLAN COMPANY

1909

Norwood Press
J. S. Cushing Co. — Berwick & Smith Co.
Norwood, Mass., U.S.A.

PREFACE

THIS volume contains selections from the works of representative American writers before Washington Irving. It is intended for use in the class-room by students who are making a fairly detailed study of American literature, and for reference and assigned reading by those whose work is more elementary or more cursory. A book of extracts always offers a poor substitute for access to complete works; but since a fairly good library of early American writings can be found in only a few cities of the country, a collection like that which follows seems to have some reason for existence.

Teachers of American literary history are coming pretty generally to recognize that some knowledge of the temper and the manner of Colonial and Revolutionary writers is necessary to the full understanding of their successors. There is less general agreement, however, as to the authors and works that best repay study. In deciding what to include in this volume I have been guided to a great extent by my own experience with college classes, though I have given much weight to suggestions kindly offered by the publishers and by other teachers. My aim has been to make the collection representative and useful for its purpose, not necessarily to give the best writings of the time. Thus, Cotton and Shepard have proved in my experience well adapted to stand as representatives of the early New England divines; but I am not rash enough to say with certainty that either of these men was greater than Hooker, Eliot, or others of their contemporaries. In some cases it will be obvious that I have chosen passages to show a writer's weakness, as well as his excellences. I cannot hope that the collection will suit any one person, but I trust that it may contain enough acceptable material to make it useful.

Although it is unlikely that a book of selections will be made the basis of any scholarly research, I have felt bound to make the text as accurate as possible. It has not always been practicable to make extracts from the latest edition revised by the author, or from original manuscripts of works not printed in the author's lifetime. I have tried, however, in every case to follow an edition sufficiently accurate to serve most of the purposes of a student engaged in careful investigation. The texts chosen I have endeavored, with a few exceptions, to reproduce as closely as ordinary typographical devices would allow. The use of the long "s," the interchange of "u" and "v," "i" and "j," and such manuscript abbreviations as "y^e" for "the" and "com̄on" for "common," have not seemed worth perpetuating. In all other respects the original spelling, capitalization, punctuation, etc., have been followed. Corrections of obvious typographical errors have usually been enclosed in brackets, as have emended readings, whether suggested by myself or by an earlier editor. Footnotes not by the author are also enclosed in brackets. The titles of most selections have, necessarily, been given by the editor; titles in the words of the author are enclosed in quotation marks in the Table of Contents. As the book may be used in mixed classes in secondary schools two brief and unimportant passages have been omitted on the ground of impropriety. These omissions are indicated in the proper places.

For kind permission to follow copyrighted reprints I am indebted to G. P. Putnam's Sons, publishers of Conway's edition of the writings of Thomas Paine, Ford's edition of the works of Jefferson, and Lodge's edition of the works of Hamilton; to Doubleday, Page & Co., publishers of Bassett's edition of the writings of William Byrd; to the Library of Princeton University, publishers of Pattee's edition of Freneau; to Mr. Charles Francis Adams, editor, and the Prince Society, publisher, of writings of Thomas Morton and John Cotton; and to Mr. Sidney S. Rider, editor and publisher of Peter Folger's "A Looking Glass for the Times," in the Rhode Island Historical Tracts. I also wish to express my thanks to the Library of Harvard University for the privilege of using, in Wisconsin, three or four rare and much needed volumes.

W. B. C.

UNIVERSITY OF WISCONSIN,
　　January, 1909.

CONTENTS

CONTENTS

SELECTIONS FROM
EARLY AMERICAN WRITERS
1607–1800

JOHN SMITH

[Captain John Smith was born in Willoughby, Lincolnshire, in 1580 (1579, O.S.). He was apprenticed to a merchant, but, finding a life of trade too tame, he ran away at the age of fifteen and became a soldier of fortune. During the next ten or eleven years he visited, if we may trust his own account, most parts of Europe where adventures might be found, and fought

"As wel in Christendom as in hethenesse."

In 1605 he was again in England, and a year and a half later he went out with the colonists who finally landed at Jamestown. Here he appears, both in his own accounts and in those of his fellow-colonists, as a rough-and-ready, energetic man, always in trouble, but probably the most practical and capable manager in the new settlement. He remained in Virginia until 1609, when he returned to England. In 1614 he made a voyage of exploration to the coast of New England; and the next year he started for that region with a colonizing party, but was captured and imprisoned by the French. After his release he lived quietly in England until his death in 1631.

While he was in Virginia Captain Smith wrote only two works of importance. The first was very likely begun soon after the colonists landed in 1607, and was sent to England early in 1608. It was published the same year under the title of "A True Relation of such occurrences and accidents of noate as hath hapned in Virginia since the first planting of that Collony, which is now resident in the South part thereof, till the last returne from thence." The second work, "A Map of Virginia, with a Description of the Countrey the Commodities, People, Government and Religion," was probably sent to England a few months later than the "True Relation" but was not published until 1612. At the same time with the "Map of Virginia," Captain Smith sent an interesting and outspoken letter in reply to the demands of the proprietors for money from the colony. After his return to England he wrote a number of works, among the more important of which were "A Description of New England" (1616), "New Englands Trials" (1620-22), "The General Historie of Virginia" (1624), "The True Travels, Adventures, and Observations of Captaine John Smith" (1630). In strictness only the "True Relation" and the "Map of Virginia" have a place in a collection of American writings, but brief selections from "A Description of New England" and the "True Travels" are given in the following pages for the sake of comparison.

Much of the criticism of Smith's writings has taken the form of discussions regarding his veracity. Some of the early exploits narrated in the "True Travels" are so marvellous as to seem improbable. Many of the statements in the writings on Virginia are corroborated by the independent testimony of others; but circumstantial evidence seems to discredit the familiar story of his rescue by Pocahontas. In his earlier accounts of his visit to Powhatan, Smith speaks of that chieftain as uniformly friendly, and refers, incidentally, to Pocahontas as a mere child. It was not till the Indian "princess," as the wife of John Rolfe, was attracting attention in London, while Smith was living in comparative obscurity, that he linked his name with hers in the anecdote that has become famous. In many cases no positive proof or disproof of Smith's statements is possible. But, though Mr. Edward Arber, the conscientious editor of all his writings, believes in his absolute truthfulness, it seems probable that in his later years he availed himself of the soldier's and traveller's privilege and magnified his own exploits.

The first American writer was typical of those Elizabethan Englishmen who were primarily men of action, and incidentally men of letters. The "True Relation" and the "Map of Virginia" were in no sense works of literature, but simply businesslike reports of the doings of the colonists, and descriptions of the country that they had found. The former was probably written for the information of the proprietors, with no thought of its publication. Some of the later works were undertaken with a less immediate practical aim. There is no evidence that the author had ever tried to write before he came to Jamestown, and the style of the "True Relation" indicates that it is the work of a novice in the art. Even the "Map of Virginia," written only a few months later, shows a decided advance in style; and some of the later works, produced with greater leisure and after more practice, have in passages here and there the sonorous effectiveness of the better Elizabethan prose.

The selections here given are from the complete edition of Smith's writings edited by Edward Arber. Except for changes in paragraphing and occasionally in punctuation, the text is that of the first editions of the respective works.]

THE BEGINNINGS OF JAMESTOWN

[From the "True Relation," etc.]

Kinde Sir, commendations remembred, &c. You shall understand that after many crosses in the downes by tempests, wee arrived safely uppon the Southwest part of the great Canaries: within foure or five daies after we set saile for Dominica, the 26. of Aprill: the first land we made, wee fell with Cape Henry, the verie mouth of the Bay of *Chissiapiacke*, which at that present we little expected, having by a cruell storme bene put to the Northward:

Anchoring in this Bay twentie or thirtie went a shore with the Captain, and in comming aboard, they were assalted with certaine Indians, which charged them within Pistoll shot: in which conflict, Captaine *Archer* and *Mathew Morton* were shot: wherupon Captaine *Newport* seconding them, made a shot at them, which the Indians little respected, but having spent their arrowes retyred without harme. And in that place was the Box opened, wherin the Counsell for *Virginia* was nominated: and arriving at the place where wee are now seated, the Counsell was sworn, and the President elected, which for that yeare was Maister *Edm. Maria Wingfield,* where was made choice for our scituation, a verie fit place for the erecting of a great cittie, about which some contention passed betwixt Captaine *Wingfield* and Captaine *Gosnold:* notwithstanding, all our provision was brought a shore, and with as much speede as might bee wee went about our fortification.

The two and twenty day of Aprill, Captain *Newport* and my selfe with divers others, to the number of twenty two persons, set forward to discover the River, some fiftie or sixtie miles, finding it in some places broader, and in some narrower, the Countrie (for the moste part) on each side plaine high ground, with many fresh Springes, the people in all places kindely intreating us, daunsing and feasting us with strawberries, Mulberries, Bread, Fish, and other their Countrie provisions wherof we had plenty: for which Captaine *Newport* kindely requited their least favours with Bels, Pinnes, Needles, beades, or Glasses, which so contented them that his liberallitie made them follow us from place to place, and ever kindely to respect us. In the midway staying to refresh our selves in a little Ile, foure or five savages came unto us which described unto us the course of the River, and after in our journey, they often met us, trading with us for such provision as wee had, and ariving at *Arsatecke*, hee whom we supposed to bee the chiefe King of all the rest, moste kindely entertained us, giving us in a guide to go with us up the River to *Powhatan*, of which place their great Emperor taketh his name, where he that they honored for King used us kindely. But to finish this discoverie, we passed on further, where within a mile we were intercepted with great

craggy stones in the midst of the river, where the water falleth
so rudely, and with such a violence, as not any boat can possibly
passe, and so broad disperseth the streame, as there is not past
five or sixe Foote at a low water, and to the shore scarce passage
with a barge, the water floweth foure foote, and the freshes by
reason of the Rockes have left markes of the inundations 8. or
9. foote: The south side is plaine low ground, and the north side
high mountaines, the rockes being of a gravelly nature, interlaced
with many vains of glistring spangles.

That night we returned to *Powhatan:* the next day (being Whit-
sunday after dinner) we returned to the fals, leaving a mariner
in pawn with the Indians for a guide of theirs, hee that they honoured for King followed us by the river. That afternoone we
trifled in looking upon the Rockes and river (further he would
not goe) so there we erected a crosse, and that night taking our
man at *Powhatans*, Captaine *Newport* congratulated his kindenes
with a Gown and a Hatchet: returning to *Arsetecke*, and stayed
there the next day to observe the height therof, and so with many
signes of love we departed.

AN ADVENTURE WITH THE INDIANS

[From the " True Relation "]

Having 2 Indians for my guide and 2 of our own company, I
set forward, leaving 7 in the barge:

Having discovered 20 miles further in this desart, the river stil
kept his depth and bredth, but much more combred with trees:

Here we went ashore (being some 12 miles higher then the barge
had bene) to refresh our selves, during the boyling of our vituals:
One of the Indians I tooke with me, to see the nature of the soile,
and to crosse the boughts of the river: the other Indian I left with
Maister *Robbinson* and *Thomas Emry*, with their matches lighted,
and order to discharge a peece, for my retreat, at the first sight of
any Indian.

But within a quarter of a houre I heard a loud cry, and a
hollowing of Indians, but no warning peece. Supposing them
surprised, and that the Indians had betraid us, presently I seazed

him and bound his arme fast to my hand in a garter, with my pistoll ready bent to be revenged on him: he advised me to fly, and seemed ignorant of what was done.

But as we went discoursing, I was struck with an arrow on the right thigh, but without harme: upon this occasion I espied 2. Indians drawing their bowes, which I prevented in discharging a french pistoll: .

By that I had charged againe, 3 or 4 more did the like: for the first fell downe and fled: At my discharge, they did the like. My hinde I made my barricado, who offered not to strive. 20. or 30. arrowes were shot at me but short. 3 or 4 times I had discharged my pistoll ere the king of *Pamaunck* called *Opeckankenough* with 200 men, invironed me, eache drawing their bowe: which done they laid them upon the ground, yet without shot:

My hinde treated betwixt them and me of conditions of peace; he discovred me to be the Captaine: my request was to retire to the boate: they demaunded my armes, the rest they saide were slaine, onely me they would reserve:

The Indian importuned me not to shoot. In retiring being in the midst of a low quagmire, and minding them more than my steps, I stept fast into the quagmire, and also the Indian in drawing me forth:

Thus surprised, I resolved to trie their mercies: my armes I caste from me, till which none durst approch me.

Being ceazed on me, they drew me out and led me to the King. I presented him with a compasse diall, describing by my best meanes the use therof: whereat he so amazedly admired, as he suffered me to proceed in a discourse of the roundnes of the earth, the course of the sunne, moone, starres and plannets.

With kinde speeches and bread he requited me, conducting me where the Canow lay and *John Robbinson* slaine, with 20 or 30. arrowes in him. *Emry* I saw not.

I perceived by the aboundance of fires all over the woods,[1] At each place I expected when they would execute me, yet they used me with what kindnes they could:

Approaching their Towne, which was within 6 miles where I

[1 The text is unintelligible here. Arber supplies some such expression as "that they were a party hunting deer."]

was taken, onely made as arbors and covered with mats, which they remove as occasion requires: all the women and children, being advertised of this accident, came foorth to meet them, the King well guarded with 20 bowmen 5 flanck and rear, and each flanck before him a sword and a peece, and after him the like, then a bowman, then I on each hand a boweman, the rest in file in the reare, which reare led foorth a mongst the trees in a bishion, eache his bowe and a handfull of arrowes, a quiver at his back grimly painted: on eache flanck a sargeant, the one running alwaies towards the front, the other towards the reare, each a true pace and in exceeding good order.

This being a good time continued, they caste themselves in a ring with a daunce, and so eache man departed to his lodging.

The Captain conducting me to his lodging, a quarter of Venison and some ten pound of bread I had for supper: what I left was reserved for me, and sent with me to my lodging:

Each morning 3. women presented me three great platters of fine bread, more venison than ten men could devour I had: my gowne, points and garters, my compas and my tablet they gave me again. Though 8 ordinarily guarded me, I wanted not what they could devise to content me: and still our longer acquaintance increased our better affection:

Much they threatned to assault our forte, as they were solicited by the King of *Paspahegh*: who shewed at our fort great signes of sorrow for this mischance. The King tooke great delight in understanding the manner of our ships, and sayling the seas, the earth and skies, and of our God: what he knew of the dominions he spared not to acquaint me with, as of certaine men cloathed at a place called *Ocanahonan*, cloathed like me: the course of our river, and that within 4 or 5 daies journey of the falles, was a great turning of salt water:

I desired he would send a messenger to *Paspahegh*, with a letter I would write, by which they shold understand how kindly they used me, and that I was well, least they should revenge my death. This he granted and sent three men, in such weather as in reason were unpossible by any naked to be indured. Their cruell mindes towards the fort I had deverted, in describing the ordinance and the mines in the fields, as also the revenge Captain

Newport would take of them at his returne. Their intent, I incerted the fort, the people of *Ocanahonum* and the back sea: this report they after found divers Indians that confirmed:

The next day after my letter, came a salvage to my lodging, with his sword, to have slaine me: but being by my guard intercepted, with a bowe and arrow he offred to have effected his purpose: the cause I knew not, till the King understanding thereof came and told me of a man a dying, wounded with my pistoll: he tould me also of another I had slayne, yet the most concealed they had any hurte: This was the father of him I had slayne, whose fury to prevent, the King presently conducted me to another Kingdome, upon the top of the next northerly river, called *Youghtanan*.

Having feasted me he further led me to another branch of the river, called *Mattapament;* to two other hunting townes they led me: and to each of these Countries, a house of the great Emperour of *Pewhakan,* whom as yet I supposed to bee at the *Fals;* to him I tolde him I must goe, and so returne to *Paspahegh.*

After this foure or five dayes march, we returned to *Rasawrack,* the first towne they brought me too: where binding the Mats in bundels, they marched two dayes journey, and crossed the River of *Youghtanan,* where it was as broad as *Thames:* so conducting me to a place called *Menapacute* in *Pamaunke,* where the King inhabited.

The next day another King of that nation called *Kekataugh,* having received some kindnes of me at the Fort, kindly invited me to feast at his house, the people from all places flocked to see me, each shewing to content me.

By this, the great King hath foure or five houses, each containing fourescore or an hundred foote in length, pleasantly seated upon an high sandy hill, from whence you may see westerly a goodly low Country, the river before the which his crooked course causeth many great Marshes of exceeding good ground. An hundred houses, and many large plaines are here togither inhabited. More abundance of fish and fowle, and a pleasanter seat cannot be imagined. The King with fortie Bowmen to guard me, intreated me to discharge my Pistoll, which they there presented me, with a mark at six score to strike therwith: but to spoil the practise, I broke the cocke, whereat they were much discontented, though a chaunce supposed.

From hence, this kind King conducted mee to a place called *Topahanocke*, a kingdome upon another River northward: The cause of this was, that the yeare before, a shippe had beene in the River of *Pamaunke*, who having beene kindly entertained by *Powhatan* their Emperour, they returned thence and discovered the River of *Topahanocke:* where being received with like kindnesse, yet he slue the King, and tooke of his people, and they supposed I were hee. But the people reported him a great man that was Captaine, and using mee kindly, the next day we departed.

This River of *Topahanock* seemeth in breadth not much lesse then that we dwell upon. At the mouth of the River is a Countrey called *Cuttata women:* upwards is *Marraugh tacum*, *Tapohanock*, *Appamatuck*, and *Nantaugs tacum:* at *Topmanahocks*, the head issuing from many Mountaines.

The next night I lodged at a hunting town of *Powhatams*, and the next day arrived at *Waranacomoco* upon the river of *Pamauncke*, where the great king is resident. By the way we passed by the top of another little river, which is betwixt the two, called *Payankatank*. The most of this Country though Desert, yet exceeding fertil; good timber, most hils and dales, in each valley a cristall spring.

Arriving at *Weramocomoco*, their Emperour proudly lying uppon a Bedstead a foote high, upon tenne or twelve Mattes, richly hung with manie Chaynes of great Pearles about his necke, and covered with a great Covering of *Rahaughcums*. At heade sat a woman, at his feete another; on each side sitting uppon a Matte uppon the ground, were raunged his chiefe men on each side the fire, tenne in a ranke, and behinde them as many yong women, each a great Chaine of white Beades over their shoulders, their heades painted in redde: and with such a grave and Majesticall countenance, as drave me into admiration to see such state in a naked Salvage.

Hee kindly welcomed me with good wordes, and great Platters of sundrie Victuals, assuring mee his friendship, and my libertie within foure days. Hee much delighted in *Opechan*

Comoughs relation of what I had described to him, and oft examined me upon the same.

Hee asked mee the cause of our comming.

I tolde him being in fight with the Spaniards our enimie, beeing overpowred, neare put to retreat, and by extreame weather put to this shore: where landing at *Chesipiack*, the people shot us, but at *Kequoughtan* they kindly used us: we by signes demaunded fresh water, they described us up the River was all fresh water: at *Paspahegh* also they kindly used us: our Pinnasse being leake, we were inforced to stay to mend her, till Captaine *Newport* my father came to conduct us away.

He demaunded why we went further with our Boate. I tolde him, in that I would have occasion to talk of the backe Sea, that on the other side the maine, where was salt water. My father had a childe slaine, whiche wee supposed *Monocan* his enemie: whose death we intended to revenge.

After good deliberation, hee began to describe mee the Countreys beyonde the Falles, with many of the rest; confirming what not onely *Opechancanoyes*, and an *Indian* which had beene prisoner to *Pewhatan* had before tolde mee: but some called it five dayes, some sixe, some eight, where the sayde water dashed amongest many stones and rockes, each storm; which caused oft tymes the heade of the River to bee brackish:

Anchanachuck he described to bee the people that had slaine my brother: whose death hee would revenge. Hee described also upon the same Sea, a mighty Nation called *Pocoughtronack*, a fierce Nation that did eate men, and warred with the people of *Moyaoncer* and *Pataromerke*, Nations upon the toppe of the heade of the Bay, under his territories: where the yeare before they had slain an hundred. He signified their crownes were shaven, long haire in the necke, tied on a knot, Swords like Pollaxes.

Beyond them he described people with short Coates, and Sleeves to the Elbowes, that passed that way in Shippes like ours. Many Kingdomes hee described mee, to the heade of the Bay, which seemed to bee a mightie River issuing from mightie Mountaines betwixt the two Seas: The people cloathed at *Ocamahowan*, he also confirmed; and the Southerly Countries also, as the rest that reported us to be within a day and a halfe of

Mangoge, two dayes of *Chawwonock,* 6. from *Roonock,* to the south part of the backe sea: He described a countrie called *Anone,* where they have abundance of Brasse, and houses walled as ours.

I requited his discourse (seeing what pride hee had in his great and spacious Dominions, seeing that all hee knewe were under his Territories) in describing to him, the territories of *Europe,* which was subject to our great King whose subject I was, the innumerable multitude of his ships, I gave him to understand the noyse of Trumpets, and terrible manner of fighting were under captain *Newport* my father: whom I intituled the *Meworames,* which they call the King of all the waters. At his greatnesse, he admired: and not a little feared. He desired mee to forsake *Paspahegh,* and to live with him upon his River, a Countrie called *Capa Howasicke.* Hee promised to give me Corne, Venison, or what I wanted to feede us: Hatchets and Copper wee should make him, and none should disturbe us.

This request I promised to performe: and thus, having with all the kindnes hee could devise, sought to content me, hee sent me home, with 4. men: one that usually carried my Gowne and Knapsacke after me, two other loded with bread, and one to accompanie me.

THE RELIGIOUS OBSERVANCES OF THE INDIANS

[From "A Map of Virginia"]

There is yet in *Virginia* no place discovered to bee so *Savage* in which the *Savages* have not a religion, Deare, and Bow and Arrowes. All thinges that were able to do them hurt beyond their prevention, they adore with their kinde of divine worship; as the fire, water, lightning, thunder, our ordinance, peeces, horses, &c.

But their chiefe God they worship is the Divell. Him they call *Oke* and serve him more of feare than love. They say they have conference with him, and fashion themselves as neare to his shape as they can imagine. In their Temples they have his image evill favouredly carved, and then painted and adorned with chaines, copper, and beades; and covered with a skin, in such manner as the deformity may well suit with such a God.

By him is commonly the sepulcher of their kings. Their bodies are first bowelled, then dryed upon hurdles till they bee verie dry, and so about the most of their jointes and necke they hang bracelets or chaines of copper, pearle, and such like, as they use to weare: their inwards they stuffe with copper beads and cover with a skin, hatchets, and such trash. Then lappe they them very carefully in white skins, and so rowle them in mats for their winding sheetes. And in the Tombe, which is an arch made of mats, they lay them orderly. What remaineth of this kinde of wealth their kings have, they set at their feet in baskets. These Temples and bodies are kept by their Priests.

For their ordinary burials, they digge a deep hole in the earth with sharpe stakes; and the corpes being lapped in skins and mats with their jewels, they lay them upon sticks in the ground, and so cover them with earth. The buriall ended, the women being painted all their faces with black cole and oile, doe sit 24 howers in the houses mourning and lamenting by turnes, with such yelling and howling as may expresse their great passions.

In every Territory of a *werowance* is a Temple and a Priest 2 or 3 or more. Their principall Temple or place of superstition is at *Uttamussack* at *Pamaunke,* neare unto which is a house Temple or place of *Powhatans.*

Upon the top of certaine redde sandy hils in the woods, there are 3 great houses filled with images of their kings and Divels and Tombes of their Predecessors. Those houses are neare 60 foot in length, built arbor wise, after their building. This place they count so holy as that none but the Priestes and kings dare come into them: nor the *Savages* dare not go up the river in boats by it, but that they solemnly cast some peece of copper, white beads, or *Pocones* into the river, for feare their *Oke* should be offended and revenged of them.

In this place commonly is resident 7 Priests. The chiefe differed from the rest in his ornaments: but inferior Priests could hardly be knowne from the common people, but that they had not so many holes in their eares to hang their jewels at.

The ornaments of the chiefe Priest was certain attires for his head made thus. They tooke a dosen or 16 or more snake skins, and stuffed them with mosse; and of weesels and other vermine skins, a good many. All these they tie by their tailes, so as all their tailes meete in the toppe of their head, like a great Tassell. Round about this Tassell is as it were a crown of feathers; the skins hang round about his head necke and shoulders, and in a manner cover his face.

The faces of all their Priests are painted as ugly as they can devise. In their hands, they had every one his Rattell, some base, some smaller. Their devotion was most in songs which the chiefe Priest beginneth and the rest followed him: sometimes he maketh invocations with broken sentences, by starts and strange passions, and at every pause, the rest give a short groane.

It could not bee perceived that they keepe any day as more holy then other: but only in some great distresse, of want, feare of enimies, times of triumph and gathering togither their fruits, the whole country of men women and children come togither to solemnities. The manner of their devotion is sometimes to make a great fire in the house or fields, and all to sing and dance about it, with rattles and shouts togither, 4 or 5 houres. Sometimes they set a man in the midst, and about him they dance and sing; he all the while clapping his hands as if he would keepe time. And after their songs and dauncings ended, they goe to their Feasts.

They have also divers conjurations. One they made when Captaine *Smith* was their prisoner; (as they reported) to know if any more of his countrymen would arrive there, and what he there intended. The manner of it was thus.

First they made a faire fire in a house. About this fire set 7 Priests setting him by them; and about the fire, they made a circle of meale. That done, the chiefe Priest attired as is expressed, began to shake his rattle; and the rest followed him in his song. At the end of the song, he laid downe 5 or 3 graines of wheat, and so continued counting his songs by the graines, till 3 times they incirculed the fire. Then they divide the graines by certaine numbers with little stickes, laying downe at the ende of every song a little sticke.

In this manner, they sat 8, 10, or 12 houres without cease, with such strange stretching of their armes, and violent passions and gestures as might well seeme strange to him they so conjured; who but every houre expected his end. Not any meat they did eat till, late in the evening, they had finished this worke: and then they feasted him and themselves with much mirth. But 3 or 4 daies they continued this ceremony.

They have also certaine Altar stones they call *Pawcorances:* but these stand from their Temples, some by their houses, other in the woodes and wildernesses. Upon these, they offer blood, deare suet, and Tobacco. These they doe when they returne from the warres, from hunting, and upon many other occasions.

They have also another superstition that they use in stormes, when the waters are rough in the rivers and sea coasts. Their Conjurers runne to the water sides, or passing in their boats, after many hellish outcries and invocations, they cast Tobacco, Copper, *Pocones*, and such trash into the water, to pacifie that God whome they thinke to be very angry in those stormes.

Before their dinners and suppers, the better sort will take the first bit, and cast it in the fire; which is all the grace they are known to use.

In some part of the Country, they have yearely a sacrifice of children. Such a one was at *Quiyoughcohanock*, some 10 miles from *James* Towne, and thus performed.

Fifteene of the properest young boyes, betweene 10 and 15 yeares of age, they painted white. Having brought them forth, the people spent the forenoone in dancing and singing about them with rattles.

In the afternoone, they put those children to the roote of a tree. By them, all the men stood in a guard, every one having a Bastinado in his hand, made of reeds bound together. This made a lane betweene them all along, through which there were appointed 5 young men to fetch these children. So every one of the five went through the guard, to fetch a child, each after other by turnes: the guard fearelessly beating them with their Bastinadoes, and they patiently enduring and receaving all; defending the children with their naked bodies from the unmercifull blowes they pay them soundly, though the children escape. All this while, the women weepe and crie out very passionately; providing mats, skinnes, mosse, and drie wood, as things fitting their childrens funerals.

After the children were thus passed the guard, the guard tore down the tree, branches and boughs, with such violence, that they rent the body, and made wreathes for their heads, or bedecked their haire with the leaves. What else was done with the children was not seene; but they were all cast on a heape in a valley, as dead: where they made a great feast for al the company.

The *Werowance* being demanded the meaning of this sacrifice, answered that the children were not al dead, but that the *Oke* or *Divell* did sucke the blood from their left breast, who chanced to be his by lot, till they were dead. But the rest were kept in the wildernesse by the yong men till nine moneths were expired, during which time they must not converse with any: and of these were made their Priests and Conjurers.

This sacrifice they held to bee so necessarie, that if they should omit it, their *Oke* or Divel and all their other *Quiyoughcosughes* (which are their other Gods) would let them have no Deare, Turkies, Corne, nor fish: and yet besides, hee would make great slaughter amongst them.

They thinke that their *Werowances* and Priestes, which they also esteeme *Quiyoughcosughes*, when they are dead, doe goe beyound the mountaines towardes the setting of the sun, and ever remaine there in forme of their *Oke*, with their heads painted with oile and *Pocones*, finely trimmed with feathers; and shal have beades, hatchets, copper, and tobacco, doing nothing but dance and sing with all their Predecessors.

But the common people, they suppose shall not live after death.

ON COLONIZATION

[From "A Description of New England"]

Who can desire more content, that hath small meanes; or but only his merit to advance his fortune, then to tread, and plant that ground hee hath purchased by the hazard of his life? If he have but the taste of virtue and magnanimitie, what to such a minde can bee more pleasant, then planting and building a foundation for his Posteritie, gotte from the rude earth, by Gods blessing and his owne industrie, without prejudice to any? if hee have any graine of faith or zeale in Religion, what can hee doe lesse hurtfull to any: or more agreeable to God then to seeke to convert those poore Salvages to know Christ, and humanitie, whose labors with discretion will tripple requite thy charge and paines? What so truely sutes with honour and honestie, as the discovering things unknowne? erecting Townes, peopling Countries, informing the ignorant, reforming things unjust, teaching virtue; and gaine to our Native mother-countrie a kingdom to attend her: finde imployment for those that are idle, because they know not what to doe: so farre from wronging any, as to cause Posteritie to remember thee; and remembering thee, ever honour that remembrance with praise?

Consider: What were the beginnings and endings of the Monarkies of the *Chaldeans*, the *Syrians*, the *Grecians*, and *Romanes*, but this one rule; What was it they would not doe, for the good of the commonwealth, or their Mother-citie? For example: *Rome*, what made her such a Monarchesse, but onely the adventures of her youth, not in riots at home; but in dangers abroade? and the justice and judgement out of their experience, when they grewe aged. What was their ruine and hurt, but this; The excesse of idlenesse, the fondnesse of Parents, the want of experience in Magistrates, the admiration of their undeserved honours, the contempt of true merit, their unjust jealosies, their politicke incredulities, their hypocriticall seeming goodnesse, and their deeds of secret lewdnesse? finally, in fine, growing onely formall temporists, all that their predecessors got in many years, they lost in a few daies. Those by their pain and vertues became Lords of the world; they by their ease and vices became slaves to their servants. This is the difference betwixt the use of Armes in the field, and on the monuments of stones; the golden age and the leaden age, prosperity and miserie, justice and corruption, substance and shadowes, words and deeds, experience and imagination, making Commonwealths and marring Commonwealths, the fruits of vertue and the conclusions of vice.

Then, who would live at home idly (or thinke in himselfe any worth to live) onely to eate, drink, and sleepe, and so die? Or by consuming that carelesly, his friends got worthily? Or by using that miserably, that maintained vertue honestly? Or for being descended nobly, pine with the vaine vaunt of great kindred, in penurie? Or (to maintaine a silly shewe of bravery) toyle out thy heart, soule, and time, basely; by shifts, tricks, cards, and dice? Or by relating newes of others actions, sharke here or there for a dinner, or supper; deceive thy friends, by faire promises and dissimulation, in borrowing where thou never intendest to pay; offend the lawes, surfeit with excesse, burden thy Country, abuse thy selfe, despaire in want, and then couzen thy kindred, yea even thine owne brother, and wish thy parents death (I will not say damnation) to have their estates? though thou seest what honours, and rewards, the world yet hath for them will seeke them and worthily deserve them.

A DIVERSION FOR THE LADIES

[From "The True Travells, Adventures, and Observations of Captain John Smith"]

Which slow proceedings the *Turkes* oft derided, that the Ordnance were at pawne, and how they grew fat for want of exercise; and fearing lest they should depart ere they could assault their Citie, sent this Challenge to any Captaine in the Armie.

That to delight the Ladies, who did long to see some court-like pastime, the Lord *Turbashaw* did defie any Captaine, that had the command of a Company, who durst combate with him for his head.

The matter being discussed, it was accepted; but so many questions grew for the undertaking, it was decided by lots: which fell upon Captaine *Smith*, before spoken of.

Truce being made for that time, the Rampiers all beset with faire Dames, and men in Armes, the *Christians* in *Battalio; Turbashaw* with a noise of Howboyes entred the fields well mounted and armed; on his shoulders were fixed a paire of great wings, compacted of Eagles feathers within a ridge of silver, richly garnished with gold and precious stones; a *Janizary* before him, bearing his Lance; on each side, another leading his horse: where long hee stayed not, ere *Smith* with a noise of Trumpets, only a Page bearing his Lance, passing by him with a courteous salute, tooke his ground with such good successe, that at the sound of the charge, he passed the *Turke* throw the sight of his Beaver, face, head, and all, that he fell dead to the ground; where alighting and unbracing his Helmet, cut off his head, and the Turkes tooke his body; and so returned without any hurt at all.

The head hee presented to the Lord *Moses*, the Generall, who kindly accepted it; and with joy to the whole armie he was generally welcomed.

The death of this Captaine so swelled in the heart of one *Grualgo*, his vowed friend, as, rather inraged with madnesse than choller, he directed a particular challenge to the Conqueror, to regaine his friends head, or lose his owne, with his horse and Armour for advantage: which according to his desire, was the next day undertaken.

As before, upon the sound of the Trumpets, their Lances flew in peeces upon a cleare passage; but the *Turke* was neere unhorsed. Their Pistolls was the next, which marked *Smith* upon the placard; but the next shot the *Turke* was so wounded in the left arme, that being not able to rule his horse, and defend himselfe, he was throwne to the ground; and so bruised with the fall, that he lost his head, as his friend before him; with his horse and Armour: but his body and his rich apparell was sent backe to the Towne.

Every day the *Turkes* made some sallies, but few skirmishes would they endure to any purpose. Our workes and approaches being not yet advanced to that height and effect which was of necessitie to be performed; to delude time, *Smith*, with so many incontradictible perswading reasons, obtained leave that the Ladies might know he was not so much enamoured of their servants heads, but if any *Turke* of their ranke would come to the place of combate to redeeme them, should have his also upon the like conditions, if he could winne it.

The challenge presently was accepted by *Bonny Mulgro.*

c

The next day both the champions entring the field as before, each discharging their Pistoll (having no Lances, but such martiall weapons as the defendant appointed), no hurt was done; their Battle-axes was the next, whose piercing bils made sometime the one, sometime the other to have scarce sense to keepe their saddles: specially the *Christian* received such a blow that he lost his Battle-axe, and failed not much to have fallen after it; whereat the supposing conquering *Turk*, had a great shout from the Rampiers. The *Turk* prosecuted his advantage to the uttermost of his power; yet the other, what by the readinesse of his horse, and his judgement and dexterity in such a businesse, beyond all mens expectation, by Gods assistance, not onely avoided the *Turkes* violence, but having drawne his Faulchion, pierced the *Turke* so under the Culets thorow backe and body, that although he alighted from his horse, he stood not long ere hee lost his head, as the rest had done.

WILLIAM STRACHEY

[Little is known of William Strachey except that he accompanied Sir Thomas Gates on his unfortunate expedition to Virginia in 1609, and served as secretary of the colony for about three years. The ship bearing Gates and Strachey was separated from the rest of the fleet and wrecked on the Bermudas, from which the survivors escaped to Jamestown nearly a year later. Strachey's chief work written while he was in America is an account of these and subsequent experiences, which he sent to London in 1610, and which was published in "Purchas His Pilgrimes" under the title of "A true reportory of the wracke, and redemption of Sir Thomas Gates Knight; upon, and from the Ilands of the Bermudas: his comming to Virginia, and the estate of that Colonie then, and after, under the government of the Lord La Warre." As secretary he compiled for the colony "Lawes Divine, Morall, and Martiall," published in London in 1612; and after his return to England he wrote "The Historie of Travaile into Virginia Brittahia," which remained in manuscript until 1849.

William Strachey was evidently a man of education who had seen something of the world. His writings are, however, very uneven, and it is only when he is inspired by his subject that he attains any distinction of style. That he is remembered above his contemporaries is due in part to the fact that the powerful description of a storm, given in the following pages, has been supposed by some critics to have given Shakespeare suggestions for "The Tempest." The evidence on this point is purely circumstantial, and unless new facts are brought to light, it will always be impossible to reach a definite conclusion. An impartial statement of the case may be found in Furness's Variorum edition of "The Tempest."

The text which follows is from "Purchas His Pilgrimes," London, 1625, reprinted Glasgow, 1906.]

A STORM AND A SHIPWRECK

[From "The Wrack and Redemption of Sir Thomas Gates"]

Excellent Lady, know that upon Friday late in the evening, we brake ground out of the Sound of Plymouth, our whole Fleete then consisting of seven good Ships, and two Pinnaces, all which from the said second of June, unto the twenty three of July, kept in friendly consort together, not a whole watch at any time loosing the sight each of other. Our course when we came about the height of betweene 26. and 27. degrees, we declined

to the Northward, and according to our Governours instructions
altered the trade and ordinary way used heretofore by Dominico,
and Mevis, in the West Indies, and found the winde to this course
indeede as friendly, as in the judgement of all Sea-men, it is upon
a more direct line, and by Sir George Summers our Admirall had
bin likewise in former time sailed, being a Gentleman of approved assurednesse, and ready knowledge in Sea-faring actions,
having often carried command, and chiefe charge in many Ships
Royall of her Majesties, and in sundry Voyages made many de-
feats and attempts in the time of the Spaniards quarrelling with
us, upon the Ilands and Indies, &c. We had followed this
course so long, as now we were within seven or eight dayes at
the most, by Cap. Newports reckoning of making Cape Henry
upon the coast of Virginia: When on S. James his day, July 24.
being Monday (preparing for no lesse all the blacke night before)
the cloudes gathering thicke upon us, and the windes singing,
and whistling most unusually, which made us to cast off our
Pinnace, towing the same untill then asterne, a dreadfull storme
and hideous began to blow from out the North-east, which swelling, and roaring as it were by fits, some houres with more violence then others, at length did beate all light from heaven;
which like an hell of darknesse turned blacke upon us, so much
the more fuller of horror, as in such cases horror and feare
use to overrunne the troubled, and overmastered sences of all,
which (taken up with amazement) the eares lay so sensible to
the terrible cries, and murmurs of the windes, and distraction of
our Company, as who was most armed, and best prepared, was
not a little shaken. For surely (Noble Lady) as death comes
not so sodaine nor apparant, so he comes not so elvish and pain-
full (to men especially even then in health and perfect habitudes
of body) as at Sea; who comes at no time so welcome, but our
frailty (so weake is the hold of hope in miserable demonstrations
of danger) it makes guilty of many contrary changes, and conflicts: For indeede death is accompanied at no time, nor place
with circumstances every way so uncapable of particularities of
goodnesse and inward comforts as at Sea. For it is most true,
there ariseth commonly no such unmercifull tempest, compound
of so many contrary and divers Nations, but that it worketh upon

the whole frame of the body, and most loathsomely affecteth all the powers thereof: and the manner of the sickenesse it laies upon the body, being so unsufferable, gives not the minde any free and quiet time, to use her judgement and Empire: which made the poet say:

> Hostium uxores, puerique caecos
> Sentiant motus orientis Haedi, &
> Æquoris nigri fremitum, & trementes
> Verbere ripas.

For foure and twenty houres the storme in a restlesse tumult, had blowne so exceedingly, as we could not apprehend in our imaginations any possibility of greater violence, yet did wee still finde it, not onely more terrible, but more constant, fury added to fury, and one storme urging a second more outragious then the former; whether it so wrought upon our feares, or indeede met with new forces: Sometimes strikes in our Ship amongst women, and passengers, not used to such hurly and discomforts, made us looke one upon the other with troubled hearts, and panting bosomes: our clamours dround in the windes, and the windes in thunder. Prayers might well be in the heart and lips, but drowned in the outcries of the Officers: nothing heard that could give comfort, nothing seene that might incourage hope. It is impossible for me, had I the voyce of Stentor, and expression of as many tongues, as his throate of voyces, to expresse the outcries and miseries, not languishing, but wasting his spirits, and art constant to his owne principles, but not prevailing. Our sailes wound up lay without their use, and if at any time wee bore but a Hollocke, or halfe forecourse, to guide her before the Sea, six and sometimes eight men were not inough to hold the whipstaffe in the steerage, and the tiller below in the Gunner roome, by which may be imagined the strength of the storme: In which, the Sea swelled above the Clouds, and gave battell unto Heaven. It could not be said to raine, the waters like whole Rivers did flood in the ayre. And this I did still observe, that wheras upon the Land, when a storme hath powred it selfe forth once in drifts of raine, the winde as beaten downe, and vanquished therewith, not long after indureth: here the glut of water (as if throatling the winde ere while) was no sooner a little emptied and qualified, but instantly the windes (as having gotten their mouthes now free, and at liberty) spake more loud, and grew more tumultuous, and malignant. What shall I say? Windes and Seas were as mad, as fury and rage could make them; for mine owne part, I had bin in some stormes before, as well upon the coast of Barbary and Algeere, in the Levant, and once more distressfull in the Adriatique gulfe, in a bottome of Candy, so as I may well say. Ego quid sit ater Adriae novi sinus, & quid albus Peccet Iapex. Yet all that I had ever suffered gathered together, might not hold comparison with this: there was not a moment in which the sodaine splitting, or instant over-setting of the Shippe was not expected.

Howbeit this was not all; It pleased God to bring a greater affliction yet upon us; for in the beginning of the storme we had received likewise a mighty leake. And the Ship in every joynt almost, having spued out her Oakam, before we were aware (a casualty more desperate then any other that a Voyage by Sea draweth with it) was growne five foote suddenly deepe with water above her ballast, and we almost drowned within, whilst we sat looking when to perish from above. This imparting no lesse terrour then danger, ranne through the whole Ship with much fright and amazement, startled and turned the bloud, and tooke downe the braves of the most hardy Marriner of them all, insomuch as he that before happily felt not the sorrow of others, now began to sorrow for himselfe, when he saw such a pond of water so suddenly broken in, and which he knew could not (without present avoiding) but instantly sinke him. So as joyning (onely for his owne sake, not yet worth the saving) in the publique safety; there might be seene Master, Masters Mate, Boateswaine, Quarter Master, Coopers, Carpenters, and who not, with candels in their hands, creeping along the ribs viewing the sides, searching every corner, and listening in every place, if they could heare the water runne. Many a weeping leake was this way found, and hastily stopt, and at length one in the Gunner roome made up with I know not how many peeces of Beefe: but all was to no purpose, the Leake (if it were but one) which drunke in our greatest Seas, and tooke in our destruction fastest, could not then be found, nor ever was, by any labour, counsell, or search. The waters still

increasing, and the Pumpes going, which at length choaked with
bringing up whole and continuall Bisket (and indeede all we had,
tenne thousand weight) it was conceived, as most likely, that the
Leake might be sprung in the Bread-roome, whereupon the Carpenter went downe, and ript up all the roome, but could not finde
it so.

I am not able to give unto your Ladiship every mans thought in
this perplexity, to which we were now brought; but to me, this
Leakage appeared as a wound given to men that were before dead.
The Lord knoweth, I had as little hope, as desire of life in the
storme, & in this, it went beyond my will; because beyond my
reason, why we should labour to preserve life; yet we did, either
because so deare are a few lingring houres of life in all mankinde,
or that our Christian knowledges taught us, how much we owed to
the rites of Nature, as bound, not to be false to our selves, or to
neglect the meanes of our owne preservation; the most despaire-
full things amongst men, being matters of no wonder nor moment
with him, who is the rich Fountaine and admirable Essence of all
mercy.

Our Governour, upon the tuesday morning (at what time, by
such who had bin below in the hold, the Leake was first discovered)
had caused the whole Company, about one hundred and forty,
besides women, to be equally divided into three parts, and opening
the Ship in three places (under the forecastle, in the waste, and hard
by the Bitacke) appointed each man where to attend; and there-
unto every man came duely upon his watch, tooke the Bucket, or
Pumpe for one houre, and rested another. Then men might be
seene to labour, I may well say, for life, and the better sort, even
our Governour, and Admirall themselves, not refusing their turne,
and to spell each the other, to give example to other. The common sort stripped naked, as men in Gallies, the easier both to hold
out, and to shrinke from under the salt water, which continually
leapt in among them, kept their eyes waking, and their thoughts
and hands working, with tyred bodies, and wasted spirits, three
dayes and foure nights destitute of outward comfort, and desperate
of any deliverance, testifying how mutually willing they were, yet
by labour to keepe each other from drowning, albeit each one
drowned whilest he laboured.

Once, so huge a Sea brake upon the poope and quarter upon us, as it covered our Shippe from stearne to stemme, like a garment or a vast cloude, it filled her brimme full for a while within, from the hatches up to the sparre decke.   This source or confluence of water was so violent, as it rusht and carried the Helm-man from the Helme, and wrested the Whip-staffe out of his hand, which so flew from side to side, that when he would have ceased the same againe, it so tossed him from Star-boord to Lar-boord, as it was Gods mercy it had not split him: It so beat him from his hold, and so bruised him, as a fresh man hazarding in by chance fell faire with it, and by maine strength bearing somewhat up, made good his place, and with much clamour incouraged and called upon others; who gave her now up, rent in pieces and absolutely lost.   Our Governour was at this time below at the Capstone, both by his speech and authoritie heartening every man unto his labour. It strooke him from the place where hee sate, and groveled him, and all us about him on our faces, beating together with our breaths all thoughts from our bosomes, else, then that wee were now sinking.   For my part, I thought her alreadie in the bottome of the Sea; and I have heard him say, wading out of the floud thereof, all his ambition was but to climbe up above hatches to dye in Aperto cœlo, and in the company of his old friends.   It so stun'd the ship in her full pace, that shee stirred no more, then if shee had beene caught in a net, or then, as if the fabulous Remora had stucke to her fore-castle.   Yet without bearing one inch of saile, even then shee was making her way nine or ten leagues in a watch.   One thing, it is not without his wonder (whether it were the feare of death in so great a storme, or that it pleased God to be gracious unto us) there was not a passenger, gentleman, or other, after hee beganne to stirre and labour, but was able to relieve his fellow, and make good his course: And it is most true, such as in all their life times had never done houres worke before (their mindes now helping their bodies) were able twice fortie eight houres together to toile with the best.

During all this time, the heavens look'd so blacke upon us, that it was not possible the elevation of the Pole might be observed: nor a Starre by night, not Sunne beame by day was to be seene. Onely upon the thursday night Sir George Summers being upon

the watch, had an apparition of a little round light, like a faint
Starre, trembling, and streaming along with a sparkeling blaze,
halfe the height upon the Maine Mast, and shooting sometimes
from Shroud to Shroud, tempting to settle as it were upon any of
the foure Shrouds: and for three or foure houres together, or
rather more, halfe the night it kept with us; running sometimes
along the Maine-yard to the very end, and then returning. At
which, Sir George Summers called divers about him, and shewed
them the same, who observed it with much wonder, and carefulnesse: but upon a sodaine, towards the morning watch, they
lost the sight of it, and knew not what way it made. The superstitious Sea-men make many constructions of this Sea-fire, which
neverthelesse is usuall in stormes: the same (it may be) which the
Grecians were wont in the Mediterranean to call Castor and
Pollux, of which, if one onely appeared without the other, they
tooke it for an evill signe of great tempest. The Italians, and
such, who lye open to the Adriatique and Tyrrene Sea, call it
(a sacred Body) Corpo sancto: the Spaniards call it Saint Elmo,
and have an authentique and miraculous Legend for it. Be it what
it will, we laid other foundations of safety or ruine, then in the
rising or falling of it, could it have served us now miraculously to
have taken our height by, it might have strucken amazement, and
a reverence in our devotions, according to the due of a miracle.
But it did not light us any whit the more to our knowne way, who
ran now (as doe hoodwinked men) at all adventures, sometimes
North, and North-east, then North and by West, and in an instant againe varying two or three points, and sometimes halfe the
Compasse. East and by South we steered away as much as we
could to beare upright, which was no small carefulnesse nor paine
to doe, albeit we much unrigged our Ship, threw over-boord much
luggage, many a Trunke and Chest (in which I suffered no meane
losse) and staved many a Butt of Beere, Hogsheads of Oyle,
Syder, Wine, and Vinegar, and heaved away all our Ordnance on
the Starboord side, and had now purposed to have cut downe the
Maine Mast, the more to lighten her, for we were much spent, and
our men so weary, as their strengths together failed them, with
their hearts, having travailed now from Tuesday till Friday morning, day and night, without either sleepe or foode; for the leakeage

taking up all the hold, wee coud neither come by Beere nor fresh water; fire we could keepe none in the Cooke-roome to dresse any meate, and carefulnesse, griefe, and our turne at the Pumpe or Bucket, were sufficient to hold sleepe from our eyes.

And surely, Madam, it is most true, there was not any houre (a matter of admiration) all these dayes, in which we freed not twelve hundred Barricos of water, the least whereof contained six gallons, and some eight, besides three deepe Pumpes continually going, two beneath at the Capstone, and the other above in the halfe Decke, and at each Pumpe foure thousand stroakes at the least in a watch; so as I may well say, every foure houres, we quitted one hundred tunnes of water: and from tuesday noone till friday noone, we bailed and pumped two thousand tunne, and yet doe what we could, when our Ship held least in her, (after tuesday night second watch) shee bore ten foote deepe, at which stay our extreame working kept her one eight glasses, forbearance whereof had instantly sunke us, and it being now Friday, the fourth morning, it wanted little, but that there had bin a generall determination, to have shut up hatches, and commending our sinfull soules to God, committed the Shippe to the mercy of the Sea: surely, that night we must have done it, and that night had we then perished: but see the goodnesse and sweet introduction of better hope, by our mercifull God given unto us. Sir George Summers, when no man dreamed of such happinesse, had discovered, and cried Land. Indeede the morning now three quarters spent, had wonne a little cleerenesse from the dayes before, and it being better surveyed, the very trees were seene to move with the winde upon the shoare side: whereupon our Governour commanded the Helme-man to beare up, the Boateswaine sounding at the first, found it thirteene fathome, & when we stood a little in seven fatham; and presently heaving his lead the third time, had ground at foure fathome, and by this, we had got her within a mile under the South-east point of the land, where we had somewhat smooth water. But having no hope to save her by comming to an anker in the same, we were inforced to runne her ashoare, as neere the land as we could, which brought us within three quarters of a mile of shoare, and by the mercy of God unto us, making out our Boates, we had ere night brought all our men, women, and children, about the number of one hundred and fifty, safe into the Iland.

WILLIAM BRADFORD

[William Bradford was born in Yorkshire, England, in 1588. He joined the Separatists in 1606, went to Holland in 1608, and though a young man was prominent in the affairs of the church at Amsterdam and Leyden. He seems to have been active in urging emigration to America, and he sailed in the *Mayflower*. When Governor Carver died, a few months after the landing at Plymouth, Bradford was chosen his successor, and was annually reëlected for many years. He died in 1657.

Although Bradford was not of high social position, and had no regular opportunities for a liberal education, he gained some knowledge of the classics, and in his later years attempted to learn Hebrew. In his exercise book he notes: "Though I am growne aged, yet I have had a longing desire, to see with my own eyes, something of that most ancient language, and holy tongue, in which the Law and oracles of God were write; and in which God, and angels, spake to the holy patriarchs, of old time; and what names were given to things, from the creation." Governor Bradford was a somewhat voluminous writer, though but one of his works was published during his lifetime. This was a journal containing the experiences of the colonists from November, 1620, to December, 1621, and was the joint work of Bradford, Edward Winslow, and others. It was published in London, without the authors' names, in 1622, and became known, on account of a prefatory note signed "G. Mourt," as "Mourt's Relation." Bradford's most important writing is "The History of Plymouth Plantation." The first book treats of the rise of the dissenters, and the causes that influenced their emigration to Holland and afterward to America. The part of the work which covers the period after 1620 is in the form of annals. Governor Bradford began the History about 1630, and after bringing the narrative to date, added an account of the events of each year till 1647. His object in writing was evidently to leave a record for posterity, and so far as is known he made no attempt to have the work published in his lifetime. After his death the manuscript passed to his relatives, and finally reached the Prince Library. During the British occupation of Boston at the time of the Revolution it disappeared, and was supposed to be lost; but in 1855 it was discovered in the library of the Bishop of London. In 1897 it was returned by the Bishop of London to the Commonwealth of Massachusetts. Many passages from the History had been used, with and without credit, in the works of Nathaniel Morton, Thomas Prince, Governor Hutchinson, and others; but the work as a whole was first printed by the Massachusetts Historical Society in 1856. A photographic facsimile was issued in London and Boston in 1896, a new edition was prepared under the direction of the Commonwealth of Massachusetts in 1898, and another edition appeared in 1907. A portion of Governor Bradford's letter-book was published by the Massachusetts Historical Society in 1794, and some of his other writings in prose and verse have since been printed. A number of them are found in Alexander Young's "Chronicles of the Pilgrim Fathers," 1841.

In some passages Governor Bradford's writings show a simple dignity and a finely pathetic quality obviously derived from the reading and contemplation of the Bible. The greater part of his work is plain and accurate, but without any graces of style. His lack of a literary sense is best shown by the ludicrous baldness of his verses, a few of which are given in the following pages.

The text of the selection from "Mourt's Relation" follows the literal reprint by Henry Martin Dexter, Boston, 1865. The text of the passages from "The History of Plymouth Plantation" is based on the edition prepared for the Commonwealth of Massachusetts by Alfred Seelye Roe in 1898, collated in some doubtful places with the zincograph facsimile of the manuscript, Boston, 1896. The verses on New England are from a fragment printed from Governor Bradford's manuscript in the Massachusetts Historical Society Collections, First Series, Vol. III, 1794.]

FIRST ACQUAINTANCE WITH THE INDIANS

[From "Mourt's Relation"[1]]

Fryday, the 16. a fayre warme day towards; this morning we determined to conclude of the military Orders, which we had began to consider of before, but were interrupted by the Savages, as we mentioned formerly; and whilst we were busied here about, we were interrupted againe, for there presented himself a *Savage*, which caused an Alarm, he very boldly came all alone and along the houses straight to the Randevous, where we intercepted him, not suffering him to goe in, as undoubtedly he would, out of his boldnesse, hee saluted us in English, and bad us well-come, for he had learned some broken English amongst the English men that came to fish at *Monchiggon*, and knew by name the most of the Captaines, Commanders, & Masters that usually come, he was a man free in speech, so farre as he could expresse his minde, and of a seemely carriage, we questioned him of many things, he was the first *Savage* we could meete withall; he sayd he was not of these parts, but of *Moratiggon*, and one of the *Sagamores* or *Lords* thereof,

[1 See the introductory note, above. This part of the journal is conjecturally ascribed to Bradford, but the authorship cannot be definitely established.]

and had beene 8. moneths in these parts, it lying hence a dayes
sayle with a great wind, and five dayes by land; he discoursed of
the whole Country, and of every Province, and of their *Sagamores*,
and their number of men, and strength; the wind beginning to
rise a little, we cast a horsemans coat about him, for he was starke
naked, onely a leather about his wast, with a fringe about a span
long, or little more; he had a bow & 2 arrowes, the one headed,
and the other unheaded; he was a tall straight man, the haire of
his head blacke, long behind, onely short before, none on his face
at all; he asked some beere, but we gave him strong water, and
bisket, and butter, and cheese, & pudding, and a peece of a mal-
lerd, all which he liked well, and had bin acquainted with such
amongst the English; he told us the place where we now live, is
called, *Patuxet*, and that about foure yeares agoe, all the Inhabitants dyed of an extraordinary plague, and there is neither man,
woman, nor childe remaining, as indeed we have found none, so
as there is none to hinder our possession, or to lay claime unto it;
all the after-noone we spent in communication with him, we would
gladly have beene rid of him at night, but he was not willing to goe
this night, then we thought to carry him on ship-boord, wherewith
he was well content, and went into the Shallop, but the winde
was high and water scant, that it could not returne backe: we
lodged him that night at *Steven Hopkins* house, and watched him;
the next day he went away backe to the *Masasoits*, from whence
he sayd he came, who are our next bordering neighbours: they
are sixtie strong, as he sayth: the *Nausites* are as neere South-
east of them, and are a hundred strong, and those were they of
whom our people were encountred, as we before related. They
are much incensed and provoked against the English, and about
eyght moneths agoe slew three English men, and two more hardly
escaped by flight to *Monhiggon;* they were Sir *Ferdinando Gorge*
his men, as this Savage told us, as he did likewise of the *Huggerie,*
that is, *Fight,* that our discoverers had with the *Nausites,* & of
our tooles that were taken out of the woods, which we willed him
should be brought againe, otherwise, we would right ourselves.
These people are ill affected towards the English, by reason of one
Hunt, a master of a ship, who deceived the people, and got them
under colour of truking with them, twentie out of this very place

where we inhabite, and seaven men from the *Nausites*, and carried them away, and sold them for slaves, like a wretched man (for 20. pound a man) that cares not what mischiefe he doth for his profit.

Saturday in the morning we dismissed the Salvage, and gave him a knife, a bracelet, and a ring; he promised within a night or two to come againe, and to bring with him some of the *Massasoyts* our neighbours, with such Bevers skins as they had to trucke with us.

Saturday and Sunday reasonable fayre dayes. On this day came againe the Savage, and brought with him five other tall proper men, they had every man a Deeres skin on him, and the principall of them had a wild Cats skin, or such like on the one arme; they had most of them long hosen up to their groynes, close made; and above their groynes to their wast another leather, they were altogether like the *Irish*-trouses; they are of complexion like our English Gipseys, no haire or very little on their faces, on their heads long haire to their shoulders, onely cut before some trussed up before with a feather, broad wise, like a fanne, another a fox tayle hanging out: these left (according to our charge given him before) their Bowes and Arrowes a quarter of a myle from our Towne, we gave them entertaynement as we thought was fitting them, they did eate liberally of our English victuals, they made semblance unto us of friendship and amitie; they song & danced after their maner, like Anticks; they brought with them in a thing like a Bow-case (which the principall of them had about his wast) a little of their Corne pownded to Powder, which put to a little water they eate; he had a little Tobacco in a bag, but none of them drunke but when he listed, some of them had their faces paynted black, from the forehead to the chin, foure or five fingers broad; others after other fashions, as they liked; they brought three or foure skins, but we would not trucke with them at all that day, but wished them to bring more, and we would trucke for all, which they promised within a night or two, and would leave these behind them, though we were not willing they should, and they brought us all our tooles againe which were taken in the woods, in our mens absence, so because of the day we dismissed them so soone as we could. But *Samoset* our first acquaintance, eyther was sicke, or fayned himselfe so, and would not goe with them, and stayed with us till Wednesday morning : Then we sent him to them, to know the reason they came not according to their words, and we gave him an hat, a payre of stockings and shooes, a shirt, and a peece of cloth to tie about his wast.

THE VOYAGE OF THE MAYFLOWER

[Chapter IX, Book I, of "The History of Plymouth Plantation"]

Septr. 6. These troubls being blowne over, and now all being compacte togeather in one shipe, they put to sea againe with a prosperus winde, which continued diverce days togeather, which was some incouragmente unto them; yet according to the usuall maner many were afflicted with sea-sicknes. And I may not omite hear a spetiall worke of Gods providence. Ther was a proud & very profane yonge man, one of the sea-men, of a lustie, able body, which made him the more hauty; he would allway be contemning the poore people in their sicknes, & cursing them dayly with gree[v]ous execrations, and did not let to tell them, that he hoped to help to cast halfe of them over board before they came to their jurneys end, and to make mery with what they had; and if he were by any gently reproved, he would curse and swear most bitterly. But it plased God before they came halfe seas over, to smite this yong man with a greeveous disease, of which he dyed in a desperate maner, and so was him selfe the first that was throwne overbord. Thus his curses light on his owne head; and it was an astonishmente to all his fellows, for they noted it to be the just hand of God upon him.

After they had injoyed faire winds and weather for a season, they were incountred many times with crosse winds, and mete with many feirce stormes, with which the shipe was shroudly shaken, and her upper works made very leakie; and one of the maine beames in the midd ships was bowed & craked, which put them in some fear that the shipe could not be able to performe the vioage. So some of the cheefe of the company, perceiveing the mariners to feare the suffisiencie of the shipe, as appeared by their mutterings, they entred into serious consulltation with the mr. & other officers of the ship, to consider in time of the danger;

and rather to returne then to cast them selves into a desperate &
inevitable perill. And truly ther was great distraction & differance of opinion amongst the mariners them selves; faine would
they doe what could be done for their wages sake, (being now
halfe the seas over,) and on the other hand they were loath to
hazard their lives too desperatly. But in examening of all opinions, the mr. & others affirmed they knew the ship to be stronge
& firme under water; and for the buckling of the maine beame,
ther was a great iron scrue the passengers brought out of Holland,
which would raise the beame into his place; the which being done,
the carpenter & mr. affirmed that with a post put under it, set
firme in the lower deck, & otherways bounde, he would make it
sufficiente. And as for the decks & uper workes they would
calke them as well as they could, and though with the workeing
of the ship they would not longe keepe stanch, yet ther would
otherwise be no great danger, if they did not overpress her with
sails. So they commited them selves to the will of God, & resolved to proseede. In sundrie of these stormes the winds were
so feirce, & the seas so high, as they could not beare a knote of
saile, but were forced to hull, for diverce days togither. And in
one of them as they thus lay at hull, in a mighty storme, a lustie
yonge man (called John Howland) coming upon some occasion
above the grattings, was, with a seele of the shipe throwne into sea;
but it pleased God that he caught hould of the top-saile halliards,
which hunge over board, & rane out at length; yet he held his
hould (though he was sundrie fadomes under water) till he was
hald up by the same rope to the brime of the water, and then with
a boat hooke & other means got into the shipe againe, & his
life saved; and though he was something ill with it, yet he lived
many years after, and became a profitable member both in church
& commone wealthe. In all this viage ther died but one of the
passengers, which was William Butten, a youth, servant to Samuell
Fuller, when they drew near the coast. But to omite other things,
(that I may be breefe,) after longe beating at sea they fell with
that land which is called Cape Cod; the which being made &
certainly knowne to be it, they were not a litle joyfull. After
some deliberation had amongst them selves & with the mr. of
the ship, they tacked aboute and resolved to stande for the south-

ward (the wind & weather being faire) to finde some place aboute
Hudsons river for their habitation. But after they had sailed
that course aboute halfe the day, they fell amongst deangerous
shoulds and roring breakers, and they were so farr intangled ther
with as they conceived them selves in great danger; & the wind
shrinking upon them withall, they resolved to bear up againe for the
Cape, and thought them selves hapy to gett out of those dangers
before night overtooke them, as by Gods providence they did.
And the next day they gott into the Cape-harbor wher they ridd
in saftie. A word or too by the way of this cape; it was thus first
named by Capten Gosnole & his company,[1] Anno 1602, and after
by Capten Smith was caled Cape James; but it retains the former
name amongst seamen. Also that pointe which first shewed those
dangerous shoulds unto them, they called Pointe Care, & Tuckers
Terrour; but the French & Dutch to this day call it Malabarr,
by reason of those perilous shoulds, and the losses they have suffered their.

Being thus arived in a good harbor and brought safe to land,
they fell upon their knees & blessed the God of heaven, who had
brought them over the vast & furious ocean, and delivered them
from all the periles & miseries therof, againe to set their feete
on the firme and stable earth, their proper elemente. And no
marvell if they were thus joyefull, seeing wise Seneca was so
affected with sailing a few miles on the coast of his owne Italy;
as he affirmed[2] that he had rather remaine twentie years on his
way by land, then pass by sea to any place in a short time; so
tedious & dreadfull was the same unto him.

But hear I cannot but stay and make a pause, and stand half
amased at this poore peoples presente condition; and so I thinke
will the reader too, when he well considers the same. Being thus
passed the vast ocean, and a sea of troubles before in their preparation (as may be remembred by that which wente before), they had
now no freinds to wellcome them, nor inns to entertaine or refresh
their weatherbeaten bodys, no houses or much less townes to repaire too, to seeke for succoure. It is recorded in scripture[3]
as a mercie to the apostle & his shipwraked company, that the
barbarians shewed them no smale kindnes in refreshing them, but

---

[1] Because they tooke much of that fishe ther.   [2] Epist. iii.   [3] Acts xxviii.

D

these savage barbarians, when they motte with them (as after will appeare) were readier to fill their sids full of arrows then otherwise. And for the season it was winter, and they that know the winters of that cuntrie know them to be sharp & violent, & subjecte to cruell & feirce stormes, deangerous to travill to known places, much more to serch an unknown coast. Besids, what could they see but a hidious & desolate wildernes, full of wild beasts & willd men? and what multituds ther might be of them they knew not. Nether could they, as it were, goe up to the tope of Pisgah, to vew from this willdernes a more goodly cuntrie to feed their hops; for which way soever they turnd their eys (save upward to the heavens) they could have litle solace or content in respecte of any outward objects. For summer being done, all things stand upon them with a wetherbeaten face; and the whole countrie, full of woods & thickets, represented a wild & savage heiw. If they looked behind them, ther was the mighty ocean which they had passed, and was now as a maine barr & goulfe to seperate them from all the civill parts of the world. If it be said they had a ship to succour them, it is trew; but what heard they daly from the mr. & company? but that with speede they should looke out a place with their shallop, wher they would be at some near distance; for the season was shuch as he would not stirr from thence till a safe harbor was discovered by them wher they would be, and he might goe without danger; and that victells consumed apace, but he must & would keepe sufficient for them selves & their returne. Yea, it was muttered by some, that if they gott not a place in time, they would turne them & their goods ashore & leave them. Let it also be considred what weake hopes of supply & succoure they left behinde them, that might bear up their minds in this sade condition and trialls they were under; and they could not but be very smale. It is true, indeed, the affections & love of their brethren at Leyden was cordiall & entire towards them, but they had litle power to help them, or them selves; and how the case stode betweene them & the marchants at their coming away, hath allready been declared. What could now sustaine them but the spirite of God & his grace? May not & ought not the children of these fathers rightly say: *Our faithers were Englishmen which came over this great ocean, and were ready to perish in this willder-*

nes; [1] *but they cried unto the Lord, and he heard their voyce, and
looked on their adversitie, &c. Let them therfore praise the Lord,
because he is good, & his mercies endure for ever.* [2] *Yea, let them
which have been redeemed of the Lord, shew how he hath delivered
them from the hand of the oppressour. When they wandered in
the deserte willdernes out of the way, and found no citie to dwell in,
both hungrie, & thirstie, their sowle was overwhelmed in them.
Let them confess before the Lord his loving kindnes, and his wonderfull works before the sons of men.*

THE SETTLEMENT AT MERRY MOUNT

[From "The History of Plymouth Plantation" for 1628]

Aboute some 3. or 4. years before this time, ther came over one
Captaine Wolastone, (a man of pretie parts,) and with him 3. or
4. more of some eminencie, who brought with them a great many
servants, with provissions & other implments for to begine a
plantation; and pitched them selves in a place within the Massachusets, which they called, after their Captains name, Mount-
Wollaston. Amongst whom was one Mr. Morton, who, it should
seeme, had some small adventure (of his owne or other mens)
amongst them; but had litle respecte amongst them, and was
sleghted by the meanest servants. Haveing continued ther some
time, and not finding things to answer their expectations, nor
profite to arise as they looked for, Captaine Wollaston takes a great
part of the sarvents, and transports them to Virginia, wher he
puts them of at good rates, selling their time to other men; and
writs back to one Mr. Rassdall, one of his cheefe partners, and
accounted their marchant, to bring another parte of them to Verginia likewise, intending to put them of there as he had done the
rest. And he, with the consente of the said Rasdall, appoynted
one Fitcher to be his Livetenante, and governe the remaines of the
plantation, till he or Rasdall returned to take further order ther-
aboute. But this Morton abovesaid, haveing more craft than
honestie, (who had been a kind of petiefogger, of Furnefells Inne,)
in the others absence, watches an oppertunitie, (commons being

---

[1] Deut. 26. 5, 7.   [2] 107 Ps. v. 1, 2, 4, 5, 8.

but hard amongst them,) and gott some strong drinck and other junkats, & made them a feast; and after they were merie, he begane to tell them, he would give them good counsell. You see (saith he) that many of your fellows are carried to Virginia; and if you stay till this Rasdall returne, you will also be carried away and sould for slaves with the rest. Therfore I would advise you to thrust out this Levetenant Fitcher; and I, having a parte in the plantation, will receive you as my partners and consociats; so may you be free from service, and we will converse, trad, plante, & live togeather as equalls, & supporte & protecte one another, or to like effecte. This counsell was easily received; so they tooke oppertunitie, and thrust Levetenante Fitcher out a dores, and would suffer him to come no more amongst them, but forct him to seeke bread to eate, and other releefe from his neigbours, till he could gett passages for England. After this they fell to great licenciousness, and led a dissolute life, powering out them selves into all profanenes. And Morton became lord of misrule, and maintained (as it were) a schoole of Athisme. And after they had gott some good into their hands, and gott much by trading with the Indeans, they spent it as vainly, in quaffing & drinking both wine & strong waters in great exsess, and, as some reported 10£. worth in a morning. They allso set up a May-pole, drinking and dancing aboute it many days togeather, inviting the Indean women, for their consorts, dancing and frisking togither, (like so many fairies, or furies rather,) and worse practises. As if they had anew revived & celebrated the feasts of the Roman Goddes Flora, or the beasly practieses of the madd Bacchinalians. Morton likwise (to shew his poetrie) composed sundry rimes & verses, some tending to lasciviousnes, and others to the detraction & scandall of some persons, which he affixed to this idle or idoll May-polle. They chainged allso the name of their place, and in stead of calling it Mounte Wollaston, they call it Merie-mounte, as if this joylity would have lasted ever. But this continued not long, for after Morton was sent for England, (as follows to be declared,) shortly after came over that worthy gentlman, Mr. John Indecott, who brought over a patent under the broad seall, for the governmente of the Massachusets, who visiting those parts caused that Maypolle to be cutt downe, and rebuked them for their profannes, and admonished them to looke ther should be better walking; so they now, or others, changed the name of their place againe, and called it Mounte-Dagon.

Now to maintaine this riotous prodigallitie and profuse excess, Morton, thinking him selfe lawless, and hearing what gaine the French & fisher-men made by trading of peeces, powder, & shotte to the Indeans, he, as the head of this consortship, begane the practise of the same in these parts; and first he taught them how to use them, to charge, & discharg, and what proportion of powder to give the peece, according to the sise or bignes of the same; and what shotte to use for foule, and what for deare. And having thus instructed them, he imployed some of them to hunte & fowle for him, so as they became farr more active in that imploymente then any of the English, by reason of ther swiftnes of foote, & nimblnes of body, being also quick-sighted, and by continuall exercise well knowing the hants of all sorts of game. So as when they saw the execution that a peece would doe, and the benefite that might come by the same, they became madd, as it were, after them, and would not stick to give any prise they could attaine too for them; accounting their bowes & arrowes but bables in comparison of them.

And here I may take occasion to bewaile the mischefe that this wicked man began in these parts, and which since base covetousnes prevailing in men that should know better, has now at length gott the upper hand, and made this thing commone, notwithstanding any laws to the contrary; so as the Indeans are full of peeces all over, both fouling peeces, muskets, pistols, &c. They have also their moulds to make shotte, of all sorts, as muskett bulletts, pistoll bullets, swane & gose shote, & of smaler sorts; yea, some have seen them have their scruplats to make scrupins them selves, when they wante them, with sundery other implements, wherwith they are ordinarily better fited & furnished then the English them selves. Yea, it is well knowne that they will have powder & shot, when the English want it, nor cannot gett it; and that in time of warre or danger, as experience hath manifested, that when lead hath been scarce, and men for their owne defence would gladly have given a groat a li, which is dear enoughe, yet hath it bene bought up & sent to other places, and sould to shuch as trade it with the Indeans, at 12. pence the li.; and it is like they give 3. or 4. s. the pound, for they will have it at any rate. And these things have been done in the same times, when some of their neighbours & freinds are daly killed by the Indeans, or are in deanger therof, and live but at the Indeans mercie. Yea, some (as they have aquainted them with all other things) have tould them how gunpowder is made, and all the materialls in it, and that they are to be had in their owne land; and I am confidente, could they attaine to make saltpeter, they would teach them to make powder. O, the horiblnes of this vilanie! how many both Dutch & English have been latly slaine by those Indeans, thus furnished; and no remedie provided, nay, the evill more increased, and the blood of their brethren sould for gaine, as is to be feared; and in what danger all these colonies are in is too well known. Oh! that princes & parlements would take some timly order to prevente this mischeefe, and at length to supprcss it, by some exemplerie punishmente upon some of these gaine thirstie murderers, (for they deserve no better title,) before their collonies in these parts be over throwne by these barbarous savages, thus armed with their owne weapons, by these evill instruments, and traytors to their neighbors and cuntrie. But I have forgott my selfe, and have been to longe in this digression; but now to returne. This Morton having thus taught them the use of peeces, he sould them all he could spare; and he and his consorts detirmined to send for many out of England, and had by some of the ships sente for above a score. The which being knowne, and his neighbours meeting the Indeans in the woods armed with guns in this sorte, it was a terrour unto them, who lived straglingly, and were of no strenght in any place. And other places (though more remote) saw this mischeefe would quictly spread over all if not prevented. Besides, they saw they should keep no servants, for Morton would entertaine any, how vile soever, and all the scume of the countrie, or any discontents, would flock to him from all places, if this nest was not broken; and they should stand in more fear of their lives & goods (in short time) from this wicked & deboste crue, then from the salvages them selves.

So sundrie of the cheefe of the stragling plantations, meeting

togither, agreed by mutuall consente to sollissite those of Plimoth
(who were then of more strength then them all) to joyne with
them, to prevente the further grouth of this mischeefe, and suppress Morton & his consortes before they grewe to further head
and strength. Those that joyned in this acction (and after contributed to the charge of sending him for England) were from
Pascataway, Namkeake, Winisimett, Weesagascusett, Natasco,
and other places wher any English were seated. Those of Plimoth being thus sought too by their messengers & letters, and
waying both their reasons, and the commone danger, were willing
to afford them their help; though them selves had least cause of
fear or hurte. So, to be short, they first resolved joyntly to
write to him, and in a freindly & neigborly way to admonish
him to forbear these courses, & sent a messenger with their
letters to bring his answer. But he was so highe as he scorned
all advise, and asked who had to doe with him; he had and
would trade peeces with the Indeans in dispite of all, with many
other scurilous termes full of disdaine. They sente to him a
second time, and bad him be better advised, and more temperate
in his termes, for the countrie could not beare the injure he did;
it was against their comone saftie, and against the king's proclamation. He answerd in high terms as before, and that the
kings proclaimation was no law; demanding what penaltie was
upon it. It was answered, more then he could bear, his majesties displeasure. But insolently he persisted, and said the king
was dead and his displeasure with him, & many the like things;
and threatened withall that if any came to molest him, let them
looke to them selves, for he would prepare for them. Upon
which they saw ther was no way but to take him by force; and
having so farr proceeded, now to give over would make him farr
more hautie & insolente. So they mutually resolved to proceed, and obtained of the Govr. of Plimoth to send Captaine
Standish, & some other aide with him, to take Morton by force.
The which accordingly was done; but they found him to stand
stifly in his defence, having made fast his dors, armed his consorts, set diverse dishes of powder & bullets ready on the table;
and if they had not been over armed with drinke, more hurt
might have been done. They sommaned him to yeeld, but he

kept his house, and they could gett nothing but scofes & scorns from him; but at length, fearing they would doe some violence to the house, he and some of his crue came out, but not to yeeld, but to shoote; but they were so steeld with drinke as their peeces were to heavie for them; him selfe with a carbine (over charged & allmost halfe fild with powder & shote, as was after found) had thought to have shot Captaine Standish; but he stept to him, & put by his peece, & tooke him. Neither was ther any hurte done to any of either side, save that one was so drunke that he rane his owne nose upon the pointe of a sword that one held before him as he entred the house; but he lost but a litle of his hott blood. Morton they brought away to Plimoth, wher he was kepte, till a ship went from the Ile of Shols for England, with which he was sente to the Counsell of New-England; and letters writen to give them information of his course & cariage; and also one was sent at their commone charge to informe their Honours more perticulerly, & to prosecute against him. But he foold of the messenger, after he was gone from hence, and though he wente for England, yet nothing was done to him, not so much as rebukte, for ought was heard; but returned the nexte year. Some of the worst of the company were disperst, and some of the more modest kepte the house till he should be heard from. But I have been too long aboute so unworthy a person, and bad a cause.

THE DESTRUCTION OF THE PEQUODS

[From "The History of Plymouth Plantation" for 1637]

I shall not take upon me exactly to describe their proceedings in these things, because I expecte it will be fully done by them selves, who best know the carrage & circumstances of things; I shall therfore but touch them in generall. From Connightecute (who were most sencible of the hurt sustained, & the present danger), they sett out a partie of men, and an other partie mett them from the Bay, at the Narigansets, who were to joyne with them. The Narigansets were ernest to be gone before the Eng-lish were well rested and refreshte, espetially some of them which came last. It should seeme their desire was to come upon the enemie sudenly, & undiscovered. Ther was a barke of this place, newly put in ther, which was come from Conightecutte, who did incourage them to lay hold of the Indeans forwardnes, and to shew as great forwardnes as they, for it would incorage them, and expedition might prove to their great advantage. So they went on, and so ordered their march, as the Indeans brought them to a forte of the enimies (in which most of their cheefe men were) before day. They approached the same with great silence, and surrounded it both with English & Indeans, that they might not breake out; and so assualted them with great courage, shooting amongst them, and entered the forte with all speed; and those that first entered found sharp resistance from the enimie, who both shott at & grapled with them; others rane into their howses, & brought out fire, and sett them on fire, which soone tooke in their matts, &, standing close togeather, with the wind, all was quickly on a flame, and therby more were burnte to death then was otherwise slaine; it burnte their bowstrings, and made them unservisable. Those that scaped the fire were slaine with the sword; some hewed to peeces, others rune throw with their rapiers, so as they were quickly dispatchte, and very few escaped. It was conceived they thus destroyed about 400. at this time. It was a fearfull sight to see them thus frying in the fyer, and the streams of blood quenching the same, and horrible was the stinck & sente ther of; but the victory seemed a sweete sacrifice, and they gave the prays therof to God, who had wrought so wonderfuly for them, thus to inclose their enimise in their hands, and give them so speedy a victory over so proud & insulting an enimie.

SOME VERSES ON NEW ENGLAND

[Printed, from a manuscript of Governor Bradford, in the "Collections of the Massachusetts Historical Society," First series, Vol. II, 1794 [1]]

Almost *ten* years we lived *here* alone,
In other places there were few or none;
For *Salem* was the next of any fame,
That began to augment New England's name;

[[1] The spelling, etc., were of course modernized by the editor. No exact reprint is available.]

But after multitudes began to flow,
More than well knew themselves where to bestow;
Boston then began her roots to spread,
And quickly soon she grew to be the head,
Not only of the Massachusetts Bay,
But all trade and commerce fell in her way.
And truly it was admirable to know,
How greatly all things here began to grow.
New plantations were in each place begun
And with inhabitants were filled soon.
All sorts of grain which our own land doth yield,
Was hither brought, and sown in every field:
As wheat and rye, barley, oats, beans, and pease
Here all thrive, and they profit from them raise,
All sorts of roots and herbs in gardens grow,
Parsnips, carrots, turnips, or what you'll sow,
Onions, melons, cucumbers, radishes,
Skirets, beets, coleworts, and fair cabbages.
Here grows fine flowers many, and 'mongst those,
The fair white lily and sweet fragrant rose.
Many good wholesome berries here you'll find,
Fit for man's use, almost of every kind,
Pears, apples, cherries, plumbs, quinces, and peach,
Are *now* no dainties; you may have of each.
Nuts and grapes of several sorts are here,
If you will take the pains them to seek for.

Cattle of every kind do fill the land;
Many now are kill'd, and their hides tann'd:
By which men are supply'd with meat and shoes,
Or what they can, though much by wolves they lose.
Here store of cows, which milk and butter yield,
And also oxen, for to till the field;
Of which great profit many now do make,
If they have a fit place and able pains do take.
Horses here likewise now do multiply,
They prosper well, and yet their price is high.
Here are swine, good store, and some goats do keep,

But now most begin to get store of sheep,
That with their wool their bodies may be clad,
In time of straits, when things cannot be had;
For merchants keep the price of cloth so high,
As many are not able the same to buy.
And happy would it be for people here,
If they could raise cloth for themselves to wear.

JOHN WINTHROP

[John Winthrop was a man of better family and wider experience in the world than most of the Puritan laymen in early New England. He was born in Suffolk in 1588, and spent two years at Trinity College, Cambridge. His religious experiences inclined him at one time to become a minister, but he finally devoted himself to the law. By 1630, when he came to America as the leader of the new colony of the Massachusetts Company, he was forty-two years of age, had been three times married, had attained some distinction in his profession, and was looked on as a man of weight and substance. For the greater part of the time until his death in 1649 he was either governor or deputy governor of the colony.

Few of Governor Winthrop's writings were printed in his lifetime. "A Short Story of the Rise, reign and ruine of the Antinomians, Familists & Libertines that infected the Churches of New England," a somewhat virulent tract published in London in 1644, has been ascribed to him. His longest and most important work was a journal, which has come to be commonly known by the too inclusive title of "The History of New England." The first part of this was edited by Noah Webster and printed in 1790; and the whole, edited by James Savage, was published in 1825, and again in 1853. Both these versions modernize the spelling, etc.; and no literal reprint of Winthrop's manuscript has been made. The latest edition, by J. K. Hosmer, 1908, follows Savage's text. As in most diaries kept by busy men, the scale of treatment in "The History of New England" is not proportioned to the importance of the events; and there are many blanks which the author evidently intended to fill up in a leisure that never came. The journal is, however, one of the most valuable and readable of the documents from which we gain a picture of early New England life, and not a little of its value comes from the fact that it gives so frank and delightful a revelation of the governor himself. "A Modell of Christian Charity," a homily written on the voyage to America, and other of Winthrop's papers have been published in the collections of the Massachusetts Historical Society.

The selections from "The History of New England" are from Savage's second edition. The selection from Winthrop's "Christian Experience," and the letters to his third wife, Margaret, are from the "Life and Letters of John Winthrop," by Robert C. Winthrop.]

A HALF YEAR IN MASSACHUSETTS BAY

[From "The History of New England" for 1630]

Thursday, July 1.] The Mayflower and the Whale arrived safe in Charlton harbour. Their passengers were all in health, but most of their cattle dead, (whereof a mare and horse of mine). Some stone horses came over in good plight.

Friday, 2.] The Talbot arrived there. She had lost fourteen passengers.

My son, Henry Winthrop, was drowned at Salem.

Saturday, 3.] The Hopewell, and William and Francis arrived.

Monday, 5.] The Trial arrived at Charlton, and the Charles at Salem.

Tuesday, 6.] The Success arrived. She had ―――― goats and lost ―――― of them, and many of her passengers were near starved, etc.

Wednesday, 7.] The Lion went back to Salem.

Thursday, 8.] We kept a day of thanksgiving in all the plantations.

Thursday, August 18.] Capt. Endecott and ―――― Gibson were married by the governour and Mr. Wilson.

Saturday, 20.] The French ship called the Gift, came into the harbour at Charlton. She had been twelve weeks at sea, and lost one passenger and twelve goats; she delivered six.

Monday we kept a court.

' Friday, 27.] We, of the congregation, kept a fast, and chose Mr. Wilson our teacher, and Mr. Nowell an elder, and Mr. Gager and Mr. Aspinwall, deacons. We used imposition of hands, but with this protestation by all, that it was only as a sign of election and confirmation, not of any intent that Mr. Wilson should renounce his ministry he received in England.

September 20.] Mr. Gager died.

30.] About two in the morning, Mr. Isaac Johnson died; his wife, the lady Arbella, of the house of Lincoln, being dead about one month before. He was a holy man, and wise, and died in sweet peace, leaving some part of his substance to the colony.

The wolves killed six calves at Salem, and they killed one wolf.

Thomas Morton adjudged to be imprisoned, till he were sent into England, and his house burnt down, for his many injuries offered to the Indians, and other misdemeanours. Capt. Brook, master of the Gift, refused to carry him.

Finch, of Watertown, had his wigwam burnt and all his goods.

Billington executed at Plimouth for murdering one.

Mr. Phillips, the minister of Watertown, and others, had their hay burnt.

The wolves killed some swine at Saugus.

A cow died at Plimouth, and a goat at Boston, with eating Indian corn.

October 23.] Mr. Rossiter, one of the assistants, died.

25.] Mr. Colburn (who was chosen deacon by the congregation a week before) was invested by imposition of hands of the minister and elder.

The governour, upon consideration of the inconveniences which had grown in England by drinking one to another, restrained it at his own table, and wished others to do the like, so as it grew, by little and little, to disuse.

29.] The Handmaid arrived at Plimouth, having been twelve weeks at sea, and spent all her masts, and of twenty-eight cows she lost ten. She had about sixty passengers, who came all well; John Grant, master.

Mr. Goffe wrote to me, that his shipping this year had utterly undone him.

She brought out twenty-eight heifers, but brought but seventeen alive.

November 11.] The master came to Boston with Capt. Standish and two gentlemen passengers, who came to plant here, but having no testimony, we would not receive them.

10.] —— Firmin, of Watertown, had his wigwam burnt.

Divers had their hay-stacks burnt by burning the grass.

27.] Three of the governour's servants were from this day to the 1 of December abroad in his skiff among the islands, in bitter frost and snow, being kept from home by the N. W. wind, and without victuals. At length they gat to Mount Wollaston, and left their boat there, and came home by land. Laus Deo.

December 6.] The governour and most of the assistants, and others, met at Roxbury, and there agreed to build a town fortified upon the neck between that and Boston, and a committee was appointed to consider of all things requisite, etc.

14.] The committee met at Roxbury, and upon further consideration, for reasons, it was concluded, that we could not have a town in the place aforesaid: 1. Because men would be forced to keep two families. 2. There was no running water; and if there were any springs, they would not suffice the town. 3. The most part of the people had built already, and would not be able to build again. So we agreed to meet at Watertown that day sen'night, and in the meantime other places should be viewed.

Capt. Neal and three other gentlemen came hither to us. He came in the bark Warwick, this summer, to Pascataqua, sent as governour there for Sir Ferdinando Gorges and others.

21.] We met again at Watertown, and there, upon view of a place a mile beneath the town, all agreed it a fit place for a fortified town, and we took time to consider further about it.

24.] Till this time there was (for the most part) fair, open weather, with gentle frosts in the night; but this day the wind came N. W., very strong, and some snow withal, but so cold as some had their fingers frozen, and in danger to be lost. Three of the governour's servants, coming in a shallop from Mistick, were driven by the wind upon Noddle's Island, and forced to stay there all that night, without fire or food; yet, through God's mercy, they came safe to Boston next day, but the fingers of two of them were blistered with cold, and one swooned when he came to the fire.

26.] The rivers were frozen up, and they of Charlton could not come to the sermon at Boston till the afternoon at high water.

Many of our cows and goats were forced to be still abroad for want of houses.

28.] Richard Garrett, a shoemaker of Boston, and one of the congregation there, with one of his daughters, a young maid, and four others, went towards Plimouth in a shallop, against the advice of his friends; and about the Gurnett's Nose the wind overblew so much at N. W. as they were forced to come to a killock at twenty fathom, but their boat drave and shaked out the stone, and they were put to sea, and the boat took in much water, which did freeze so hard as they could not free her; so they gave themselves for lost, and, commending themselves to God, they disposed themselves to die; but one of their company espying land near Cape Cod, they made shift to hoist up part of their sail, and, by God's special providence, were carried through the rocks to the shore, where some gat on land, but some had their legs frozen into the ice, so as they were forced to be cut out. Being come on shore they kindled a fire, but, having no hatchet, they could get little wood, and were forced to lie in the open air all night, being extremely cold. In the morning two of their company went towards Plimouth, (supposing it had been within seven or eight miles, whereas it was near fifty miles from them). By the way they met with two Indian squaws, who, coming home, told their husbands that they had met two Englishmen. They thinking (as it was) that they had been shipwrecked, made after them, and brought them back to their wigwam, and entertained them kindly; and one of them went with them the next day to Plimouth, and the other went to find out their boat and the rest of their company, which were seven miles off, and having found them, he holp them what he could, and returned to his wigwam, and fetched a hatchet, and built them a wigwam and covered it, and gat them wood (for they were so weak and frozen, as they could not stir;) and Garrett died about two days after his landing; and the ground being so frozen as they could not dig his grave, the Indian hewed a hole about half a yard deep, with his hatchet, and having laid the corpse in it, he laid over it a great heap of wood to keep it from the wolves. By this time the governour of Plimouth had sent three men to them with provisions, who being come, and not able to launch their boat, (which with the strong N. W. wind was driven up to the high water mark,) the Indian returned to Plimouth and fetched three more; but before they came, they had launched their boat, and with a fair southerly wind were gotten to Plimouth, where another of their company died, his flesh being mortified with the frost; and the two who went towards Plimouth died also, one of them being not able to get thither, and the other had his feet so frozen as he died of it after. The girl escaped best, and one Harwood, a godly man of the congregation of Boston, lay long under the surgeon's hands; and it was above six weeks before they could get the boat from Plimouth; and in their return they were much distressed; yet their boat was very well manned, the want whereof before was the cause of their loss.

THE INSTITUTING OF A CHURCH

[From "The History of New England" for 1635]

Mr. Shepherd, a godly minister, come lately out of England, and divers other good Christians, intending to raise a church body, came and acquainted the magistrates therewith, who gave their approbation. They also sent to all the neighboring churches for their elders to give their assistance, at a certain day, at Newtown, when they should constitute their body. Accordingly, at this day, there met a great assembly, where the proceeding was as followeth:

Mr. Shepherd and two others (who were after to be chosen to office) sate together in the elder's seat. Then the elder of them began with prayer. After this, Mr. Shepherd prayed with deep confession of sin, etc., and exercised out of Eph. v. — that he might make it to himself a holy, etc.; and also opened the cause of their meeting, etc. Then the elder desired to know of the churches assembled, what number were needful to make a church, and how they ought to proceed in this action. Whereupon some of the ancient ministers, conferring shortly together, gave answer: That the scripture did not set down any certain rule for the number. Three (they thought) were too few, because by Matt. xviii. an appeal was allowed from three; but that seven might be a fit number. And, for their proceeding, they advised, that such as were to join should make confession of their faith, and declare what work of grace the Lord had wrought in them; which accordingly they did, Mr. Shepherd first, then four others, then the elder, and one who was to be deacon, (who had also prayed,) and another member. Then the covenant was read, and they all gave a solemn assent to it. Then the elder desired of the churches, that, if they did approve them to be a church, they would give them the right hand of fellowship. Whereupon Mr. Cotton, (upon short speech with some others near him,) in the name of their churches, gave his hand to the elder, with a short speech of their assent, and desired the peace of the Lord Jesus to be with them. Then Mr. Shepherd made an exhortation to the rest of his body, about the nature of their covenant, and to stand firm to it, and commended them to the Lord in a most heavenly prayer.

z

Then the elder told the assembly, that they were intended to choose Mr. Shepherd for their pastor, (by the name of the brother who had exercised,) and desired the churches, that, if they had any thing to except against him, they would impart it to them before the day of ordination. Then he gave the churches thanks for their assistance, and so left them to the Lord.

A REMARKABLE PROVIDENCE

[From "The History of New England" for 1638]

A remarkable providence appeared in a case, which was tried at the last court of assistants. Divers neighbors of Lynn, by agreement, kept their cattle by turns. It fell out to the turn of one Gillow to keep them, and, as he was driving them forth, another of these neighbors went along with him, and kept him so earnestly in talk, that his cattle strayed and gate in the corn. Then this other neighbor left him, and would not help him recover his cattle, but went and told another how he had kept Gillow in talk, that he might lose his cattle, etc. The cattle, getting into the Indian corn, eat so much ere they could be gotten out, that two of them fell sick of it, and one of them died presently; and these two cows were that neighbor's, who had kept Gillow in talk, etc. The man brings his action against Gillow for his cow (not knowing that he had witness of his speech); but Gillow, producing witness, etc., barred him of his action, and had good costs, etc.

ON THE NATURE OF LIBERTY [1]

[From "The History of New England" for 1645]

I suppose something may be expected from me, upon this charge that is befallen me, which moves me to speak now to you; yet I intend not to intermeddle in the proceedings of the court, or with any of the persons concerned therein. Only I bless God,

[1] This is Winthrop's report of a speech which he delivered before the General Court after his acquittal of a charge of exceeding his powers as deputy governor. The account of the whole controversy, which arose from a neighborhood dispute over a trainband captaincy, is interesting, and significant to the student of early New England social and political conditions, but is too long to quote entire.]

that I see an issue of this troublesome business. I also acknowledge the justice of the court, and, for mine own part, I am well satisfied, I was publicly charged, and I am publicly and legally acquitted, which is all I did expect or desire. And though this be sufficient for my justification before men, yet not so before the God, who hath seen so much amiss in my dispensations (and even in this affair) as calls me to be humble. For to be publicly and criminally charged in this court, is matter of humiliation, (and I desire to make a right use of it,) notwithstanding I be thus acquitted. If her father had spit in her face, (saith the Lord concerning Miriam,) should she not have been ashamed seven days? Shame had lien upon her, whatever the occasion had been. I am unwilling to stay you from your urgent affairs, yet give me leave (upon this special occasion) to speak a little more to this assembly. It may be of some good use, to inform and rectify the judgments of some of the people, and may prevent such distempers as have arisen amongst us. The great questions that have troubled the country, are about the authority of the magistrates and the liberty of the people. It is yourselves who have called us to this office, and being called by you, we have our authority from God, in way of an ordinance, such as hath the image of God eminently stamped upon it, the contempt and violation whereof hath been vindicated with examples of divine vengeance. I entreat you to consider, that when you choose magistrates, you take them from among yourselves, men subject to like passions as you are. Therefore when you see infirmities in us, you should reflect upon your own, and that would make you bear the more with us, and not be severe censurers of the failings of your magistrates, when you have continual experience of the like infirmities in yourselves and others. We account him a good servant, who breaks not his covenant. The covenant between you and us is the oath you have taken of us, which is to this purpose, that we shall govern you and judge your causes by the rules of God's laws and our own, according to our best skill. When you agree with a workman to build you a ship or house, etc., he undertakes as well for his skill as for his faithfulness, for it is his profession, and you pay him for both. But when you call one to be a magistrate, he doth not profess nor undertake to have sufficient skill for that office, nor can you furnish him with gifts, etc., therefore you must run the hazard of his skill and ability. But if he fail in faithfulness, which by his oath he is bound unto, that he must answer for. If it fall out that the case be clear to common apprehension, and the rule clear also, if he transgress here, the error is not in the skill, but in the evil of the will: it must be required of him. But if the case be doubtful, or the rule doubtful, to men of such understanding and parts as your magistrates are, if your magistrates should err here, yourselves must bear it.

For the other point concerning liberty, I observe a great mistake in the country about that. There is a twofold liberty, natural (I mean as our nature is now corrupt) and civil or federal. The first is common to man with beasts and other creatures. By this, man, as he stands in relation to man simply, hath liberty to do what he lists; it is a liberty to evil as well as to good. This liberty is incompatible and inconsistent with authority, and cannot endure the least restraint of the most just authority. The exercise and maintaining of this liberty makes men grow more evil, and in time to be worse than brute beasts: omnes sumus licentia deteriores. This is that great enemy of truth and peace, that wild beast, which all the ordinances of God are bent against, to restrain and subdue it. The other kind of liberty I call civil or federal, it may also be termed moral, in reference to the covenant between God and man, in the moral law, and the politic covenants and constitutions, amongst men themselves. This liberty is the proper end and object of authority, and cannot subsist without it; and it is a liberty to that only which is good, just, and honest. This liberty you are to stand for, with the hazard (not only of your goods, but) of your lives, if need be. Whatsoever crosseth this, is not authority, but a distemper thereof. This liberty is maintained and exercised in a way of subjection to authority; it is of the same kind of liberty wherewith Christ hath made us free. The woman's own choice makes such a man her husband; yet being so chosen, he is her lord, and she is to be subject to him, yet in a way of liberty, not of bondage; and a true wife accounts her subjection her honor and freedom, and would not think her condition safe and free, but in her sub-

jection to her husband's authority. Such is the liberty of the
church under the authority of Christ, her king and husband; his
yoke is so easy and sweet to her as a bride's ornaments; and if
through frowardness or wantonness, etc., she shake it off, at any
time, she is at no rest in her spirit, until she take it up again;
and whether her lord smiles upon her, and embraceth her in his
arms, or whether he frowns, or rebukes, or smites her, she appre-
hends the sweetness of his love in all, and is refreshed, supported,
and instructed by every such dispensation of his authority over
her. On the other side, ye know who they are that complain of
this yoke and say, let us break their bands, etc., we will not have
this man to rule over us. Even so, brethren, it will be between
you and your magistrates. If you stand for your natural corrupt
liberties, and will do what is good in your own eyes, you will not
endure the least weight of authority, but will murmur, and oppose,
and be always striving to shake off that yoke; but if you will be
satisfied to enjoy such civil and lawful liberties, such as Christ
allows you, then will you quietly and cheerfully submit unto that
authority which is set over you, in all the administrations of it,
for your good. Wherein, if we fail at any time, we hope we
shall be willing (by God's assistance) to hearken to good advice
from any of you, or in any other way of God; so shall your liberties be preserved, in upholding the honor and power of authority
amongst you.

SOME EDIFYING CASUALTIES

[From "The History of New England" for 1648]

About eight persons were drowned this winter, all by adven-
turing upon the ice, except three, whereof two (one of them being
far in drink) would needs pass from Boston to Winisemett in a
small boat and a tempestuous night. This man (using to come
home to Winisemett drunken) his wife would tell him, he would
one day be drowned, etc., but he made light of it. Another went
aboard a ship to make merry the last day at night, (being the
beginning of the Lord's day,) and returning about midnight with
three of the ship's company, the boat was overset by means of
the ice, they guiding her by a rope, which went from the ship to

the shore. The seamen waded out, but the Boston man was drowned, being a man of good conversation and hopeful of some work of grace begun in him, but drawn away by the seamen's invitation. God will be sanctified in them that come near him. Two others were the children of one of the church of Boston. While the parents were at the lecture, the boy (being about seven years of age,) having a small staff in his hand, ran down upon the ice towards a boat he saw, and the ice breaking, he fell in, but his staff kept him up, till his sister, about fourteen years old, ran down to save her brother (though there were four men at hand, and called to her not to go, being themselves hasting to save him) and so drowned herself and him also, being past recovery ere the men could come at them, and could easily reach ground with their feet. The parents had no more sons, and confessed they had been too indulgent towards him, and had set their hearts over much upon him.

This puts me in mind of another child very strangely drowned a little before winter. The parents were also members of the church of Boston. The father had undertaken to maintain the mill-dam, and being at work upon it, (with some help he had hired,) in the afternoon of the last day of the week, night came upon them before they had finished what they intended, and his conscience began to put him in mind of the Lord's day, and he was troubled, yet went on and wrought an hour within night. The next day, after evening exercise, and after they had supped, the mother put two children to bed in the room where themselves did lie, and they went out to visit a neighbor. When they returned, they continued about an hour in the room, and missed not the child, but then the mother going to the bed, and not finding her youngest child, (a daughter about five years of age,) after much search she found it drowned in a well in her cellar; which was very observable, as by a special hand of God, that the child should go out of that room into another in the dark, and then fall down at a trap door, or go down the stairs, and so into the well in the farther end of the cellar, the top of the well and the water being even with the ground. But the father, freely in the open congregation, did acknowledge it the righteous hand of God for his profaning his holy day against the checks of his own conscience.

RELIGIOUS EXPERIENCES

[From Winthrop's "Christian Experience," written on his forty-ninth birthday]

About 18 years of age, (being a man in stature, & understanding as my parents conceived me) I married into a family under Mr. Culverwell his ministry in Essex; & living there sometimes I first found the ministry of the Word to come home to my heart with power, (for in all before I found only light) & after that I found the like in the ministry of many others. So as there began to be some change which I perceived in myself, & others took notice of. Now I began to come under strong exercises of conscience, (yet by fits only). I could no longer dally with religion. God put my soule to sad tasks sometimes, which yet the flesh would shake off, & outwear still. I had withal many sweet invitations, which I would willingly have entertained, but the flesh would not give up her interest. The merciful Lord would not thus bee answered, but notwithstanding all my stubbornnesse & unkind rejections of mercy, hee left me not till he had overcome my heart to give up itself to him, & to bid farewell to all the world, & until my heart could answer, "Lord! what wilt thou have mee doe?"

Now came I to some peace & comfort in God & in his wayes, my chief delight was therein. I loved a Christian & the very ground hee went upon. I honoured a faythful minister in my heart & could have kissed his feet: Now I grew full of zeal (which outranne my knowledge & carried mee sometimes beyond my calling), & very liberall to any good work. I had an unsatiable thirst after the word of God & could not misse a good sermon, though many miles off, especially of such as did search deep into the conscience. I had also a great striving in my heart to draw others to God. It pitied my heart to see men so little to regard their soules, & to despise that happiness which I knew to be better than all the world besides, which stirred mee up to take any opportunity to draw men to God, & by successe in my endeavours I took much encouragement hereunto. But these affections were not constant, but very unsettled. By these occasions I grew to bee of some note for religion (which did not a little puff mee up) & divers would come to mee for advice in cases of conscience;

— & if I heard of any that were in trouble of mind I usually went to comfort them; so that upon the bent of my spirit this way & the success I found of my endeavours, I gave up myself to the study of Divinity, & intended to enter into the ministry, if my friends had not diverted me.

But as I grew into employment & credit thereby; so I grew also in pride of my guifts, & under temptations which sett mee on work to look to my evidence more narrowly than I had done before (for the great change which God had wrought in mee, & the generall approbation of good ministers & other Christians, kept me from making any great question of my good estate,) though my secret corruptions, & some tremblings of heart (which was greatest when I was among the most godly persons) put me to some plunges; but especially when I perceived a great decay in my zeal & love, &c. And hearing sometimes of better assurance by the seale of the Spirit, which I also knew by the word of God, but could not, nor durst say that ever I had it; & finding by reading of Mr. Perkin's & other books, that a reprobate might (in appearance) attaine to as much as I had done; finding withal much hollowness & vaine glory in my heart, I began to grow very sad, & knew not what to do: I was ashamed to open my case to any minister that knew mee; I feared it would shame myself & religion also, that such an eminent professor as I was accounted, should discover such corruptions as I found in myself; & had in all this time attained no better evidence of salvation; & [if] I should prove a hypocrite, it was too late to begin anew: I should never repent in truth; having repented so oft as I had done. It was like Hell to mee to think of that in Hebr. 6. Yet I should sometimes propound questions afarre off to such of the most godly ministers as I mett, which gave mee ease for the present, but my heart could not find where to rest; but I grew very sad & melancholy; & now to hear others applaud mee, was a dart through my liver; for still I feared I was not sound at the root, and sometimes I had thoughts of breaking from my profession, & proclaim myself an hypocrite. But these troubles came not all at once but by fits, for sometimes I should find refreshing in prayer, & sometimes in the love that I had had to the Saints: which though it were but poor comfort (for I durst not say before the Lord that

I did love them in truth), yet the Lord upheld mee, and many times outward occasions put these fears out of my thoughts. And though I had knowne long before, the Doctrine of free Justification by Christ, & had often urged it upon my owne soul & others, yet I could not close with Christ to my satisfaction. — I have many times striven to lay hold upon Christ in some promise, & have brought forth all the arguments that I had for my part in it. But instead of finding it to bee mine, I have lost sometimes the faith of the very general truth of the promise, sometimes after much striving by prayer for faith in Christ, I have thought I had received some power to apply Christ unto my soul: but it was so doubtfull as I could have little comfort in it, & it soon vanished.

LETTERS TO MRS. WINTHROP

I

To Mrs. Marg. Winthrop, the elder, at Groton.

MY FAITHFUL AND DEAR WIFE, — It pleaseth God, that thou shouldst once again hear from me before our departure, and I hope this shall come safe to thy hands. I know it will be a great refreshing to thee. And blessed be his mercy, that I can write thee so good news, that we are all in very good health, and, having tried our ship's entertainment now more than a week, we find it agree very well with us. Our boys are well and cheerful, and have no mind of home. They lie both with me, and sleep as soundly in a rug (for we use no sheets here) as ever they did at Groton; and so I do myself, (I praise God). The wind hath been against us this week and more; but this day it has come fair to the north, so as we are preparing (by God's assistance) to set sail in the morning. We have only four ships ready, and some two or three Hollanders go along with us. The rest of our fleet (being seven ships) will not be ready this sennight. We have spent now two Sabbaths on shipboard very comfortably, (God be praised,) and are daily more and more encouraged to look for the Lord's presence to go along with us. Henry Kingsbury hath a child or two in the Talbot sick of the measles, but like to do well. One of my men had them at Hampton, but he was soon well again. We are, in all our eleven ships, about seven hundred persons, passengers, and two hundred and forty cows, and about sixty horses. The ship, which went from Plimouth, carried about one hundred and forty persons, and the ship, which goes from Bristowe, carrieth about eighty persons. And now (my sweet soul) I must once again take my last farewell of thee in Old England. It goeth very near to my heart to leave thee; but I know to whom I have committed thee, even to him who loves thee much better than any husband can, who hath taken account of the hairs of thy head, and puts all thy tears in his bottle, who can, and (if it be for his glory) will bring us together again with peace and comfort. Oh, how it refresheth my heart, to think, that I shall yet again see thy sweet face in the land of the living! — that lovely countenance, that I have so much delighted in, and beheld with so great content! I have hitherto been so taken up with business, as I could seldom look back to my former happiness; but now, when I shall be at some leisure, I shall not avoid the remembrance of thee, nor the grief for thy absence. Thou hast thy share with me, but I hope the course we have agreed upon will be some ease to us both. Mondays and Fridays, at five of the clock at night, we shall meet in spirit till we meet in person. Yet, if all these hopes should fail, blessed be our God, that we are assured we shall meet one day, if not as husband and wife, yet in a better condition. Let that stay and comfort thy heart. Neither can the sea drown thy husband, nor enemies destroy, nor any adversary deprive thee of thy husband or children. Therefore I will only take thee now and my sweet children in mine arms, and kiss and embrace you all, and so leave you with my God. Farewell, farewell. I bless you all in the name of the Lord Jesus. I salute my daughter Winth. Matt. Nan. and the rest, and all my good neighbors and friends. Pray all for us. Farewell. Commend my blessing to my son John. I cannot now write to him; but tell him I have committed thee and thine to him. Labor to draw him yet nearer to God, and he will be the surer staff of comfort to thee. I cannot name the rest of my good friends, but thou canst supply it. I wrote, a week since, to thee and Mr. Leigh, and divers others.

Thine wheresoever,

Jo. Winthrop.

From aboard the Arbella, riding at the Cowes, March 28, 1630.

I would have written to my brother and sister Gostling, but it is near midnight. Let this excuse; and commend my love to them and all theirs.

II

ffor Mrs. Winthrop at her house in Boston.

SWEET HEART, — I was unwillingly hinderd from comminge to thee, nor am I like to see thee before the last daye of this weeke: therefore I shall want a band or 2: & cuffes. I pray thee also send me 6: or 7: leaves of Tobacco dried and powdred. Have care of thy selfe this colde weather, & speak to the folkes to keepe the goates well out of the Garden; & if my brother Peter hath not fetched away the sheep ramme, let them looke him up & give him meate, the green pease in the Garden &c are good for him: If any lettres be come for me send them by this bearer. I will trouble thee no further, the Lorde blesse & keepe thee my sweet wife & all our familye: & send us a comfortable meetinge, so I kisse thee & love thee ever & rest

Thy faithfull husband,

Jo: WINTHROP

This 6th of the 9th, 1637.·

THOMAS MORTON

[Thomas Morton, though of no great importance as an author or as a man, affords a pleasing relief from the severity of most of the early New England writers. He was born in England about 1575, and became a lawyer of Clifford's Inn, London. He seems to have been in America at least four times, but the events of his expeditions are so confused in his own writings that the details of his career are hard to trace. It was on his second visit, in 1625, that he established himself at Mount Wollaston, or Merry (Ma-re) Mount. Here, with a few congenial companions, he traded with the Indians, and enjoyed life after his own fashion. His more austere neighbors charged, probably with truth, that he furnished spirits and fire-arms to the Indians, and that he was guilty of personal immoralities. It is probable, however, that their dislike for him arose in large measure from his ridicule of the Puritans, from his nominal adherence to the Church of England, and from his indulgence in abhorred English festivities, especially those about his famous May-pole, which he erected in 1627. Governor Bradford's account of his plantation, and of his arrest, has been given on an earlier page, and may be compared with his own story of the same occurrences in some of the selections that follow. After being sent to England he at once returned to plague the colonists, and in 1630 was again arrested and deported. It is probable that Morton was an undesirable citizen, but it is doubtful if he committed any serious offence punishable by English law. At all events he was not punished on either occasion when he was sent to England, but allied himself with the party that was working for the revocation of the Massachusetts charter, and succeeded in causing the colonists much trouble. On his fourth visit to America, in 1643, he was imprisoned at Boston for a year, ostensibly to wait for further evidence; but no further evidence was produced, and he was set at liberty. By this time the Puritan successes had destroyed the hopes of his party in England, and, broken in health and fortune, he retired to Agamenticus, Maine, and died there in 1646. His picturesque career has always appealed to students of early New England life, and has inspired more than one literary attempt. Especially notable are Motley's novel of "Merry Mount" and Hawthorne's tale, "The May-Pole of Merry Mount."

Morton's only book was the "New English Canaan, or New Canaan." There has been considerable discussion regarding the history of this work, but it seems reasonably certain that it was written in 1634 or 1635, to create a prejudice against the Massachusetts Puritans at the time when their charter was attacked; and that it was first published at Amsterdam in 1637. To this foreign printing may be due the crudities and inaccuracies of the text, which is in many places obviously corrupt.

As is indicated on the title-page, the "New English Canaan" is divided into three books: "The first Booke setting forth the originall of the Natives, their Manners and Customes, together with their tractable Nature and Love towards the English. The second Booke setting forth the naturall Indowments of the Country, and what staple Commodities it yealdeth. The third Booke setting forth, what people are planted there, their prosperity, what remarkable accidents have happened since the first planting of it, together with their Tenents and practise of their Church." The third book is the most interesting, and also the most obviously biased and unfair. Morton is notable for a certain coarse but quick-witted cleverness which will be observed more than once in the selections that follow. One of his cruder devices is that of using nicknames. Miles Standish is always "Captaine Shrimp," Governor Winthrop is "Joshua Temperwell"; "Bubble," "Eacus," and other characters in his narrative are less readily identified.

The text of the following selections follows the edition made for the Prince Society by Charles Francis Adams, Jr., in 1883. All the selections except the "Dedication" are complete chapters, and the titles assigned to each are Morton's own chapter headings.]

DEDICATION OF THE NEW ENGLISH CANAAN

To the right honorable, the Lords and
others of his Majesties most honorable privy Councell, Commissioners, for the Government of all his
Majesties forraigne Provinces.

Right honorable,

The zeale which I beare to the advauncement of the glory of God, the honor of his Majesty, and the good of the weale publike hath incouraged mee to compose this abstract, being the modell of a Rich, hopefull and very beautifull Country worthy the Title of Natures Masterpeece, and may be lost by too much sufferance. It is but a widowes mite, yet all that wrong and rapine hath left mee to bring from thence, where I have indevoured my best, bound by my allegeance, to doe his Majesty service. This in all humility I present as an offering, wherewith I prostrate my selfe at your honorable footstoole. If you please to vouchsafe it may receave a blessing from the Luster of your gracious Beames, you shall make your vassaile happy, in that hee yet doth live to shew how ready hee is, and alwayes hath bin, to sacrifice his dearest blood, as becometh a loyall subject, for the honor of his native Country. Being

your honors humble vassaile

THOMAS MORTON.

THE GENERALL SURVEY OF THE COUNTRY

[From "New English Canaan," Book II, Chap. I]

In the Moneth of June, Anno Salutis 1622, it was my chaunce to arrive in the parts of New England with 30. Servants, and provision of all sorts fit for a plantation: and whiles our howses were building, I did indeavour to take a survey of the Country: The more I looked, the more I liked it. And when I had more seriously considered of the bewty of the place, with all her faire indowments, I did not thinke that in all the knowne world it could be paralel'd, for so many goodly groves of trees, dainty fine round rising hillucks, delicate faire large plaines, sweete cristall fountaines, and cleare running streames that twine in fine meanders through the meads, making so sweete a murmering noise to heare as would even lull the sences with delight a sleepe, so pleasantly doe they glide upon the pebble stones, jetting most jocundly where they doe meete and hand in hand runne downe to Neptunes Court, to pay the yearely tribute which they owe to him as soveraigne Lord of all the springs. Contained within the volume of the Land, Fowles in abundance, Fish in multitude; and discovered, besides, Millions of Turtledoves one the greene boughes, which sate pecking of the full ripe pleasant grapes that were supported by the lusty trees, whose fruitfull loade did cause the armes to bend: which here and there dispersed, you might see Lillies and of the Daphnean-tree: which made the Land to mee seeme paradice: for in mine eie t'was Natures Masterpeece; Her cheifest Magazine of all where lives her store: if this Land be not rich, then is the whole world poore.

What I had resolved on, I have really performed; and I have endeavoured to use this abstract as an instrument, to bee the meanes to communicate the knowledge which I have gathered, by my many yeares residence in those parts, unto my Countrymen: to the end that they may the better perceive their error, who cannot imagine that there is any Country in the universall world which may be compared unto our native soyle. I will now discover unto them a Country whose indowments are by learned men allowed to stand in a paralell with the Israelites Canaan, which none will deny to be a land farre more excellent then Old England, in her proper nature.

This I consider I am bound in duety (as becommeth a Christian man) to performe for the glory of God, in the first place; next, (according to Cicero,) to acknowledge that, *Non nobis solum nati sumus, sed partim patria, partim parentes, partim amici vindicant.*

For which cause I must approove of the indeavoures of my Country men, that ha$ve bin studious to inlarge the territories of his Majesties empire by planting Colonies in America.

And of all other, I must applaude the judgement of those that have made choise of this part, (whereof I now treat,) being of all other most absolute, as I will make it appeare hereafter by way of paralell. Among those that have setled themselvs in new England, some have gone for their conscience sake, (as they professe,) and I wish that they may plant the Gospel of Jesus Christ, as becommeth them, sincerely and without satisme or faction, whatsoever their former or present practises are, which I intend not to justifie: howsoever, they have deserved (in mine opinion) some commendationes, in that they have furnished the Country so commodiously in so short a time; although it hath bin but for their owne profit, yet posterity will taste the sweetnes of it, and that very sodainly.

And since my taske, in this part of mine abstract, is to intreat of the naturall indowments of the Country, I will make a breife demonstration of them in order, severally, according to their severall qualities: and shew you what they are, and what profitable use may be made by them of industry.

OF THOMAS MORTONS ENTERTAINEMENT AT PLIMMOUTH, AND CASTINGE AWAY UPON AN ISLAND

[From "New English Canaan," Book III, Chap. VII]

This man arrived in those parts, and, hearing newes of a Towne that was much praised, he was desirous to goe thither, and see how thinges stood; where his entertainement was their best, I dare be bould to say: for, although they had but 3. Cowes in all, yet had they fresh butter and a sallet of egges in dainty wise, a dish not common in a wildernes. There hee bestowed some time in the survey of this plantation. His new come servants, in the meane time, were tane to taske, to have their zeale appeare, and questioned what preacher was among their company; and finding none, did seeme to condole their estate as if undone, because no man among them had the guift to be in Jonas steade, nor they the meanes to keepe them in that path so hard to keepe.

Our Master, say they, reades the Bible and the word of God, and useth the booke of common prayer: but this is not the meanes, the answere is: the meanes, they crie, alas, poore Soules where is the meanes? you seeme as if betrayed, to be without the meanes: how can you be stayed from fallinge headlonge to perdition? *Facilis descensus averni:* the booke of common prayer, sayd they, what poore thinge is that, for a man to reade in a booke? No, no, good sirs, I would you were neere us, you might receave comfort by instruction: give me a man hath the guiftes of the spirit, not a booke in hand. I doe professe sayes one, to live without the meanes is dangerous, the Lord doth know.

By these insinuations, like the Serpent, they did creepe and winde into the good opinion of the illiterate multitude, that were desirous to be freed and gone to them, no doubdt, (which some of them after confessed); and little good was to be done one them after this charme was used: now plotts and factions how they might get loose: and here was some 35. stout knaves; and some plotted how to steale Master Westons barque, others, exasperated knavishly to worke, would practise how to gett theire Master to an Island, and there leave him; which hee had notice of, and fitted him to try what would be done; and steps aborde his shallop bound for Cape Anne, to the Massachusetts, with an Hogshead of Wine; Sugar hee tooke along, the Sailes hoist up, and one of the Conspirators aboard to steere; who in the mid way pretended foule weather at the harboure mouth, and therefore, for a time, hee would put in to an Island neere, and make some stay where hee thought to tempt his Master to walke the woods, and so be gone: but their Master to prevent them caused the sales and oares to be brought a shore, to make a tilt if neede showld be, and kindled fire, broched that Hogshed, and caused them fill the can with lusty liquor,

Claret sparklinge neate; which was not suffered to grow pale and flatt, but tipled of with quick dexterity: the Master makes a shew of keepinge round, but with close ljpps did seeme to make longe draughts, knowinge the wine would make them Protestants; and so the plot was then at large disclosed and discovered, and they made drowsie; and the inconstant windes shiftinge at night did force the kellecke home, and billedge the boat, that they were forced to leave her so, and cut downe trees that grew by the shore, to make Caffes: two of them went over by helpe of a fore saile almost a mile to the maine; the other two stayed five dayes after, till the windes would serve to fill the sailes. The first two went to cape Ann by land, and had fowle enough, and fowle wether by the way; the Islanders had fish enough, shel-fish and fire to roast, and they could not perish for lacke of foode, and wine they had to be sure; and by this you see they were not then in any want: the wine and goodes brought thence; the boat left ther so billedgd that it was not worth the labor to be mended.

OF A MAN INDUED WITH MANY SPETIALL GUIFTS SENT OVER TO BE MASTER OF THE CERE-MONIES

[From "New English Canaan," Book III, Chap. X]

This was a man approoved of the Brethren, both for his zeale and guiftes, yet but a Bubble, and at the publike Chardge conveyed to New England, I thinke to be Master of the Ceremonies betweene the Natives, and the Planters: for hee applied himselfe cheifly to pen the language downe in Stenography: But there for want of use, which hee rightly understood not, all was losse of labor; some-thinge it was when next it came to view, but what hee could not tell.

This man, Master Bubble, was in the time of John Oldams absence made the howse Chaplaine there, and every night hee made use of his guifts, whose oratory luld his auditory fast a sleepe, as Mercuries pipes did Argus eies: for, when hee was in, they sayd hee could not tell how to get out; nay, hee would hardly out till hee were fired out, his zeale was such: (one fire they say drives

F

out another): hee would become a great Merchant, and by any thinge that was to be sold so as hee might have day and be trusted never so litle time: the price it seemed hee stood not much upon, but the day: for to his freind he shewed commodities, so priced as caused him to blame the buyer, till the man this Bubble did declare that it was tane up at day, and did rejoyce in the bargaine, insistinge on the day; the day, yea, marry, quoth his friend, if you have doomesday for payment you are then well to passe. But if he had not, it were as good hee had; they were payed all alike.

And now this Bubbles day is become a common proverbe. Hee obtained howse roome at Passonagessit and remooved thether, because it stood convenient for the Beaver trade: and the rather because the owner of Passonagessit had no Corne left, and this man seemed a bigg boned man, and therefore thought to be a good laborer, and to have store of corne; but, contrary wise, hee had none at all, and hoped upon this freind his host: thithere were brought the trophies of this Master Bubbles honor, his water tankard and his Porters basket, but no provision; so that one gunne did serve to helpe them both to meat; and now the time for fowle was almost past.

This man and his host at dinner, Bubble begins to say grace; yea, and a long one to, till all the meate was cold; hee would not give his host leave to say grace: belike, hee thought mine host past grace, and further learned as many other Schollers are: but in the usage and custom of this blinde oratory his host tooke himselfe abused, and the whiles fell to and had halfe done before this man Bubble would open his eies to see what stood afore him, which made him more cautius, and learned that *brevis oratio penetrat Cœlum*. Together Bubbles and hee goes in the Canaw to Nut Island for brants, and there his host makes a shotte and breakes the winges of many: Bubble, in hast and single handed, paddels out like a Cow in a cage: his host cals back to rowe two handed like to a pare of oares; and, before this could be performed, the fowle had time to swimme to other flockes, and so to escape: the best part of the pray being lost mayd his host to mutter at him, and so to parte for that time discontended.

OF A GREAT MONSTER SUPPOSED TO BE AT MA-RE-MOUNT; AND THE PREPARATION MADE TO DESTROY IT

[From "New English Canaan," Book III, Chap. XV]

The Seperatists, envying the prosperity and hope of the Plantation at Ma-re Mount, (which they perceaved beganne to come forward, and to be in a good way for gaine in the Beaver trade,) conspired together against mine Host especially, (who was the owner of that Plantation,) and made up a party against him; and mustred up what aide they could, accounting of him as of a great Monster.

Many threatening speeches were given out both against his person and his Habitation, which they divulged should be consumed with fire: And taking advantage of the time when his company, (which seemed little to regard theire threats,) were gone up into the Inlands to trade with the Salvages for Beaver, they set upon my honest host at a place called Wessaguscus, where, by accident, they found him. The inhabitants there were in good hope of the subvertion of the plantation at Mare Mount, (which they principally aymed at;) and the rather because mine host was a man that indeavoured to advaunce the dignity of the Church of England; which they, (on the contrary part,) would laboure to vilifie with uncivile termes: enveying against the sacred booke of common prayer, and mine host that used it in a laudable manner amongst his family, as a practise of piety.

There hee would be a meanes to bring sacks to their mill, (such is the thirst after Beaver,) and helped the conspiratores to surprise mine host, (who was there all alone;) and they chargded him, (because they would seeme to have some reasonable cause against him to sett a glosse upon their mallice,) with criminall things; which indeede had beene done by such a person, but was of their conspiracy; mine host demaunded of the conspirators who it was that was author of that information, that seemed to be their ground for what they now intended. And because they answered they would not tell him, hee as peremptorily replyed, that hee would not say whether he had, or he had not done as they had bin informed.

The answere made no matter, (as it seemed,) whether it had bin negatively or affirmatively made; for they had resolved that hee should suffer, because, (as they boasted,) they were now become the greater number: they had shaked of their shackles of servitude, and were become Masters, and masterles people.

It appeares they were like beares whelpes in former time, when mine hosts plantation was of as much strength as theirs, but now, (theirs being stronger,) they, (like overgrowne beares,) seemed monsterous. In'breife, mine host must indure to be their prisoner untill they could contrive it so that they might send him for England, (as they said,) there to suffer according to the merrit of the fact which they intended to father upon him; supposing, (belike,) it would proove a hainous crime.

Much rejoycing was made that they had gotten their capitall enemy, (as they concluded him;) whome they purposed to hamper in such sort that hee should not be able to uphold his plantation at Ma-re Mount.

The Conspirators sported themselves at my honest host, that meant them no hurt, and were so joccund that they feasted their bodies, and fell to tippeling as if they had obtained a great prize; like the Trojans when they had the custody of Hippeus pinetree horse.

Mine host fained greefe, and could not be perswaded either to eate or drinke; because hee knew emptines would be a meanes to make him as watchfull as the Geese kept in the Roman Cappitall: whereon, the contrary part, the conspirators would be so drowsy that hee might have an opportunity to give them a slip, insteade of a tester. Six persons of the conspiracy were set to watch him at Wessaguscus: But hee kept waking; and in the dead of night, (one lying on the bed for further suerty,) up gets mine Host and got to the second dore that hee was to passe, which, notwithstanding the lock, hee got open, and shut it after him with such violence that it affrighted some of the conspirators.

The word, which was given with an alarme, was, ô he's gon, he's gon, what shall wee doe, he's gon! The rest, (halfe a sleepe,) start up in a maze, and, like rames, ran theire heads one at another full butt in the darke.

Theire grande leader, Captaine Shrimp, tooke on most furiously and tore his clothes for anger, to see the empty nest, and their bird gone.

The rest were eager to have torne theire haire from theire heads; but it was so short that it would give them no hold. Now Captaine Shrimp thought in the losse of this prize, (which hee accoumpted his Master peece,) all his honor would be lost for ever.

In the meane time mine Host was got home to Ma-re Mount through the woods, eight miles round about the head of the river Monatoquit that parted the two Plantations, finding his way by the helpe of the lightening, (for it thundred as hee went terribly;) and there hee prepared powther, three pounds dried, for his present imployement, and foure good gunnes for him and the two assistants left at his howse, with bullets of severall sizes, three houndred or thereabouts, to be used if the conspirators should pursue him thether: and these two persons promised theire aides in the quarrell, and confirmed that promise with health in good rosa solis.

Now Captaine Shrimp, the first Captaine in the Land, (as hee supposed,) must doe some new act to repaire this losse, and, to vindicate his reputation, who had sustained blemish by this oversight, begins now to study, how to repaire or survive his honor: in this manner, callinge of Councell, they conclude.

Hee takes eight persons more to him, and, (like the nine Worthies of New Canaan,) they imbarque with preparation against Ma-re Mount, where this Monster of a man, as theire phrase was, had his denne; the whole number, had the rest not bin from home, being but seaven, would have given Captaine Shrimpe, (a quondam Drummer,) such a wellcome as would have made him wish for a Drume as bigg as Diogenes tubb, that hee might have crept into it out of sight.

Now the nine Worthies are approached, and mine Host prepared: having intelligence by a Salvage, that hastened in love from Wessaguscus to give him notice of their intent.

One of mine Hosts men prooved a craven: the other had prooved his wits to purchase a little valoure, before mine Host had observed his posture.

The nine worthies comming before the Denne of this supposed Monster, (this seaven headed hydra, as they termed him,) and began, like Don Quixote against the Windmill, to beate a parly, and to offer quarter, if mine Host would yeald; for they resolved to send him for England; and bad him lay by his armes.

But hee, (who was the Sonne of a Souldier,) having taken up armes in his just defence, replyed that hee would not lay by those armes, because they were so needefull at Sea, if hee should be sent over. Yet, to save the effusion of so much worty bloud, as would have issued out of the vaynes of these 9. worthies of New Canaan, if mine Host should have played upon them out at his port holes, (for they came within danger like a flocke of wild geese, as if they had bin tayled one to another, as coults to be sold at a faier,) mine Host was content to yeelde upon quarter; and did capitulate with them in what manner it should be for more certainety, because hee knew what Captaine Shrimpe was.

Hee expressed that no violence should be offered to his person, none to his goods, nor any of his Howsehold: but that hee should have his armes, and what els was requisit for the voyage: which theire Herald retornes, it was agreed upon, and should be performed.

But mine Host no sooner had set open the dore, and issued out, but instantly Captaine Shrimpe and the rest of the worthies stepped to him, layd hold of his armes, and had him downe: and so eagerly was every man bent against him, (not regarding any agreement made with such a carnall man,) that they fell upon him as if they would have eaten him: some of them were so violent that they would have a slice with scabbert, and all for haste; untill an old Souldier, (of the Queenes, as the Proverbe is,) that was there by accident, clapt his gunne under the weapons, and sharply rebuked these worthies for their unworthy practises. So the matter was taken into more deliberate consideration.

Captaine Shrimp, and the rest of the nine worthies, made themselves, (by this outragious riot,) Masters of mine Host of Ma-re Mount, and disposed of what hee had at his plantation.

This they knew, (in the eye of the Salvages,) would add to their glory, and diminish the reputation of mine honest Host; whome they practised to be ridd of upon any termes, as willingly as if hee had bin the very Hidra of the time.

HOW THE 9. WORTHIES PUT MINE HOST OF MA-RE-
MOUNT INTO THE INCHAUNTED CASTLE AT
PLIMMOUTH, AND TERRIFIED HIM WITH THE
MONSTER BRIAREUS

[From "New English Canaan," Book III, Chap. XVI]

The nine worthies of New Canaan having now the Law in their
owne hands, (there being no generall Governour in the Land;
nor none of the Seperation that regarded the duety they owe their
Soveraigne, whose naturall borne subjects they were, though
translated out of Holland, from whence they had learned to worke
all to their owne ends, and make a great shewe of Religion, but
no humanity,) for they were now to sit in Counsell on the
cause.

And much it stood mine honest Host upon to be very circum-
spect, and to take Eacus to taske; for that his voyce was more
allowed of then both the other: and had not mine Host confounded all the arguments that Eacus could make in their
defence, and confuted him that swaied the rest, they would
have made him unable to drinke in such manner of merriment
any more. So that following this private counsell, given him by
one that knew who ruled the rost, the Hiracano ceased that els
would split his pinace.

A conclusion was made and sentence given that mine Host
should be sent to England a prisoner. But when hee was brought
to the shipps for that purpose, no man durst be so foole hardy as to
undertake carry him. So these Worthies set mine Host upon an
Island, without gunne, powther, or shot or dogge or so much as a
knife to get any thinge to feede upon, or any other cloathes to
shelter him with at winter then a thinne suite which hee had one at
that time. Home hee could not get to Ma-re Mount. Upon this
Island hee stayed a moneth at least, and was releeved by Salvages
that tooke notice that mine Host was a Sachem of Passonagessit,
and would bringe bottles of strong liquor to him, and unite themselves into a league of brother hood with mine Host; so full of
humanity are these infidels before those Christians.

From this place for England sailed mine Host in a Plimmouth

shipp, (that came into the Land to fish upon the Coast,) that landed him safe in England at Plimmouth: and hee stayed in England untill the ordinary time for shipping to set forth for these parts, and then retorned: Noe man being able to taxe him of any thinge.

But the Worthies, (in the meane time,) hoped they had bin ridd of him.

"THE BAY PSALM BOOK"

[The extreme punctiliousness of the early New England Puritans in all matters pertaining to worship led many of them to take offence at the lack of literalness in Sternhold and Hopkins's version of the Psalms, which was at first used in the churches of Massachusetts Bay. Accordingly "the chief Divines of the Country" undertook a new and more faithful metrical rendering. The greater part of the work was done by Richard Mather, who probably wrote the preface, Thomas Welde, and John Eliot. The result of their labors was published at Cambridge, in 1640, and has the distinction of being the first book printed in America. The title-page reads "The Whole Booke of Psalmes Faithfully Translated into English Metre. Whereunto is prefixed a discourse declaring not only the lawfullnes, but also the necessity of the heavenly Ordinance of singing Scripture Psalmes in the Churches of God." The work seems always to have been known, however, as "The Bay Psalm Book." It was generally used in New England churches until it was supplanted by Watts's "Psalms and Hymns" in the middle of the eighteenth century; and it attained some use in England and Scotland.

The modern reader finds it hard to understand how our forefathers could have endured so rough and barbarous a rendering of the Hebrew poems. It must be remembered that the sense of form in English verse was not high, as is shown by other poetic attempts of New England divines; that extreme reverence for the Bible blinded Christians to its literary excellences, so that they failed to see the contrast between this rendering and the sonorous grandeur of the King James version; and that the one test imposed on this work, as a matter of sacred principle, was that of literal exactness.

The selections follow the facsimile reprint of the first edition edited by Wilberforce Eames in 1903.]

METRICAL TRANSLATION OF THE PSALMS DEFENDED

[From the "Preface"]

As for the scruple that some take at the translation of the book of psalmes into meeter, because Davids psalmes were sung in his owne words without meeter: wee answer — First. There are many verses together in several psalmes of David which run in rithmes (as those that know the hebrew and as Buxtorf shews

73

Thesau. pa. 62.) which shews at least the lawfullnes of singing psalmes in english rithmes.

Secondly. The psalmes are penned in such verses as are sutable to the poetry of the hebrew language, and not in the common style of such other bookes of the old Testament as are not poeticall; now no protestant doubteth but that all the bookes of the scripture should by Gods ordinance be extant in the mother tongue of each nation, that they may be understood of all, hence the psalmes are to be translated into our english tongue: and if in our english tongue we are to sing them, then as all our english songs (according to the course of our english poetry) do run in metre, soe ought Davids psalmes to be translated into meeter, that soe wee may sing the Lords songs, as in our English tongue soe in such verses as are familiar to an english eare which are commonly metricall: and as it can be no just offence to any good conscience, to sing Davids hebrew songs in english words, soe neither to sing his poeticall verses in english poeticall metre: men might as well stumble at singing the hebrew psalmes in our english tunes (and not in the hebrew tunes) as at singing them in english meeter, (which are our verses) and not in such verses as are generally used by David according to the poetry of the hebrew language: but the truth is, as the Lord hath hid from us the hebrew tunes, lest wee should think our selves bound to imitate them; soe also the course and frame (for the most part) of their hebrew poetry, that wee might not think our selves bound to imitate that, but that every nation without scruple might follow as the grave sort of tunes of their owne country songs, soe the graver sort of verses of their owne country poetry.

Neither let any think, that for the meetre sake wee have taken liberty or poeticall license to depart from the true and proper sence of Davids words in the hebrew verses, noe; but it hath beene one part of our religious care and faithfull indeavour, to keepe close to the originall text.

As for other objections taken from the difficulty of *Ainsworths* tunes, and the corruptions in our common psalme books, wee hope they are answered in this new edition of psalmes which wee here present to God and his Churches. For although wee have cause to blesse God in many respects for the religious indeavours of the translaters of the psalmes into meetre usually annexed to our

Bibles, yet it is not unknowne to the godly learned that they have
rather presented a paraphrase then the words of David translated
according to the rule 2 *chron.* 29. 30. and that their addition to
the words, detractions from the words are not seldome and rare,
but very frequent and many times needles, (which wee suppose
would not be approved of if the psalmes were so translated into
prose) and that their variations of the sense, and alterations of the
sacred text too frequently, may justly minister matter of offence to
them that are able to compare the translation with the text; of
which failings, some judicious have oft complained, others have
been grieved, whereupon it hath bin generally desired, that as wee
doe injoye other, soe (if it were the Lords will) wee might injoye
this ordinance also in its native purity: wee have therefore done
our indeavour to make a plaine and familiar translation of the
psalmes and words of David into english metre, and have not soe
much as presumed to paraphrase to give the sense of his meaning
in other words; we have therefore attended heerin as our chief
guide the originall, shunning all additions, except such as even the
best translators of them in prose supply, avoiding all materiall
detractions from words or sence.   The word ו which wee translate
and as it is redundant sometime in the Hebrew, soe somtime
(though not very often) it hath been left out and yet not then, if
the sence were not faire without it.

As for our translations, wee have with our english Bibles (to
which next to the Originall wee have had respect) used the Idioms
of our owne tongue in stead of Hebraismes, lest they might seeme
english barbarismes.

Synonimaes wee use indifferently: as *folk* for *people*, and *Lord*
for *Jehovah*, and sometime (though seldome) *God* for *Jehovah;*
for which (as for some other interpretations of places cited in the
new Testament) we have the scriptures authority ps. 14. with 53.
Heb. 1. 6. with psalme 97. 7.   Where a phrase is doubtfull wee
have followed that which (in our owne apprehension) is most
genuine & edifying:

Somtime wee have contracted, somtime dilated the same hebrew
word, both for the sence and the verse sake: which dilatation wee
conceive to be no paraphrasticall addition no more then the con-
traction of a true and full translation to be any unfaithfull detrac-

tion or diminution: as when wee dilate *who healeth* and say *he it is who healeth;* soe when wee contract, *those that stand in awe of God* and say *Gods fearers.*

Lastly. Because some hebrew words have a more full and emphaticall signification then any one english word can or doth somtime expresse, hence wee have done that somtime which faithfull translators may doe, *viz.* not only to translate the word but the emphasis of it; as אֵל *mighty God* for *God.* בָּרַך *humbly blesse* for *blesse; rise to stand,* psalm 1. for *stand truth and faithfullnes* for *truth.* Howbeit, for the verse sake wee doe not alway thus, yet wee render the word truly though not fully; as when wee somtime say *rejoyce* for *shout for joye.*

As for all other changes of numbers, tenses, and characters of speech, they are either such as the hebrew will unforcedly beare, or our english forceably calls for, or they no way change the sence; and such are printed usually in an other character.

If therefore the verses are not always so smooth and elegant as some may desire or expect; let them consider that Gods Altar needs not our pollishings: Ex. 20. for wee have respected rather a plaine translation, then to smooth our verses with the sweetnes of any paraphrase, and soe have attended Conscience rather than Elegance, fidelity rather then poetry, in translating the hebrew words into english language, and Davids poetry into english meetre; that soe wee may sing in Sion the Lords songs of prayse according to his owne will; untill hee take us from hence and wipe away all our teares, & bid us enter into our masters joye to sing eternall Halleluliahs.

PSALME 1

O Blessed man, that in th' advice
    of wicked doeth not walk;
nor stand in sinners way, nor sit
    in chayre of scornfull folk,
2 But in the law of Jehovah,
    is his longing delight:
and in his law doth meditate,
    by day and eke by night.

3 And he shall be like to a tree
  planted by water-rivers:
that in his season yeilds his fruit,
  and his leafe never withers.
4 And all he doth, shall prosper well,
  the wicked are not so:
but they are like unto the chaffe,
  which winde drives to and fro.
5 Therefore shall not ungodly men,
  rise to stand in the doome,
nor shall the sinners with the just,
  in their assemblie *come*.
6 For of the righteous men, the Lord
  acknowledgeth the way:
but the way of ungodly men,
  shall utterly decay.

PSALME 19

The heavens doe declare
  the majesty of God:
also the firmament shews forth
  his handy-work abroad.
2 Day speaks to day, knowledge
  night hath to night declar'd.
3 There neither speach nor language is,
  where their voyce is not heard.
4 Through all the earth their line
  is gone forth, & unto
the.utmost end of all the world,
  their speaches reach also:
A Tabernacle hee
  in them pitcht for the Sun.
5 Who Bridegroom like from's chamber goes
  glad Giants-race to run.
6 From heavens utmost end,
  his course and compassing;

.

to ends of it, & from the heat
thereof is hid nothing.

(2)

7 The Lords law perfect is,
    the soule converting back:
  Gods testimony faithfull is,
    makes wise who-wisdome-lack.
8 The statutes of the Lord,
    are right, & glad the heart:
  the Lords commandement is pure,
    light doth to eyes impart.
9 Jehovahs feare is cleane,
    and doth indure for ever:
  the judgements of the Lord are true,
    and righteous altogether.
10 Then gold, then much fine gold,
    more to be prized are,
  then hony, & the hony-comb,
    sweeter they are by farre.
11 Also thy servant is
    admonished from hence:
  and in the keeping of the same
    is a full recompence.
12 Who can his errors know?
    from secret faults cleanse mee.
13 And from presumptuous-sins, let thou
    kept back thy servant bee:
  Let them not beare the rule
    in me, & then shall I
  be perfect, and shall cleansed bee
    from much iniquity.
14 Let the words of my mouth,
    and the thoughts of my heart,
  be pleasing with thee, Lord, my Rock
    who my redeemer art.

23 A PSALME OF DAVID

The Lord to mee a shepheard is,
  want therefore shall not I.
2 Hee in the folds of tender-grasse,
  doth cause mee downe to lie:
To waters calme me gently leads
3   Restore my soule doth hee:
he doth in paths of righteousnes:
  for his names sake leade mee.
4 Yea though in valley of deaths shade
  I walk, none ill I'le feare:
because thou are with mee, thy rod,
  and staffe my comfort are.
5 For mee a table thou hast spread,
  in presence of my foes:
thou dost annoynt my head with oyle,
  my cup it over-flowes.
6 Goodnes & mercy surely shall
  all my dayes follow mee:
and in the Lords house I shall dwell
  so long as dayes shall bee.

PSALME 95

O Come, let us unto the Lord
  shout loud with singing voyce.
to the rock of our saving health
  let us make joyfull noyse.
2 Before his presence let us then
  approach with thanksgiving:
also let us triumphantly
  with Psalmes unto him sing.
3 For the Lord a great God: & great
  King above all gods is.
4 In whose hands are deepes of the earth,
  & strength of hills are his

5 The sea to him doth appertaine,
   also he made the same:
  & also the drye land is his
   for it his hands did frame.
6 O come, & let us worship give.
   & bowing downe adore:
  he that our maker is, the Lord
   o let us kneele before.
7 Because hee is our God, & wee
   his pasture people are,
  & of his hands the sheep: today
   if yee his voyce will heare,
8 As in the provocation,
   o harden not your heart:
 , as in day of temptation,
   within the vast desart.
9 When mee your fathers tryde, & prov'd,
   & my works lookt upon:
10 Fourty yeares long I griev'd was with
   this generation:
  And sayd, this people erre in heart:
   my wayes they doe not know.
11 To whom I sware in wrath: if they
   into my rest should goe.

PSALME 100

Make yee a joyfull sounding noyse
   unto Jehovah, all the earth:
2 Serve yee Jehovah with gladnes:
  before his presence come with mirth.
3   Know, that Jehovah he is God,
  who hath us formed it is hee,
   & not ourselves: his owne people
   & sheepe of his pasture are wee.
4   Enter into his gates with prayse,
  into his Courts with thankfullnes:

make yee confession unto him,
& his name reverently blesse.

5   Because Jehovah he is good,
for evermore is his mercy:
& unto generations all
continue doth his verity.

PSALME 121

1 I to the hills lift up mine eyes,
   from whence shall come mine aid
2 Mine help doth from Jehovah come,
   which heav'n & earth hath made.
3 Hee will not let thy foot be mov'd,
   nor slumber; that thee keeps.
4 Loe hee that keepeth Israell,
   hee slumbreth not, nor sleeps.
5 The Lord thy keeper is, the Lord
   on thy right hand the shade.
6 The Sun by day, nor Moone by night,
   shall thee by stroke *invade*.
7 The Lord will keep the from all ill:
   thy soule hee keeps alway,
8 Thy going out, & thy income,
   the Lord keeps now & aye.

JOHN COTTON

[John Cotton, perhaps the most famous in his day of the early New England ministers, was born in 1585. He was educated at Cambridge, where he first entered Trinity College, and afterward became a fellow of Emanuel. Here he became a Puritan, and when, later, he settled as minister of a congregation in Boston, Lincolnshire, he refused to conform to parts of the Church ritual. His influence was such, however, that he held his pastorate for over twenty years, and became famous among Puritans everywhere. It was in honor of the town in which he ministered that the new Boston was named. When he was finally ousted by Archbishop Laud, he fled to America. From his arrival in 1633 to his death in 1652 he was connected, as teacher and pastor, with the First Church of Boston.

John Cotton was a profound and diligent student, and a voluminous writer, though to the reader of to-day his writings seem less interesting and less valuable than those of many of his contemporaries. He was the author of the classic catechism, "Milk for Boston Babes,"[1] and of many sermons and controversial writings. One of the most interesting controversies in which he was engaged was that with Roger Williams respecting persecution for cause of conscience. Something of his method in this discussion may be inferred from the selection from Williams's reply on a later page.

The first of the following selections is from a sermon delivered at Southampton before Winthrop's expedition, some three years before his own emigration. The text follows the reprint in Old South Leaflets, Number 53. The second selection, from "The Way of Congregational Churches cleared," Cotton's famous defence of the policy and method of New England Congregationalists, follows the reprint in the publications of the Prince Society, edited by Charles Francis Adams. The subject of this selection is of interest because Mrs. Hutchinson had placed Cotton in an embarrassing position by praising him above the other ministers. The third selection is the first part of a letter to Roger Williams, printed in London in 1643, but written some years earlier. The text is that of the reprint in the Publications of the Narragansett Club, 1866.]

[1] The full title is " Milk for Babes, drawn out of the Breasts of both Testaments, chiefly for the Spiritual Nourishment of Boston Babes in either England, but may be of use for any Children."

GOD'S PROMISE TO HIS PLANTATIONS

[From a sermon, " God's Promise to his Plantations "]

The placing of a people in this or that Countrey is from the appointment of the Lord.

This is evident in the Text,[1] and the Apostle speakes of it as grounded in nature, *Acts* 17. 26. *God hath determined the times before appointed, and the bounds of our habitation. Dut. 2 chap.* 5. 9. God would not have the *Israelites* meddle with the *Edomites*, or the *Moabites*, because he had given them their land for a possession. God assigned out such a land for such a posterity, and for such a time.

Quest. Wherein doth this worke of God stand in appointing a place for a people?

Answ. First, when God espies or discovers a land for a people, as in *Ezek.* 20. 6. he brought them into a land that he had espied for them: And that is, when either he gives them to discover it themselves, or heare of it discovered by others, and fitting them.

Secondly, after he hath espied it, when he carrieth them along to it, so that they plainly see a providence of God leading them from one Country to another: As in *Exod.* 19. 4. *You have seene how I have borne you as on Eagles wings, and brought you unto my selfe.* So that though they met with many difficulties, yet hee carried them high above them all, like an eagle, flying over seas and rockes, and all hindrances.

Thirdly, when he makes roome for a people to dwell there, as in *Psal.* 80. 9. *Thou preparedst roome for them.* When *Isaac* sojourned among the *Philistines*, he digged one well, and the *Philistines* strove for it, and he called it *Esek.* and he digged another well, and for that they strove also, therefore he called it *Sitnah:* and he removed thence, and digged an other well, and for that they strove not, and he called it *Rohoboth*, and said, *For now the Lord hath made roomee for us, and we shall be fruitfull in the Land.* Now no *Esek*, no *Sitnah*, no quarrel or contention, but now he sits downe in *Rohoboth* in a peaceable roome.

Now God makes room for a people 3 wayes:

[1] [2 Sam. vii, 10.]

First, when he casts out the enemies of a people before them by lawfull warre with the inhabitants, which God cals them unto: as in *Ps.* 44. 2. *Thou didst drive out the heathen before them.* But this course of warring against others, & driving them out without provocation, depends upon speciall Commission from God, or else it is not imitable.

Secondly, when he gives a forraigne people favour in the eyes of any native people to come and sit downe with them either by way of purchase, as *Abraham* did obtaine the field of *Machpelah;* or else when they give it in courtesie, as *Pharaoh* did the land of *Goshen* unto the sons of *Jacob.*

Thirdly, when hee makes a Countrey though not altogether void of inhabitants, yet voyd in that place where they reside. Where there is a vacant place, there is liberty for the sonne of *Adam* or *Noah* to come and inhabite, though they neither buy it, nor aske their leaves. *Abraham* and *Isaac*, when they sojourned [1] amongst the Philistines, they did not buy that land to feede their cattle, because they said There is roome enough. And so did *Jacob* pitch his tent by *Sechem, Gen.* 34. 21. There was *roome enough* as *Hamor* said, *Let them sit down amongst us.* And in this case if the people who were former inhabitants did disturbe them in their possessions, they complained to the King, as of wrong done unto them: As *Abraham* did because they took away his well, in *Gen.* 21, 25. For his right whereto he pleaded not his immediate calling from God, (for that would have seemed frivolous amongst the Heathen) but his owne industry and culture in digging the well, verse 30. Nor doth the King reject his plea, with what had he to doe to digge wells in their soyle? but admitteth it as a Principle in Nature, That in a vacant soyle, hee that taketh possession of it, and bestoweth culture and husbandry upon it, his Right it is. And the ground of this is from the grand Charter given to Adam and his posterity in Paradise, *Gen.* 1. 28. *Multiply, and replenish the earth, and subdue it.* If therefore any sonne of *Adam* come and

---

[1] This sojourning was a constant residence there, as in a possession of their owne; although it be called sojourning or dwelling as strangers, because they neither had the soveraigne government of the whole Countrey in their owne hand, nor yet did incorporate themselves into the Commonwealth of the Natives, to submit themselves unto their government.

finde a place empty, he hath liberty to come, and fill, and subdue the earth there. This Charter was renewed to *Noah, Gen.* 9. 1. *Fulfill the earth and multiply:* So that it is free from that comon Grant for any to take possession of vacant Countries. Indeed no Nation is to drive out another without speciall Commission from heaven, such as the Israelites had, unless the Natives do unjustly wrong them, and will not recompence the wrongs done in peaceable sort, & then they may right themselves by lawfull war, and subdue the Countrey unto themselves.

This placeing of people in this or that Countrey, is from Gods soveraignty over all the earth, and the inhabitants thereof: as in *Psal.* 24. 1 *The earth is the Lords, and the fulnesse thereof.* And in *Jer.* 10. 7. God is there called, *The King of Nations:* and in *Deut.* 10. 14. Therefore it is meete he should provide a place for all Nations to inhabite, and have all the earth replenished. Onely in the Text here is meant some more speciall appointment, because God tells them it by his owne mouth; he doth not so with other people, he doth not tell the children of *Sier*, that hee hath appointed a place for them: that is, He gives them the land by promise; others take the land by his providence, but Gods people take the land by promise: And therefore the land of *Canaan* is called a land of promise. Which they discerne, first, by discerning themselves to be in Christ, in whom all the promises are yea, and amen.

Secondly, by finding his holy presence with them, to wit, when he plants them in the holy Mountaine of his Inheritance: *Exodus.* 15. 17. And that is when he giveth them the liberty and purity of his Ordinances. It is a land of promise, where they have provision for soule as well as for body. *Ruth* dwelt well for outward respects while shee dwelt in *Moab*, but when shee cometh to dwell in *Israel*, shee is said to come under the wings of God: *Ruth* 2. 12. When God wrappes us in with his Ordinances, and warmes us with the life and power of them as with wings, there is a land of promise.

This may teach us all where we doe now dwell, or where after wee may dwell, be sure you looke at every place appointed to you, from the hand of God: wee may not rush into any place, and never say to God, By your leave; but we must discerne how God appoints us this place. There is poore comfort in sitting down in any place, that you cannot say, This place is appointed me of God. Canst thou say that God spied out this place for thee, and there hath setled thee above all hinderances? didst thou finde that God made roome for thee either by lawfull descent, or purchase, or gift, or other warrantable right? Why then this is the place God hath appointed thee; here hee hath made roome for thee, he hath placed thee in *Rehoboth*, in a peaceable place: This we must discerne, or els we are but intruders upon God. And when wee doe withall discerne, that God giveth us these outward blessings from his love in Christ, and maketh comfortable provision as well for our soule as for our bodies, by the meanes of grace, then doe we enjoy our present possession as well by gracious promise, as by the common, and just, and bountifull providence of the Lord. Or if a man doe remove he must see that God hath espied out such a Countrey for him.

Secondly, though there be many difficulties yet he hath given us hearts to overlook them all, as if we were carried upon eagles wings.

And thirdly, see God making roome for us by some lawfull means.

Quest. But how shall I know whether God hath appointed me such a place, if I be well where I am, what may warrant my removeall?

Answ. There be foure or five good things, for procurement of any of which I may remove. Secondly, there be some evill things, for avoiding of any of which wee may transplant ourselves. Thirdly, if withall we find some speciall providence of God concurring in either of both concerning our selves, and applying general grounds of removall to our personall estate.

First, wee may remove for the gaining of knowledge. Our Saviour commends it in the Queene of the south, that she came from the utmost parts of the earth to heare the wisdom of *Solomon: Matth.* 12. 42. And surely with him she might have continued for the same end, if her personall calling had not recalled her home.

Secondly, some remove and travaile for merchandize and gainesake; *Daily bread may be sought from farre, Prov.* 31. 14. Yea our Saviour approveth travaile for Merchants, *Matth.* 13. 45, 46.

when hee compareth a Christian to a Merchantman seeking pearles: For he never fetcheth a comparison from any unlawfull thing to illustrate a thing lawfull. The comparison from the unjust Steward, and from the Theefe in the night, is not taken from the injustice of the one, or the theft of the other; but from the wisdome of the one, and the sodainnesse of the other; which in themselves are not unlawfull.

Thirdly, to plant a Colony, that is, a company that agree together to remove out of their owne Country, and settle a Citty or commonwealth elsewhere. Of such a Colony wee reade in *Acts* 16. 12. which God blessed and prospered exceedingly, and made it a glorious Church. Nature teacheth Bees to doe so, when as the hive is too full, they seeke abroad for new dwellings: So when the hive of the Common wealth is so full, that Tradesmen cannot live one by another, but eate up one another, in this case it is lawfull to remove.

Fourthly, God alloweth a man to remove, when he may employ his Talents and gift better elsewhere, especially when where he is, he is not bound by any speciall engagement. Thus God sent *Joseph* before to preserve the Church: *Josephs* wisedome and spirit was not fit for a shepheard, but for a Counsellour of State, and therefore God sent him into *Egypt*. *To whom much is given of him God will require the more: Luk* 12. 48.

Fifthly, for the liberty of the Ordinances. 2 *Chron.* 11. 13, 14, 15. When *Jeroboam* made a desertion from *Judah*, and set up golden Calves to worship, all that were well affected, both Priests and people, sold their possessions, and came to *Jerusalem* for the Ordinances sake. This case was of seasonable use to our fathers in the dayes of Queene Mary; who removed to *France* and *Germany* in the beginning of her Reign, upon Proclamation of alteration of religion, before any persecution began.

Secondly, there be evills to be avoyded that may warrant removeall. First, when some grievous sinnes overspread a Country that threaten desolation. *Mic.* 2. 6 to 11 verse: When the people say to them that prophecie, *Prophecie not;* then verse 10. *Arise then, this is not your rest.* Which words though they be a threatning, not a commandement; yet as in a threatning a wise man foreseeth the plague, so in the threatning he seeth a com-

mandement, to hide himselfe from it.   This case might have been
of seasonable use unto them of the *Palatinate*, when they saw their
Orthodox Ministers banished, although themselves might for a
while enjoy libertie of conscience.

Secondly, if men be overburdened with debts and miseries, as
Davids followers were; they may then retire out of the way (as
they retired to *David* for safety) not to defraud their creditors (for
God is an avenger of such things, 1 *Thess*. 4. 6.) but to gaine fur-
ther opportunity to discharge their debts, and to satisfie their
Creditors. 1 *Sam*. 22. 1, 2.

Thirdly, in case of persecution, so did the Apostle in *Acts* 13. 46,
47.

Thirdly, as these generall cases, where any of them doe fall out,
doe warrant removeall in generall: so there be some speciall
providences or particular cases which may give warrant unto such
or such a person to transplant himselfe, and which apply the former
generall grounds to particular persons.

First, if soveraigne Authority command and encourage such
Plantations by giving way to subjects to transplant themselves,
and set up a new Commonwealth.   This is a lawfull and expedient case for such particular persons as be designed and sent:
Matth. 8. 9. and for such as they who are sent, have power to
command.

Secondly, when some speciall providence of God leades a man
unto such a course.   This may also single out particulars.   *Psal*.
32. 8.   *I will instruct, and guide thee with mine eye.*   As the childe
knowes the pleasure of his father in his eye, so doth the child of
God see Gods pleasure in the eye of his heavenly Fathers providence.   And this is done in three wayes.

First, if God give a man an inclination to this or that course,
for that is the spirit of man; and *God is the father of spirits: Rom*.
1. 11, 12. 1 *Cor*. 16. 12. *Paul* discerned his calling to goe to Rom,
by his τὸ πρόθυμον, his ready inclination to that voyage;   and
Apollos his loathing to goe to *Corinth*, *Paul* accepted as a just
reason of his refusall of a calling to goe thither.   And this holdeth,
when in a mans inclination to travaile, his heart is set on no by-
respects, as to see fashions, to deceive his Creditours, to fight
Duels, or to live idly, these are vaine inclinations; but if his heart

be inclined upon right judgement to advance the Gospell, to maintaine his family, to use his Talents fruitfully, or the like good end, this inclination is from God. As the beames of the Moone darting into the Sea leades it to and fro, so doth a secret inclination darted by God into our hearts leade and bowe (as a byas) our whole course.

Secondly, when God gives other men hearts to call us as the men of *Mecedon* did *Paul, Come to us into Macedonia, and helpe us.* When wee are invited by others who have a good calling to reside there, we may goe with them, unlesse we be detained by waightier occasions. One member hath interest in another, to call to it for helpe, when it is not diverted by greater employment.

Thirdly, there is another providence of God concurring in both these, that is, when a mans calling and person is free, and not tyed by parents, or Magistrates, or other people that have interest in him. Or when abroad hee may doe himselfe and others more good than he can doe at home. Here is then an eye of God that opens a doore there, and sets him loose here, inclines his heart that way, and outlookes all difficulties. When God makes roome for us, no binding here, and an open way there, in such a case God tells them, he will appoint a place for them.

AN ACCOUNT OF MRS. ANNE HUTCHINSON

[From "The Way of Congregational Churches Cleared"]

At her first comming she was well respected and esteemed of me, not onely because herself and her family were well beloved in *England* at *Allford* in *Lincolnshire* (not far beyond *Boston:*) nor onely because she with her family came over hither (as was said) for conscience sake: but chiefly for that I heard, shee did much good in our Town, in womans meeting at Childbirth-Travells, wherein shee was not onely skilfull and helpfull, but readily fell into good discourse with the women about their spirituall estates: And therein cleared it unto them, That the soul lying under a Spirit of Bondage, might see and sensibly feel the hainous guilt, and deep desert of sin, and thereby not onely undergoe affliction of Spirit but also receive both restraining, and constraining

Grace likewise, (in some measure:) restraining from all known evill (both courses, and companies) (at least for a season) and constraining to all knowen duties, as secret Prayer, Family Exercises, Conscience of Sabbaths, Reverence of Ministers, Frequenting of Sermons, Diligence in calling, honesty in dealing and the like: yea and that the Soul might find some tastes and flashes of spirituall comfort in this estate, and yet never see or feel the need of Christ, much lesse attain any saving Union, or Communion with him, being no more but Legall work, even what the Law, and the Spirit of bondage (breathing in it) might reach unto. By which means many of the women (and by them their husbands) were convinced, that they had gone on in a Covenant of Works, and were much shaken and humbled thereby, and brought to enquire more seriously after the Lord Jesus Christ, without whom all their Gifts and Graces would prove but common, and their duties but legall, and in the end wizzen and vanish. All this was well (as is reported truely, *page* 31 of her Story) and suited with the publike Ministery, which had gone along in the same way, so as these private conferences did well tend to water the seeds publikely sowen. Whereupon all the faithfull embraced her conference, and blessed God for her fruitfull discourses. And many whose spirituall estates were not so safely layed, yet were hereby helped and awakened to discover their sandy foundations, and to seek for better establishment in Christ: which caused them also to blesse the Lord for the good successe, which appeared to them by this discovery.

Hitherto therefore shee wrought with God, and with the Ministers, the work of the Lord. No marvell therefore if at that time, shee found loving and dear respect both from our Church-Elders and Brethren, and so from my self also amongst the rest.

Afterwards, it is true, she turned aside not only to corrupt opinions, but to dis-esteem generally the Elders of the churches, (though of them shee esteemed best of Mr. *Shepheard:*) and for my selfe, (in the repetitions of Sermons in her house) what shee repeated and confirmed, was accounted sound, what shee omitted, was accounted Apocrypha. This change of hers was long hid from me: and much longer the evidence of it, by any two clear witnesses. I sent some Sisters of the Church on purpose to her

Repetitions, that I might know the truth: but when shee discerned any such present, no speech fell from her, that could be much excepted against. But further discourse about her course is not pertinent to the present businesse. But by this Mr. *Baylie* may discerne, how farre Ms. *Hutchinson* was dear unto mee, and if hee speak of her as my deare friend, till shee turned aside, I refuse it not.

But yet thus much I must professe to him, That in the times of her best acceptance, shee was not so dear unto mee, but that (by the help of Christ) I dealt faithfully with her about her spirituall estate. Three things I told her, made her spirituall estate unclear to mee. 1. "That her Faith was not begotten nor (by her "relation) scarce at any time strengthened by publick Ministry, "but by private Meditations, or Revelations onely.

"2. That shee clearly discerned her Justification (as shee "professed:) but little or nothing at all, her Sanctification: though "(she said) shee beleeved, such a thing there was by plain Scripture.

"3. That she was more sharply censorious of other mens spir-"ituall estates and hearts, then the servants of God are wont to "be, who are more taken up with judging of themselves before the "Lord, then of others."

AN ADMONITION TO ROGER WILLIAMS

[From "A Letter of Mr. *John Cottons,* Teacher of the Church in *Boston,* in New-England, to Mr. Williams a Preacher there"]

Beloved in Christ,

Though I have little hope (when I consider the uncircumcision of mine owne lips, *Exod.* 6. 12.) that you will hearken to my voyce, who hath not hearkened to the body of the whole Church of Christ, with you, and the testimony, and judgement of so many Elders and Brethren of other Churches, yet I trust my labour will be accepted of the Lord; and who can tell but that he may blesse it to you also, if (by his helpe) I indevour to shew you the sandinesse of those grounds, out of which you have banished yours from the fellowship of all the Churches in these Countries. Let not any prejudice against my person (I beseech you) forestall either your affection or judgement, as if I had hastened forward the sentence of your civill banishment; for what was done by the Magistrates, in that kinde, was neither done by my counsell nor consent, although I dare not deny the sentence passed to be righteous in the eyes of God, who hath said that he that with-holdeth the Corne (which is the staffe of life) from the people, the multitude shall curse him, *Prov.* 11. 26. how much more shall they separate such from them as doe with-hold and separate them from the Ordinances or the Ordinances from them (which are in Christ the bread of life). And yet it may be they passed that sentence against you not upon that ground, but for ought I know, upon your other corrupt doctrines, which tend to the disturbance both of civill and holy peace, as may appeare by that answer which was sent to the Brethren of the Church of *Salem*, and to your selfe. And to speake freely what I thinke, were my soule in your soules stead, I should thinke it a worke of mercy of God to banish me from the civill society of such a Common wealth, when I could not injoy holy fellowship with any Church of God amongst them without sin. What should the Daughter of *Zion* doe in *Babell?* why should she not hasten to flee from thence ? *Zach.* 2. 6, 7.

I speake not these things (the God of Truth is my witnes) to adde affliction to your affliction, but (if it were the holy will of God) to move you to a more serious sight of your sin, and of the justice of Gods hand against it. Against your corrupt Doctrines, it pleased the Lord Jesus to fight against you with the sword of his mouth (as himselfe speaketh, *Rev.* 2. 16.) in the mouthes and testimonies of the Churches and Brethren. Against whom, when you over-heated your selfe in reasoning and disputing against the light of his truth, it pleased him to stop your mouth by a suddaine disease, and to threaten to take your breath from you. But you in stead of recoyling (as even Balaam offered to doe in the like case) you chose rather to persist in your way, and to protest against all the Churches and Brethren that stood in your way: and thus the good hand of Christ that should have humbled you, to see and turne from the errour of your way, hath rather hardened you therein, and quickned you onely to see failings (yea intolerable errours) in all the Churches and brethren, rather then in your selfe. In which course though you say you doe not remember an houre wherein the countenance of the Lord was darkned to you, yet be not deceived, it is no new thing with Satan to transforme himselfe into an Angell of light, and to cheare the soule with false peace, and with flashes of counterfeit consolation. Sad and wofull is the memory of Master *Smiths* strong consolations on his death-bed, which are set as a Seale to the grosse and damnable Arminianisme and Enthusiasmes delivered in the confession of his faith, prefixed to the story of his life and death. The countenance of God is upon his people when they feare him, not when they presume of their owne strength; and his consolations are found not in the way of presidence in errour, but in the wayes of humility and truth.

Two stumbling blockes (I perceive by your letter) have turned you off from fellowship with us. First, the want of fit matter of our Church. Secondly, disrespect of the separate Churches in England under afflictions, who doe our selves practise separation in peace.

'For the first, you acknowledge (as you say) with joy that 'godly persons are the visible matter of these Churches, but yet 'you see not that godly persons are matter fitted to constitute a 'Church, no more then trees or Quarries are fit matter propor- 'tioned to the building.'

Answ. This exception seemeth to mee to imply a contradiction to it selfe, for if the matter of our Churches be as you say godly persons, they are not then as trees unfelled, or stones unhewen. Godlinesse cutteth men downe from the former roote, and heweth them out of the pit of corrupt nature, and fitteth them for fellowship with Christ and with his people.

ROGER WILLIAMS

[Roger Williams, famous as the founder of Rhode Island and the chief advocate of religious toleration in early New England, was born in Wales in 1599. He studied at Pembroke College, Cambridge, and took orders in the Church of England, but soon became a Puritan. In 1630 he sailed for America, and served as minister at Salem, and for a time at Plymouth. His views on religious and political matters became more radical, and after various less drastic proceedings it was resolved to send him to England as a dangerous man. He eluded the officers, and took refuge among the Indians, with whom he was always on friendly terms. In 1636 he established a settlement at Providence, and afterward secured a charter for the colony of Rhode Island. He continued as a leading spirit in this colony until his death in 1683.

Roger Williams was a man of wide interests, and of intense and sometimes erratic beliefs. He was especially stanch in maintaining that the colonists had no right to their lands until they had acquired them of the Indians by purchase, and in arguing for religious toleration. The latter subject he debated with John Cotton in one of the most famous of early New England controversies. A prisoner in Newgate, confined because of his religious belief, had written a "letter" arguing against persecution for cause of conscience. A copy of this was sent to John Cotton, who wrote a reply. In answer to this Williams wrote in 1643–1644 "The Bloudy Tenent of Persecution for cause of Conscience, discussed in a Conference betweene Truth and Peace." Cotton responded with "The Bloody Tenent washed and made white in the Blood of the Lamb"; and Williams published as a rejoinder "The Bloody Tenent yet More Bloody: by Mr. Cottons endevour to wash it white in the Blood of the Lambe." The selection from "The Bloody Tenent" which follows will illustrate the method of religious controversy of the time — the reliance on the letter even more than the spirit of Scripture, and the minute and exhaustive study of figurative passages in an attempt to throw light on practical questions. Though Williams was always consistent in preaching and practising religious toleration, so far as actual persecution was concerned, he was not always charitable towards the beliefs of others. It was chiefly due to his efforts that the Quakers were permitted in Rhode Island; but in "George Fox Digg'd out of his Burrowes," his account of an oral debate which he held with champions of the Quakers at Newport, he is often bitter and vituperative. Besides the works already mentioned, Roger Williams wrote a key to the Indian languages, other controversial and religious works, and many letters, some of them of great interest.

The selections given follow the reprints of Williams's works in the "Publications of the Narragansett Club," Vols. III, IV, and V.]

THE MEANING OF THE PARABLE OF THE TARES

[From "The Bloudy Tenent of Persecution" [1]]

Peace. We are now come to the second part of the *Answer,* which is a particular examination of such *grounds* as are brought against such *persecution.*

The first sort of grounds are from the *Scriptures.*

CHAP. XVIII

First, *Matth.* 13. 30, 38. because *Christ* commandeth to let alone the *Tares* to grow up together with the *Wheat,* untill the *Harvest.*

Unto which he [2] answereth: That *Tares* are not *Bryars* and *Thornes,* but partly *Hypocrites,* like unto the *godly,* but indeed *carnall* (as the *Tares* are like to *Wheat,* but are not *Wheat,*) or partly such corrupt *doctrines* or *practices* as are indeed unsound, but yet such as come very near the truth (as *Tares* do to the *Wheat*) and so neer that *good* men may be taken with them, and so the persons in whom they grow cannot bee rooted out, but good *Wheat* will be rooted out with them. In such a case (saith he) *Christ* calleth for *peaceable toleration,* and not for *penall prosecution,* according to the third Conclusion.

Truth. The *substance* of this *Answer* I conceive to be first *negative,* that by *Tares* are not meant persons of another *Religion* and *Worship,* that is (saith he) they are not *Briars* and *Thornes.*

Secondly, *affirmative,* by *Tares* are meant either *persons,* or *doctrines,* or *practices; persons,* as *hypocrites,* like the *godly:* *doctrines* or *practices* corrupt, yet like the *truth.*

[[1] Both " The Bloudy Tenent " and "The Bloudy Tenent yet more Bloudy " were originally printed with a marginal gloss that summarized the argument. This is omitted in the selections here given.]

[[2] John Cotton. The first paragraph of the chapter is a paraphrase of the statement by the prisoner in Newgate whose paper started the controversy (see introduction). The second paragraph is almost a literal quotation of Cotton's reply.]

For answer hereunto I confesse that not onely those worthy *witnesses* (whose memories are sweet with all that feare God) *Calvin, Beza, &c.* but of later times many conjoyne with this worthy *Answerer*, to satisfie themselves and others with such an *Interpretation.*

But alas, how darke is the soule left that desires to walke with the Lord in holy feare and trembling, when in such a waighty and mighty point as this is, that in matters of *conscience* concerneth the spilling of the *bloud of thousands*, and the *Civill Peace* of the *World* in the taking up *Armes* to suppresse all false *Religions!* when I say no *evidence* or *demonstration* of the *Spirit* is brought to prove such an *interpretation*, nor *Arguments* from the place it selfe or the Scriptures of truth to confirme it; but a bare Affirmation that these *Tares* must signifie *persons*, or *doctrines* and *practices.*

I will not imagine any deceitfull purpose in the Answerers thoughts in the proposall of these three, *persons, doctrines,* or *practices*, yet dare I confidently avouch that the *Old Serpent* hath deceived their precious soules, and by *Tongue* and *Pen* would deceive the soules of others by such a *method* of dividing the word of *truth.* A threefold *Cord*, and so a threefold *Snare*, is strong, and too like it is that one of the three, either *Persons, Doctrines,* or *Practices* may catch some feet.

Chap. XIX

Peace. The place then being of such great importance as concerning the *truth of God*, the *bloud of thousands*, yea the bloud of *Saints*, and of the *Lord Jesus* in them, I shall request your more diligent search (by the Lords holy assistance) into this Scripture.

[*Truth.*] I shall make it evident, that by these Tares in this Parable are meant *persons* in respect of their *Religion* and way of *Worship, open* and *visible professours*, as bad as *briars* and *thornes;* not onely suspected *Foxes*, but as bad as those *greedy Wolves* which *Paul* speakes of, *Acts* 20. who with perverse and evill *doctrines* labour spiritually to devoure the *flocke*, and to draw away Disciples after them, whose mouthes must be stopped,

and yet no carnall *force* or *weapon* to be used against them, but
their *mischiefe* to bee resisted with those mighty *weapons* of the
holy *Armoury* of the *Lord Jesus*, wherein there hangs a *thousand
shields, Cant.* 4.

That the *Lord Jesus* intendeth not *doctrines* or *practices* by the
tares in this Parable is cleare: for

First, the *Lord Jesus* expresly interpreteth the *good seed* to be
persons, and those the children of the *Kingdome;* and the *tares*
also to signifie *Men*, and those the *children* of the *Wicked one,
ver.* 38.

Secondly, such corrupt *doctrines* or *practices* are not to bee
tolorated now as those *Jewish* observations (the *Lords* owne
Ordinances) were for a while to be permitted, *Rom.* 14. Nor so
long as till the Angels the *Reapers* come to reape the Harvest in
the end of the *world*. For can we thinke that because the tender
Consciences of the *Jewes* were to be tendred in their *differences*
of *meats*, that therefore persons must now bee tolerated in the
Church (for I speake not of the *Civill State*) and that to the
worlds end, in superstitious forbearing and forbidding of *flesh* in
Popish Lents, and *superstitious Fridayes, &c.* and that because
they were to be tendred in their observation of *Jewish Holidayes*,
that therefore untill the *Harvest* or *Worlds end*, persons must
now be tolerated (I meane in the *Church*) in the observation of
Popish *Christmas, Easter, Whitsontide*, and other superstitious
Popish *Festivals?*

I willingly acknowledge, that if the members of a *Church of
Christ* shall upon some *delusion* of *Sathan kneele* at the *Lords
Supper*, keep *Christmas*, or any other Popish *observation*, great
tendernesse ought to bee used in winning his soule from the
errour of his way: and yet I see not that persons so practising
were fit to be received into the Churches of Christ now, as the
Jews weake in the Faith, (that is, in the *Liberties* of *Christ*) were
to be received, *Rom.* 14. 1. And least of all (as before) that the
toleration or *permission* of such ought to continue till *Doomes
day*, or the end of the *world*, as this Parable urgeth the *Toleration;* Let them alone untill the *Harvest*.

H

Chap. XX

Againe, *Hypocrites* were not intended by the *Lord Jesus* in this famous Parable.

First, the Originall word ζιζάνια, signifying all those *Weeds* which spring up with the *Corne*, as *Cockle, Darnell, Tares, &c.* seemes to imply such a kinde of people as commonly and generally are knowne to bee manifestly different from, and opposite to the true *worshippers* of *God*, here called the *children* of the *Kingdom;* as these *weeds, tares, cockle, darnell, &c.* are commonly and presently knowne by every *husbandman* to differ from the *wheat*, and to be opposite, and contrary, and hurtfull unto it.

Now whereas it is pleaded that these *tares* are like the *wheat*, and so like that this *consimilitude* or likenesse is made the ground of this *interpretation*, viz. That *tares* must needs signifie *hypocrites*, or *doctrines*, or *practices*, who are like *Gods children, Truth, &c.*

I answer, first, the *Parable* holds forth no such thing, that the likenesse of the *tares* should deceive the servants to cause them to suppose for a time that they were good *wheat*, but that as soone as ever the *tares* appeared, ver. 26. the *servants* came to the *housholder* about them, ver. 27. the Scripture holds forth no such time wherein they doubted or suspected what they were.

Peace. It may be said they did not appeare to be *tares* untill the *corne* was in the blade, and put forth its fruit.

Truth. I answer,[1] The one appeared as soone as the other, for so the word clearly carries it, that the *seed* of both having been sowne, when the *wheat* appeared and put forth its blade and fruit, the *tares* also were as early, and put forth themselves as appeared also.

Secondly, there is such a *dissimilitude* or *unlikenesse*, I say such a *dissimilitude*, that as soone as *tares* and *wheat* are sprung up to blade and fruit, every *husbandman* can tell which is *wheat*, and which are *tares* and *cockle, &c.*

Peace. It may be said true: So when the *hypocrite* is manifested, then all may know him, *&c.*, but before *hypocrites* be manifested by *fruits* they are unknowne.

---

[1] The false and counterfeit Christians appeare as soon as the true and faithfull.

[*Truth.*] I answer, search into the *Parable*, and aske when was it that the *servants* first complained of the *tares* to the *housholder*, but when they appeared or came in sight, there being no *interim*, wherein the servants could not tell what to make of them, but doubted whether they were *wheat* or *tares*, as the Answerer implies.

Secondly, when was it that the *housholder* gave charge to let them alone, but after that they appeared, and were known to be *tares*, which should imply by this *interpretation* of the *Answerer*, that when men are discovered and knowne to be *Hypocrites*, yet still such a *generation* of *Hypocrites* in the *Church* must be let alone and tolerated untill the *harvest* or end of the world, which is contrary to all *order*, *piety* and *safety* in the *Church* of the *Lord Jesus*, as doubtlesse the *Answerers* will grant; so that these Tares being notoriously knowne to be different from the Corne, I conclude that they cannot here be intended by the *Lord Jesus* to signifie secret *Hypocrites*, but more open and apparent Sinners.

CHAP. XXI

The second reason why these *tares* cannot signifie *hypocrites* in the *Church*, I take from the *Lord Jesus* His own *Interpretation* of the *field* (in which both *wheat* and *tares* are sowne, which saith he is the *World*, out of which God chooseth and calleth His *Church*.

The *World* lyes in *wickednesse*, is like a *Wildernesse* or a *Sea* of *wilde Beasts* innumerable, *fornicators*, *covetous*, *Idolators*, &c. with whom *Gods people* may lawfully converse and cohabit in *Cities*, *Townes*, &c. else must they not live in the *World*, but goe out of it. In which *world* as soone as ever the *Lord Jesus* had sowne the *good seed*, the *children* of the *Kingdome*, true *Christianity*, or the true *Church;* the *Enemy Sathan* presently in the *night* of *security*, *Ignorance* and *Errour* (whilst men slept) sowed also these *tares* which are *Antichristians* or *false Christians*. These *strange Professours* of the Name of *Jesus*, the *Ministers* and *Prophets* of *God* beholding, they are ready to runne to *Heaven* to fetch *fiery judgements* from thence to consume these strange *Christians*, and to pluck them by the *roots* out of the world: But the Son of Man, the *meek Lamb* of *God* (for the *Elect* sake which must be gathered out of *Jew* and *Gentile, Pagan, Anti-christian*) commands a permission of them in the *World,* untill the time of the end of the *World,* when the *Goats* and *Sheep,* the *Tares* and *Wheat* shall be eternally separated each from other.

Peace. You know some excellent *Worthies* (dead and living) have laboured to turne this *Field* of the *World* into the *Garden* of the *Church.*

Truth. But who can imagine that the *Wisdome* of the *Father,* the *Lord Jesus Christ,* would so open this *Parable* (as He professedly doth) as that it should be close shut up, and that one *difficulty* or *locke* should be opened by a greater and harder, in calling the *World* the *Church?* contrary also to the way of the Light and Love that is in Jesus, when he would purposely teach and instruct His scholars; contrary to the nature of *Parables* and *similitudes.*

And lastly, to the nature of the *Church* or *Garden* of *Christ.*

CHAP. XXII

In the former *Parable* the *Lord Jesus* compared the *Kingdome* of *Heaven* to the sowing of *Seed.* The true *Messengers* of *Christ* are the *Sowers,* who cast the *Seed* of the *Word* of the *Kingdome* upon *foure sorts* of ground, which foure *sorts* of *ground* or *hearts* of men, cannot be supposed to be of the *Church,* nor will it ever be proved that the *Church* consisteth of any more sorts or natures of ground properly, but *one,* to wit, the *honest* and *good* ground, and the proper worke of the *Church* concernes the flourishing and prosperity of this sort of ground, and not the other *unconverted* three sorts, who it may be seldome or never come neare the *Church* unlesse they be forced by the *Civill sword,* which the *patterne* or first *sowers* never used, and being forced they are put into a way of *Religion* by such a course, if not so, they are forced to live without a *Religion,* for one of the two must necessarily follow, as I shall prove afterward.

In the *field* of the *World* then are all those *sorts* of *ground, high way hearers, stony* and *thorny* ground hearers, as well as the *honest* and good ground; and I suppose it will not now be said by the Answerer, that those three sorts of *bad* grounds were *hypocrites* or *tares* in the *Church*.

Now after the *Lord Jesus* had propounded that great *leading Parable* of the *Sower* and the *Seed*, He is pleased to propound this *Parable* of the *Tares*, with admirable *coherence* and sweet *consolation* to the honest and good ground, who with glad and honest hearts having received the *word* of the *Kingdome*, may yet seem to be discouraged and troubled with so many *Antichristians* and false *Professours* of the *Name* of *Christ*. The *Lord Jesus* therefore gives *direction* concerning these *tares*, that unto the end of the World successively in all the *sorts* and *generations* of them they must be (not approved or countenanced, but) let alone or *permitted* in the *World*.

Secondly, he gives to His owne *good seed* this *consolation*, that those heavenly *Reapers* the *Angells* in the *harvest* or end of the *World*, will take an order and course with them, to wit, they shall binde them into *bundles*, and cast them into the *everlasting burnings*, and to make the cup of their *consolation* run over: He adds vers. 4. Then, then at that time shall the *Righteous* shine as the *Sun* in the *Kingdome* of their *Father*.

These *tares* then neither being erronious *doctrines*, nor corrupt *practises*, nor *hypocrites* in the true *Church* intended by the Lord Jesus in this Parable; I shall in the third place (by the helpe of the same Lord Jesus) evidently prove that these *tares* can be no other sort of sinners, but false *worshippers*, *Idolaters*, and in particular properly, *Antichristians*.

CHAP. XXIII

First then, these Tares are such sinners as are opposite and contrary to the *children* of the *Kingdome* visibly so declared and manifest, ver. 38. Now the Kingdome of *God* below, is the *visible Church* of Christ Jesus, according to *Matth*. 8. 12. The children of the *Kingdome* which are threatned to be cast out, seeme to be the *Jewes*, which were then the onely *visible Church* in Covenant with the Lord, when all other *Nations* followed other *gods* and *worships*. And more plaine is that fearfull *threatning*, *Matth*. 21. 43. The *Kingdome* of *God* shall be taken from you, and given to a *Nation* that will bring forth the fruits thereof.

Such then are the *good seed, good wheat, children of the Kingdome,* as are the *disciples, members* and *subjects* of the Lord *Jesus Christ* his *Church & Kingdom:* and therefore consequently such are the *tares,* as are opposite to these, *Idolaters, Will-worshippers,* not truly but falsly submitting to *Jesus:* and in especiall, the children of the *wicked* one, visibly so appearing. Which wicked one I take not to be the *Devill;* for the Lord *Jesus* seemes to make them distinct: He that sowes the good seed (saith he) is the *Son* of *man,* the *field* is the *World,* the good seed are the *Children* of the *Kingdome,* but the *Tares* are the *children* of the *wicked,* or wickednesse, the *enemy* that sowed them, is the *Devill.*

The Originall here, τοῦ πονηροῦ, agrees with that, *Luk.* II. 4. Deliver us, ἀπο τ᾽πονηροῦ, from evill or *wickednesse;* opposite to the children of the *Kingdome* and the *righteousnesse* thereof.

Chap. XXIV

Peace. It is true, that all *drunkards, thieves, uncleane persons, &c.* are opposite to *Gods children.*

Truth. Answ. Their opposition here against the *children* of the *Kingdome,* is such an opposition as properly fights against the *Religious state* or Worship of the *Lord Jesus Christ.*

Secondly, it is manifest, that the Lord Jesus in this parable intends no other sort of sinners, unto whom he saith, Let them alone, in *Church* or *State;* for then he should contradict other holy and blessed *ordinances* for the punishment of offenders both in *Christian* and *Civill State.*

First, in *Civill state,* from the beginning of the World, God hath armed *Fathers, Masters, Magistrates,* to punish evill doers, that is, such of whose actions *Fathers, Masters, Magistrates* are to judge, and accordingly to punish such sinners as transgresse against the good and peace of their Civill state, *Families, Townes, Cities, Kingdomes:* their *States, Governments, Governours, Lawes, Punishments* and *Weapons* being all of a *Civill nature;* and therefore neither *disobedience* to *parents* or *magistrates,* nor *murther* nor *quarrelling, uncleannesse* nor *laciviousnesse, stealing* nor *extor-*

tion, neither ought of that kinde ought to be let alone, either in lesser or greater *families, townes, cities, kingdomes*, Rom. 13. but seasonably to be supprest, as may best conduce to the *publike safetie*.

Againe secondly, in the *Kingdome of Christ Jesus*, whose *kingdome, officers, lawes, punishments, weapons*, are spirituall and of a Soule-nature, he will not have *Antichristian idolators, extortioners, covetous, &c.* to be let alone, but the *uncleane* and *lepers* to be thrust forth, the old *leaven* purged out, the *obstinate* in sinne spiritually *stoned* to *death*, and put away from Israel; and this by many degrees of gentle *admonition* in *private* and *publique*, as the case requires.

Therefore if neither *offenders* against the *civill Lawes, State* and *peace* ought to be let alone; nor the *Spirituall estate*, the *Church* of *Jesus Christ* ought to beare with them that are *evill*, Revel. 2. I conclude, that these are sinners of another nature, *Idolaters, False-worshippers, Antichristians*, who without discouragement to true Christians must be let alone and permitted in the world to grow and fill up the measure of their sinnes, after the *image* of him that hath sowen them, untill the great Harvest shall make the *difference*.

CHAP. XXV

Thirdly, in that the *officers* unto whom these *Tares* are referred, are the *Angels* the heavenly *Reapers* at the last day, it is cleare as the *light*, that (as before) these *Tares* cannot signifie *Hypocrites* in the *Church*, who when they are discovered and seen to be *Tares* opposite to the good fruit of the good seed, are not to be let alone to the *Angels* at Harvest or end of the world, but purged out by the *Governors* of the *Church*, and the whole *Church* of *Christ*. Againe, they cannot be offenders against the *civill state* and Common welfare, whose dealing with is not suspended unto the comming of the *Angels*, but [is committed] unto Men, who (although they know not the Lord *Jesus Christ*, yet) are lawfull *Governours* and *Rulers* in *Civill things*.

Accordingly in the 4. and last place, in that the plucking up of these *tares* out of this *field* must bee let alone unto the very *harvest* or end of the *world*, it is apparent from thence, that (as before)

they could not signifie *hypocrites* in the *Church*, who when they
are discovered to be so, (as these *tares* were discovered to be
tares) are not to be suffered (after the first and second Admonition) but to be rejected, and every Brother that walketh disorderly to be withdrawen or separated from: So likewise no
offendour against the *Civill state*, by *robbery, murther, adultery,
oppression, sedition, mutinie*, is for ever to be connived at, and to
enjoy a perpetuall *toleration* unto the *Worlds end*, as these *tares*
must.

Moses for a while held his peace against the *sedition* of *Korah,
Dathan*, and *Abiram*. *David* for a season tolerated *Shimei,
Joab, Adonijah;* but till the *Harvest* or end of the World, the
Lord never intended that any but these *spirituall* and *mysticall
Tares* should be so permitted.

Chap. XXVI

Now if any imagine that the time or date is long, that in the
meane season they may doe a *world of mischiefe* before the *Worlds
end*, as by infection, &c.

Truth. First, I answer, that as the *civill State* keepes it selfe
with a *civill Guard*, in case these *Tares* shall attempt ought against
the *peace* and *welfare* of it, let such *civill offences* be punished,
and yet as *Tares* opposite to *Christs Kingdome*, let their *Worship*
and *Consciences* be tolerated.

Secondly, the *Church* or *spirituall State, City*, or *Kingdome*
hath *lawes*, and *orders*, and *armories*, (whereon there hang a
thousand *Bucklers, Cant.* 4.) *Weapons* and *Ammunition*, able to
break down the strongest *Holds*, 1 *Cor.* 10. and so to defend it
selfe against the very *Gates* of *Earth* or *Hell*.

Thirdly, the *Lord* himself knows who are his, & his *foundation*
remaineth sure, his *Elect* or chosen cannot perish nor be finally
deceived.

Lastly, the *Lord Jesus* here in this Parable layes downe two
Reasons, able to content and satisfie our *hearts*, to beare patiently
this their *contradiction* and *Antichristianity*, and to permit or let
them alone.

First, let the good Wheat bee pluckt up and rooted up also

out of this *Field* of the *World:* if such *combustions* and *fightings* were, as to pluck up all the false professours of the name of *Christ,* the *good wheat* also would enjoy little peace, but be in danger to bee pluckt up and torne out of this world by such bloody *stormes and tempests.*

And therefore as *Gods people* are commanded, *Jer.* 29. to pray for the peace of *materiall Babell,* wherein they were captivated, and 1 *Tim.* 2. to pray for all men, and specially *Kings and Governors,* that in the peace of the *civill State* they may have peace: So contrary to the opinion and practice of most (drunke with the Cup of the *Whores fornication*) yea, and of *Gods* owne people fast asleepe in *Antichristian Dalilahs* laps, *obedience* to the command of *Christ* to let the *tares* alone, will prove the onely meanes to preserve their Civill Peace, and that without obedience to this command of Christ, it is impossible (without great transgression against the *Lord* in carnall policy, which will not long hold out) to preserve the *civill* peace.

Beside, Gods people the good Wheat are generally pluckt up and persecuted, as well as the vilest idolaters, whether Jewes or Antichristians, which the Lord Jesus seemes in this *Parable* to foretell.

The second *Reason* noted in the *Parable* which may satisfie any man from wondering at the *patience* of *God,* is this: when the *world* is ripe in sinne, in the sinnes of *Antichristianisme* (as the Lord spake of the sinnes of the *Amorites, Gen.* 12.) then those holy and mighty *Officers* and *Executioners,* the *Angels,* with their sharpe and cutting *sickles* of eternall vengeance, shall downe with them, and bundle them up for the *everlasting burnings.*

Then shall that Man of Sin, 2. *Thess.* 2. be consumed by the breath of the mouth of the *Lord Jesus,* and all that *worship* the *Beast* and his picture, and receive his *mark* into their *forehead* or their *hands,* shall drink of the Wine of the *wrath of God* which is poured out without mixture into the Cup of his *indignation,* and he shall be tormented with *fire and brimstone* in the presence of the holy *Angels,* and in the presence of the *Lambe,* and the smoake of their *torment* shall ascend up forever and ever, *Rev.* 14. 10. 11.

"THE PORTRAITURE OF THE BLOUDIE TENENT"

[From "The bloody Tenent yet more bloody"]

And for my selfe I must proclaime, before the most holy *God*, *Angells* and *Men*, that (what ever other *white* and heavenly *Tenents* Mr. *Cotton* houlds) yet this is a *fowle*, a *black*, and a *bloudie Tenent*.

A *Tenent* of high *Blasphemie* against the *God* of *Peace*, the *God* of *Order*, who hath of one *Bloud*, made all *Mankinde*, to dwell upon the face of the Earth, now, all *confounded* and *destroyed* in their *Civill Beings* and *Subsistences*, by mutuall flames of *warre* from their severall respective *Religions* and *Consciences*.

A *Tenent warring* against the *Prince* of *Peace*, *Christ Jesus*, denying his *Appearance* and *Comming* in the *Flesh*, to put an end to, and *abolish* the *shadowes* of that *ceremoniall* and *typicall* Land of *Canaan*.

A *Tenent* fighting against the sweete *end* of his *comming*, which was not to destroy mens *Lives*, for their *Religions*, but to save them, by the meeke and peaceable *Invitations* and *perswasions* of his peaceable *wisdomes Maidens*.

A *Tenent* fowly charging his *Wisdome*, *Faithfullnes* and *Love*, in so poorly providing such *Magistrates* and *Civill Powers* all the *World* over, as might effect so great a *charge* pretended to be committed to them.

A *Tenent* lamentably guilty of his most precious *bloud*, shed in the *bloud* of so many hundreth thousand of his poore *servants* by the *civill powers* of the *World*, pretending to suppresse *Blasphemies*, *Heresies*, *Idolatries*, *Superstition*, &c.

A *Tenent* fighting with the *Spirit* of *Love*, *Holines*, and *Meeknes*, by kindling fiery *Spirits* of *false zeale* and *Furie*, when yet such *Spirits* know not of what *Spirit* they are.

A *Tenent* fighting with those mighty *Angels* who stand up for the peace of the *Saints*, against *Persia*, *Grecia*, &c. and so consequently, all other *Nations*, who fighting for their severall *Religions*, and against the *Truth*, leave no *Roome* for such as feare and love the *Lord* on the Earth.

A *Tenent*, against which the blessed *Soules* under the *Altar* cry loud for *vengeance*, this *Tenent* having cut their *Throats*, torne out their *Hearts*, and powred forth their *Bloud* in all *Ages*, as the onely *Hereticks* and *Blasphemers* in the World.

A *Tenent* which no *Uncleannes*, no *Adulterie*, *Incest*, *Sodomie*, or *Beastialitie* can equall, this *ravishing* and forcing (*explicitly* or *implicitly*) the very *Soules* and *Consciences* of all the *Nations* and *Inhabitants* of the *World*.

A *Tenent* that puts out the very *eye* of all true *Faith*, which cannot but be as free and voluntarie as any *Virgin* in the *World*, in *refusing* or *embracing* any *spirituall offer* or *object*.

A *Tenent* loathsome and ugly (in the eyes of the *God of Heaven*, and serious sonnes of men) I say, loathsome with the palpable *filths* of *grosse dissimulation* and *hypocrisie:* Thousands of *Peoples* and whole *Nations*, compelld by this *Tenent* to put on the fowle *vizard* of *Religious hypocrisie*, for feare of *Lawes, losses* and *punishments*, and for the keeping and hoping for of *favour, libertie, wordly commoditie*, &c.

A *Tenent* wofully guiltie of hardning all false and *deluded Consciences* (of whatsoever *Sect, Faction, Heresie*, or *Idolatrie*, though never so *horrid* and *blasphemous*) by *cruelties* and *violences* practiced against them: all false *Teachers* and their *Followers* (ordinarily) contracting a *Brawnie* and *steelie hardnesse* from their *sufferings* for their *Consciences*.

A *Tenent* that shuts and bars out the gracious *prophecies* and *promises* and *discoveries* of the most glorious *Sun* of *Righteousnes, Christ Jesus*, that burnes up the holy *Scriptures*, and forbids them (upon the point) to be read in *English*, or that any *tryall* or *search*, or (truly) free *disquisition* be made by them: when the most able, diligent and conscionable *Readers* must pluck forth their own *eyes*, and be forced to reade by the (which soever *prædominant) Cleargies Spectacles*.

A *Tenent* that *seales up* the spirituall *graves* of all men, *Jewes* and *Gentiles*, (and consequently stands guiltie of the *damnation* of all men) since no *Preachers*, nor *Trumpets* of *Christ* himselfe may call them out, but such as the severall and respective *Nations* of the *World* themselves allow of.

A *Tenent* that fights against the *common principles* of all *Civilitie*, and the very *civill being* and *combinations* of *men* in *Nations*,

Cities, &c. by commixing (*explicitly* or *implicitly*) a *spirituall* and *civill State* together, and so confounding and overthrowing the *puritie* and *strength* of both.

A *Tenent* that kindles the devouring *flames* of *combustions* and *warres* in most *Nations* of the *World*, and (if *God* were not infinitely gracious) had almost ruind the *English, French, the Scotch* and *Irish*, and many other *Nations, Germane, Polonian, Hungarian, Bohemian*, &c.

A *tenent* that bowes downe the *backs* and *necks* of all *civill States* and *Magistrates, Kings* and *Emperours*, under the proud feet of that *man* and *monster* of *sinne* and *pride* the *Pope*, and all *Popish* and proud *Cleargie-men* rendring such *Laicks* and *Seculars* (as they call them) but slavish *Executioners* (upon the point) of their most imperious *Synodicall Decrees* and *Sentences*.

A *Tenent* that renders the highest *civill Magistrates* and *Ministers* of *Justice* (the *Fathers* and *Gods* of their *Countries*) either odious or lamentably grievous unto the very best *Subjects* by either clapping or keeping on, the *iron yoakes* of cruellest *oppression*. No *yoake* or *bondage* comparably so griveous, as that upon the *Soules necke* of mens *Religion* and *Consciences*.

A *Tenent*, all besprinckled with the *bloudie murthers, stobs, poysonings, pistollings, powder-plots*, &c. against many famous *Kings, Princes*, and *States*, either actually performed or attempted in *France, England, Scotland, Low-Countries*, and other *Nations*.

A *Tenent* all *red* and *bloudie* with those most *barbarous* and *Tyger*-like *Massacres*, of so many thousand and ten thousands formerly in *France*, and other parts, and so lately and so horribly in *Ireland*: of which, whatever causes be assigned, this chiefly will be found the true, and while this continues (to wit, *violence* against *Conscience*) this *bloudie Issue*, sooner or later, must *breake forth* againe (except *God* wonderfully stop it) in *Ireland* and other places too.

A *Tenent* that *stunts* the *growth* and *flourishing* of the most likely and hopefullest *Common-weales* and *Countries*, while *Consciences*, the *best*, and the *best* deserving *Subjects* are forct to flie (by enforced or voluntary *Banishment*) from their native *Countries*; The lamentable proofe whereof *England* hath felt in the flight of so many worthy *English*, into the *Low Countries* and

New England, and from *New England* into old againe and other forraigne parts.

A *Tenent* whose grosse partialitie denies the *Principles* of *common Justice*, while *Men* waigh out to the *Consciences* of all others, that which they judge not fit nor right to be waighed out to their owne: Since the *persecutours Rule* is, to take and persecute all *Consciences*, onely, *himselfe* must not be touched.

A *Tenent* that is but *Machevilisme*, and makes a *Religion*, but a *cloake* or *stalking horse* to *policie* and *private Ends* of *Jeroboams Crowne*, and the *Priests Benefice*, &c.

A *Tenent* that *corrupts* and *spoils* the very *Civill Honestie* and *Naturall Conscience* of a *Nation*. Since *Conscience* to *God* violated, proves (without *Repentance*) ever after, a very *Jade*, a *Drug*, loose and *unconscionable* in all converse with men.

Lastly, a *Tenent* in *England* most unseasonable, as powering *Oyle* upon those *Flames* which the high *Wisdome* of the *Parliament* (by easing the yoakes on *Mens Consciences*) had begun to quench.

In the sad Consideration of all which (Deare *Peace*) let *Heaven* and *Earth* judge of the *washing* and *colour* of this *Tenent*. For thee (*sweete heavenly Guest*) goe lodge thee in the *breasts* of the *peaceable* and humble *Witnesses* of *Jesus*, that love the *Truth* in *peace!* Hide thee from the Worlds *Tumults* and *Combustions*, in the breasts of thy truely *noble children*, who professe and *endeavour* to breake the *irony* and insupportable *yoakes* upon the *Soules* and *Consciences* of any of the sonnes of Men.

ON CHRIST WITHOUT AND WITHIN

[From "George Fox Digg'd out of his Burrowes"]

In Pag. 221. He brings in the Author to a Book called *Hosanna to the Son of David*, saying, [*Christ is without the Saints in respect of his Bodily presence*,] He Answereth, (They are of his Flesh and of his Bone, and eat his Flesh and drink his Blood: and how have the Saints his Mind and Spirit, and he with them and they with him, and sit with him in Heavenly places, and he is the *Head* of the *Church:* how then is he absent? Ye poor

Apostates from him who feel not Christ with you, but he is with the Saints, and they feel him.)

I Reply, I observe this *Viperous Tongue* saying to the unknown, heavenly *Author*, and *Fox* his other *Oppositee* [*Ye poor Apostates &c.*] what is it but a heighth of Devilish Pride going before destruction and condemnation? this proud swelling Bladder puft up with a *Timpany* of *Wind* and *Vanity*, what a huge swelling shew he makes? what a breadth of confident boldness and bruitish impudencie he carries before him? what a gross, Frantick *Papist* is he become, that cannot, will not distinguish between *Christs Spiritual presence* and his bodily? that cannot, will not consider the difference between *Spirits* and *Bodies*, a *Spirit* that hath no Flesh nor Bones, and a Body which hath both, as Christ his Body had? that cannot, will not distinguish between their sinful *Flesh* and *Bones*, and the sinless *Flesh* and *Bones* of that Man Christ Jesus? that cannot, will not distinguish between God manifested in the *Flesh* and *Bones* of that Man Christ Jesus, and manifested in the *Flesh* and *Bones* of *Believers* in him: O most Holy and Righteous are thy Judgements, O thou most High Judge of the World, who art a devouring fire and Justice it self, who thus casteth down the *Proud* and *Self-conceited* into the Dungeon of such *Black* and *Hellish* Ignorance!

Pag. 217, Out of a Book mentioning the *Quakers Cause*, saying, [*To say Christ within is never to mention Christ without*]. He Answers, There is none knows Christ within, but he knows him without: the same yesterday, and to day, and for ever: And there is none knows him but they know him within, revealed of the Father, which is beyond Flesh and Blood.

I Observe, This foolish *Fox* (for all his hiding Craft) is here found out: He professeth (against his Will and Heart) a Christ that *died at Jerusalem*, and therefore is he forced to name a Christ without: but when the *Hole and Burrough is Digged* the *Fox* is found: For Examine what is this *Christ without?* is he that litteral, real and material Person the Son of *Mary* (as all professing Christs Name generally agree)? Is this he whom the *Quakers* acknowledge to have *lived* and *died* at *Jerusalem?* and do they intend a *Material Crosse*, a literal Death, a literal and real *Jerusalem?* some of them will say yes, but therein give the lye to others

of themselves, and also to the rest of their own story, in acknowledging no other Christ but such as is in *every man:* such a Christ
as really and bodily *died at Jerusalem,* they scorn and hate and fly
from as the *Devils did,* crying out, *What have we to do with thee
Jesus thou Son of the most High God, art thou come to torment us
before the time?* Hence the former *Arch-deacon* or *Arch-bishop* of
these parts *Humphrey Norton:* he mocks at an outward Christ,
he asks what Countryman he was and shall be: He reproves the
Fools that have their Eyes abroad, and gazing after a man into
Heaven, he jeers at the Crosse, and asks what manner of wood
it was made of, seeing we must take it up dayly? And *Fox* saith,
this Jesus Christ without and within, is Jesus Christ yesterday,
and to day, and the same for ever: therefore in the *Logick* or *Reason* of this *Bruite,* Christ had no body that was born at *Bethlehem,*
or died at *Jerusalem;* For he was born yesterday, and to day, and
he is born forever: he dyed yesterday, and he dies to day, and
he dies forever, which is a most Heavenly Truth relating to
Gods purpose, Christs Merit, and to Forefathers, our present
times, and such as yet must be born and follow after us.

But such Mystical and figurative Scriptures (which are in
themselves like *Sampsons Lion* and *Riddle*) through *Satans Policy,* and the proud simplicity of these simple *Foxes,* are made the
common *Holes* and *Burroughs* where you may be sure to find
them: just like the Jesuites (whose Cosens, if not Brethren of one
belly of Hell they are) who usually confound clear Scriptures with
Spirituall and Mystical Illusions, and fly from Distinctions and
openings necessary in places more dark, figurative and allegorical.

NATHANIEL WARD

["The Simple Cobler of Aggawamm" is one of the most interesting of American literary curiosities, though it is valuable chiefly as a curiosity. Its author, the Rev. Nathaniel Ward, was a graduate of Cambridge, who had been a barrister and had travelled extensively on the Continent before he became a clergyman. After coming into conflict with Laud because of his Puritanism, he sailed for America in 1634, and remained until 1647. He served as minister at Ipswich, then known as Aggawam, from 1634 to 1636, when he laid down his pastorate on account of poor health. About 1645 he began to write the pamphlet which was published in London early in 1647, inscribed on the title-page "The Simple Cobler of Aggawamm in America. Willing to help 'mend his Native Country, lamentably tattered, both in the upper-Leather and sole, with all the honest stitches he can take. And as willing never to bee paid for his work, by Old English wonted pay. *It is his trade to patch all the year long, gratis.* Therefore I pray Gentlemen keep your purses. By *Theodore de la Guard.*" Though written in America, and dealing to some extent with American themes, "The Simple Cobler" is evidently addressed to the people and parliament of Great Britain, and owes its inception to the political and religious condition of the mother country. It begins with a protest against religious toleration, and passes to a tirade against women's fashions and long hair; but the greater part of the work, though somewhat rambling, is given to a discussion of the political state of England. One of the best written and least intemperate parts of the pamphlet is a long address to "My Dearest Lord, and my more than dearest King"; but the work owes its fame to the more virulent passages which are fairly represented in the pages that follow. The oddity of these has distracted attention from the narrowness and bitterness of the ideas that they express, and has allowed the author's name to live with a more creditable reputation than it would have had if his prejudices had been less curiously phrased.

Ward returned to England in time to revise the second, third, and fourth editions of "The Simple Cobler," all of which appeared in London in 1647. While in the colonies he had compiled "The Body of Liberties," a code of laws adopted by Massachusetts in 1641, and after his return to England he published a number of sermons and other writings. The selections that follow are from the reprint of the fourth edition of "The Simple Cobler," issued by the Ipswich Historical Society in 1905.]

ON TOLERATION OF RELIGIOUS OPINIONS

[From "The Simple Cobler of Aggawamm"]

Either I am in an Appoplexie, or that man is in a Lethargie, who doth not now sensibly feele God shaking the heavens over his head, and the earth under his feet: The Heavens so, as the Sun begins to turne into darknesse, the Moon into blood, the Starres to fall down to the ground; So that little Light of Comfort or Counsell is left to the sonnes of men: The Earth so, as the foundations are failing, the righteous scarce know where to finde rest, the inhabitants stagger like drunken men: it is in a manner dissolved both in Religions and Relations: And no marvell; for, they have defiled it by transgressing the Lawes, changing the Ordinances, and breaking the Everlasting Covenant. The Truths of God are the Pillars of the world, whereon States and Churches may stand quiet if they will; if they will not, Hee can easily shake them off into delusions, and distractions enough.

Sathan is now in his passions, he feeles his passion approaching; hee loves to fish in royled waters. Though that Dragon cannot sting the vitals of the Elect mortally, yet that Beelzebub can fly-blow their Intellectuals miserably: The finer Religion grows, the finer hee spins his Cobwebs, hee will hold pace with Christ so long as his wits will serve him. Hee sees himselfe beaten out of grosse Idolatries, Heresies, Ceremonies, where the Light breakes forth with power; he will therefore bestirre him to prevaricate Evangelicall Truths, and Ordinances, that if they will needs be walking, yet they shall *laborare varicibus*, and not keep their path, he will put them out of time and place; Assassinating for his Engineers, men of Paracelsian parts; well complexioned for honesty; for, such are fittest to Mountebanke his Chimistry into sicke Churches and weake Judgements.

Nor shall hee need to stretch his strength overmuch in this worke: Too many men having not laid their foundations sure, nor ballasted their Spirits deepe with humility and feare, are prest enough of themselves to evaporate their owne apprehensions. Those that are acquainted with Story know, it hath ever beene so in new Editions of Churches: Such as are least able, are most busie to pudder in the rubbish, and to raise dust in the eyes of

I

more steady Repayrers. Civill Commotions make roome for uncivill practises: Religious mutations, for irreligious opinions: Change of Aire, discovers corrupt bodies; Reformation of Religion, unsound mindes. Hee that hath any well-faced phansy in his Crowne, and doth not vent it now, fears the pride of his owne heart will dub him dunce for ever. Such a one will trouble the whole *Israel* of God with his most untimely births, though he makes the bones of his vanity stick up, to the view and griefe of all that are godly wise. The devill desiers no better sport then to see light heads handle their heels, and fetch their carreers in a time, when the Roofe of Liberty stands open.

The next perplexed Question, with pious and ponderous men, will be: What should bee done for the healing of these comfortlesse exulcerations. I am the unablest adviser of a thousand, the unworthiest of ten thousand; yet I hope I may presume to assert what follows without just offence.

First, such as have given or taken any unfriendly reports of us *New-English*, should doe well to recollect themselves. Wee have beene reputed a Colluvies of wild Opinionists, swarmed into a remote wildernes to find elbow-roome for our phanatick Doctrines and practices: I trust our diligence past, and constant sedulity against such persons and courses, will plead better things for us. I dare take upon me, to bee the Herauld of *New-England* so farre, as to proclaime to the world, in the name of our Colony, that all Familists, Antinomians, Anabaptists, and other Enthusiasts shall have free Liberty to keepe away from us, and such as will come to be gone as fast as they can, the sooner the better.

Secondly, I dare averre, that God doth no where in his word tolerate Christian States, to give Toleration to such adversaries of his Truth, if they have power in their hands to suppresse them.

Here is lately brought us an extract of a *Magna Charta*, so called, compiled between the Sub-planters of a *West-Indian* Island; whereof the first Article of constipulation, firmly provides free stable-room and litter for all kinde of consciences, be they never so dirty or jadish; making it actionable, yea, treasonable, to disturbe any man in his Religion, or to discommend it, whatever it be. Wee are very sorry to see such professed prophanenesse in

English Professors, as industriously to lay their Religious foundations on the ruine of true Religion; which strictly binds every conscience *to contend earnestly for the Truth: to preserve unity of spirit, Faith and Ordinances, to be all like minded, of one accord; every man to take his brother into his Christian care: to stand fast with one spirit, with one mind, striving together for the faith of the Gospel.* and by no meanes to permit Heresies or erronious opinions: But God abhorring such loathsome beverages, hath in his righteous judgement blasted that enterprize, which might otherwise have prospered well, for ought I know; I presume their case is generally knowne ere this.

If the devill might have his free option, I beleeve he would ask nothing else, but liberty to enfranchize all false Religions, and to embondage the true; nor should hee need: It is much to be feared, that laxe Tolerations upon State-pretences and planting necessities, will be the next subtle Stratagem he will spread to distate the Truth of God and supplant the peace of the Churches. Tolerations in things tolerable, exquisitely drawn out by the lines of the Scripture, and pensill of the Spirit, are the sacred favours of Truth, the due latitudes of Love, the faire Compartiments of Christian fraternity: but irregular dispensations, dealt forth by the facilities of men, are the frontiers of error, the redoubts of Schisme, the perillous irritaments of carnall and spirituall enmity.

My heart hath naturally detested foure things: The standing of the Apocrypha in the Bible; Forrainers dwelling in my Countrey, to crowd out native Subjects into the corners of the Earth; Alchymized coines; Tolerations of divers Religions, or of one Religion in segregant shapes: He that willingly assents to the last, if he examines his heart by day-light, his conscience will tell him, he is either an Atheist, or an Heretique, or an Hypocrite, or at best a captive to some Lust: Poly-piety is the greatest impiety in the world. True Religion is *Ignis probationis*, which doth *congregare homogenea & segregare heterogenea.*

Not to tolerate things meerly indifferent to weak consciences, argues a conscience too strong: pressed uniformity in these, causes much disunity: To tolerate more then indifferents, is not to deale indifferently with God: He that doth it, takes his Scepter out of his hand, and bids him stand by. Who hath to doe to institute

Religion but God. The power of all Religion and Ordinances,
lies in their purity: their purity in their simplicity: then are mix-
tures pernicious. I lived in a City, where a Papist preached in
one Church, a Lutheran in another, a Calvinist in a third; a
Lutheran one part of the day, a Calvinist the other, in the same
Pulpit: the Religion of that place was but motly and meagre,
their affections Leopard-like.

If the whole Creature should conspire to doe the Creator a mischiefe, or offer him an insolency, it would be in nothing more,
than in erecting untruths against his Truth, or by sophisticating
his Truths with humane medleyes: the removing of some one iota
in Scripture, may draw out all the life, and traverse all the Truth
of the whole Bible: but to authorise an untruth, by a Toleration
of State, is to build a Sconce against the walls of heaven, to batter
God out of his Chaire: To tell a practicall lye, is a great sin, but
yet transient; but to set up a Theoricall untruth, is to warrant every
lye that lyes from its root to the top of every branch it hath, which
are not a few.

I would willingly hope that no Member of the Parliament hath
skilfully ingratiated himselfe into the hearts of the House, that he
might watch a time to midwife out some ungracious Toleration
for his owne turne, and for the sake of that, some other, I would
also hope that a word of generall caution should not be particularly misapplied. I am the freer to suggest it, because I know
not one man of that mind, my aime is generall, and I desire may
be so accepted. Yet good Gentlemen, look well about you, and
remember how Tiberius play'd the Fox with the Senate of *Rome*,
and how *Fabius Maximus* cropt his ears for his cunning.

MORE ARGUMENTS AGAINST TOLERATION

[From "The Simple Cobler"]

It is said, Though a man have light enough himselfe to see the
Truth, yet if he hath not enough to enlighten others, he is bound
to tolerate them, I will engage my self, that all the Devills in
Britanie shall sell themselves to their shirts, to purchase a Lease
of this Position for three of their Lives, under the Seale of the
Parliament.

It is said, That Men ought to have Liberty of their Conscience, and that it is persecution to debarre them of it: I can rather stand amazed then reply to this: it is an astonishment to think that the braines of men should be parboyl'd in such impious ignorance; Let all the wits under the Heavens lay their heads together and finde an Assertion worse then this (one excepted) I will petition to be chosen the universall Ideot of the world.

It is said, That Civill Magistrates ought not to meddle with Ecclesiasticall matters.

I would answer to this so well as I could, did I not know that some papers lately brought out of *New-England*, are going to the Presse, wherein the Opinions of the Elders there in a late Synod, concerning this point are manifested, which I suppose will give clearer satisfaction then I can.

The true English of all this their false Latine, is nothing but a generall Toleration of all Opinions; which motion if it be like to take, it were very requisite, that the City would repaire *Pauls* with all the speed they can, for an English *Pantheon*, and bestow it upon the Sectaries, freely to assemble in, then there may be some hope that London will be quiet in time.

But why dwell I so intolerable long about Tolerations, I hope my fears are but panick, against which I have a double cordiall. First, that the Parliament will not though they could: Secondly, that they cannot though they would grant such Tolerations. God who hath so honoured them with eminent wisdome in all other things, will not suffer them to cast both his, and their Honour in the dust of perpetuall Infamy, doe what they can; nor shall those who have spent so great a part of their substance in redeeming their Civill Liberties from Usurpation, lose all that remaines in enthralling their spirituall Liberty by Toleration.

It is said Opinionists are many, and strong, that *de sunt Vires*, that it is *turbata respublica*, I am very sorry for it, but more sorry, if despondency of minde shall cause the least tergiversation in Gods Worthies, who have receiv'd such pledges of his presence in their late Counsels, and Conflicts. It is not thousands of Opinionists that can pinion his Everlasting armes, I can hardly beleeve there is a greater unbeleever then my Selfe, yet I can verily beleeve that the God of Truth will in a short time scatter them

all like smoak before the wind. I confesse I am troubled to see
Men so over-troubled about them; I am rather glad to heare the
Devill is breaking up house in *England,* and removing some-
whither else, give him leave to sell all his rags, and odd-eends by
the out-cry; and let his petty Chapmen make their Market while
they may, upon my poore credit it will not last long.   Hee that
hath done so much for *England* will go on to perfect his owne
praise, and his Peoples Peace: Let good men stand still, and
behold his further Salvation. He that sitteth in the Heavens
laughs at them, the most High hath them in Derision, and their
folly shall certainly be manifested to all men.

Yet I dare not but adde, and in the Name of God will adde, that
if any Publique members of Church or State, have been either
open fautors, or private abetters of any blasphemous, contagious
Opinions, It will be their wisdome to proportion their repentance
to their Sin, before God makes them Publique monuments of
Ignominie, and Apostasie.

Thirdly, that all Christian States, ought to disavow and decry
all such Errors, by some peremptory Statutary Act, and that in
time, that Subjects knowing fully the minde of the State, might
not delude themselves with vaine hopes of unsufferable Liberties.
It is lesse to say, *Statuatur veritas, ruat Regnum,* than *Fiat justitia,
ruat Coelum;* but there is no such danger in either of them.   Feare
nothing Gentlemen, *Rubiconemtransiistis, jacta est alea,* ye have
turned the Devill out of doores; fling all his old parrell after him
out at the windows, lest he makes another errand for it againe.
*Quae relinquuntur in morbis post indicationem, recidivas facere
confuevere.*   Christ would have his Church without spot or
wrinckle; They that help make it so, shall lose neither honour
nor labour: If yee be wise, suffer no more thorns in his sides or
your owne.   When God kindles such fires as these, hee doth not
usually quench them, till the very scum on the pot sides be boyled
cleane away, *Ezek.* 24. 10, 11.   Yee were better to doe it yourselves, than leave it to him: the Arme of the Lord is mighty, his
hand very heavy; who can dwell with his devouring fire, and long
lasting burnings?

Fourthly, to make speedy provision against Obstinates and
Disseminaries: where under favour, two things will be found

requisite. First, variety of penaltyes, I meane certaine, not in-
definite: I am a Crabbat against Arbitrary Government. Experience hath taught us here, that politicall, domesticall, and personall respects, will not admit one and the same remedy for all,
without sad inconveniences. Secondly, just severity: persecution hath ever spread Truth, prosecution scattered Errour: Ten
of the most Christian Emperors, found that way best; Schollars
know whom I meane: Five of the ancient Fathers perswaded to
it, of whom *Augustine* was one, who for a time argued hard for
indulgency: but upon conference with other prudent Bishops,
altered his judgement, as appears in three of his Epistles, to
Marcellinus, Donatus, and *Boniface.* I would be understood, not
onely an Allower, but an humble Petitioner, that ignorant and
tender conscienced Anabaptists may have due time and means of
conviction.

Fifthly, That every Prophet, to whom God hath given the
tongue of the learned, should teach, and every Angel who hath
a pen and inkehorne by his side write against these grieving extravagancies: writing of many books, I grant is irksome, reading
endlesse. A reasonable man would thinke Divines had declaimed
sufficiently upon these Themes. I have ever thought the Rule
given, *Titus* 3. 10. which cuts the work short and sharpe to be
more properly prevelant, then wearisome waiting upon unwear-
iable Spirits. It is a most toylsome taske to run the wild-goose
chase after a well-breath'd Opinionist: they delight in vitilitigation:
it is an itch that loves alife to be scrub'd: they desire not satisfaction, but satisdiction, whereof themselves must be judges:
yet in new eruptions of Error with new objections, silence is
sinfull.

ON WOMEN'S FASHIONS

[From "The Simple Cobler"]

Should I not keepe promise in speaking a little to Womens
fashions, they would take it unkindly: I was loath to pester
better matter with such stuffe; I rather thought it meet to let
them stand by themselves, like the *Quae Genus* in the Grammer,
being Deficients, or Redundants, not to be brought under any

Rule: I shall therefore make bold for this once, to borrow a little of their loose tongued Liberty, and mis-spend a word or two upon their long-wasted, but short-skirted patience: a little use of my stirrup will doe no harme.

Ridentem dicere verum, quid prohibet?

Gray Gravity it selfe can well beteam,
That Language be adapted to the Theme.
He that to Parrots speaks, must parrotise:
He that instructs a foole, may act th' unwise.

It is known more then enough, that I am neither Nigard, nor Cinick, to the due bravery of the true Gentry: if any man dislikes a bullymong drossock more then I, let him take her for his labour: I honour the woman that can honour her selfe with her attire: a good Text alwayes deserves a fair Margent; I am not much offended, if I see a trimme, far trimmer than she that weares it: in a word, whatever Christianity or Civility will allow, I can afford with *London* measure: but when I heare a nugiperous Gentledame inquire what dresse the Queen is in this week: what the nudiustertian fashion of the Court; with egge to be in it in all haste, whatever it be; I look at her as the very gizzard of a trifle, the product of a quarter of a cypher, the epitome of Nothing, fitter to be kickt, if shee were of a kickable substance, than either honour'd or humour'd.

To speak moderately, I truly confesse it is beyond the ken of my understanding to conceive, how those women should have any true grace, or valuable vertue, that have so little wit, as to disfigure themselves with such exotick garbes, as not only dismantles their native lovely lustre, but transclouts them into gant-bar-geese, ill-shapen-shotten-shell-fish, Egyptian Hyeroglyphicks, or at the best into French flurts of the pastery, which a proper English woman should scorne with her heels: it is no marvell they weare draills on the hinder part of their heads, having nothing as it seems in the fore-part, but a few Squirrils brains to help them frisk from one ill-favour'd fashion to another.

These whimm' Crown'd shees, these fashion-fansying wits,
Are empty thin brain'd shells, and fidling Kits.

The very troublers and impoverishers of mankind, I can hardly forbeare to commend to the world a saying of a Lady living sometime with the Queen of *Bohemia,* I know not where shee found it, but it is pitty it should be lost.

The world is full of care, much like unto a bubble;
Women and care, and care and women, and women and care and trouble.

The Verses are even enough for such odde pegma's I can make my selfe sicke at any time, with comparing the dazling splender wherewith our Gentlewomen were imbellished in some former habits, with the gut-foundred goosdom, wherewith they are now surcingled and debauched. Wee have about five or six of them in our Colony: if I see any of them accidentally, I cannot cleanse my phansie of them for a moneth after. I have been a solitary widdower almost twelve yeares, purposed lately to make a step over to my Native Country for a yoke-fellow: but when I consider how women there have tripe-wifed themselves with their cladments, I have no heart to the voyage, least their nauseous shapes and the Sea, should work too sorely upon my stomach. I speak sadly; me thinkes it should breake the hearts of Englishmen, to see so many goodly English-women imprisoned in French Cages, peering out of their hood-holes for some men of mercy to help them with a little wit, and no body relieves them.

It is a more common then convenient saying, that nine Taylors make a man: it were well if nineteene could make a woman to her minde: if Taylors were men indeed, well furnished but with meer morall principles, they would disdain to be led about like Apes, by such mymick Marmosets. It is a most unworthy thing, for men that have bones in them, to spend their lives in making fidle-cases for futulous womens phansies; which are the very pettitoes of Infirmity, the giblets of perquisquilian toyes. I am so charitable to think, that most of that mystery would worke the cheerfuller while they live, if they might bee well discharged of the tyring slavery of mis-tyring women: it is no little labour to be continually putting up English-women into Out-landish caskes; who if they be not shifted anew, once in a few months, grow too sowre for their Husbands. What this Trade will answer for themselves when God shall take measure of Taylors con-

sciences is beyond my skill to imagine. There was a time
when

The joyning of the Red-Rose with the White,
Did set our State into a Damask plight.

But now our Roses are turned to *Flore de lices*, our Carnations
to Tulips, our Gilliflowers to Dayzes, our City-Dames, to an in-
denominable Quæmalry of overturcas'd things. Hee that makes
Coates for the Moone, had need to take measure every noone:
and he that makes for women, as often, to keepe them from
Lunacy.

I have often heard divers Ladies vent loud feminine complaints
of the wearisome varieties and chargable changes of fashions: I
marvell themselves preferre not a Bill of Redresse. I would
Essex [1] Ladies would lead the *Chore*, for the honour of their
County and persons; or rather the thrice honorable Ladies of
the Court, whom it best besemes: who may well presume of a *Le
Roy le veult* from our sober King, a *Les Seigneurs ont assentus*
from our prudent Peers, and the like *Assentus*, from our considerate, I dare not say wife-worne Commons: who I beleeve
had much rather passe one such Bill, than pay so many Taylors
Bills as they are forced to doe.

Most deare and unparallel'd Ladies, be pleased to attempt it:
as you have the precellency of the women of the world for beauty
and feature; so assume the honour to give, and not take Law
from any in matter of attire: if ye can transact so faire a
motion among yourselves unanimously, I dare say, they that
most renite, will least repent. What greater Honour can your
Honors desire, then to build a Promontory president to all
foraigne Ladies, to deserve so eminently at the hands of all the
English Gentry present and to come: and to confute the opinion
of all the wise men in the world; who never thought it possible
for women to doe so good a work?

If any man think I have spoken rather merrily than seriously
he is much mistaken, I have written what I write with all the indignation I can, and no more then I ought. I confesse I veer'd

---

[1] All the counties and shires of England have had wars in them since the
Conquest, but Essex, which is onely free, and should be thankfull. [Printed in
the original edition as a marginal gloss.]

my tongue to this kinde of Language *de industria* though un-willingly, supposing those I speak to are uncapable of grave and rationall arguments.

I desire all Ladies and Gentlewomen to understand that all this while I intend not such as through necessary modesty to avoyd morose singularity, follow fashions slowly, a flight shot or two off, shewing by their moderation, that they rather draw counter-mont with their hearts, then put on by their examples.

I point my pen only against the light-heel'd beagles that lead that chase so fast, that they run all civility out of breath, against these Ape-headed pullets, which invent antique foole-fangles, meerly for fashion and novelty sake.

In a word, if I begin once to declaime against fashions, let men and women look well about them, there is somewhat in the busi-nesse; I confesse to the world, I never had grace enough to be strict in that kinde; and of late years, I have found syrrope of pride very wholesome in a due *Dos*, which makes mee keep such store of that drugge by me, that if any body comes to me for a question-full or two about fashions, they never complain of me for giving them hard measure, or under-weight.

But I addresse my self to those who can both hear and mend all if they please: I seriously fear, if the pious Parliament doe not find a time to state fashions, as ancient Parliaments have done in part, God will hardly finde a time to state Religion or Peace: They are the surquedryes of pride, the wantonnesse of idlenesse, provoking sins, the certain prodromies of assured judgement, *Zeph.* 1. 7, 8.

It is beyond all account, how many Gentlemens and Citizens estates are deplumed by their feather-headed wives, what useful supplies the pannage of *England* would afford other Countries, what rich returnes to it selfe, if it were not sliced out into male and female fripperies: and what a multitude of mis-imploy'd hands, might be better improv'd in some more manly Manufactures for the publique weale: it is not easily credible, what may be said of the preterpluralities of Taylors in *London:* I have heard an honest man say, that not long since there were numbered between *Temple-barre* and *Charing-Crosse*, eight thou-sand of that Trade: let it be conjectured by that proportion how

many there are in and about *London*, and in all *England*, they will
appear to be very numerous. If the Parliament would please to
mend women, which their Husbands dare not doe, there need not
so many men to make and mend as there are. I hope the present
dolefull estate of the Realme, will perswade more strongly to some
considerate course herein, than I now can.

A WORD OF IRELAND

NOT OF THE NATION UNIVERSALLY, NOR OF ANY MAN IN IT, THAT HATH SO
   MUCH AS ONE HAIRE OF CHRISTIANITY OR HUMANITY GROWING ON HIS
   HEAD OR BEARD, BUT ONELY OF THE TRUCULENT CUT-THROATS, AND
   SUCH AS SHALL TAKE UP ARMES IN THEIR DEFENCE.

[From "The Simple Cobler"]

These *Irish* anciently called *Antropophagi*, man-eaters: Have a
Tradition among them, That when the Devill shewed our Saviour
all the Kingdomes of the Earth and their glory, that he would not
shew him *Ireland*, but reserved it for himselfe: it is probably true,
for he hath kept it ever since for his own peculiar; the old Fox
foresaw it would eclipse the glory of all the rest: he thought it
wisdome to keep the land for a Boggards for his unclean spirits
imployed in this Hemisphere, and the people, to doe his Son and
Heire, I mean the Pope, that service for which *Lewis* the eleventh
kept his Barbor *Oliver*, which makes them so blood-thirsty. They
are the very Offall of men, Dregges of Mankind, Reproach of
Christendom, the Bots that crawle on the Beasts taile, I wonder
Rome it self is not ashamed of them.

I begge upon my hands and knees, that the Expedition against
them may be undertaken while the hearts and hands of our Soul-
diery are hot, to whom I will be bold to say briefly: Happy is he
that shall reward them as they have served us, and Cursed be he
that shall do that work of the Lord negligently, Cursed be he
that holdeth back his Sword from blood: yea, Cursed be he that
maketh not his Sword starke drunk with *Irish* blood, that doth not
recompence them double for their hellish treachery to the *English*, that maketh them not heaps upon heaps, and their Country
a dwelling place for Dragons, an Astonishment to Nations: Let
not that eye look for pity, nor that hand to be spared, that pities
or spares them, and let him be accursed, that curseth not them
bitterly.

THOMAS SHEPARD

[Thomas Shepard was another of the famous Massachusetts divines who were educated at Emmanuel College, Cambridge, and who were later driven from the Church of England by Archbishop Laud. He came to Boston in 1635 at the age of thirty, and from 1636 till his death in 1649 was pastor of the church at Cambridge. His many published writings were almost all on religious and theological subjects. His style is at times unusually modern, and he is more readable than many of his contemporaries, but none of his works stands out with especial distinction. His brief "Autobiography" remained in manuscript until 1832, when it was privately printed. It was first published in Alexander Young's "Chronicles of the First Planters of Massachusetts Bay," in 1846.

The first passage given below was quoted by Thomas Prince in his "Annals of New England" from "A manuscript of Master Shepard's written in his own hand." The text is that of the reprint of the "Annals" in Edward Arber's "English Garner." The second selection is from Shepard's pamphlet, "The Cleare Sunshine of the Gospell breaking forth upon the Indians in New England," originally published in London in 1648, and reprinted in the Collections of the Massachusetts Historical Society, 1834. The selection from "The Sincere Convert" is from the first London edition, 1659. A marginal gloss, which summarizes each paragraph without comment, is here omitted. The extract from the "Autobiography" is from Young's reprint, referred to above. This modernizes the spelling.]

AN INTERVIEW WITH BISHOP LAUD

December 16, 1630. I was inhibited from preaching in the diocese of London by Doctor LAUD, Bishop of that diocese.

As soon as I came, in the morning, about eight o'clock; falling into a fit of rage, he asked me, "What degree I had taken in the University?" I answered him, "I was a Master of Arts." He asked, "Of what College?" I answered, "Of Emmanuel." He asked me, "How long I had lived in his diocese?" I answered, "Three years and upwards." He asked, "Who maintained me all this while?" Charging me to deal plainly with him; adding withal, that he had been more cheated and equivocated with by

some of my malignant faction, than ever was man by Jesuit. At
the speaking of which words, he looked as though blood would
have gushed out of his face, and did shake as if he had been
haunted with an ague fit: to my apprehension, by reason of his
extreme malice and secret venom. I desired him "to excuse me."
He fell then to threaten me, and withal to bitter railing; calling
me all to naught: saying, "You prating coxcomb! Do you think
all the learning is in your brain?"

He pronounced his sentence thus. "I charge you, that you
neither preach, read, marry, bury, nor exercise any ministerial
function in any part of my diocese! for if you do, and I hear of it,
I'll be upon your back; and follow you wherever you go, in any
part of the kingdom: and so everlastingly disenable you!" I be-
sought him not to deal so, in regard of a poor town. And here he
stopped me, in what I was going on to say, "A poor town! You
have made a company of seditious, factious bedlams! And what
do you prate to me of a poor town!" I prayed him "to suffer me
to catechize on the Sabbath days, in the afternoon." He replied,
"Spare your breath! I will have no such fellows prate in my
diocese! Get you gone! And now make your complaints to
whom you will!" So away I went. And blessed be GOD! that I
may go to Him.

QUESTIONS IN INDIAN MEETING

[From "The Cleare Sunshine of the Gospell Breaking forth upon the
Indians in New England"]

As soone as ever the fiercenesse of the winter was past, March.
3. 1647. I went out to *Noonanetum* to the *Indian* Lecture, where
Mr. *Wilson*, Mr. *Allen*, of *Dedham*, Mr. *Dunster*, beside many other
Christians were present; on which day perceiving divers of the
Indian women 'well affected, and considering that their soules
might stand in need of answer to their scruples as well as the mens;
& yet because we knew how unfit it was for women so much as to
aske questions publiquely immediately by themselves; wee did
therefore desire them to propound any questions they would be
resolved about by first acquainting either their Husbands, or the
Interpreter privately therewith: whereupon we heard two ques-

tions thus orderly propounded; which because they are the first
that ever were propounded by *Indian* women in such an ordinance
that ever wee heard of, and because they may bee otherwise usefull,
I shall therefore set them downe.

The first question was propounded by the wife of one *Wampooas*
a well affected *Indian, viz.* "Whether (said she) do I pray
"when my husband prayes if I speak nothing as he doth, yet if
"I like what he saith, and my heart goes with it? (for the *Indians*
will many times pray with their wives, and with their children also
sometime in the fields) shee therefore fearing lest prayer should
onely be an externall action of the lips, enquired if it might not be
also an inward action of the heart, if she liked of what he said.

The second question was propounded by the Wife of one
Totherswampe, her meaning in her question (as wee all perceived)
was this *viz.* "Whether a husband should do well to pray with
"his wife, and yet continue in his passions, & be angry with his
wife? But the modesty and wisdome of the woman directed her
to doe three things in one, for thus shee spake to us, *viz.* "Before
"my husband did pray hee was much angry and froward, but since
"hee hath begun to pray hee was not angry so much, but little
"angry: wherein first shee gave an honorable testimony of her
husband and commended him for the abatement of his passion;
secondly, shee gave implicitly a secret reproofe for what was past,
and for somewhat at present that was amisse; and thirdly, it was
intended by her as a question whether her husband should pray to
God, and yet continue in some unruly passions; but she wisely
avoyded that, lest it might reflect too much upon him, although wee
desired her to expresse if that was not her meaning.

At this time (beside these questions) there were sundry others
propounded of very good use, in all which we saw the Lord Jesus
leading them to make narrow inquiries into the things of God,
that so they might see the reality of them. I have heard few Christians when they began to looke toward God, make more searching
questions that they might see things really, and not onely have
a notion of them: I forbeare to mention any of them, because I
forget the chiefe of them; onely this wee tooke notice of at this
dayes meeting, that there was an aged *Indian* who proposed his
complaint in propounding his question concerning an unruly

disobedient son, and "what one should do with him in case of "obstinacy and disobedience, and that will not heare Gods Word, "though his Father command him, nor will not forsake his drunk- "ennesse, though his father forbid him? Unto which there were many answers to set forth the sinne of disobedience to parents; which were the more quickned and sharpned because wee knew that this rebellious sonne whom the old man meant, was by Gods providence present at this Lecture: Mr *Wilson* was much inlarged, and spake so terribly, yet so graciously as might have affected a heart not quite shut up, which this young *desperado* hearing (who well understood the *English* tongue) instead of humbling himself before the Lords Word, which touched his conscience and condition so neare, hee was filled with a spirit of Satan, and as soone as ever Mr. *Wilsons* speech was ended hee brake out into a loud contemptuous expression; *So*, saith he: which we passed by without speaking againe, leaving the Word with him, which we knew would one day take its effect one way or other upon him.

THE SENTENCE AT THE LAST JUDGMENT

[From "The Sincere Convert"]

4. In regard of the fearful sentence that then shall be passed upon thee; *Depart thou cursed creature into everlasting fire, prepared for the devil and his Angels.* Thou shalt then cry out. Oh mercy, Lord! Oh a little mercy! No, will the Lord Jesus say, I did indeed once offer it you, but you refused, therefore *Depart.* Then thou shalt plead again, Lord if I must depart, yet blesse me before I go: No, no, Depart *thou cursed.* Oh but, Lord, If I must depart cursed, let me go into some good place: No, depart thou cursed *into hell fire.* Oh Lord, that's a torment I cannot bear; but if it must be so, Lord, let me come out again quickly; No, depart thou cursed into *everlasting* fire. Oh Lord, if this be thy pleasure, that here I must abide, let me have good company with me. No depart thou cursed into everlasting fire *prepared for the Devil and his Angels.* This shall be thy sentence. The hearing of which may make the rocks to rent, so that, go on in thy sin and prosper, despise and scoff at Gods Ministers and prosper, abhorre

the power and practise of Religion, as a too precise course, and prosper; yet know it, there will a day come, when thou shalt meet with a dreadfull Judge, a dolefull sentence. Now is thy day of sinning, but God will have shortly his day of condemning.

5. When the Judgement day is done then the fearfull wrath of God shall be poured out, and piled upon their bodies and soules, and the breath of the Lord, like a stream of brimstone shall kindle it, and here thou shalt lie burning, and none shall ever quench it. This is the execution of a sinner after judgement, *Rev.* 21. 8.

Now this wrath of God consists in these things.

1. Thy soul shall be banished from the face, and blessed sweet presence of God and Christ, and thou shalt never see the face of God more. It is said *Acts* 20. that *they wept sore, because they should see* Pauls *face no more.* Oh, thou shalt never see the face of *God, Christ, Saints* and *Angels* more. Oh, heavy doom to famish and pine away for ever without one bit of bread to comfort thee, one smile of God to refresh thee! Men that have their sores running upon them, must be shut up from the presence of men sound and hole. Oh, thy sinnes like plague-sores, run on thee, therefore thou must be shut out like a Dog from the presence of God and all his people, 2 *Thes*, 1. 9.

2. God shall set himself like a consuming infinite fire against thee, and tread thee under his feet, who hast by sin trod him & his glory under foot all thy life. A man may devise exquisite torments for another, and great power may make a little stick to lay on heavy strokes: but great power stirred up to strike from great fury and wrath, makes the stroak deadly: I tell thee, all the wisdom of God shall then be set against thee to devise torments for thee, *Mich.* 2. 3. There was never such wrath felt or conceived, as the Lord hath devised against thee, that livest and diest in thy natural estate: hence it is called *wrath to come, I Thess. I. ult.* The torment which wisdome shall devise, the Almighty power of God shall inflict upon thee, so as there was never such power seen in making the world, as in holding a poor creature under this wrath, that holds up the soul in being with one hand, and beats it with the other, ever burning like fire against a creature, and yet that creature never burnt up, *Rom.* 9. 22. Think not this cruelty, it's justice; what cares God for a vile wretch, whom nothing can

K

make good while it lives? If we have been long in hewing a block, and we can make no meet vessel of it, put it to no good use for our selves, we cast it into the fire: God heweth thee by *Sermons, sickness, losses,* and *crosses, sudden death, mercies* and *miseries,* yet nothing makes the better; what should God do with thee, but cast thee hence? Oh, consider of this wrath before you feel it. I had rather have all the world burning about my ears, than to have one blasting frown from the blessed face of an infinite and dreadful God. Thou canst not endure the torments of a little Kitchin fire on the tip of thy finger, not one half hour together; how wilt thou bear the fury of this infinite, endlesse, consuming fire in body and soul throughout all eternity?

3. The never-dying worm of a guilty conscience shall torment thee, as if thou hadst swallowed down a living poisonfull snake, which shall lie gnawing and biting thine heart for sin past, day and night. And this worm shall torment by shewing the cause of thy misery, that is, that thou didst never care for him that would have saved thee. By shewing thee also thy sins against the Law, by shewing thee thy sloath, whereby thy happiness is lost. Then shall thy conscience gnaw to think so many nights I went to bed without prayer, and so many dayes and hours I spent in feasting and foolish sporting. Oh, if I had spent half that time, now mispent, in praying, in mourning, in meditation, yonder in Heaven had I been. By shewing thee also the means that thou once hadst to avoid this misery; Such a Minister I heard once, that told me of my particular sins, as if he had been told of me; such a friend per-swaded me once to turn over a new leaf: I remember so many knocks God gave at this Iron heart of mine, so many mercies the Lord sent; but oh, no meanes could prevail with me. Lastly, by shewing thee how easily thou mightest have avoided all these miseries. Oh, once I was almost perswaded to be a Christian, but I suffered my heart to grow dead, and fell to *loose company,* and so lost all. The Lord Jesus came unto my door and knocked, and if I had done that for Christ which I did for the Devil many a time to open at his knocks, I had been saved. A thousand such bites will this worm give at thine heart, which shall make thee cry out, Oh time, time! Oh Sermons, Sermons! Oh my hopes and my helps are now lost, that once I had to save my lost soul!

4. Thou shalt take up thy lodging for ever with Devils, and they shall be thy companions: him thou hast served here, with him must thou dwell there. It scares men out of their wits almost, to see the Devil, as they think, when they be alone; but what horrour shall fill thy soul, when thou shalt be banished from Angels society, and come into the fellowship of Devils for ever?

5. Thou shalt be filled with finall despair. If a man be grievously sick, it comforts him to think it will not last long. But if the Physitian tell him he must live all his life time in this extreamity, he thinks the poorest beggar in a better estate than himself. Oh to think when thou hast been millions of years in thy sorrows, then thou art no nearer thy end of bearing thy misery, then at the first coming in: Oh I might once have had mercy and Christ, but no hope now ever to have one glimpse of his face, or one good look from him any more.

6. Thou shalt vomit out blasphemous oathes and curses in the face of God the Father for ever, and curse God that never elected thee, and curse the Lord Jesus that never shed one drop of bloud to redeem thee, and curse God the holy Ghost that passed by thee and never called thee, *Rev.* 16. 9. And here thou shalt lie and weep, and gnash thy teeth in spight against God and thy self, and roar, and stamp, and grow mad, that there thou must lie under the curse of God for ever. Thus (I say) thou shalt lie blaspheming, with Gods wrath like a pile of fire on thy soul burning, and floods, nay seas, nay more, seas of tears (for thou shalt forever lie weeping) shall never quench it. And here which way soever thou lookest thou shalt see matter of everlasting grief. Look up to Heaven, and there thou shalt see (Oh) that God is for ever gone. Look about thee, thou shalt see Devils quaking, cursing God; and thousands, nay millions of sinfull, damned creatures crying and roaring out with dolefull shriekings: Oh the day that ever I was born! Look within thee, there is a guilty conscience gnawing, Look to time past; Oh those golden days of grace, and sweet seasons of mercy are quite lost and gone! Look to time to come, there thou shalt behold evils, troops and swarms of sorrows, and woes, and raging waves, and billows of wrath coming roaring upoh thee. Look to time present, Oh not one hour or moment of ease or refreshing, but all curses meet together, and feeding upon one

poor lost immortal soul, that never can be recovered again! No God, no Christ, no Spirit to comfort thee, no Minister to preach unto thee, no friend to wipe away thy continual *Tears*, no Sun to shine upon thee, not a bit of bread, not one drop of water to cool thy tongue.

This is the misery of every naturall man.

ON THE DEATH OF HIS SECOND WIFE

[From the "Autobiography"]

But the Lord hath not been wont to let me live long without some affliction or other; and yet ever mixed with some mercy. And therefore, April the 2d, 1646, as he gave me another son, John, so he took away my most dear, precious, meek, and loving wife, in child-bed, after three weeks' lying-in; having left behind her two hopeful branches, my dear children, Samuel and John. This affliction was very heavy to me; for in it the Lord seemed to withdraw his tender care for me and mine, which he graciously manifested by my dear wife; also refused to hear prayer, when I did think he would have hearkened and let me see his beauty in the land of the living, in restoring of her to health again; also, in taking her away in the prime of her life, when she might have lived to have glorified the Lord long; also, in threatening me to proceed in rooting out my family, and that he would not stop, having begun here, as in Eli, for not being zealous enough against the sins of his sons. And I saw that if I had profited by former afflictions of this nature, I should not have had this scourge. But I am the Lord's, and He may do with me what he will. He did teach me to prize a little grace, gained by a cross, as a sufficient recompense for all outward losses.

But this loss was very great. She was a woman of incomparable meekness of spirit, toward myself especially, and very loving; of great prudence to take care for and order my family affairs, being neither too lavish nor sordid in anything, so that I knew not what was under her hands. She had an excellency to reprove for sin, and discern the evils of men. She loved God's people dearly, and [was] studious to profit by their fellowship, and therefore loved their company. She loved God's word exceedingly, and hence was glad she could read my notes, which she had to muse on every week. She had a spirit of prayer, beyond ordinary of her time and experience. She was fit to die long before she did die, even after the death of her first-born, which was a great affliction to her. But her work not being done then, she lived almost nine years with me, and was the comfort of my life to me; and the last sacrament before her lying-in, seemed to be full of Christ, and thereby fitted for heaven. She did oft say she should not outlive this child; and when her fever first began, by taking some cold, she told me so, that we should love exceedingly together, because we should not live long together. Her fever took away her sleep; want of sleep wrought much distemper in her head, and filled it with fantasies and distractions, but without raging. The night before she died, she had about six hours' unquiet sleep. But that so cooled and settled her head, that when she knew none else, so as to speak to them, yet she knew Jesus Christ, and could speak to him; and therefore, as soon as she awakened out of sleep, she brake out into a most heavenly, heart-breaking prayer, after Christ, her dear Redeemer, for the spirit of life, and so continued praying until the last hour of her death, "Lord, though I [am] unworthy, Lord, one word, one word," &c.; and so gave up the ghost.

Thus God hath visited and scourged me for my sins, and sought to wean me from this world. But I have ever found it a difficult thing to profit even but a little by the sorest and sharpest afflictions.

EDWARD JOHNSON

[Captain Edward Johnson's one book, "The Wonder-Working Providence," stands as an example of literary composition by a vigorous and devout, but uncultured, Puritan layman. The author was born in Kent in 1599, came to America with Governor Winthrop in 1630, aided in founding Woburn, Mass., in 1642, and from that time till his death in 1672 was prominent in the affairs of the town and the colony. His book, first published anonymously in London in 1654, was sedately designated on the title-page as "A History of New England from the English planting in the Yeere 1628 untill the Yeere 1652," but it has come to be all but universally known by the running title of "The Wonder-Working Providence of Sions Saviour in New England." A later edition was prefixed by a title-page erroneously ascribing the book to Sir Ferdinando Gorges.

Captain Johnson wrote with the object of showing the immediate hand of God in the planting and development of New England. He mentions the results of each annual election for governor and deputy-governor, records in detail the founding of each new church, and narrates other events of interest. His work is, however, more valuable as a literary curiosity than as history. His freedom from the pedantry that characterized his more learned contemporaries, the freshness and originality of his diction and figures of speech, his formless sentences, perhaps made more rude by an unintelligent printer, all give the book a delightful individuality. Even the spelling is more than usually original. It is a pleasure to meet the Mohicans as "Mawhiggins," or to find the good governor of Massachusetts designated as "John Indicat." Not the least amusing part of the book are the attempts at verse, which the author introduces for the especial commemoration of men and events. But while the reader finds much in "The Wonder-Working Providence" that is ridiculous, he should notice that the author always reveals himself as a man worthy of respect, and to some extent of admiration.

The selections follow the reprint of "The Wonder-Working Providence" in the Collections of the Massachusetts Historical Society, Second Series.]

OF THE FIRST PREPARATION OF THE MARCHANT ADVENTURERS, IN THE MATTACHUSETS

[Chap. IX, Book I, of "The Wonder-Working Providence of Sions Saviour in New England"]

Now it will be time to returne againe to England, to speake further of the people that wee left in way of preparation; who in the yeare 1628, sent forth some store of servants to provide against the wants of a Desart Wildernesse, amongst whom came over a mixt multitude, insomuch that very little appeared of the following worke, onely the much honoured Mr. John Indicat, came over with them to governe, a fit instrument to begin this Wildernesse-worke, of courage bold undanted, yet sociable, and of a cheerfull spirit, loving and austere, applying himselfe to either as occasion served. And now let no man be offended at the Authors rude Verse, penned of purpose to keepe in memory the Names of such Worthies as Christ made strong for himselfe, in this unwonted worke of his.

John Endicat twice Gover[n]our of the English, inhabiting the Mattachusets Bay in N. England

Strong valiant John wilt thou march on, and take up station first,
   Christ cal'd hath thee, his Souldier be, and faile not of thy trust;
Wilderness wants Christs grace supplants, then plant his Churches pure,
   With Tongues gifted, and graces led, help thou to his procure;
Undanted thou wilt not allow, Malignant men to wast:
   Christs Vineyard heere, whose grace should cheer, his well-beloved's tast.
Then honoured be, thy Christ hath thee their Generall promoted:
   To shew their love, in place above, his people have thee voted.
Yet must thou fall, to grave with all the Nobles of the Earth,
   Thou rotting worme, to dust must turn, and worse but for new birth.

The place picked out by this People to settle themselves in, was in the bosome of the out-stretched arme of Cape Anne, now called Gloster, but at the place of their abode they began to build a Town, which is called Salem, after some little space of time having made tryall of the Sordid spirits of the Neighbouring Indians, the most bold among them began to gather to divers places, which they began to take up for their owne, those that were sent over servants, having itching desires after novelties, found a reddier way to make an end of their Masters provision, then they could find meanes to get more; They that came over their own men had but little left to feed on, and most began to repent when their strong Beere and full cups ran as small as water in a large Land, but little Corne, and the poore Indian so far from relieving them, that they were forced to lengthen out their owne food with Acorns, and that

which added to their present distracted thoughts, the Ditch betweene England and their now place of abode was so wide, that they
could not leap over with a lope-staffe, yet some delighting their
Eye with the rarity of things present, and feeding their fancies
with new discoveries at the Springs approach, they made shift to
rub out the Winters cold by the Fire-side, having fuell enough
growing at their very doores, turning down many a drop of the
Bottell, and burning Tobacco with all the ease they could, discoursing betweene one while and another, of the great progresse
they would make after the Summers-Sun had changed the Earths
white furr'd Gowne into a greene Mantell.   Now the vernall of
thirty [twenty] nine being come, they addrest themselves to coste
it as far as they durst for feare of losing themselves, or falling into
the hands of unknown Indians, being kept in awe by a report of
a cruell people, not far of called the Tarratines.   All this while
little like-lihood there was building the Temple for Gods worship,
there being only two that began to hew stones in the Mountaines,
the one named Mr. Bright, and the other Mr. Blaxton, and one of
them began to build, but when they saw all sorts of stones would
not fit in the building, as they supposed, the one betooke him to the
Seas againe, and the other to till the Land, retaining no simbole of
his former profession, but a Canonicall Coate.

OF THE VOLUNTARY BANISHMENT, CHOSEN BY THIS PEOPLE OF CHRIST, AND THEIR LAST FAREWELL TAKEN OF THEIR COUNTRY AND FRIENDS

[Chap. XII, Book I, of "The Wonder-Working Providence"]

And now behold the severall Regiments of these Souldiers of
Christ, as they are shipped for his service in the Western World,
part thereof being come to the Towne and Port of Southampton
in England, where they were to be shipped, that the[y] might
prosecute this designe to the full, one Ship called the Eagle, they
wholly purchase, and many more they hire, filling them with the
seede of man and beast to sow this yet untilled Wildernesse withall, making sale of such Land as they possesse, to the great ad-

miration of their Friends and Acquaintance, who thus expostulate with them, What, will not the large income of your yearly revenue content you, which in all reason cannot chuse but be more advantageous both to you and yours, then all that Rocky Wildernesse, whither you are going, to run the hazard of your life? Have you not here your Tables filled with great variety of Foode, your Coffers filled with Coyne, your Houses beautifully built and filled with all rich Furniture? (or otherwise) have you not such a gainfull Trade as none the like in the Towne where you live? Are you not inriched daily? Are not your Children very well provided for as they come to years? (nay) may you not here as pithily practise the two chiefe Duties of a Christian (if Christ give strength) namely Mortification and Sanctification as in any place of the World? What helps can you have there that you must not carry from hence? With bold resolvednesse these stout Souldiers of Christ reply; as Death, the King of terror with all his dreadfull attendance inhumane and barbarous, tortures doubled and trebled by all the infernall furies have appeared but light and momentary to the Souldiers of Christ Jesus, so also the Pleasure, Profits and Honours of this World set forth in their most glorious splendor, and magnitude by the alluring Lady of Delight, proffering pleasant embraces, cannot intice with her Syren Songs, such Souldiers of Christ, whose aymes are elevated by him, many Millions above that brave Warrier Ulysses.

Now seeing all can be said will but barely set forth the immoveable Resolutions that Christ continued in these men; Passe on and attend with teares, if thou hast any, the following discourse, while these Men, Women and Children are taking their last farewell of their Native Country, Kindred, Friends and Acquaintance, while the Ships attend them; Many make choise of some solitary place to eccho out their bowell-breaking affections in bidding their Friends farewell, deare friends (sayes one) as neare as my owne soule doth thy love lodge in my brest, with thought of the heart-burning Ravishments, that thy Heavenly speeches have wrought; my melting soule is poured out at present with these words, both of them had their farther speach strangled from the depth of their inward dolor, with breast-breaking sobs, till leaning their heads each on others shoulders, they let fall the salt-dropping dews of vehement affection, striving to exceede one another, much like the departure of David and Jonathan: having a little eased their hearts with the still streames of Teares, they recovered speech againe. Ah! my much honoured friend, hath Christ given thee so great a charge as to be Leader of his People into that far remote, and vast Wildernesse, I, oh, and alas thou must die there and never shall I see thy Face in the flesh againe, wert thou called to so great a taske as to passe the pretious Ocean, and hazard thy person in Battell against thousands of Malignant Enemies there? there were hopes of thy return with triumph, but now after two, three, or foure moneths spent with daily expectation of swallowing Waves, and cruell Pirates, you are to be landed among barbarous Indians, famous for nothing but cruelty, where you are like to spend your days in a famishing condition for a long space; Scarce had he uttered this, but presently hee lockes his friend fast in his armes, holding each other thus for some space of time, they weepe againe, But as Paul to his beloved flock: the other replies what doe you weeping and breaking my heart? I am now prest for the service of our Lord Christ, to re-build the most glorious Edifice of Mount Sion in a Wildernesse, and as John Baptist, I must cry prepare yee the way of the Lord, make his paths strait, for behold hee is comming againe, hee is comming to destroy Antichrist, and give the whore double to drinke the very dregs of his wrath.

Then my deare friend unfold thy hands, for thou and I have much worke to doe, I and all Christian Souldiers the World throughout, then hand in hand they leade each other to the Sandy-banks of the brinish Ocean, when clenching their hands fast, they unloose not til inforced to wipe their watery-eyes, whose constant streames forced a watery-path upon their Cheeks, which to hide from the eyes of others they shun society for a time, but being called by occasion, whose bauld back-part none can lay hold one; They thrust in among the throng now ready to take Ship, where they beheld the like affections with their own among divers Relations, Husbands and Wives with mutuall consent are now purposed to part for a time 900 Leagues asunder, since some providence at present will not suffer them to goe together, they resolve their tender affections shall not hinder this worke of Christ, the new Married and betrothed man, exempt by the Law of God from war, now will not claime their priviledge, but being constrained by the Love of Christ, lock up their naturall affections for a time, till the Lord shall be pleased to give them a meeting in this Westerne World, sweetly mixing it with spirituall love, in the meane time many Fathers now take their yong Samuells, and give them to this service of Christ all their Lives. Brethren, Sisters, Unkles, Nephewes, Neeces, together with all Kindred of bloud that binds the bowells of affection in a true Lovers knot, can now take their last farewell, each of other, although naturall affection will still claime her right, and manifest her selfe to bee in the body by looking out at the Windowes in a mournefull manner among this company, thus disposed doth many Reverend and godly Pastors of Christ present themselves, some in a Seamans Habit, and their scattered sheepe comming as a poore Convoy loftily take their leave of them as followeth, what dolefull dayes are these, when the best choise our Orthodox Ministers can make is to take up a perpetuall banishment from their native soile, together with their Wives and Children, wee their poore sheepe they may not feede, but by stoledred should they abide here. Lord Christ, here they are at thy command, they go, this is the doore thou hast opened upon our earnest request, and we hope it shall never be shut: For Englands sake they are going from England to pray without ceasing for England, O England! thou shalt finde New England prayers prevailing with their God for thee, but now woe alas, what great hardship must these our indeared Pastors indure for a long season, with these words they lift up their voyces and wept, adding many drops of salt liquor to the ebbing Ocean; Then shaking hands they bid adue with much cordiall affection to all their Brethren, and Sisters in Christ, yet now the Scorne and Derision of those times, and for this their great enterprise counted as so many cracktbraines, but Christ will make all the Earth know the wisdome he hath indued them with, shall over-top all the humane policy in the World, as the sequell wee hope will shew; Thus much shall suffice in generall to speak of their peoples farewell they tooke from time to time of their Country and Friends.

OF THE GREAT CHEEREFULNESSE OF THEIR SOULDIERS OF CHRIST, IN AND UNDER THE PENURIES OF A WILDERNESSE

[Chap. XXIV, Book I, of "The Wonder-Working Providence"]

These were the beginnings of these resolute Souldiers of Christ Jesus in the yeare, 1631. Even to lay the foundation of their severall Churches of Christ, built onely on him as their chiefe Corner Stone. But as his chosen Israel met with many difficulties after their returne from Captivity, in building the Temple and City, which they valiantly waded through; So these weake wormes (Oh Christ to thy praise be it spoken,) were most wonderfully holpen in such distresses, as to appearance of man seemed to be both hopelesse, and helplesse, threatening destruction to the whole building, and far from accomplishing such great things as you have in part seene already, and shall in the following discourse (God willing) see more abundantly, adding a strong testimony to the work, that as it was begun by Christ, so hath it beene carried on by him, and shall to the admiration of the whole World be perfected in his time, and unlesse men will be wilfully blinde, they must needs see and confesse the same, and that the influence thereof hath already run from one end of the Earth unto the other.

This yeare 1631 John Winthrop Esq. was chosen Governour, pickt out for the worke, by the provident hand of the most high, and inabled with gifts accordingly, then all the folke of Christ, who have seene his face and beene partaker of the same, remember him in this following Meeter.

John Winthrope Esq. Eleven times Governour of the English Nation, inhabiting the Mattacusets Bay in New England

Why leavest thou John, thy station, in Suffolk, thy own soile,
    Christ will have thee a pillar be, for's people thou must toyle,
He chang'd thy heart, then take his part, 'gainst prelates proud invading.
    (His Kingly throne) set up alone, in wildernesse their shading.
His little flocks from Prelates knocks, twice ten years rul'd thou hast,
    With civill sword at Christs word and eleven times been trast.
By Name and Note, with peoples vote, their Governour to be.
    Thy means hast spent, 'twas therefore lent, to raise this work by thee.

Well arm'd and strong, with sword among, Christ armies marcheth he,
　　Doth valiant praise, and weak one raise, with kind benignity.
To lead the Van, 'gainst Babylon, doth worthy Winthrop call,
　　Thy Progeny, shall Battell try, when Prelacy shall fall.
With fluent Tongue thy Pen doth run, in learned Latine Phrase,
　　To Sweads, French, Dutch, thy Neighbours, which thy lady rhetorick
　　　praise.
Thy bounty feeds, Christs servants needs, in wildernesse of wants
　　To Indians thou Christs Gospell now, 'mongst heathen people plants.
Yet thou poore dust, now dead and must, to rottennesse be brought,
　　Till Christ restore thee glorious, more then can of dust be thought.

The much honoured Thomas Dudly Esquire was chosen Deputy Governour, and the number of Free-men added was about 83.
Those honoured persons who were now in place of Government,
having the propagation of the Churches of Christ, in their eye
laboured by all meanes to make room for Inhabitants, knowing
well that where the dead carkass is, thither will the Eagles resort.
But herein they were much opposed by certaine persons, whose
greedy desire for land much hindered the worke for a time, as
indeed all such persons do at this very day, and let such take notice
how these were cured of this distemper, some were taken away by
death, and then to be sure they had Land enough, others fearing
poverty, and famishment, supposing the present scarcity would
never be turned into plenty, removed themselves away, and so
never beheld the great good the Lord hath done for his people,
but the valiant of the Lord waited with patience, and in the misse
of beere supplied themselves with water, even the most honoured
as well as others, contentedly rejoycing in a Cup of cold water,
blessing the Lord that had given them the taste of that living water,
and that they had not the water that slackes the thirst of their
naturall bodies, given them by measure, but might drinke to the
full; as also in the absence of Bread they feasted themselves with
fish, the Women once a day, as the tide gave way, resorted to the
Mussells and Clambankes, which are a fish as big as Horse-mussels,
where they daily gathered their Families food with much heavenly
discourse of the provisions Christ had formerly made for many
thousands of his followers in the wildernesse. Quoth one, my Husband hath travailed as far as Plimoth (which is neere 40 miles,)
and hath with great toile brought a little Corne home with him, and

before that is spent the Lord will assuredly provide: quoth the
other, our last peck of meale is now in the Oven at home a baking,
and many of our godly Neighbours have quite spent all, and wee
owe one Loafe of that little wee have; Then spake a third, my
husband hath ventured himselfe among the Indians for Corne,
and can get none, as also our honoured Governour hath distributed
his so far, that a day or two more will put an end to his store, and
all the rest, and yet methinks our Children are as cheerefull, fat,
and lusty with feeding upon those Mussells, Clambanks and other
Fish as they were in England, with their fill of Bread, which makes
mee cheerfull in the Lords providing for us, being further confirmed by the exhortation of our Pastor to trust the Lord with providing for us; whose is the Earth and the fulnesse thereof. And
as they were incouraging one another in Christs carefull providing
for them, they lift up their eyes and saw two Ships comming in,
and presently this newes came to their Eares, that they were come
from Jacland full of Victualls, now their poore hearts were not so
much refreshed in regard of the food they saw they were like to
have, as their soules rejoyced in that Christ would now manifest
himselfe to be the Commissary Generall of this his Army, and that
hee should honour them so far as to be poore Sutlers for his Camp,
they soone up with their Mussells, and hie them home to stay
their hungry stomacks. After this manner did Christ many times
graciously provide for this his people, even at the last cast.

THE EXTERMINATION OF THE PEQUOTS

[From "The Wonder-Working Providence," Book II, Chap. VI]

After the Ministers of Christ had, through the grace that was
given them, exhorted and encouraged these Souldiers appointed
for the work, they being provided with certaine Indian guides,
who with the close of the day brought them to a small river, where
they could perceive many persons had been dressing of fish; upon
the sight thereof, the Indian guides concluded they were now a
feasting it at their fort, which was hard at hand; the English calling a Councill of warre, being directed by the speciallist providence of the most high God, they concluded to storm the fort a
little before break of day; at which time they supposed the Indians

being up late in their jolly feasting, would bee in their deepest sleepe; and surely so it was, for they now slept their last; the English keeping themselves as covertly as they could, approached the fort at the time appointed, which was builded of whole Trees set in the ground fast, and standing up an end about twelve foot high, very large, having pitcht their Wigwams within it, the entrance being on two sides, with intricate Meanders to enter. The chiefe Leaders of the English made some little stand before they offered to enter, but yet boldly they rushed on, and found the passages guarded at each place with an Indian Bow-man, ready on the string, they soone let fly, and wounded the foremost of the English in the shoulder, yet having dispatch'd the Porters, they found the winding way in without a Guide, where they soone placed themselves round the Wigwams, and according to direction they made their first shot with the muzzle of their Muskets downe to the ground, knowing the Indian manner is to lie on the ground to sleep, from which they being in this terrible manner awakened, unlesse it were such as were slaine with the shot.

After this some of the English entred the Wigwams, where they received some shot with their Arrowes, yet catching up the firebrands, they began to fire them, and others of the English Souldiers with powder, did the same: the day now began to break; the Lord intending to have these murtherers know he would looke out of the cloudy pillar upon them: and now these women and children set up a terrible out-cry; the men were smitten down, and slaine, as they came forth with a great slaughter, the Sqawes crying out, oh much winn it Englishman, who moved with pitty toward them, saved their lives: and hereupon some young youth cried, I squaw, I squaw, thinking to finde the like mercy. There were some of these Indians, as is reported, whose bodyes were not to be pierced by their sharp rapiers or swords of a long time, which made some of the Souldiers think the Devil was in them, for there were some Powwowes among them, which work strange things, with the help of Satan. But this was very remarkable, one of them being wounded to death, and thrust thorow the neck with a Halbert; yet after all, lying groaning upon the ground, he caught the halberts speare in his hand, and wound it quite round. After the English were thus possessed of this first victory, they sent their prisoners to the pinnaces, and prosecute the warre in hand, to the next Battalia of the Indians, which lay on a hill about two miles distant, and indeed their stoutest Souldiers were at this place, and not yet come to the fort; the English being weary with their night worke, and wanting such refreshing as the present worke required, began to grow faint, yet having obtained one victory, they were very desirous of another: and further, they knew right-well, till this cursed crew were utterly rooted out, they should never be at peace; therefore they marched on toward them. Now assuredly, had the Indians knowne how much weakened our Souldiers were at present, they might have born them downe with their multitude, they being very strong and agile of body, had they come to handy-gripes; but the Lord (who would have his people know their work was his, and he onely must order their Counsels, and war-like work for them) did bring them timely supply from the vessels, and also gave them a second victory, wherein they slew many more of their enemies, the residue flying into a very thick swamp, being unaccessible, by reason of the boggy holes of water, and thick bushes; the English drawing up their company beleagered the swamp, and the Indians in the mean time skulking up and down, and as they saw opportunity they made shot with their Arrowes at the English, and then suddainly they would fall flat along in the water to defend themselves from the retalliation of the Souldiers Muskets. This lasted not long, for our English being but a small number, had parted themselves far asunder, but by the providence of the most high God, some of them spyed an Indian with a kettle at his back going more in-wardly into the swamp, by which they perceived there was some place of firm land in the midst thereof, which caused them to make way for the passage of their Souldiers, which brought this warre to a period: For although many got away, yet were they no such considerable number as ever to raise warre any more; the slaine or wounded of the English were (through the mercy of Christ) but a few: One of them being shot through the body, neere about the breast, regarding it not till of a long time after, which caused the bloud to dry and thicken on eitheir end of the arrow so that it could not be drawne forth his body without great difficulty and much paine, yet did he scape his life, and the wound healed.

Thus the Lord was pleased to assist his people in this warre, and deliver them out of the Indians hands, who were very lusty proper men of their hands, most of them, as may appear by one passage which I shall here relate: thus it came to passe, As the Souldiers were uppon their march, close by a great thicket, where no eye could penetrate farre, as it often falls out in such wearisom wayes, where neither men nor beast have beaten out a path; some Souldiers lingering behinde their fellowes, two Indians watching their opportunity, much like a hungry hauke, when they supposed the last man was come up, who kept a double double double distance in his march, they sudden and swiftly snatched him up in their tallens, hoising him upon their shoulders, ran into the swamp with him; the Souldier being unwilling to be made a Pope by being borne on mens shoulders, strove with them all he could to free himselfe from their hands; but, like a carefull Commander, one Captaine Davenport, then Lieutenant of this company, being diligent in his place to bring up the reare, coming up with them, followed with speed into the swamp after him, having a very severe cutlace tyed to his wrist, and being well able to make it bite sore when he set it on, resolving to make it fall foul on the Indians bones, he soone overtooke them, but was prevented by the buckler they held up from hitting them, which was the man they had taken: It was matter of much wonder to see with what dexterity they hurled the poore Souldier about, as if they had been handling a Lacedæmonian shield, so that the nimble Captaine Davenport could not, of a long time, fasten one stroke upon them; yet, at last, dying their tawny skin into a crimson colour, they cast downe their prey, and hasted thorow the thickets for their lives. The Souldier thus redeemed, had no such hard usage, but that he is alive, as I suppose, at this very day: The Lord in mercy toward his poore Churches, having thus destroyed these bloudy barbarous Indians, he returnes his people in safety to their vessels, where they take account of their prisoners: the Squawes and some young youths they brought home with them, and finding the men to be deeply guilty of the crimes they undertooke the warre for, they brought away onely their heads as a token of their victory. By this means the Lord strook a trembling terror into all the Indians round about, even to this very day.

L

ANNE BRADSTREET

[The chief poetess of the colonial time was born in England about 1612, the daughter of Thomas Dudley; and was married in 1628 to Simon Bradstreet. In 1630 she came to America, where both her father and her husband later served as governors of Massachusetts. Here she became the mother of eight children, and performed faithfully the manifold household and social duties that devolved on a woman of her station; and in some way she also found time to write a considerable body of verse. A great part of this was taken to England by her brother-in-law, and published in London in 1650, with the title "The Tenth Muse Lately sprung up in America. Or Severall Poems, compiled with great Variety of Wit and Learning," etc. The author appears to have been far too modest and too sensible to approve this absurd designation, and it is unfortunate that her work was weighted down with it. A second edition, published in Boston in 1678, six years after Mrs. Bradstreet's death, contained a number of additional poems, and showed many changes made by the author in those that had appeared earlier. Mrs. Bradstreet seems never to have sought publicity, and it is probable that many of her more personal poems, such as the last two in the selections that follow, were never intended to be printed. Besides her poems, she wrote for members of her family a short account of her religious experiences, and a series of "Meditations, Divine and Morall," of which a few specimens are given later.

Anne Bradstreet's avowed master was the French poet Du Bartas, whose works had been translated into English by Sylvester; though some of her later poems show influence of the school of Spenser. Her ambitious verses — those not relating to personal affairs and intended for her family — were didactic. The greater part of "The Tenth Muse" was taken up by five poems: "The Four Elements," "The Four Humours in Man's Constitution," "The Four Ages of Man," "The Four Seasons of the Year," and "The Four Monarchies." The last and longest of these "quaternions" is based on Sir Walter Raleigh's "History of the World." "Contemplations," which is usually considered the author's best poem, first appeared in the edition of 1678. It is given complete in the following pages, and serves to illustrate most of her excellences and her weaknesses. A few stanzas show genuine emotion, an appreciation of nature unusual in her day, and an ear for musical verse; others show lapses into the prosaic, and above all, the author's tendency to sacrifice everything to rather profitless moralizing. Faulty as Mrs. Bradstreet's work is, however, it gives evidence of more genuine poetic feeling than any other body of verse written in America in the seventeenth century, and deserves study as the work of a pioneer.

The selections follow the edition of Anne Bradstreet's works, by John Harvard Ellis, 1867. The poem entitled "Longing for Heaven," and the "Meditations," were first printed in this edition, from the author's manuscript. "Contemplations" and "To my Dear and Loving Husband" first appeared in the edition of 1678. The others were included in "The Tenth Muse." The text of all these poems, except the two printed for the first time by Mr. Ellis, is that of the edition of 1678.]

PROLOGUE

1

To sing of Wars, of Captains, and of Kings,
Of Cities founded, Common-wealths begun,
For my mean pen are too superiour things:
Or how they all, or each their dates have run
Let Poets and Historians set these forth,
My obscure Lines shall not so dim their worth.

2

But when my wondring eyes and envious heart
Great *Bartas* sugar'd lines, do but read o're
Fool I do grudg the Muses did not part
'Twixt him and me that overfluent store;
A *Bartas* can, do what a *Bartas* will
But simple I according to my skill.

3

From school-boyes tongue no rhet'rick we expect
Nor yet a sweet Consort from broken strings,
Nor perfect beauty, where's a main defect:
My foolish, broken, blemish'd Muse so sings
And this to mend, alas, no Art is able,
'Cause nature, made it so irreparable.

4

Nor can I, like that fluent sweet tongu'd Greek,
Who lisp'd at first, in future times speak plain
By Art he gladly found what he did seek

A full requital of his, striving pain
Art can do much, but this maxime's most sure
A weak or wounded brain admits no cure.

5

I am obnoxious to each carping tongue
Who says my hand a needle better fits,
A Poets pen all scorn I should thus wrong,
For such despite they cast on Female wits:
If what I do prove well, it won't advance,
They'l say it's stoln, or else it was by chance.

6

But sure the Antique Greeks were far more mild
Else of our Sexe, why feigned they those Nine
And poesy made, *Calliope's* own Child;
So 'mongst the rest they placed the Arts Divine,
But this weak knot, they will full soon untie,
The Greeks did nought, but play the fools & lye.

7

Let Greeks be Greeks, and women what they are
Men have precedency and still excell,
It is but vain unjustly to wage warre:
Men can do best, and women know it well
Preheminence in all and each is yours;
Yet grant some small acknowledgement of ours.

8

And oh ye high flown quills that soar the Skies,
And ever with your prey still catch your praise,
If e're you daigne these lowly lines your eyes
Give Thyme or Parsley wreath, I ask no bayes,
This mean and unrefined ure of mine
Will make you glistring gold, but more to shine.

OF THE FOUR AGES OF MAN

[The introductory section of the poem]

Lo now four other act upon the stage,
Childhood and Youth, the Manly & Old age;
The first son unto flegm, Grand-child to water,
Unstable, supple, cold and moist's his nature.
The second frolick, claims his pedegree
From blood and air, for hot and moist is he.
The third of fire and Choler is compos'd
Vindicative and quarrelsome dispos'd.
The last of earth, and heavy melancholy,
Solid, hating all lightness and all folly.
Childhood was cloth'd in white & green to show
His spring was intermixed with some snow:
Upon his head nature a Garland set
Of Primrose, Daizy & the Violet.
Such cold mean flowrs the spring puts forth betime
Before the sun hath throughly heat the clime.
His Hobby striding did not ride but run,
And in his hand an hour-glass new begun,
In danger every moment of a fall,
And when tis broke then ends his life and all:
But if he hold till it have run its last,
Then may he live out threescore years or past.
Next Youth came up in gorgeous attire,
(As that fond age doth most of all desire)
His Suit of Crimson and his scarfe of green,
His pride in's countenance was quickly seen,
Garland of roses, pinks and gilli-flowers
Seemed on's head to grow bedew'd with showers:
His face as fresh as is *Aurora* fair,
When blushing she first 'gins to light the air.
No wooden horse, but one of mettal try'd,
He seems to fly or swim, and not to ride.
Then prancing on the stage, about he wheels,
But as he went death waited at his heels.

The next came up in a much graver sort,
As one that cared for a good report,
His sword by's side, and choler in his eyes,
But neither us'd as yet, for he was wise:
Of Autumns fruits a basket on his arm,
His golden God in's purse, which was his charm.
And last of all to act upon this stage
Leaning upon his staff came up Old Age,
Under his arm a sheaf of wheat he bore,
An harvest of the best, what needs he more?
In's other hand a glass ev'n almost run,
Thus writ about *This out then am I done.*
His hoary hairs, and grave aspect made way,
And all gave ear to what he had to say.
These being met each in his equipage
Intend to speak according to their age:
But wise Old age did with all gravity
To childish Childhood give precedency,
And to the rest his reason mildly told,
That he was young before he grew so old.
To do as he each one full soon assents,
Their method was that of the Elements,
That each should tell what of himself he knew,
Both good and bad, but yet no more then's true.
With heed now stood three ages of frail man,
To hear the child, who crying thus began:

SPRING

[From " The Four Seasons of the Year "]

Another four I've left yet to bring on,
Of four times four the last *Quaternion,*
The Winter, Summer, Autumn & the Spring,
In season all these Seasons I shall bring:
Sweet Spring like man in his Minority,
At present claim'd and had priority.
With smiling face and garments somewhat green,
She trim'd her locks, which late had frosted been,

Nor hot nor cold, she spake, but with a breath,
Fit to revive, the nummed earth from death.
Three months (quoth she) are 'lotted to my share
March, April, May of all the rest most fair.
Tenth of the first, *Sol* into *Aries* enters,
And bids defiance to all tedious winters,
Crosseth the Line, and equals night and day,
(Stil adds to th' last til after pleasant *May*)
And now makes glad the darkned northern wights
Who for some months have seen but starry lights.
Now goes the Plow-man to his merry toyle,
He might unloose his winter locked soyl:
The Seeds-man too, doth lavish out his grain,
In hope the more he casts, the more to gain:
The Gardner now superfluous branches lops,
And poles erects for his young clambring hops.
Now digs then sowes his herbs, his flowers & roots
And carefully manures his trees of fruits.
The *Pleiades their influence* now give,
And all that seem'd as dead afresh doth live.
The croaking frogs, whom nipping winter kil'd,
Like birds now chirp, and hop about the field,
The Nightingale, the black-bird and the Thrush
Now tune their layes, on sprayes of every bush.
The wanton frisking Kid, and soft-fleec'd Lambs
Do jump and play before their feeding Dams,
The tender tops of budding grass they crop,
They joy in what they have, but more in hope:
For though the frost hath lost his binding power,
Yet many a fleece of snow and stormy shower
Doth darken *Sol's* bright eye, makes us remember
The pinching North-west wind of cold *December.*
My second moneth is *April*, green and fair,
Of longer dayes, and a more temperate Air.
The Sun in *Taurus* keeps his residence,
And with his warmer beams glanceth from thence
This is the month whose fruitful showrs produces
All set and sown for all delights and uses:

The Pear, the Plum, and Apple-tree now flourish
The grass grows long the hungry beast to nourish.
The Primrose pale, and azure violet
Among the virduous grass hath nature set,
That when the Sun on's Love (the earth) doth shine
These might as lace set out her garment fine.
The fearfull bird his little house now builds
In trees and walls, in Cities and in fields.
The outside strong, the inside warm and neat;
A natural Artificer compleat.
The clocking hen her chirping chickins leads
With wings & beak defends them from the gleads
My next and last is fruitfull pleasant *May*.
Wherein the earth is clad in rich aray,
The Sun now enters loving *Gemini*,
And heats us with the glances of his eye,
Our thicker rayment makes us lay aside
Lest by his fervor we be torrifi'd.
All flowers the Sun now with his beams discloses,
Except the double pinks and matchless Roses.
Now swarms the busy, witty honey-Bee,
Whose praise deserves a page from more then me
The cleanly Huswifes Dary's now in th' prime,
Her shelves and firkins fill'd for winter time.
The meads with Cowslips, Honey-suckles dight,
One hangs his head, the other stands upright:
But both rejoyce at th'heavens clear smiling face,
More at her showers, which water them a space.
For fruits my Season yields the early Cherry,
The hasty Peas, and wholesome cool Strawberry.
More solid fruits require a longer time,
Each Season hath his fruit, so hath each Clime:
Each man his own peculiar excellence,
But none in all that hath preheminence.
Sweet fragrant Spring, with thy short pittance fly
Let some describe thee better then can I.
Yet above all this priviledg is thine,
Thy dayes still lengthen without least decline:

THE FOUNDING OF ROME

[From "The Four Monarchies"]

Stout *Romulus*, *Romes* founder, and first King,
Whom vestal *Rhea* to the world did bring:
His Father was not *Mars* as some devis'd,
But *Æmulus* in Armour all disguiz'd:
Thus he deceiv'd his *Neece*, she might not know
The double injury he then did do.
Where sheperds once had Coats & sheep their folds
Where Swains & rustick Peasants kept their holds,
A City fair did *Romulus* erect,
The Mistress of the World, in each respect,
His brother *Rhemus* there by him was slain,
For leaping o're the wall with some disdain.
The stones at first was cemented with blood,
And bloody hath it prov'd, since first it stood.
This City built and Sacrifices done,
A Form of Government, he next begun;
A hundred Senators he likewise chose,
And with the style of *Patres*, honoured those,
His City to replenish, men he wants,
Great priviledges then to all he grants;
That will within those strong built walls reside,
And this new gentle Government abide.
Of wives there was so great a scarcity,
They to their neighbours sue for a supply;
But all disdain Alliance, then to make,
So *Romulus* was forc'd this course to take:
Great shews he makes at *Tilt* and *Turnament*,
To see these sports, the *Sabins* all are bent.
Their daughters by the Romans then were caught,
Then to recover them a Field was fought;
But in the end, to final peace they come,
And *Sabins* as one people dwelt in *Rome*.
The Romans now more potent 'gin to grow,
And *Fedinates* they wholly overthrow.
But *Romulus* then comes unto his end.

Some feigning to the Gods he did ascend:
Others the seven and thirtyeth of his reign,
Affirm, that by the Senate he was slain.

CONTEMPLATIONS

Some time now past in the Autumnal Tide,
When *Phœbus* wanted but one hour to bed,
The trees all richly clad, yet void of pride,
Where gilded o're by his rich golden head.
Their leaves & fruits seem'd painted, but was true
Of green, of red, of yellow, mixed hew,
Rapt were my sences at this delectable view.

2

I wist not what to wish, yet sure thought I,
If so much excellence abide below;
How excellent is he that dwells on high?
Whose power and beauty by his works we know.
Sure he is goodness, wisdome, glory, light,
That hath this under world so richly dight:
More Heaven then Earth was here no winter & no night.

3

Then on a stately Oak I cast mine Eye,
Whose ruffling top the Clouds seem'd to aspire;
How long since thou wast in thine Infancy?
Thy strength, and stature, more thy years admire,
Hath hundred winters past since thou wast born?
Or thousand since thou brakest thy shell of horn,
If so, all these as nought, Eternity doth scorn.

4

Then higher on the glistering Sun I gaz'd,
Whose beams was shaded by the leavie Tree,
The more I look'd, the more I grew amaz'd,

And softly said, what glory's like to thee?
Soul of this world, this Universes Eye,
No wonder, some made thee a Deity:
Had I not better known, (alas) the same had I.

5

Thou as a Bridegroom from thy Chamber rushes,
And as a strong man, joyes to run a race,
The morn doth usher thee, with smiles & blushes,
The Earth reflects her glances in thy face.
Birds, insects, Animals with Vegative,
Thy heart from death and dulness doth revive:
And in the darksome womb of fruitful nature dive.

6

Thy swift Annual, and diurnal Course,
Thy daily streight, and yearly oblique path,
Thy pleasing fervor, and thy scorching force,
All mortals here the feeling knowledg hath.
Thy presence makes it day, thy absence night,
Quaternal Seasons caused by thy might:
Hail Creature, full of sweetness, beauty & delight.

7

Art thou so full of glory, that no Eye
Hath strength, thy shining Rayes once to behold?
And is thy splendid Throne erect so high?
As to approach it, can no earthly mould.
How full of glory then must thy Creator be?
Who gave this bright light luster unto thee:
Admir'd, ador'd for ever, be that Majesty.

8

Silent alone, where none or saw, or heard,
In pathless paths I lead my wandring feet,
My humble Eyes to lofty Skyes I rear'd

To sing some Song, my mazed Muse thought meet.
My great Creator I would magnifie,
That nature had, thus decked liberally:
But Ah, and Ah, again, my imbecility!

9

I heard the merry grashopper then sing,
The black clad Cricket, bear a second part,
They kept one tune, and plaid on the same string,
Seeming to glory in their little Art.
Shall Creatures abject, thus their voices raise?
And in their kind resound their makers praise:
Whilst I as mute, can warble forth no higher layes.

10

When present times look back to Ages past,
And men in being fancy those are dead,
It makes things gone perpetually to last,
And calls back moneths and years that long since fled
It makes a man more aged in conceit,
Then was *Methuselah*, or's grand-sire great:
While of their persons & their acts his mind doth treat.

11

Sometimes in *Eden* fair, he seems to be,
Sees glorious *Adam* there made Lord of all,
Fancyes the Apple, dangle on the Tree,
That turn'd his Sovereign to a naked thral.
Who like a miscreant's driven from that place,
To get his bread with pain, and sweat of face:
A penalty impos'd on his backsliding Race.

12

Here sits our Grandame in retired place,
And in her lap, her bloody *Cain* new born,
The weeping Imp oft looks her in the face,

Bewails his unknown hap, and fate forlorn;
His Mother sighs, to think of Paradise,
And how she lost her bliss, to be more wise,
Believing him that was, and is, Father of lyes.

13

Here *Cain* and *Abel* come to sacrifice,
Fruits of the Earth, and Fatlings each do bring,
On *Abels* gift the fire descends from Skies,
But no such sign on false *Cain's* offering;
With sullen hateful looks he goes his wayes.
Hath thousand thoughts to end his brothers dayes,
Upon whose blood his future good he hopes to raise.

14

There *Abel* keeps his sheep, no ill he thinks,
His brother comes, then acts his fratricide,
The Virgin Earth, of blood her first draught drinks
But since that time she often hath been cloy'd;
The wretch with gastly face and dreadful mind,
Thinks each he sees will serve him in his kind,
Though none on Earth but kindred near then could he find.

15

Who fancyes not his looks now at the Barr,
His face like death, his heart with horror fraught,
Nor Male-factor ever felt like warr,
When deep dispair, with wish of life hath fought,
Branded with guilt, and crusht with treble woes,
A Vagabond to Land of *Nod* he goes.
A City builds, that wals might him secure from foes.

16

Who thinks not oft upon the Fathers ages.
Their long descent, how nephews sons they saw,
The starry observations of those Sages,

And how their precepts to their sons were law,
How Adam sigh'd to see his Progeny,
Cloath'd all in his black sinfull Livery,
Who neither guilt, nor yet the punishment could fly.

17

Our Life compare we with their length of dayes
Who to the tenth of theirs doth now arrive?
And though thus short, we shorten many wayes,
Living so little while we are alive;
In eating, drinking, sleeping, vain delight
So unawares comes on perpetual night,
And puts all pleasures vain unto eternal flight.

18

When I behold the heavens as in their prime,
And then the earth (though old) stil clad in green,
The stones and trees, insensible to time,
Nor age nor wrinkle on their front are seen;
If winter come, and greeness then do fade,
A Spring returns, and they more youthfull made;
But Man grows old, lies down, remains where once he's laid.

19

By birth more noble then those creatures all,
Yet seems by nature and by custome curs'd,
No sooner born, but grief and care makes fall
That state obliterate he had at first:
Nor youth, nor strength, nor wisdom spring again
Nor habitations long their names retain,
But in oblivion to the final day remain.

20

Shall I then praise the heavens, the trees, the earth
Because their beauty and their strength last longer
Shall I wish there, or never to had birth,

Because they're bigger, & their bodyes stronger?
Nay, they shall darken, perish, fade and dye,
And when unmade, so ever shall they lye,
But man was made for endless immortality.

21

Under the cooling shadow of a stately Elm
Close sate I by a goodly Rivers side,
Where gliding streams the Rocks did overwhelm;
A lonely place, with pleasures dignifi'd.
I once that lov'd the shady woods so well,
Now thought the rivers did the trees excel,
And if the sun would ever shine, there would I dwell.

22

While on the stealing stream I fixt mine eye,
Which to the long'd for Ocean held its course,
I markt, nor crooks, nor rubs that there did lye
Could hinder ought, but still augment its force:
O happy Flood, quoth I, that holds thy race
Till thou arrive at thy beloved place,
Nor is it rocks or shoals that can obstruct thy pace

23

Nor is't enough, that thou alone may'st slide,
But hundred brooks in thy cleer waves do meet,
So hand in hand along with thee they glide
To *Thetis* house, where all imbrace and greet:
Thou Emblem true, of what I count the best,
O could I lead my Rivolets to rest,
So may we press to that vast mansion, ever blest.

24

Ye Fish which in this liquid Region 'bide,
That for each season, have your habitation,
Now salt, now fresh where you think best to glide

To unknown coasts to give a visitation,
In Lakes and ponds, you leave your numerous fry,
So nature taught, and yet you know not why,
You watry folk that know not your felicity.

25

Look how the wantons frisk to tast the air,
Then to the colder bottome streight they dive,
Eftsoon to *Neptun's* glassie Hall repair
To see what trade they great ones there do drive,
Who forrage o're the spacious sea-green field,
And take the trembling prey before it yield,
Whose armour is their scales, their spreading fins their shield.

26

While musing thus with contemplation fed,
And thousand fancies buzzing in my brain,
The sweet-tongu'd Philomel percht ore my head,
And chanted forth a most melodious strain
Which rapt me so with wonder and delight,
I judg'd my hearing better then my sight,
And wisht me wings with her a while to take my flight.

27

O merry Bird (said I) that fears no snares,
That neither toyles nor hoards up in thy barn,
Feels no sad thoughts, nor cruciating cares
To gain more good, or shun what might thee harm
Thy cloaths ne're wear, thy meat is every where,
Thy bed a bough, thy drink the water cleer,
Reminds not what is past, nor whats to come dost fear.

28

The dawning morn with songs thou dost prevent,
Sets hundred notes unto thy feathered crew,
So each one tunes his pretty instrument,

And warbling out the old, begin anew,
And thus they pass their youth in summer season,
Then follow thee into a better Region,
Where winter's never felt by that sweet airy legion

29

Man at the best a creature frail and vain,
In knowledg ignorant, in strength but weak,
Subject to sorrows, losses, sickness, pain,
Each storm his state, his mind, his body break,
From some of these he never finds cessation,
But day or night, within, without, vexation,
Troubles from foes, from friends, from dearest, near'st Relation

30

And yet this sinfull creature, frail and vain,
This lump of wretchedness, of sin and sorrow,
This weather-beaten vessel wrackt with pain,
Joyes not in hope of an eternal morrow;
Nor all his losses, crosses, and vexation,
In weight, in frequency and long duration
Can make him deeply groan for that divine Translation.

31

The Mariner that on smooth waves doth glide,
Sings merrily, and steers his Barque with ease,
As if he had command of wind and tide,
And now become great Master of the seas;
But suddenly a storm spoiles all the sport,
And makes him long for a more quiet port,
Which 'gainst all adverse winds may serve for fort.

32

So he that saileth in this world of pleasure,
Feeding on sweets, that never bit of th' sowre,
That's full of friends, of honour and of treasure,

M

Fond fool, he takes this earth ev'n for heav'ns bower.
But sad affliction comes & makes him see
Here's neither honour, wealth, nor safety;
Only above is found all with security.

33

O Time the fatal wrack of mortal things,
That draws oblivions curtains over kings,
Their sumptuous monuments, men know them not,
Their names without a Record are forgot,
Their parts, their ports, their pomp's all laid in th'dust
Nor wit nor gold, nor buildings scape times rust;
But he whose name is graved in the white stone [1]
Shall last and shine when all of these are gone.

TO MY DEAR AND LOVING HUSBAND

If ever two were one, then surely we.
If ever man were lov'd by wife, then thee;
If ever wife was happy in a man,
Compare with me ye women if you can.
I prize thy love more then whole Mines of gold,
Or all the riches that the East doth hold.
My love is such that Rivers cannot quench,
Nor ought but love from thee, give recompence.
Thy love is such I can no way repay,
The heavens reward thee manifold I pray.
Then while we live, in love lets so persever,
That when we live no more, we may live ever.

LONGING FOR HEAVEN

As weary pilgrim, now at rest,
   Hugs with delight his silent nest
His wasted limbes, now lye full soft
   That myrie steps, have troden oft
Blesses himself, to think upon
   his dangers past, and travailes done

[1] Rev. ii. 17.

The burning sun no more shall heat
 Nor stormy raines, on him shall beat.
The bryars and thornes no more shall scratch
 nor hungry wolves at him shall catch
He erring pathes no more shall tread
 nor wild fruits eate, in stead of bread,
for waters cold he doth not long
 for thirst no more shall parch his tongue
No rugged stones his feet shall gaule
 nor stumps nor rocks cause him to fall
All cares and feares, he bids farwell
 and meanes in safity now to dwell.
A pilgrim I, on earth, perplext
 with sinns with cares and sorrows vext
By age and paines brought to decay
 and my Clay house mouldring away
Oh how I long to be at rest
 and soare on high among the blest.
This body shall in silence sleep
 Mine eyes no more shall ever weep
No fainting fits shall me assaile
 nor grinding paines my body fraile
With cares and feares ne'r cumbred be
 Nor losses know, nor sorrowes see
What tho.my flesh shall there consume
 it is the bed Christ did perfume
And when a few yeares shall be gone
 this mortall shall be cloth'd upon
A Corrupt Carcasse downe it lyes
 a glorious body it shall rise
In weaknes and dishonour sowne
 in power 'tis rais'd by Christ alone
Then soule and body shall unite
 and of their maker have the sight
Such lasting joyes shall there behold
 as eare ne'r heard nor tongue e'er told
Lord make me ready for that day
 then Come deare bridgrome Come away.
Aug: 31, 69.

MEDITATIONS, DIVINE AND MORALL

I

There is no object that we see; no action that we doe; no good that we injoy; no evill that we feele, or fear, but we may make some spirituall advantage of all: and he that makes such improvement is wise, as well as pious.

II

Many can speak well, but few can do well. We are better scholars in the Theory then the practique part, but he is a true Christian that is a proficient in both.

III

Youth is the time of getting, middle age of improving, and old age of spending; a negligent youth is usually attended by an ignorant middle age, and both by an empty old age. He that hath nothing to feed on but vanity and lyes must needs lye down in the Bed of sorrow.

IV

A ship that beares much saile, and little or no ballast, is easily overset; and that man, whose head hath great abilities, and his heart little or no grace, is in danger of foundering.

V

It is reported of the peakcock that, prideing himself in his gay feathers, he ruffles them up; but, spying his black feet, he soon lets fall his plumes, so he that glories in his gifts and adornings, should look upon his Corruptions, and that will damp his high thoughts.

VI

The finest bread hath the least bran; the purest hony, the least wax; and the sincerest christian, the least self-love.

MICHAEL WIGGLESWORTH

[Michael Wigglesworth, the most popular versifier of early New England Puritanism, was born in England, but came to America with his parents in 1638, at the age of seven. He was graduated from Harvard in 1651, and was for a time tutor in that institution. For nearly half a century he was pastor of the church at Malden, Mass., though for long periods of time he was unable to preach on account of ill health. During these periods his avocations seem to have been medicine and versifying. He became a skilful physician, and some of his poems show his familiarity with medical phraseology. The poem which made him famous was "The Day of Doom, or a Poetical Description of the Great and Last Judgment." This was published in 1662, and has been many times reprinted in both England and America. It consists of two hundred and twenty-four eight-line stanzas of jigging octosyllabics, and describes in detailed and graphic manner the events of the Judgment Day. In the part of the poem which the author's contemporaries probably found most edifying, different classes of sinners offer pleas for mercy, and are in turn answered by the Judge. The popularity of the poem was doubtless due in part to the vivid descriptions, which must have been especially striking to readers who knew little poetry except that which presented abstract moralizing; and in part to the fact that the answers to different sinners expounded in easily remembered jingles many of the chief doctrines of Calvinism. At all events "The Day of Doom" was long considered a religious classic. It was almost universally read, and innumerable children were required to learn it with their catechisms. Of late years the want of dignity and fitness in its form, together with the harshness of the pictures that it presents, have combined to make it as notorious as it was once famous.

Michael Wigglesworth also wrote a few other poems, including "Meat out of the Eater, or Meditations concerning the Necessity, End, and Usefulness of Affliction to God's Children," published in 1669, and "God's Controversy with New England, written in the Time of the Great Drought, anno 1662, by a Lover of New England's Prosperity," first printed in the Proceedings of the Massachusetts Historical Society, for 1871.

As no copy of the "Day of Doom" published in Wigglesworth's lifetime is available, the selections that follow are taken from the edition prepared by William Henry Burr in 1867. This is based on the edition of 1715, compared with the London edition of 1673. The spelling and, to some extent, the punctuation have been modernized. The closing stanzas of "God's Controversy with New England" are from the Proceedings of the Massachusetts Historical Society.]

THE CALL TO JUDGMENT

[From "The Day of Doom"]

X

No heart so bold, but now grows cold,   Rev. 6 : 15.
   and almost dead with fear;
No eye so dry but now can cry,
   and pour out many a tear.
Earth's Potentates and pow'rful States,
   Captains and Men of Might,
Are quite abasht, their courage dasht,
   at this most dreadful sight.

XI

Mean men lament, great men do rent   Mat. 24 : 30.
   their Robes and tear their hair;
They do not spare their flesh to tear
   through horrible despair.
All kindreds wail; all hearts do fail;
   Horror the World doth fill
With weeping eyes and loud out-cries,
   yet knows not how to kill.

XII

Some hide themselves in Caves and Delves,   Rev. 6 : 15, 16.
   in places under ground:
Some rashly leap into the Deep
   to 'scape by being drown'd:
Some to the Rocks (O senseless blocks!)
   And woody Mountains run,
That there they might this fearful sight,
   and dreaded Presence shun.

XIII

In vain do they to Mountains say,
   "Fall on us and us hide

From Judge's ire, more hot than Fire,
    for who may it abide?"
No hiding place can from his Face
    sinners at all conceal,
Whose flaming Eye hid things doth spy,
    and darkest things reveal.

XIV

The Judge draws nigh, exalted high   Mat. 25 : 21.
    upon a lofty Throne,
Amidst the throng of Angels strong,
    lo, Israel's Holy One!
The excellence of whose Presence
    and awful Majesty,
Amazeth Nature, and every Creature
    doth more than terrify.

XV

The Mountains smoke, the Hills are shook,   Rev. 6 : 14.
    the Earth is rent and torn,
As if she should be clear dissolv'd
    or from her center borne.
The sea doth roar, forsakes the shore,
    and shrinks away for fear;
The wild beasts flee into the sea,
    so soon as he draws near,

XVI

Whose Glory bright, whose wond'rous Might
    whose Power Imperial,·
So far surpass whatever was
    in Realms Terrestrial,
That tongues of men (nor Angel's pen)
    Cannot the same express;
And therefore I must pass it by,
    lest speaking should transgress.   Thes. 4 : 16.

XVII

Before his Throne a Trump is blown,
    proclaiming th' Day of Doom;
Forthwith he cries, "*Ye Dead arise*
    and unto Judgment come."
No sooner said, but 'tis obey'd;
    Sepulchers open'd are;
Dead bodies all rise at his call,
    and's mighty Power declare.

Resurrection of the Dead. John 5:28, 29.

XVIII

Both Sea and Land at his command,
    their Dead at once surrender;
The Fire and Air constrainéd are
    also their dead to tender.
The mighty Word of this great Lord
    links Body and Soul together,
Both of the Just and the unjust,
    to part no more forever.

XIX

The same translates from Mortal states
    To Immortality,
All that survive and be alive,
    in th' twinkling of an eye;
That so they may abide for aye,
    to endless weal or woe:
Both the Renate and Reprobate
    are made to die no moe.

The living changed. Luke 20:36. 1 Cor. 15:52.

XX

His wingéd Hosts fly through all coasts,
    together gathering
Both good and bad, both Quick and Dead,
    and all to Judgment bring.

All brought to Judgment. Mat. 24:31.

Out of their holes those creeping Moles,
    that hid themselves for fear,
By force they take, and quickly make
    before the Judge appear.

XXI

Thus every one before the Throne
    of Christ the Judge is brought,
Both rightéous and impious,
    that good or ill hath wrought.
A separation and diff'ring station
    by Christ appointed is
(To sinners sad) 'twixt good and bad,
    'twixt Heirs of woe and bliss.

*2 Cor. 5 : 10.
The Sheep
separated
from the
Goats.
Mat. 25 : 32.*

THE HEATHEN AND THE INFANTS PLEAD

[From " The Day of Doom "]

Then were brought near with trembling fear,
    a number numberless,
Of Blind Heathen, and brutish men
    that did God's Law transgress;

CLVII

Whose wicked ways Christ open lays,
    and makes their sins appear,
They making pleas their case to ease,
    if not themselves to clear.
"Thy Written Word," say they, "good Lord,
    we never did enjoy; ˙
We ne'er refus'd, nor it abus'd;
    Oh, do not us destroy!"

*Heathen men
plead want of
the Written
Word.*

CLVIII

"You ne'er abus'd, nor yet refus'd
    my Written Word, you plead;

That's true," quoth he, "therefore shall ye
    the less be punishéd.
You shall not smart for any part
    of other men's offense,
But for your own transgressi-on
    receive due recompense."

Mat. 11 : 12.
Luke 12 : 48.

CLIX

"But we were blind," say they, "in mind;
    too dim was Nature's Light,
Our only guide, as hath been tried,
    to bring us to the sight
Of our estate degenerate,
    and curs'd by Adam's Fall;
How we were born and lay forlorn
    in bondage and in thrall.

1 Cor. 1 : 21.
Insufficiency
of the light
of Nature.

CLX

"We did not know a Christ till now,
    nor how fall'n men be savéd,
Else would we not, right well we wot,
    have so ourselves behavéd.
We should have mourn'd, we should have turn'd
    from sin at thy Reproof,
And been more wise through thy advice,
    for our own soul's behoof.

Mat. 11 : 22.

CLXI

"But Nature's light shin'd not so bright,
    to teach us the right way:
We might have lov'd it and well improv'd it,
    and yet have gone astray."
The Judge most High makes this Reply:
    "You ignorance pretend,
Dimness of sight, and want of light,
    your course Heav'nward to bend.

They are
answered.

CLXII

"How came your mind to be so blind?
  I once you knowledge gave,
Clearness of sight and judgment right:
  who did the same deprave?
If to your cost you have it lost,
  and quite defac'd the same,
Your own desert hath caus'd the smart;
  you ought not me to blame.

Gen. 1 : 27.
Eccl. 7 : 29.
Hos. 13 : 9.

CLXIII

"Yourselves into a pit of woe,
  your own transgression led;
If I to none my Grace had shown,
  who had been injured?
If to a few, and not to you,
  I shew'd a way of life,
My Grace so free, you clearly see
  gives you no ground of strife.

Mat. 11 : 25,
compared
with 20 : 15.

CLXIV

" 'Tis vain to tell, you wot full well,
  if you in time had known
Your misery and remedy,
  your actions had it shown:
You, sinful Crew, have not been true
  unto the Light of Nature,
Nor done the good you understood,
  nor ownéd your Creator.

Rom. 1 : 20,
21, 22.

CLXV

"He that the Light, because 'tis slight,
  hath uséd to despise,
Would not the Light shining more bright,
  be likely for to prize.

Rom. 2 : 12,
15, and 1 : 32.
Mat. 12 : 41.

If you had lov'd, and well improv'd
  your knowledge and dim sight,
Herein your pain had not been vain,
  your plagues had been more light."

CLXVI

Then to the Bar all they drew near   Reprobate In-
  Who died in infancy,   fants plead for
And never had or good or bad   themselves.
  effected pers'nally;   Rev. 20 : 12,
But from the womb unto the tomb   15, compared
  were straightway carriéd,   with Rom. 5 :
(Or at the least ere they transgress'd)   12, 14, and
  Who thus began to plead: 9 : 11, 13.
                                            Ezek. 18 : 2.

CLXVII

"If for our own transgressi-on,
  or disobedience,
We here did stand at thy left hand,
  just were the Recompense;
But Adam's guilt our souls hath spilt,
  his fault is charg'd upon us;
And that alone hath overthrown
  and utterly undone us.

CLXVIII

"Not we, but he ate of the Tree,
  Whose fruit was interdicted;
Yet on us all of his sad Fall
  the punishment's inflicted.
How could we sin that had not been,
  or how is his sin our,
Without consent, which to prevent
  we never had the pow'r?

CLXIX

"O great Creator why was our Nature
   depravéd and forlorn?
Why so defil'd, and made so vil'd,
   whilst we were yet unborn?
If it be just, and needs we must
   transgressors reckon'd be,
Thy Mercy, Lord, to us afford,   Psal. 51 : 5.
   which sinners hath set free.

CLXX

"Behold we see Adam set free,
   and sav'd from his trespass,
Whose sinful Fall hath split us all,
   and brought us to this pass.
Canst thou deny us once to try,
   or Grace to us to tender,
When he finds grace before thy face,
   who was the chief offender?"

CLXXI

Then answeréd the Judge most dread:
   "God doth such doom forbid,   Their argu-
That men should die eternally   ments taken off.
   for what they never did.   Ezek. 18 : 20.
But what you call old Adam's Fall,   Rom. 5 : 12, 19.
   and only his Trespass,
You call amiss to call it his,
   both his and yours it was.

CLXXII

"He was design'd of all Mankind
   to be a public Head;   1 Cor. 15 : 48,
A common Root, whence all should shoot, 49.
   and stood in all their stead.

He stood and fell, did ill or well,
    not for himself alone,
But for you all, who now his Fall
    and trespass would disown.

CLXXIII

"If he had stood, then all his brood
    had been establishéd
In God's true love never to move,
    nor once awry to tread;
Then all his Race my Father's Grace
    should have enjoy'd for ever,
And wicked Sprites by subtile sleights
    could them have harméd never.

CLXXIV

"Would you have griev'd to have receiv'd
    through Adam so much good,
As had been your for evermore,
    if he at first had stood?
Would you have said, 'We ne'er obey'd
    nor did thy laws regard;
It ill befits with benefits,
    us, Lord, to so reward?'

CLXXV

"Since then to share in his welfare,
    you could have been content,
You may with reason share in his treason,
    and in the punishment.   Rom. 5 : 12.
Hence you were born in state forlorn,   Psal. 51 : 5.
    with Natures so depravéd;   Gen. 5 : 3.
Death was your due because that you
    had thus yourselves behavéd.

CLXXVI

"You think 'If we had been as he,
   whom God did so betrust,
We to our cost would ne'er have lost
   all for a paltry lust.'
Had you been made in Adam's stead,   Mat. 23 : 30, 31.
   you would like things have wrought,
And so into the self-same woe,
   yourselves and yours have brought.

CLXXVII

"I may deny you once to try,
   or Grace to you to tender,
Though he finds Grace before my face   Rom. 9 : 15, 18.
   who was the chief offender;   The free gift.
Else should my Grace cease to be Grace,   Rom. 5 : 15.
   for it would not be free,
If to release whom I should please
   I have no liberty.

CLXXVIII

"If upon one what's due to none
   I frankly shall bestow,
And on the rest shall not think best
   compassion's skirt to throw,
Whom injure I? will you envy
   and grudge at others' weal?
Or me accuse, who do refuse
   yourselves to help and heal?

CLXXIX

"Am I alone of what's my own,
   no Master or no Lord?
And if I am, how can you claim   Mat. 20 : 15.
   what I to some afford?

Will you demand Grace at my hand,
    and challenge what is mine?
Will you teach me whom to set free,
    and thus my Grace confine?

CLXXX

"You sinners are, and such a share
    as sinners, may expect;
Such you shall have, for I do save
    none but mine own Elect.
Yet to compare your sin with their
    who liv'd a longer time,
I do confess yours is much less,
    though every sin's a crime.

Psal. 58 : 8.
Rom. 6 : 23.
Gal. 3 : 10.
Rom. 8 : 29,
30, and 11 : 7.
Rev. 21 : 27.
Luke 12 : 14, 8.
Mat. 11 : 22.

CLXXXI

"A crime it is, therefore in bliss
    you may not hope to dwell;
But unto you I shall allow
    the easiest room in Hell."
The glorious King thus answering,
    they cease, and plead no longer;
Their Consciences must needs confess
    his Reasons are the stronger.

The wicked
all convinced
and put to si-
lence.
Rom. 3 : 19.
Mat. 22 : 12.

CLXXXII

Thus all men's pleas the Judge with ease
    doth answer and confute,
Until that all, both great and small,
    are silencéd and mute.
Vain hopes are cropt, all mouths are stopt,
    sinners have naught to say,
But that 'tis just and equal most
    they should be damn'd for aye.

Behold the
formidable
estate of all
the ungodly as
they stand
hopeless and
helpless be-
fore an impar-
tial Judge ex-
pecting their
final Sentence.
Rev. 6 : 16, 17.

EPILOGUE TO "GOD'S CONTROVERSY WITH NEW ENGLAND"

Ah dear New England! dearest land to me;
    Which unto God hast hitherto been dear,
And mayst be still more dear than formerlie,
    If to his voice thou wilt incline thine ear.

Consider wel & wisely what the rod,
    Wherewith thou art from yeer to yeer chastized,
Instructeth thee. Repent, & turn to God,
    Who wil not have his nurture be despized.

Thou still hast in thee many praying saints,
    Of great account, and precious with the Lord,
Who dayly powre out unto him their plaints,
    And strive to please him both in deed & word.

Cheer on, sweet souls, my heart is with you all,
    And shall be with you, maugre Sathan's might:
And whereso'ere this body be a Thrall,
    Still in New-England shall be my delight.

N

PETER FOLGER

[The greater part of the New England writings that have been preserved from the seventeenth century are the work of ministers and other members of the theological and intellectual oligarchy that dominated the government. Many of the contemporaries of these authors were, however, practical, hard-headed Yankees who were inclined to criticise the opinions and the acts of their superiors. These men were not in the habit of writing much, and they doubtless refrained, through fear for their personal safety, from expressing their most radical ideas openly. The few of their rude utterances that have been preserved have, therefore, an especial interest. One of these works is "A Looking Glass for the Times, or The former Spirit of *New-England* revived in this generation," a doggerel poem of some four hundred lines, written by Peter Folger in 1675. Folger was one of the first settlers of Nantucket, a land-surveyor, who, if he had written nothing, would still have been remembered as the grandfather of Benjamin Franklin. At the outbreak of the Indian troubles he took the ground that the afflictions of the colonists were a divine punishment for their religious intolerance, and he criticised the interference of the ministers with affairs of state. A mistaken reading of a passage in Franklin's "Autobiography" once led to the belief that the verses were published in the year that they were written; but it now seems certain that Folger had the discretion common to men of his class, and that he gave his work no publicity that was likely to get him into trouble. It is probable that if Cotton Mather had seen the poem, he would not have used some complimentary terms with which he refers to the author in the "Magnalia." The first known edition of the verses, now very rare, was published in 1763. The brief selection here given is from the reprint of this edition made by Sidney S. Rider in the Rhode Island Historical Tracts.]

A WORD CONCERNING MAGISTRATES AND MINISTERS

[From "A Looking Glass for the Times"]

I would not have you for to think,
　　tho' I have wrote so much,
That I hereby do throw a Stone
　　at Magistrates *as such*.
The Rulers in the Country I
　　do own them in the Lord;
And such as are for Government,
　　with them I do accord.

But that which I intend hereby,
  is that they would keep bound,
And meddle not with God's Worship,
  for which they have no ground.
And I am not alone herein,
  there's many hundreds more
That have for many Year's ago
  spake much upon that Score,
Indeed I really believe
  it's not your Business
To meddle with the Church of Christ,
  in Matters more or less,
There's work enough to do besides,
  to judge in *mine* and *thine*,
To succour Poor and Fatherless,
  that is the Work in fine.
And I do think that now you find
  enough of that to do;
Much more at such a Time as this
  as there is War also,
Indeed I count it very low
  for People in these Days,
To ask the Rulers for their leave
  to serve God in his Ways.
I count it worse in Magistrates
  to use the Iron Sword,
To do that Work which Christ alone
  will do by his own Word.
The Church may now go stay at home,
  there's nothing for to do;
Their Work is all cut out by Law,
  and almost made up too.
Now Reader, least you should mistake,
  in what I said before
Concerning Minister's, I think
  to write a few Words more,
I would not have you for to think
  that I am such a Fool,

To write against Learning, as such,
　　or to cry down a School.
But 'tis that *Popish College* way,
　　that I intend hereby,
Where Men are mew'd up in a Cage,
　　fit for all Villany.
But I shall leave this puddle Stuff
　　to neighbours at the Door,
That can speak more unto such things,
　　upon a knowing Score.
And now these Men though ne'er so bad,
　　when they have learn'd their Trade,
They must come in and bear a Part,
　　whatever Laws are made.
I can't but wonder for to see
　　our Magistrates and Wise,
That they sit still, and suffer them,
　　to ride on them, not rise,
And stir them up to do that Work
　　that Scripture Rule there wants,
To persecute and persecute
　　Those that they judge are Saints.
There's one thing more that I believe
　　is worse than all the rest,
They vilify the Spirit of God,
　　and count School Learning Best.
If that a Boy hath learn'd his Trade,
　　and can the Spirit disgrace,
Then he is lifted up on high,
　　and needs must have a Place,
But I shall leave this dirty Stuff,
　　and give but here a hint,
Because that you have *Cradock's* Book,
　　and may see more in Print.
There are some few, it may be, that
　　are clear of this same Trade;
And of those Men, I only say,
　　these Verses are not made.

THE BURWELL PAPERS

[The so-called "Burwell Papers" are contained in an incomplete and imperfect manuscript which, early in the last century, was in the possession of the Burwell family in Virginia. It treats of "Bacon's Rebellion," the civil disturbance that agitated the Virginia colony in 1676. The name of the author and the exact time of composition are matters of conjecture; but it was evidently written by a partisan of the royal governor, very soon after the occurrence of the events that it narrates. It offers an interesting contrast to the writings of the earliest settlers in Virginia, and shows how Southern writers followed the literary fashions of England. It illustrates the conceits, the prolixity, and the striving after effect that characterize the most artificial Restoration prose. Two poems on Bacon's death, at least one of which is by some other person than the author of the main narrative, are interesting specimens of the verse of the period.

The Burwell Papers have been twice printed by the Massachusetts Historical Society — first, from an inaccurate copy, in the Collections, Series II, Vol. I; and again in the Proceedings for 1866–1867. The selections that follow are from the latter reprint.]

THE SIEGE OF JAMESTOWN

The Towne being thus forsaken, by the Baconians, his Honour enters the same the next day, about noone; where after he had rendered thanks unto God for his safe arivall (which he forgot not to perform upon his knees, at his first footeing the shore) hee applyes himselfe not onely to secure what he had got posesion of, but to increace and inlarge the same to his best advantage. And knowing that the people of ould useally painted the God of war with a belly to be fed, as well as with hands to fight, he began to cast about for the bringing in of provissions for to feed his soulders; and in the next place for soulders, as well to reinforce his strength with in, as to inlarge his quarters abrode: But as the saying is, Man may propose, but God will dispose; when that his honour thought him selfe so much at liberty, that he might have the liberty to go when and where he pleased, his expectations became very speedily & in a moment frusterated.

For Bacon haveing don his buisness against the Indians, or at least so much as he was able to do, haveing marched his men with a grate deale of toyle & haserd som hundreds of miles, one way and another, killing som and takeing others prissoners, and haveing spent his provissions, draws in his forces with in the verge of the English Plantations, from whence he dismiseth the gratest part of his Army to gether strength against the next designed March, which was no sooner don but he incounters the newes of the Governours being arived at town. Of which being informed he with a marvellous cellerity (outstriping the swift wings of fame) marcheth those few men now with him (which hee had onely resarved as a gard to his parson) and in a trice blocks up the Governour in Towne, to the generall astonishment of the wholl Countrey; especially when that Bacons numbers was knowne; which at this time did not exseed above a hundred and fifty, and these not above two thirds at worke neather. An action of so strange an Aspect, that who ever tooke notis of it, could not chuse but thinke but that the Accomackians eather intended to receve their promised pay, without disart; or other ways to establish such signall testimonies of there cowerdize or disaffections, or both, that posterity might stand & gaze at there reched stupidety.

Bacon soone perceved what easey worke he was likely to have, in this servis, and so began to set as small an esteeme upon these mens curages, as they did upon there owne credits. Hee saw, by the Prolog, what sport might be expected in the play, and soe began to dispose of his affaires accordingly. Yet not knowing but that the paucity of his numbers being once knowne, to those in Towne, it might raise there hearts to a degree of curage, haveing so much the ods, and that mani-times number prevales against ressalution, he thought it not amiss, since the Lions strength was too weake, to strengthen the same with the Foxes Braines: and how this was to be efected you shall heare.

For emediately he despacheth two or three parties of Horss, and about so many in each party, for more he could not spare, to bring in to the Camp some of the prime Gent: Women, whose Husbands were in towne. Where when arived he sends one of them to inform her owne, and others Husbands, for what purposes he had brought them into the camp, namely, to be plac'd in the fore frunt of his Men, at such time as those in towne should sally forth upon him.

The poore Gent: Women were mightely astonish'd at this project; neather were there Husbands voide of amazements at this subtill invention. If Mr. Fuller thought it strange, that the Divells black gard should be enrouled Gods soulders, they made it no less wonderfull, that there innocent and harmless Wives should thus be entred a white garde to the Divell. This action was a Method, in war, that they were not well aquainted with (no not those the best inform'd in millitary affaires) that before they could com to pearce their enimies sides, they must be obliged to dart there wepons through there wives brest: By which meanes though they (in there owne parsons) might escape without wounds; yet it might be the lamentable fate of there better halfe to drop by gunshott, or other ways be wounded to death.

Whether it was these Considerations, or som others, I do not know, that kep their swords in there scabards: But this is manifest, That Bacon knit more knotts by his owne head in one day, then all the hands in Towne was able to untye in a wholl weeke: While these Ladyes white Aprons became of grater force to keepe the beseiged from salleing out then his works (a pittifull trench) had strength to repell the weakest shot, that should have bin sent into his Legure, had he not made use of this invention.

For it is to be noted that rite in his frunt, where he was to lodge his Men, the Governour had planted 3 grate Guns, for to play poynt blank upon his Men, as they were at worke, at about 100 or a 150 paces distance; and then againe, on his right hand, all most close aborde the shore, lay the ships, with ther broade sides, to thunder upon him if he should offer to make an onslaute: this being the onely place, by land, for him to make his entry, into the Towne: But for your better satisfaction, or rather those who you may show this Naritive to, who have never bin upon the place, take this short description.

The place, on which the Towne is built, is a perfict Peninsulla, or tract of Land, all most wholly incompast with Water. Haveing on the Sowth side the River (Formerly Powhetan, now called James River) 3 miles brode, Incompast on the North, from the east point, with a deep Creeke, rangeing in a cemicircle, to the west, with in 10 paces of the River; and there, by a smalle Istmos, tacked to the Continent. This Iseland (for so it is denominate) hath for Longitud (east and west) nere upo 2 miles, and for Lattitude about halfe so much, beareing in the wholl compass about

5 miles, litle more or less. It is low-ground, full of Marches and Swomps, which makes the Aire, especially in the Sumer, insalubritious & unhelty: It is not at all replenish'd with springs of fresh water, & that which they have in ther Wells, brackish, ill sented, penurious, and not gratefull to the stumack; which render the place improper to indure the commencement of a seige. The Towne is built much about the midle of the Sowth line, close upon the River, extending east and west, about 3 quarters of a mile; in which is comprehended som 16 or 18 howses, most as is the Church, built of Brick, faire and large; and in them about a dozen ffamilles (for all the howses are not inhabited) getting there liveings by keepeing of ordnaries, at exstreordnary rates.

The Governour understanding that the Gent: Women, at the Legure, was, by order, drawne out of danger, resalved, if posible, to beate Bacon out of his trench; which he thought might easely be performed, now that his Gardian Angles had forsaken his Camp. For the efecting of which he sent forth 7 or (as they say) 800 of his Accomackians, who (like scholers goeing to schoole) went out with hevie harts, but returnd hom with light heeles; thinkeing it better to turne there backs upon that storme, that there brests could not indure to strugle against, for feare of being gauled in there sides, or other parts of there bodys, through the sharpness of the wether; which (after a terable noyse of thunder and lightning out of the Easte) began to blow with a powder (and som leade too as big as musquitt boolitts) full in there faces, and that with so grate a violence, that som off them was not able to stand upon there leggs, which made the rest betake them selves to there heeles; as the onely expedient to save there lives; which som amongst them had rather to have lost, then to have own'd there safty at the price of such dishonourable rates.

The Governour was exstremly disgusted at the ill management of this action, which he exprest in som passionate terms, against those who merited the same. But in ernist, who could expect the event to be other ways then it was, when at the first notis given, for the designed salley to be put in execution, som of the officers made such crabed faces at the report of the same, that the Guner of Yorke Fort did proffer to purchase, for any that would buy, a Collonells, or a Captains, Commission, for a chunke of a pipe.

The next day Bacon orders 3 grate Guns to be brought into the Camp, two where of he plants upon his trench. The one he sets to worke (playing som calls itt, that takes delight to see stately structurs beated downe, and Men blowne up into the aire like Shutle Cocks) against the Ships, the other against the enterance into Towne, for to open a pasage to his intended Storm, which now was resalved upon as he said, & which was prevented by the Governours forsakeing the place, and shiping himselfe, once more to Accomack; takeing along with him all the Towne people, and there goods, leaveing all the grate Guns naled up, and the howses emty, for Bacon to enter at his pleasure, and which he did the next morning before day: Where, contrary to his hopes, he met with nothing that might satisfie eather him selfe or soulders desires, except few Horsses, two or three sellers of wine, and som small quantety of Indian Corne with a grate many Tan'd hides.

THE DEATH OF BACON AND THE ACCESSION OF INGRAM

Bacon haveing for som time, bin beseiged by sickness, and now not able to hould out any longer; all his strength, and provissions being spent, surrendred up that Fort he was no longer able to keepe, into the hands of that grim and all conquering Captaine, Death; after that he had implor'd the assistance of the above mentioned Minester, for the well makeing his Artickles of Rendition. The onely Religious duty (as they say) he was observ'd to perform dureing these Intregues of affaires, in which he was so considerable an actor, and soe much consearn'd, that rather then he would decline the cause, he be came so deeply ingaged in, in the first rise there of, though much urged by arguments of dehortations, by his nearest Relations and best friends, that he subjected him selfe to all those inconvenences that, singly, might bring a Man of a more Robust frame to his last hom. After he was dead he was bemoned in these following lines (drawne by the Man that waited upon his person, as it is said) and who attended his Corps to there Buriall place: But where depossited till the Generall day, not knowne, onely to those who are ressalutly silent in that particuler. There was many coppes of Verces made after his departure, calculated to the Lattitude of there affections who composed them; as a rellish taken from both appetites I have here sent you a cuple.

Bacons Epitaph, made by his Man.

Death why soe crewill! what no other way
To manifest thy splleene, but thus to slay
Our hopes of safety; liberty, our all
Which, through thy tyrany, with him must fall
To its late Caoss? Had thy riged force
Bin delt by retale, and not thus in gross
Griefe had bin silent: Now wee must complaine
Since thou, in him, hast more then thousand slane
Whose lives and safetys did so much depend
On him there lif, with him there lives must end.
   If't be a sin to thinke Death brib'd can bee
Wee must be guilty; say twas bribery
Guided the fatall shaft. Verginias foes
To whom for secrit crimes, just vengeance owes
Disarved plagues, dreding their just disart
Corrupted Death by Parasscellcian art
Him to destroy; whose well tride curage such
There heartless harts, nor arms, nor strength could touch.
   Who now must heale those wounds, or stop that blood
The Heathen made, and drew into a flood?
Who i'st must pleade our Cause? nor Trump nor Drum
Nor Deputations; these alass are dumb.
And Cannot speake. Our Arms (though nere so strong)
Will want the aide of his Commanding tongue,
Which Conquer'd more than Ceaser: He orethrew
Onely the outward frame; this Could subdue
The ruged workes of nature. Soules repleate
With dull Child could, he'd annemate with heate
Drawne forth of reasons Lymbick. In a word
Marss and *Minerva*, both in him Concurd
For arts, for arms, whose pen and sword alike
As *Catos* did, may admireation strike

In to his foes; while they confess with all
It was there guilt stil'd him a Criminall.
Onely this differance doth from truth proceed
They in the guilt, he in the name must bleed
While none shall dare his *Obseques* to sing
In disarv'd measures; untill time shall bring
Truth Crown'd with freedom, and from danger free
To sound his praises to posterity.

Here let him rest; while wee this truth report
Hee's gon from hence unto a higher Court
To pleade his Cause: where he by this doth know
WHETHER TO CEASER HEE WAS FRIEND, OR FOE.

Upon the Death of G: B.

Whether to Ceaser he was Friend or Foe?
Pox take such Ignorance, do you not know?
Can he be Friend to Ceaser, that shall bring
The Arms of Hell, to fight against the King?
(Treason, Rebellion) then what reason have
Wee for to waite upon him to his Grave,
There to express our passions? Wilt not bee
Worss then his Crimes, to sing his Ellegie
In well tun'd numbers; where each Ella beares
(To his Flagitious name) a flood of teares?
A name that hath more soules with sorow fed,
Then reched Niobe, single teares ere shed;
A name that fil'd all hearts, all eares, with paine,
Untill blest fate proclamed, Death had him slane.
Then how can it be counted for a sin
Though Death (nay though my selfe) had bribed bin,
To guide the fatall shaft? we honour all
That lends a hand unto a T[r]ators fall.
What though the well paide Rochit soundly ply
And box the Pulpitt, in to flatterey;
Urging his Rhethorick, and straind elloquence,
T' adorne incoffin'd filth and excrements;
Though the Defunct (like ours) nere tride

A well intended deed untill he dide?
'Twill be nor sin, nor shame, for us, to say
A two fould Passion checker-workes this day
Of Joy and Sorow; yet the last doth move
On feete impotent, wanting strength to prove
(Nor can the art of Logick yeild releife)
How Joy should be surmounted, by our greife.
Yet that wee Grieve it cannot be denide,
But 'tis because he was, not cause he dide.
So wep the poore destresed, Ilyum Dames
Hereing those nam'd, there Citty put in flames,
And Country ruing'd; If wee thus lament
It is against our present Joyes consent.
For if the rule, in Phisick, trew doth prove,
Remove the cause, th' effects will after move,
We have outliv'd our sorows; since we see
The Causes shifting, of our miserey.
   Nor is't a single cause, that's slipt away,
That made us warble out, a well-a-day.
The Braines to plot, the hands to execute
Projected ills, Death Joyntly did nonsute
At his black Bar.   And what no Baile could save
He hath committed Prissoner to the Grave;
From whence there's no repreive.   Death keep him close
We have too many Divells still goe loose.

Ingrams Proceedings.

The Lion had no sooner made his exitt, but the Ape (by indubitable right) steps upon the stage.   Bacon was no sooner removed by the hand of good providence, but another steps in, by the wheele of fickle fortune.   The Countrey had, for som time, bin guided by a company of knaves, now it was to try how it would behave it selfe under a foole.   Bacon had not long bin dead, (though it was a long time be fore som would beleive that he was dead) but one Ingram (or Isgrum, which you will) takes up Bacons Commission (or ells by the patterne of that cuts him out a new one) and as though he had bin his natureall heire, or that

Bacons Commission had bin granted not onely to him selfe, but to his Executors, Administraters, and Assignes, he (in the Millitary Court) takes out a Probit of Bacons will, and proclames him selfe his Successer.

This Ingram, when that he came first into the Countrey, had gott upon his Back the title of an Esquire, but how he came by it may pussell all the Herolds in England to finde out, u[n]till he informs them of his right name: how ever, by the helpe of this (and his fine capering, for it is saide that he could dance well upon a rope) he caper'd him selfe in to a fine (though short liv'd) estate: by marying, here, with a rich Widow, vallued at som hundreds of pounds.

The first thing that this fine fellow did, after that he was mounted upon the back of his Commission, was to Spur, or Switch, those who were to pay obedience unto his Authorety, by geting him selfe proclaimed Generall of all the forces, now raised, or here after to be raised, in Verginia: Which while it was performing at the head of the Army, the Milke-sop stoode with his hatt in his hand, lookeing as demurely as the grate Turks Mustie, at the readeing som holy sentance, extracted forth of the Alchron. The Bell-man haveing don, he put on his hat, and his Janessarys threw up there Caps; crying out as lowde as they could Bellow, God save our new Generall, hopeing, no dout, but he, in imitation of the grat Sultaine, at his election, would have inlarged there pay, or ells have given them leave to have made Jewes of the best Christians in the Countrey: but he being more than halfe a jew him self, at present forbad all plundrings, but such as he him selfe should be parsonally at.

MARY ROWLANDSON

[The early accounts of captivity among the Indians are interesting for the pictures they give of pioneer hardships and of the life of the savages; and they are important because in early New England they were almost the only form of writing that gratified the love for tales of adventure. One of the most notable of these accounts is that of Mary Rowlandson, wife of the pastor at Lancaster, Mass., who suffered an especially trying period of captivity in 1676. According to the preface, "This Narrative was penned by the Gentlewoman her self, to be to her a memorandum of Gods dealing with her." She was persuaded, however, to make it public, and it was printed at Cambridge in 1682 with the title "The Soveraignty & Goodness of God Together With the Faithfulness of his Promises Displayed; Being a Narrative of the Captivity and Restauration of Mrs. Mary Rowlandson." The narrative went through two American editions and one English edition in 1682, and has since been many times reprinted. It owes its interest not only to the graphic account of fascinating though horrible events, but to the unconscious revelation of the author's character.

No copy of the first edition is known to exist. The selections here given follow the rare second edition, Cambridge, 1682, as reprinted in facsimile by Henry Stedman Nourse and John Eliot Thayer, Lancaster, 1903. The work of the colonial printer was very crude and inaccurate, but the reader will ordinarily find no difficulty in making necessary emendations in the text.]

THE BEGINNING OF THE CAPTIVITY

[From "The Narrative of the Captivity," etc.]

On the tenth of *February* 1675, Came the *Indians* with great numbers upon *Lancaster:* Their first coming was about Sunrising; hearing the noise of some Guns, we looked out; several Houses were burning, and the Smoke ascending to Heaven. There were five persons taken in one house, the Father, and the Mother and a sucking Child they knockt on the head; the other two they took and carried away alive. Their were two others, who being out of their Garison upon some occasion, were set upon; one was knockt on the head, the other escaped: Another their was who running along was shot and wounded, and fell down; he begged of them his life, promising them Money (as they told me) but they would not hearken to him but knockt him in head, and stript him naked, and split open his Bowels. Another seeing many of the *Indians* about his Barn, ventured and went out, but was quickly shot down. There were three others belonging to the same Garison who were killed; the *Indians* getting up upon the roof of the Barn, had advantage to shoot down upon them over their Fortification. Thus these murtherous wretches went on, burning, and destroying before them,

At length they came and beset our own house, and quickly it was the dolefullest day that ever mine eyes saw. The House stood upon the edg of a hill; some of the *Indians* got behind the hill, others into the Barn, and others behind any thing that could shelter them; from all which places they shot against the House, so that the Bullets seemed to fly like hail; and quickly they wounded one man among us, then another, and then a third, About two hours (according to my observation, in that amazing time) they had been about the house before they prevailed to fire it (which they did with Flax and Hemp, which they brought out of the Barn, and there being no defence about the House, only two Flankers at two opposite corners and one of them not finished) they fired it once and one ventured out and quenched it, but they quickly fired it again, and that took Now is the dreadfull hour come, that I have often heard of (in time of War, as it was the case of others) but now mine eyes see it. Some in our house were fighting for their lives, others wallowing in their blood, the House on fire over our heads, and the bloody Heathen ready to knock us on the head, if we stired out. Now might we hear Mothers & Children crying out for themselves, and one another, *Lord, what shall we do?* Then I took my Children (and one of my sisters, hers) to go forth and leave the house: but as soon as we came to the dore and appeared, the *Indians* shot so thick that the bulletts rattled against the House, as if one had taken an handfull of stones and threw them, so that we were fain to give back. We had six stout Dogs belonging to our Garrison, but none of them would stir, though another time, if any *Indian* had come to the door, they were ready to fly upon him and tear him down. The Lord hereby would make us the more to acknowledge his hand, and to see that our help is always in him. But out we must go, the fire increasing, and coming along behind us, roaring, and the *Indians* gaping before us with their Guns, Spears and Hatchets to devour us. No sooner were we out of the House, but my Brother in Law (being before wounded, in defending the house, in or near the throat) fell down dead, whereat the *Indians* scornfully shouted, and hallowed, and were presently upon him, stripping off his cloaths, the bulletts flying thick, one went through my side, and the same (as would seem) through the bowels and hand of my dear Child in my arms. One of my elder Sisters Children, named *William*, had then his Leg broken, which the *Indians* perceiving, they knockt him on head. Thus were we butchered by those merciless Heathen, standing amazed, with the blood running down to our heels. My eldest Sister being yet in the House, and seeing those wofull sights, the Infidels haling Mothers one way, and Children another, and some wallowing in their blood: and her elder Son telling her that her Son *William* was dead, and my self was wounded, she said, And, *Lord, let me dy with them;* which was no sooner said, but she was struck with a Bullet, and fell down dead over the threshold. I hope she is reaping the fruit of her good labours, being faithfull to the service of God in her place. In her younger years she lay under much trouble upon spiritual accounts, till it pleased God to make that precious Scripture take hold of her heart, 2 *Cor.* 12. 9. *And he said unto me my Grace is sufficient for thee.* More then twenty years after I have heard her tell how sweet and comfortable that place was to her, But to return: The *Indians* laid hold of me, pulling me one way, and the Children another, and said, *Come go along with us;* I told them they would kill me: they answered, *If I were willing to go along with them they would not hurt me.*

Oh the dolefull sight that now was to behold at this House! *Come, behold the works of the Lord, what dissolations he has made in the Earth.* Of thirty seven persons who were in this one House, none escaped either present death, or a bitter captivity, save only one, who might say as he. *Job.* 1. 15. *And I only am escaped alone to tell the News.* There were twelve killed, some shot, some stab'd with their Spears, some knock'd down with their Hatchets. When we are in prosperity, Oh the little that we think of such dreadfull sights, and to see our dear Friends, and Relations ly bleeding out their heart-blood upon the ground. There was one who was chopt into the head with a Hatchet, and stript naked, and yet was crawling up and down. It is a solemn sight to see so many Christians lying in their blood, some here, and some there, like a company of Sheep torn by Wolves. All of them stript naked by a company of hell-hounds, roaring, sing-ing, ranting and insulting, as if they would have torn our very hearts out; yet the Lord by his Almighty power preserved a num-ber of us from death, for there were twenty-four of us taken alive and carried Captive.

I had often before this said, that if the Indians *should come, I should chuse rather to be killed by them then taken alive* but when it came to the tryal my mind changed; their glittering weapons so daunted my spirit, that I chose rather to go along with those (as I may say) ravenous Bears, then that moment to end my dayes; and that I may the better declare what happened to me during thaf grievous Captivity I shall particularly speak of the severall Removes we had up and down the Wilderness.

The first Remove.

Now away we must go with those Barbarous Creatures, with our bodies wounded and bleeding, and our hearts no less than our bodies. About a mile we went that night, up upon a hill within sight of the Town where they intended to lodge. There was hard by a vacant house (deserted by the English before, for fear of the *Indians*) I asked them whether I might not lodge in the house that night to which they answered, what will you love *English men* still? this was the dolefullest night that ever my eyes saw. Oh the roaring, and singing and danceing, and yelling of those black creatures in the night, which made the place a lively resemblance of hell And as miserable was the wast that was there made, of Horses, Cattle, Sheep, Swine, Calvès, Lambs, Roasting Pigs, and Fowl [which they had plundered in the Town] some roasting, some lying and burning, and some boyling to feed our merciless Enemies; who were joyful enough though we were disconsolate To add to the dolefulness of the former day, and

o

the dismalness of the present night: my thoughts ran upon my losses and sad bereaved condition. All was gone, my Husband gone (at least separated from me, he being in the Bay; and to add to my grief, the *Indians* told me they would kill him as he came homeward) my Children gone, my Relations and Friends gone, our House and home and all our comforts within door, and without, all was gone, (except my life) and I knew not but the next moment that might go too. There remained nothing to me but one poor wounded Babe, and it seemed at present worse than death that it was in such a pitiful condition, bespeaking, Compassion, and I had no refreshing for it, nor suitable things to revive it, Little do many think what is the savageness and bruitishness of this barbarous Enemy; even those that seem to profess more than others among them, when the *English* have fallen into their hands.

Those seven that were killed at *Lancaster* the summer before upon a Sabbath day, and the one that was afterward killed upon a week day, were slain and mangled in a barbarous manner, by one-ey'd *John*, and *Marlborough's* Praying *Indians*, which Capt. *Mosely* brought to *Boston*, as the *Indians* told me.

The second Remove.

But now, the next morning, I must turn my back upon the Town, and travel with them into the vast and desolate Wilderness, I knew not whither. It is not my tongue, or pen can express the sorrows of my heart, and bitterness of my spirit, that I had at this departure: but God was with me, in a wonderfull manner, carrying me along, and bearing up my spirit, that it did not quite fail One of the *Indians* carried my poor wounded Babe upon a horse, it went moaning all along I shall dy, I shall dy. I went on foot after it, with sorrow that cannot be exprest. At length I took it off the horse, and carried it in my armes till my strength failed, and I fell down with it: Then they set me upon a horse with my wounded Child in my lap, and there being no furniuure upon the horse back; as we were going down a steep hill, we both fell over the horses head, at which they like inhumane creatures laught, and rejoyced to see it, though I thought we should there have ended our dayes, as overcome with so many difficulties. But the Lord renewed my strength still, and carried me along, that I might see more of his Power; yea, so much that I could never have thought of, had I not experienced it.

After this it quickly began to snow, and when night came on, they stopt: and now down I must sit in the snow, by a little fire, and a few boughs behind me, with my sick Child in my lap; and calling much for water, being now (through the wound) fallen into a violent Fever. My own wound also growing so stiff, that I could scarce sit down or rise up; yet so it must be, that I must sit all this cold winter night upon the cold snowy ground, with my sick Child in my armes, looking that every hour would be the last of its life; and having no Christian friend near me, either to comfort or help me. *Oh, I may see the wonderfull power of God, that my Spirit did not utterly sink under my affliction: still the Lord upheld me with his gracious and mercifull Spirit, and we were both alive to see the light of the next morning.*

SOME INCIDENTS OF THE EIGHTH REMOVE

[From "The Narrative of the Captivity," etc.]

We travelled on till night; and in the morning, we must go over the River to *Philip's* Crew. When I was in the Cannoe, I could not but be amazed at the numerous crew of Pagans that were on the Bank on the other side. When I came ashore, they gathered all about me, I sitting alone in the midst: I observed they asked one another questions, and laughed, and rejoyced over their Gains and Victories. Then my heart began to fail: and I fell a weeping which was the first time to my remembrance, that I wept before them. Although I had met with so much Affliction, and my heart was many times ready to break, yet could I not shed one tear in their sight: but rather had been all this while in a maze, and like one astonished: but now I may say as, *Psal* 137. 1. *By the Rivers of Babylon, there we sat down: yea, we wept when we remembered Zion.* There one of them asked me, why I wept, I could hardly tell what to say: yet I answered, they would kill me: No, said he, none will hurt you. Then came one of them and gave me two spoon-fulls of Meal to comfort me, and another gave me half a pint of Pease; which was more worth than many Bushels at another time. Then I went to see King *Philip*, he bade me come in and sit down, and asked me whether I would smoke it (a usual Complement now adayes amongst Saints and Sinners) but this no way suited me. For though I had formerly used Tobacco, yet I had left it ever since I was first taken. *It seems to be a Bait, the Devil layes to make men loose their precious time:* I remember with shame, how formerly, when I had taken two or three pipes, I was presently ready for another, such a bewitching thing it is: But I thank God, he has now given me power over it; surely there are many who may be better imployed than to ly sucking a stinking Tobacco-pipe.

Now the *Indians* gather their Forces to go against *North-Hampton:* over-night one went about yelling and hooting to give notice of the design. Whereupon they fell to boyling of Ground-nuts, and parching of Corn (as many as had it) for their Provision: and in the morning away they went: *During my abode in this place, Philip spake to me to make a shirt for his boy, which I did, for which he gave me a shilling: I offered the mony to my master, but he bade me keep it: and with it I bought a piece of Horse flesh.* Afterwards he asked me to make a Cap for his boy, for which he invited me to Dinner. I went, and he gave me a Pancake, about as big as two fingers; it was made of parched wheat, beaten, and fryed in Bears grease, but I thought I never tasted pleasanter meat in my life. There was a *Squaw* who spake to me to make a shirt for her *Sannup*, for which she gave me a piece of Bear. Another asked me to knit a pair of Stockins, for which she gave me a quart of Pease: I boyled my Pease and Bear together, and invited my master and mistriss to dinner, but the proud Gossip, because I served them both in one Dish, would eat nothing, except on bit that he gave her upon the point of his knife. Hearing that my son was come to this place, I went to see him, and found him lying flat upon the ground: I asked him how he could sleep so? he answered me, *That he was not asleep, but at Prayer;* and lay so that they might not observe what he was doing. I pray God he may remember these things now he is returned in safety. At this Place (the sun now getting higher) what with the beams and heat of the Sun, and the smoak of the

Wigwams, I thought I should have been blind, I could scarce discern one *Wigwam* from another. There was here one *Mary Thurston* of *Medfield*, who seeing how it was with me, lent me a Hat to wear: but as soon as I was gone, the *Squaw* who owned that *Mary Thurston* came running after me, and got it away again. *Here was the* Squaw *that gave me one spoonfull of Meal.* I put it in my Pocket to keep it safe: yet notwithstanding some body stole it, but put five *Indian* Corns in the room of it: which Corns were the greatest Provisions I had in my travel for one day.

THE CONCLUDING MEDITATION

[From "The Narrative of the Captivity," etc.]

I can remember the time, when I used to sleep quietly without workings in my thoughts, whole nights together, but now it is other-wayes with me. When all are fast about me, and no eye open, but his who ever waketh, my thoughts are upon things past, upon the awfull dispensation of the Lord towards us; upon his wonder-full power and might, in carrying of us through so many difficulties, in returning us in safety, and suffering none to hurt us. I remember in the night season, how the other day I was in the midst of thousands of enemies, & nothing but death before me: It was then hard work to perswade my self, that ever I should be satisfied with bread again. But now we are fed with the finest of the Wheat, and, as I may say, *With honey out of the rock:* In stead of the Husk, we have the fatted Calf: The thoughts of these things in the particulars of them, and of the love and good-ness of God towards us, make it true of me, what *David* said of himself, *Psal.* 6. 5. *I watered my Couch with my tears.* Oh! the wonderfull power of God that mine eyes have seen, affording matter enough for my thoughts to run in, that when others are sleeping mine eyes are weeping.

I have seen the extrem vanity of this World: One hour I have been in health, and wealth, wanting nothing: But the next hour in sickness and wounds, and death, having nothing but sorrow and affliction.

Before I knew what affliction means, I was ready sometimes to wish for it. When I lived in prosperity; having the comforts of the World about me, my relations by me, my Heart chearfull: and taking little care for any thing: and yet seeing many, whom I preferred before my self, under many tryals and afflictions, in sickness, weakness, poverty, losses, crosses, and cares of the World, I should be sometimes jealous least I should have my portion in this life, and that Scripture would come to my mind, *Heb.* 12. 6. *For whom the Lord loveth he chasteneth, and scourgeth every Son whom he receiveth.*   But now I see the Lord had his time to scourge and chasten me.   The portion of some is to have their afflictions by drops, now one drop and then another; but the dregs of the Cup, the Wine of astonishment: like a sweeping rain that leaveth no food, did the Lord prepare to be my portion Affliction I wanted, and affliction I had, full measure (I thought) pressed down and running over; yet I see, when God calls a person to any thing, and through never so many difficulties, yet he is fully able to carry them through, and make them see, and say they have been gainers thereby.   And I hope I can say in some measure, as *David* did, *It is good for me that I have been afflicted.* The Lord hath shewed me the vanity of these outward things. That they are the *Vanity of vanities, and vexation of spirit;* that they are but a shadow, a blast, a bubble, and things of no continuance.   That we must rely on God himself, and our whole dependence must be upon him.   If trouble from smaller matters began to arise in me, I have something at hand to check myself with, and say, why am I troubled?   It was but the other day that if I had had the world, I would have given it for my freedom, or to have been a Servant to a Christian.   I have learned to look beyond present and smaller troubles, and to be quieted under them, as *Moses.* said, *Exod.* 14. 13. *Stand still and see the salvation of the Lord.*

INCREASE MATHER

[Increase Mather was born in Dorchester, Mass., in 1639. His father, Richard Mather, was one of the ministers who left England in the time of Archbishop Laud, and has already been mentioned as one of the authors of the "Bay Psalm Book." Increase was graduated from Harvard, and afterward studied in Dublin and preached in various parts of Great Britain. Like his father, he was driven out for nonconformity, and returned to America, where he at length became pastor of the North Church, Boston.

Increase Mather's active life, which extended until 1723, coincided with a troubled period in the history of New England. The wars with the Indians, which began about 1675, were followed by serious difficulties with the English authorities regarding the form of colonial government. At the same time a change was taking place in the Church. The power of the ministers was declining, and the people were becoming, as Conservatives like the Mathers believed, hopelessly lax in their beliefs and practices. In this time of change, Increase Mather was a leader in both political and religious movements. He maintained that the afflictions of the colonies were a divine punishment for lack of religious devotion, and his "Brief History of the War with the Indians in New-England" (1676), and "A Relation of the Troubles which have hapned in New-England by reason of the Indians there" (1677) were written to emphasize this lesson. He opposed the "half-way covenant" and all liberal tendencies in the church, and was instrumental in the calling of the "Reforming Synod" which proposed to remove God's displeasure at New England by returning to a stricter and purer faith. He served as president of Harvard College from 1685 to 1701, when the Liberal party secured legislation that forced him to resign. Meanwhile he had visited England as the agent of the colony, and had attempted to have the old charter restored. Finding this impossible, he procured a new charter, which was probably as liberal as could have been secured, but which was unsatisfactory to the Radical party in the colony.

Both Increase Mather and his son Cotton incurred something of the obloquy which is sure to devolve on Conservatives who fight for a hopeless cause. He has been charged, in particular, with responsibility for the witchcraft persecutions. It is true that he seems to have been eagerly credulous regarding the direct workings of Satan, as is shown in his "Essay for the Recording of Illustrious Providences" (1684), and other writings; but he had little direct connection with the affairs at Salem, and he always advised against proceeding on insufficient evidence.

Increase Mather was the author of nearly one hundred and fifty published works, including many sermons, and some pamphlets on the political

situation printed anonymously. His style, while not wholly free from pedantry, is more direct and simple than that of his son. Perhaps his most
readable work, though not the one that does most credit to his judgment,
is the "Essay for the Recording of Illustrious Providences."

The selections from the "Historical Discourse Concerning the Preva-
lency of Prayer" and from the "History of the War with the Indians" are
from the editions edited by Samuel G. Drake; the passages from "An
Essay for the Recording of Illustrious Providences" are from the first edition,
Boston, 1684; the Letter to Governor Dudley is from the Massachusetts
Historical Society Collections.]

THE POWER OF PRAYER

[From "An Historical Discourse Concerning the Prevalency of Prayer"]

It was a great Word (and if rightly understood, a true Word)
which *Luther* spake when he said, *Est quaedam precum omni-
potentia*, there is a kind of Omnipotency in Prayer; and the
Reason is obvious, *viz*. In that the Almighty doth suffer himself
to be prevailed upon and overcome by Prayer. Had not Jacob
in this respect Power with God? Yea when he made his Suplica-
tion, he had Power, and prevailed over the Angel, even that
Angel who is the Lord of Hosts, the Lord is his Memorial. Where
do we find in all the Books of God a more wonderfull Expression,
then that of the Lord to praying Moses, *Now let me alone?* That
ever the eternal God should become thus a Petitioner to a poor
mortal Man! *Feriendi licentiam petit a Mose qui fecit Mosen.*
Prayer then is like the Sword of Saul, or the Bow of Jonathan,
which never returned empty from the Battle. Prayer is stronger
than iron Gates. At the Prayers of the Church the iron Gates
fly open, and the Apostles Fetters fall off. Sometimes the Prayers
of one Man that hath an eminent Interest in God, are a Means
to preserve a whole Town, yea a whole Land from Destruction,
wel might the Antient say, *Homine probo orante nihil potentius.*
How far did Abrahams Prayers prevail for Sodom? Did not
Elijahs Prayers open and shut the Windows of Heaven? Did
they not bring down Showers when the gasping Earth was ready
to dy for Thirst? When a fiery Drought had like to have devoured
the Land of Israel, and the Prophet Amos prayed and cried to
the Lord, saying, *O Lord God, Cease I beseech thee, by whom shall*

Jacob arise? for he is small; the Lord repented for this, and sqid this shall not be.

Wars, when justly undertaken, have been successful through the prevalency of Prayer.

Moses in the Mount praying, is too strong for all the Armies in the Valley fighting. When the Philistines went up against the Children of Israel, *Samuel* ceased not to cry to the Lord for Israel, and the Lord thundered with a great thunder that Day upon the Philistines, and discomfited them, that they were smitten before Israel. *Jehoshaphat*, when surrounded by a Multitude of heathen Enemyes, by Prayer overcame them. When *Zera* the Ethiopian came against the Lords People with an Host of a thousand thousand Men, Asa by Prayer and Faith overcame them all. *Hezekiah* and *Isaiah* by their prayers brought an Angel down from Heaven, who slew an hundred and fourscore and five thousand Assyrians, in the Host of Sennacherib in one Night.

And besides these and many Scriptural Examples in ecclesiastical Story, Instances to this Purpose are frequently observed. The History of the thundering Legion is famously known. Thus it was.

The Emperour *Marcus Aurelius* going to war against the *Quads*, *Vandals*, *Sarmats* and *Germans*, who were nine hundred seventy and five thousand fighting Men; The Imperialists were so cooped up by their numerous Enemies, in strait, dry, and hot Places, that the Souldiers having been destitute of Water for five Days together, they were all like to have perished for thirst. In this extremity, a Legion of Christian Souldiers being in the Army, withdrew themselves apart from the Rest, and falling prostrate on the Earth, by ardent Prayers prevailed with God, that he imediately sent a most plentiful Rain, whereby the Army that otherwise had perished, was refreshed and dreadfull Lightnings flashed in the Faces of their Enemies, so as that they were discomfited and put to flight. The Effect of which was, that the Persecution which before that the Emperour designed against the Christians, was diverted; and that *praying Legion* did afterwards, bear the Name of κερυνοβολος the *Lightning Legion*.

Constantine the Great, being to join the Battle with the Heathen Tyrant *Licinius*, singled out a number of godly Ministers of Christ, and with them betook himself to earnest Prayer and Supplication, after which God gave him a notable and glorious Victory over his Enemies. But *Licinius* himselfe escaped at that Time, and raised another Army, which was pursued by *Constantine*, who before he would engage with the Enemy, caused a Tent to be erected, wherein he did spend some Time in Fasting and Prayer, being attended with a Company of holy praying Men round about him, after which marching against his Enemies, he fought them, and obtained a more glorious Victory than the former, and the Grand Rebel *Licinius* was then taken Prisoner.

Theodosius being in no small Danger by Reason of the potent Army of Adversaryes he had to do with, in his Distress cryed unto Heaven for Help, and behold! the Lord sent such a terrible Tempest, as the like was not known, whereby the Darts of the Enemy were driven back upon themselves, to their own Confusion, which caused *Claudian* the Poet, (though no great Friend to the Christian Name) to say concerning *Theodosius*,

> *O nimium dilecte Deo cui militat Æther,*
> *Et conjurati veniunt ad Classica Venti.*

It is storied concerning the City of *Nisibis* that being straitly besieged by *Sapores* King of Persia, the distressed Citizens desired a devout and holy Man amongst them (whose Name was *James*) to be earnest with the Lord in their Behalf. He was so: and the Effect was, God sent an Army of Gnats and Flyes among the *Persians*, which so vexed and tormented them, as that they were forced to raise the Seige and depart.

Amongst the *Waldenses* sometimes an inconsiderable Number have prevailed over their popish Adversaryes. At one Time five hundred of these poor praying Saints overthrew two thousand and five hundred of their Enemies who scoffed at them because they would fall upon their knees and pray before they would fight.

In the Land of our Father's Sepulchres, when *Oswald* (who succeded his Father *Ethelfride* in the Northern Kingdom) was assaulted by *Cedwalla* and *Penda*, two Heathen Kings, that raised a great Army, designing the Ruin of Oswald and his People, he humbly and earnestly addressed himself to the Lord of Hosts, the great Giver of Victory, entreating him to shew his own Power in saving and protecting his People from the Rage of heathen Adversaryes: which, joyning battle with his Enemyes, albeit their Army was far greater than his, he obtained a wonderful Victory, wherein *Cedwalla* himself was slain.

When *England* was invaded by the Danes under the Conduct of their King *Osrick*, who encamped at *Ashdon*, King *Ethelred* betook himself to Prayer; and marching against the Danish Army, put them to flight, and slew the greatest Part of them.

Gustavus Adolphus the King of Sweden, no sooner landed in his Enemies Terrjtoryes, but he addressed himself to Heaven for Victory, and encouraged his Counsellors and Commanders by saying *The greater the Army of Prayers is, the greater and more assured shall be our Victory.* Yea it was his Manner when the Armyes were set in Battle array, to lift up his Eyes to Heaven and say, *Lord prosper the Battle of this Day, according as thou seest my Heart dost aim at thy Glory, and the good of thy Church.* And how successful did God make that excellent Prince to be?

But what need we go far to find Examples confirming the Truth of this Assertion, that *Prayer is of Wonderfull Prevelancy*, since our own Eyes have seen it? New England may now say, if the Lord (even the Prayer hearing God) had not been on our Side when Men rose up against us, they had swallowed us up; then the proud Waters had gone over our Soul. And thus hath it been more than once or twice, especially since the late Insurrection and Rebellion of the Heathen Nations round about us. We cannot but acknowledge, and Posterity must know, that we were in Appearance a gone and ruined People, and had been so ere this Day, if the Lord had not been a God that heareth Prayer.

THE BEGINNING OF KING PHILIP'S WAR

[From "Brief History of the War with the Indians in New England"]

June 24. (Midsummer-day) was appointed and attended as a day of solemn Humiliation throughout that Colony, by fasting and praying, to intreat the Lord to give success to the present Expedition respecting the Enemy. At the conclusion of that day of Humiliation, as soon as ever the People in Swanzy were come from the place where they had been praying together, the *Indians* discharged a volley of shot, whereby they killed one man, and wounded others. Two men were sent to call a Surgeon for the relief of the wounded, but the *Indians* killed them by the way: And in another part of the Town six men were killed, so that there were Nine *Englishmen* murthered this day.

Thus did the *War* begin, this being the first English blood which was spilt by the *Indians* in an Hostile way. The Providence of God is deeply to be observed, that the Sword should be first drawn upon a day of Humiliation, the Lord thereby declaring from Heaven that he expected something else from his People besides Fasting and Prayer.

Plymouth being thus suddenly involved in trouble, send to the other united Colonies for aid, and their desires were with all readiness complied with.

Souldiers marched out of *Boston* towards *Mount-hope*, June 26, and continued marching that night, when there hapned a great Eclipse of the Moon, which was totally darkned above an hour. Only it must be remembred, that some days before any Souldiers went out of *Boston*, Commissioners were sent to treat with *Philip*, that so if possible, ingaging in a war might be prevented. But when the Commissioners came near to *Mount-hope*, they found divers *Englishmen* on the ground, weltering in their own blood, having been newly murdered by the *Indians*, so that they could not proceed farther. Yea, the *Indians* killed a man of this Colony as he was travelling on the road before such time as we took up arms: In which respect no man can doubt of the *justness* of our Cause, since the Enemy did shed the blood of some of ours who never did them (our Enemies themselves being judges) the least wrong before we did at all offend them, or attempt any act of hostility towards them.

June 29th was a day of publick *Humiliation* in this Colony, appointed by the Council in respect of the war which is now begun.

This morning our Army would have ingaged with the Enemy. The *Indians* shot the Pilot who was directing our Souldiers in their way to *Philips* Country, and wounded several of our Men, and ran into Swamps, rainy weather hindred a further pursuit of the Enemy. An awful Providence happened at this time: For a Souldier (a stout man) who was sent from *Water-town*, seeing the *English Guide* slain, and hearing many profane oaths among some of our Souldiers (namely those Privateers, who were also Volunteers) and considering the unseasonableness of the weather was such, as that nothing could be done against the Enemy; this man was possessed with a strong conceit, that God was against the *English;* whereupon he immediately ran distracted, and so was returned home a lamentable Spectacle.

In the beginning of *July*, there was another Skirmish with the Enemy, wherein several of the *Indians* were killed, amongst whom were *Philips* chief Captain, and one of his Counsellors.

Now it appears that *Squaw-Sachem* of *Pocasset*, her men were conjoyned with the *Womponoags* (that is *Philips* men) in this Rebellion.

About this time they killed several *English* at *Taunton*, and Burnt divers Houses there. Also at *Swanzy*, they caused about half the Town to be consumed with merciless Flames. Likewise *Middlebury* and *Dartmouth*, in *Plimouth* Colony, did they burn with Fire, and barbarously murdered both men and women in those places, stripping the slain, whether Men or Women, and leaving them in the open Field, as naked as in the day wherein they were born. Such also is their Inhumanity, as that they flay off the skin from their Faces and Heads of those they get into their hands, and go away with the hairy Scalps of their Enemies.

July 19. Our Army pursued *Philip*, who fled into a dismal Swamp for refuge: The *English Souldiers* followed him, and killed many of his men, also about fifteen of the *English* were then slain. The Swamp was so Boggy, and thick of Bushes, as that it was judged to proceed further therein would be but to throw away Mens lives. It could not there be descerned who were *English*, and who the *Indians*. Our Men when in that hideous place if they did but see a Bush stir would fire presantly, whereby 'tis verily feared they did sometimes unhappily shoot *English Men* instead of *Indians*. Wherefore a Retreat was sounded, and night coming on, the Army withdrew from that place. This was because the desperate Distress which the Enemy was in was unknown to us, for the *Indians* have since said, that if the *English* had continued at the Swamp all night, nay, if they had but followed them but one half hour longer, *Philip* had come and yielded up himself. But God saw we were not yet fit for Deliverance, nor could Health be restored unto us except a great deal more Blood be first taken from us: and other places as well as *Plimouth* stood in need of such a Course to be taken with them. It might rationally be conjectured, that the unsuccessfulness of this Expedition against *Philip* would embolden the *Heathen* in other parts to do as he had done, and so it came to pass. For *July* 14, the *Nipnep* (or *Nipmuck*) *Indians* began their mischief at a Town called *Mendam* (had we mended our ways as we should have done, this Misery might have been prevented) where they committed *Barbarous Murders*. This day deserves to have a *Remark* set upon it, considering that Blood was never shed in *Massachusetts Colony* in a way of Hostility before this day. Moreover the Providence of God herein is the more awful and tremendous, in that this very day the Church in *Dorchester* was before the Lord, humbling themselves by Fasting and Prayer, on account of *the day of trouble* now begun amongst us.

The news of this Blood-shed came to us at *Boston* the next day in Lecture time, in the midst of the Sermon, the Scripture then improved being that *Isai.* 42, 24. *Who gave Jacob to the spoil and Israel to the robbers? did not the Lord, he against whom ye have sinned?*

A BEWITCHED HOUSE

[From "An Essay for the Recording of Illustrious Providences"]

As there have been several Persons vexed with evil Spirits, so divers Houses have been wofully Haunted by them. In the Year 1679, the House of *William Morse* in *Newberry* in *New-England*, was strangely disquieted by a *Dæmon*. After those troubles began, he did by the Advice of Friends write down the particulars of those unusual Accidents. And the Account which he giveth thereof is as followeth;

On *December* 3. In the night time, he and his Wife heard a noise upon the roof of their House, as if Sticks and Stones had been thrown against it with great violence; whereupon he rose out of his Bed, but could see nothing. Locking the Doors fast, he returned to Bed again. About midnight they heard an Hog making a great noise in the House, so that the Man rose again, and found a great Hog in the House, the door being shut, but upon the opening of the door it ran out.

On *December* 8. in the Morning, there were five great Stones and Bricks by an *invisible hand* thrown in at the west end of the house while the Mans Wife was making the Bed, the Bedstead was lifted up from the floor, and the Bedstaff flung out of the Window, and a Cat was hurled at her; a long staff danced up and down in the Chimney; a burnt Brick, and a piece of a weatherboard were thrown in at the Window: The Man at his going to Bed put out his Lamp, but in the Morning found that the Saveall of it was taken away, and yet it was unaccountably brought into its former place. On the same day, the long Staff but now spoken of, was hang'd up by a line, and swung to and fro, the Mans Wife laid it in the fire, but she could not hold it there, inasmuch as it would forcibly fly out; yet after much ado with joynt strength they made it to burn. A shingle flew from the Window, though no body near it, many sticks came in at the same place, only one of these was so scragged that it could enter the hole but a little way, whereupon the Man pusht it out, a great Rail likewise was thrust in at the Window, so as to break the Glass.

At another time an Iron Crook that was hanged on a Nail, violently flew up and down, also a Chair flew about, and at last lighted on the Table where Victuals stood ready for them to eat, and was likely to spoil all, only by a nimble catching they saved some of their Meal with the loss of the rest, and the overturning of their Table.

People were sometimes Barricado'd out of doors, when as yet there was no body to do it: and a Chest was removed from place to place, no hand touching it. Their Keys being tied together, one was taken from the rest, & the remaining two would fly about making a loud noise by knocking against each other. But the greatest part of this *Devils* feats were his mischievous ones, wherein indeed he was sometimes Antick enough too, and therein the chief sufferers were, the Man and his Wife, and his Grand-Son. The Man especially had his share in these *Diabolical* Molestations. For one while they could not eat their Suppers quietly, but had the Ashes on the Hearth before their eyes thrown into their Victuals; yea, and upon their heads and Clothes, insomuch that they were forced up into their Chamber, and yet they had no rest there; for one of the Man's Shoes being left below, 'twas filled with Ashes and Coals, and thrown up after them. Their Light was beaten out, and they being laid in their Bed with their little Boy between them, a great stone (from the Floor of the Loft) weighing above three pounds was thrown upon the mans stomach, and he turning it down upon the floor, it was once more thrown upon him. A Box, and a Board were likewise thrown upon them all. And a Bag of Hops was taken out of their Chest, wherewith they were beaten, till some of the Hops were scattered on the floor, where the Bag was then laid, and left.

In another Evening, when they sat by the fire, the Ashes were whirled at them, that they could neither eat their Meat, nor endure the House. A Peel struck the Man in the face. An Apron hanging by the fire, was flung upon it, and singed before they could snatch it off. The Man being at Prayer with his Family, a Beesom gave him a blow on his head behind, and fell down before his face.

On another day, when they were Winnowing of Barley, some hard dirt was thrown in, hitting the Man on the Head, and both the Man and his Wife on the back; and when they had made themselves clean, they essayed to fill their half Bushel but the foul Corn was in spite of them often cast in amongst the clean, and the Man being divers times thus abused was forced to give over what he was about.

On *January* 23 (in particular) the Man had an iron Pin twice thrown at him, and his Inkhorn was taken away from him while he was writing, and when by all his seeking it he could not find it, at last he saw it drop out of the Air, down by the fire: a piece of Leather was twice thrown at him; and a shoe was laid upon his shoulder, which he catching at, was suddenly rapt from him. An handful of Ashes was thrown at his face, and upon his clothes: and the shoe was then clapt upon his head, and upon it he clapt his hand, holding it so fast, that somewhat unseen pulled him with it backward on the floor.

THE PROBATION BY COLD WATER

[From "An Essay for the Recording of Illustrious Providences"]

There is another Case of Conscience which may here be enquired into, viz. *Whether it be lawful to bind persons suspected for Witches, and so cast them into the Water, in order to making a discovery of their innocency or guiltiness; so as that if they keep above the Water, they shall be deemed as confœderate with the Devil, but if they sink they are to be acquitted from the crime of Witchcraft.* As for this way of purgation it cannot be denied but that some learned men have indulged it. King JAMES approveth of it, in his Discourse of Witch-craft *B. 3 Chap.* 6. supposing that the water refuseth to receive Witches into its Bosom, because they have perfidiously violated their Covenant with God, confirmed by Water in Baptism. *Kornmannus* and *Scribonius* do upon the same ground justifie this way of tryal. But a worthy *Casuist* of our own giveth a judicious reply to this supposal, *viz.* that all Water is not the Water of Baptism, but that only which is used in the very act of Baptism. Moreover, according to this notion the *Proba* would serve only for such persons as have been Baptized. *Wierus* and *Bodinus* have written against this Experiment. So hath *Hemmingius;* who saith, that is *both superstitious and ridiculous.* Likewise, that learned Physitian *John Heurnius* has published a Treatise, which he calls, *Responsum ad supremam curiam Hollandiæ, nullum esse æquæ innatationem lamiarum indicium.* That Book I have not seen, but I find it mentioned in *Meursius* his *Athenæ Batavæ.* Amongst *English* Authors, Dr. *Cott* hath endeavoured to shew the unlawfulness of using such a practice. Also Mr. *Perkins* is so far from approving of this *Probation by cold water,* as that he rather inclines to think that the persons who put it in practice are themselves after a sort practisers of Witch-craft. That most Learned, Judicious, and Holy Man, *Gisbertus Vœtius* in his so ementioned Exercitation *de Magia,* P. 573. endeavours to evince that the custom of trying Witches by casting them into the Water is *unlawful, a Tempting of God, and indirect Magic.* And that it is utterly unlawful, I am by the following Reasons, convinced:

P

1. This practice has no Foundation in nature, nor in Scripture. If the Water will bear none but Witches, this must need proceed either from some natural or some supernatural cause. No natural cause is or can be assigned why the bodies of such persons should swim rather than of any other. The Bodies of Witches have not lost their natural Properties, they have weight in them as well as others. Moral changes and viceousness of mind, make no alteration as to these natural proprieties which are inseparable from the body. Whereas some pretend that the Bodies of Witches are possessed with the Devil, and on that account are uncapable of sinking under the water; *Malderus* his reply is rational, *viz.* that the Allegation has no solidity in it, witness the *Gadarens* Hoggs, which were no sooner possessed with the Devil but they ran into the Water, and there perished. But if the experiment be supernatural, it must either be Divine or Diabolical. It is not divine; for the Scripture does no where appoint any such course to be taken to find out whether persons are in league with the Devil or no. It remains then that the experiment is Diabolical. If it be said, that the Devil has made a compact with Wizards, that they shall not be drowned, and by that means that Covenant is discovered; the Reply is, we may not in the least build upon the Devils word. By this Objection the matter is ultimately resolved into a Diabolical Faith. And shall that cast the scale, when the lives of men are concerned? Suppose the Devil saith these persons are Witches, must the Judge therefore condemn them?

2. Experience hath proved this to be a fallacious way of trying Witches, therefore it ought not to be practised. Thereby guilty persons may happen to be acquitted, and the innocent to be condemned. The Devil may have power to cause supernatation on the water in a person that never made any compact with him. And many times known and convicted Wizards have sunk under the water when thrown thereon. In the *Bohemian* History mention is made of several Witches, who being tried by cold water were as much subject to submersion as any other persons. *Delrio* reports the like of another Witch. And *Godelmannus* speaks of six Witches in whom this way of trial failed. *Malderus* saith it has been known that the very same persons being often brought to this probation by Water, did at one time swim and another

time sink; and this difference has sometimes hapned according to the different persons making the experiment upon them; in which respect one might with greater reason conclude that the persons who used the experiment were Witches, then that the persons tried were so.

3. This way of purgation is to be accounted of, like other provocations or appeals to the Judgement of God, invented by men: such as *Camp-fight, Explorations by hot water, &c.* In former times it hath been customary (and I suppose tis so still among the *Norwegians*) that the suspected party was to put his hand into scalding water, and if he received no hurt thereby then he was reputed innocent; but if otherwise, judged as guilty. Also, the trial by *fire Ordeal* has been used in our Nation in times of Darkness. Thus *Emma* the Mother of King *Edward* the Confessor, was led barefoot and blindfold over certain hot irons, and not hapning to touch any of them, was judged innocent of the crime which some suspected her as guilty of. And *Kunegund* Wife to the Emperour *Henry II.* being accused of Adultery, to clear her self, did in a great and honourable Assembly take up seven glowing irons one after onother with her bare hand, and had no harm thereby. These bloody kind of Experiments are now generally banished out of the World. It is pity the *Ordeal* by cold water is not exploded with the other.

4. This *vulgar probation* (as it useth to be called) was first taken up in times of Superstition, being (as before was hinted of other Magical Impostures) propagated from *Pagans* to *Papists*, who would (as may be gathered from *Bernards* 66 Serm. *in Cantica*) sometimes bring those that were under suspicion for Heresie unto their Purgation in this way. We know that our *Ancestors*, the old *Pagan Saxons* had amongst them four sorts of *Ordeal* (*i.e.* Trial or *Judgement* as the *Saxon* word signifies) whereby when sufficient proof was wanting, they sought (according as the Prince of darkness had instructed them) to find out the truth concerning suspected persons, one of which *Ordeals* was this, the persons surmised to be guilty, having Cords tied under their Arms, were thrown with it into some River, to see whether they would sink or swim. So that this Probation was not originally confined to Witches, but others supposed to be Criminals were

thus to be tried: but in some Countries they thought meet thus to examine none but those who have been suspected for familiarity with the Devil. That this custom was in its first rise superstitious is evident from the Ceremonies of old used about it. For the *Proba* is not canonical, except the person be cast into the Water with his right hand tied to his left foot. Also, by the Principle which some approvers of this Experiment alledge to confirm their fansies; their Principle is, *Nihil quod per Necromantian fit, potest in aqua fallere aspectum intuentium.* Hence *William* of *Malmsbury, Lib.* 2. *P.* 67. tells a fabulous Story (though he relates it not as such) of a Traveller in *Italy* that was by a Witch transformed into an Asse, but retaining his humane understanding would do such feats of activity, as one that had no more wit than an Asse could not do; so that he was sold for a great price; but breaking his Halter he ran into the Water, and thence was instantly unbewitched, and turned into a Man again. This is as true as *Lucian's* Relation about his own being by Witch-craft transformed into an Asse; and I suppose both are as true as that cold water will discover who are Witches. It is to be lamented, that *Protestants* should in these days of light, either practise or plead for so Superstitious an Invention, since *Papists* themselves have of later times been ashamed of it. *Verstegan* in his Antiquities, *Lib.* 3, *P.* 53. speaking of the trials by *Ordeal*, and of this by cold water in particular, has these words; *These aforesaid kinds of* Ordeals, *the* Saxons *long after their Christianity continued: but seeing they had their beginnings in* Paganism *and were not thought fit to be continued amongst Christians; at the last by a Decree of Pope* Stephen II. *they were abolished.* Thus he. Yea, this kind of trial by Water, was put down in *Paris* A. D. 1594. by the supream Court there. Some learned *Papists* have ingenuously acknowledged that such *Probations* are Superstitious. It is confessed that they are so, by *Tyræus, Binsfeldius, Delrio,* and by *Malderus de magia,* Tract. 10. *Cap.* 8. *Dub.* 11. who saith, that they who shall practise this Superstition, and pass a judgement of Death upon any persons on this account, will (without repentance) be found guilty of Murder before God.

It was in my thoughts to have handled some other Cases of the like nature with these insisted on: but upon further consideration, I suppose it less needful, the practises which have given occasion for them being so grosly Superstitious, as that they are ashamed to show their heads openly. The *Chaldæans* and other Magicians amongst the Heathen Nations of old, practised a sort of *Divination* by *Sieves* (which kind of *Magic* is called *Coscinomantia*). The like Superstition has been frequent in Popish Countries, where they have been wont to utter some words of Scripture, and the Names of certain Saints over a *Sieve*, that so they might by the motion thereof, know where something stollen or lost was to be found. Some also have believed that if they should cast Lead into the Water, then *Saturn* would discover to them the thing they enquired after. It is not *Saturn* but *Satan* that maketh the discovery, when any thing is in such a way revealed. And of this sort is the foolish Sorcery of those Women that put the white of an Egg into a Glass of Water, that so they may be able to divine of what Occupation their future Husbands shall be. It were much better to remain ignorant than thus to consult with the Devil. These kind of practices appear at first blush to be Diabolical; so that I shall not multiply Words in evincing the evil of them. It is noted that *the Children of Israel did secretly those things that are not right against the Lord their God*, 2 King. 17. 9. I am told that there are some who do secretly practice such Abominations as these last mentioned, unto whom the Lord in mercy give deep and unfeigned Repentance and pardon for their grievous Sin.

INCREASE MATHER TO GOVERNOR DUDLEY

Sir,

That I have had a singular respect for you, the Lord knows; but that since your arrival to the government, my charitable expectations have been greatly disappointed, I may not deny. Without any further preface or compliments, I think it my duty freely and faithfully to let you understand what my sad fears concerning you are.

1st. I am afraid you cannot clear yourself from the guilt of bribery and unrighteousness: For you to declare to Mr. Newton, that he should not do what his office as judge in the admiralty obliged him unto, unless he would give you an hundred pounds, was surely a sin of that nature. And for you not to consent that some, whose titles to their land the General Assembly had confirmed, should enjoy their right, except they would give you a sum of money, is unrighteousness. To deny men their right, except they will by some gift purchase it, is certainly the sin of bribery, let who will be guilty of it. These and other things Mr. Newton and Mr. Partridge have given their affidavits of; and I hear that many things of this nature will shortly be discovered; There is a scripture that makes me think it will be so. Numb. xxxii. 23.

2d. I am afraid that you have not been true to the interest of your country, as God (considering his marvellous dispensations towards you) and his people have expected from you. Sir H. Ashurst writes to me, that it would fill a quire of paper for him to give a full account of your contrivances to ruin your country, both this and the neighbour colony. Your son Paul's letter, dated January 12, 1703-4, to W. Wharton, seems to those that have read it, to be nothing short of a demonstration, that both of you have been contriving to destroy the charter privileges of the province; and to obtain a commission for a court of chancery, alias, a court of bribery. A gentleman in London gave ten pounds for that letter, that so his friends in New England might see what was plotting against them.

3d. I am afraid that you cannot clear yourself from the guilt of much hypocrisy and falseness in the affair of the college. In 1686, when you accepted of an illegal arbitrary commission from the late K. James, you said, that the cow was dead, and therefore the calf in her belly: meaning the charter of the college and colony. You said (and truly enough) that it was not in the power of that government to constitute a corporation, it being contrary to a maxim in law, for a corporation to make a corporation. And all writers who handle the subject, say, that a college cannot be erected without sovereign authority. But how much have you of late, to serve a design, said and done contrary to your former assertions! What an happiness would it have been to the country and a glory to the college, to have had what was by the General Assembly in my Lord Bellamont's time, sent to and confirmed by royal authority. It is your fault, Sir, that it has not been done. For both Mr. Blathwait and Mr. Phips wrote, that if you desired it, the thing would be immediately dispatched. You promised me, you would endeavour it: yet some of the representatives told me at the same time, that you promised them the contrary. And I have been informed, that you have discouraged the matter from proceeding by letters home. Alas! Sir, your friends are not faithful as they ought to be. Some whom you have promoted will backbite you, and say you are the falsest man in the world. But which of them have attended the divine precept? Lev. xix. 17.

4th. I am afraid that the guilt of innocent blood is still crying in the ears of the Lord against you. I mean the blood of Leister and Milburn. My Lord Bellamont said to me, that he was one of the committee of Parliament who examined the matter; and that those men were not only murdered, but barbarously murdered. However, the murdered men have been cleared by the King, Lords, and Commons. It is out of my province to be a judge in things of this nature. Nevertheless, considering what the proper judges, who have had an impartial hearing of the case, have said, and what the gentleman who drew up a bill for taking off the attainder from those poor men, have written to me about it, I think you ought, for your family's sake, as well as your own, to lay that matter to heart, and consider whether you ought not to pray as Psalms, li. 14.

5th. I am afraid that the Lord is offended with you, in that you ordinarily forsake the worship of God in the holy church to which you are related, in the afternoon on the Lord's day, and after the publick exercise, spend the whole time with some persons reputed very ungodly men. I am sure your father did not so. Can you sanctify the Sabbath in a conversation with such men? Would you choose to be with them or such as they are in another world, unto which you are hastening? 2 Chron. xix. 2. I had like to have said, my heart mourns for you, because I believe greater troubles are very near unto you, than any that have befallen you from your youth unto this day; but I forbear, and may not at present acquaint you with.

But, Sir, there are at present two reasons which induced me

to discharge my conscience in laying before you my fears. One is, in that you have sometimes said, that if ever you had a spiritual father, I was the man. And there was a time when I encouraged the church, with whom I have been labouring in the work of the Lord these forty-six years and more, to call you to be my assistant in the ministry. The other is, that a letter thought to have been written by me, induced the late K. William to give you a commission for the government here. Sir H. Ashurst, in a letter dated the 25th of July last, says, that the day before a Right Honourable person, one of her Majesty's Privy Council, assured him, that it was a letter of my son's which you read to the King, that inclined him to give you a commission, and that the King thought the letter had been mine.

How glad should I be, if I could receive satisfaction that my fears of your being faulty, in the matters I have faithfully mentioned to you, are groundless; but if otherwise considering such scriptures as these, Isai. lviii. 1. Jer. xxiii. 28. Math. xiv. 4, 5. 1 Tim. v. 21. I am under pressures of conscience to bear a publick testimony without respect of persons; and I shall rejoice if it may be my dying testimony. I am now aged, expecting and longing for my departure out of the world every day. I trust in Christ that when I am gone, I shall obtain a good report of my having been faithful before him. To his mercy I commend you, and remain in him,

Yours to serve,

I. MATHER.

Boston, January 20, 1707–8.
  To the Governour.

COTTON MATHER

[Cotton Mather, the son of Increase, and the grandson, on his mother's side, of John Cotton, was born in 1663, graduated at Harvard in 1678, and died in 1728. His active life was, therefore, largely contemporaneous with that of his father, with whom he was associated in the pastorate of the North Church after 1685. Here the two men worked side by side as leaders of the movement to retain the old beliefs, and the old prerogatives of the ministers. Their connection with the witchcraft excitement, perhaps the best-known episode in their lives, shows how seriously they took to heart the backsliding of New England, and how ready they were to see in any occurrence a judgment of God on the apostasy of his followers. Unlike Increase Mather, Cotton never travelled out of New England; and he seems to have differed from his father in being more learned, more self-centred, more violent in his prejudices, and less urbane. A comparison between the extract from his letter to Governor Dudley and Increase Mather's letter on the same occasion will show the difference in the literary styles of the two men, and throw some interesting side-lights on their respective characters.

Cotton Mather was a man not only of great learning, but of great industry, and the amount of his writings was prodigious. The catalogue of his publications appended to his life by Samuel Mather contains three hundred and eighty-two titles, and it is known that he left still other printed works, besides many in manuscript. His publications range in size from sermons, which are of course most numerous, to the bulky "Magnalia Christi Americana: or, the Ecclesiastical History of New England, from its First Planting in the Year 1620, unto the Year of our Lord, 1698." This is his most representative and most considerable work, and contains seven books. The first tells of the founding of the colonies, the second of the lives of the governors, the third of the lives of sixty ministers, the fourth of Harvard College, the fifth of the "Acts and Monuments of the Faith and Order in the Churches of New England," the sixth of wonderful providences, and the seventh of "The Wars of the Lord." One of the most famous of Cotton Mather's works is "The Wonders of the Invisible World: being an Account of the Tryals of several Witches Lately Executed in New England," "Published by the Special Command of his Excellency the Governour of the Province of the Massachusetts-Bay in New-England," with the evident purpose of defending the action of the authorities in the proceedings at Salem. Another work which deserves mention is that commonly known as "Essays to do Good," which shows the practical side of the author, and had great influence on Benjamin Franklin. Cotton Mather is most readable in straightforward narratives, like his accounts of witchcraft, or his "Life of Sir William Phips";

and in his exhortations on practical matters. In dealing with religious and philosophical subjects he is likely to be pompously and ridiculously pedantic. It must not be inferred from the fact that several of the selections given below deal with witchcraft that this is the subject of any great proportion of the author's work.

The selections from "The Wonders of the Invisible World" are from the reprint in the "Library of Old Authors," London, 1862. The Letter to Governor Dudley is printed in the Collections of the Massachusetts His- · torical Society. All the other selections are from the first edition of the "Magnalia," London, 1702.]

SOME EVIDENCE THAT SUSANNA MARTIN WAS A WITCH

[From "The Wonders of the Invisible World"]

IV. *John Atkinson* testifi'd, That he exchanged a Cow with a Son of *Susanna Martin's*, whereat she muttered, and was unwilling he should have it. Going to receive this Cow, tho' he Hamstring'd her, and Halter'd her, she, of a Tame Creature, grew so mad, that they could scarce get her along. She broke all the Ropes that were fastned unto her, and though she were ty'd fast unto a Tree, yet she made her escape, and gave them such further trouble, as they could ascribe to no cause but Witchcraft.

V. *Bernard Peache* testifi'd, That being in Bed, on the Lord's-day Night, he heard a scrabbling at the Window, whereat he then saw *Susanna Martin* come in, and jump down upon the Floor. She took hold of this Deponent's Feet, and drawing his body up into an Heap, she lay upon him near Two Hours; in all which time he could neither speak nor stir. At length, when he could begin to move, he laid hold on her Hand, and pulling it up to his Mouth, he bit three of her Fingers, as he judged, unto the Bone. Whereupon she went from the Chamber, down the Stairs, out at the Door. This Deponent thereupon called unto the People of the House, to advise them of what passed; and he himself did follow her. The People saw her not; but there being a Bucket at the Left-hand of the Door, there was a drop of Blood found upon it; and several more drops of Blood upon the Snow newly fallen abroad: There was likewise the print of her 2 Feet just without the Threshold; but no more sign of any Footing further off.

At another time this Deponent was desired by the Prisoner, to come unto an Husking of Corn, at her House; and she said, *If he did not come, it were better that he did!* He went not; but the Night following, *Susanna Martin*, as he judged, and another came towards him. One of them said, *Here he is!* but he having a Quarter-staff, made a Blow at them. The Roof of the Barn, broke his Blow; but following them to the Window, he made another Blow at them, and struck them down; yet they got up, and got out, and he saw no more of them.

About this time, there was a Rumour about the Town, that *Martin* had a Broken Head; but the Deponent could say nothing to that.

The said *Peache* also testifi'd the Bewitching the Cattle to Death, upon *Martin's* Discontents.

VI. *Robert Downer* testified, That this Prisoner being some Years ago prosecuted at Court for a Witch, he then said unto her, *He believed she was a Witch.* Whereat she being dissatisfied said, *That some She-Devil would shortly fetch him away!* Which words were heard by others, as well as himself. The Night following, as he lay in his Bed, there came in at the Window, the likeness of a *Cat*, which flew upon him, took fast hold of his Throat, lay on him a considerable while, and almost killed him. At length he remembred what *Susanna Martin* had threatned the Day before; and with much striving he cried out, *Avoid, thou She-Devil! In the Name of God the Father, the Son, and the Holy Ghost, Avoid!* Whereupon it left him, leap'd on the Floor, and flew out at the Window.

And there also came in several Testimonies, that before ever *Downer* spoke a word of this Accident, *Susanna Martin* and her Family had related, *How this* Downer *had been handled!*

VII. *John Kembal* testified, that Susanna Martin, upon a Causeless Disgust, had threatned him, about a certain Cow of his, *That she should never do him any more Good:* and it came to pass accordingly. For soon after the Cow was found stark dead on the dry Ground, without any Distemper to be discerned upon her. Upon which he was followed with a strange Death upon more of his Cattle, whereof he lost in one Spring to the Value of Thirty Pounds. But the said *John Kembal* had a further Testimony to give in against the Prisoner which was truly admirable.

Being desirous to furnish himself with a Dog, he applied himself to buy one of this *Martin*, who had a Bitch with Whelps in her House. But she not letting him have his choice, he said, he would supply himself then at one *Blezdels*. Having mark'd a Puppy, which he lik'd at *Blezdels*, he met *George Martin*, the Husband of the Prisoner, going by, who asked him, *Whether he would not have one of his Wife's Puppies?* and he answered *No*. The same Day, one *Edmond Eliot*, being at *Martin's* House, heard *George Martin* relate, where this *Kembal* had been, and what he had said. Whereupon *Susanna Martin* replied, *If I live, I'll give him Puppies enough!* Within a few days after, this *Kembal*, coming out of the Woods, there arose a little Black Cloud in the N. W. and *Kembal* immediately felt a force upon him, which made him not able to avoid running upon the stumps of Trees, that were before him, albeit he had a broad, plain Cartway, before him; but tho' he had his Ax also on his Shoulder to endanger him in his Falls, he could not forbear going out of his way to tumble over them. When he came below the Meeting House, there appeared unto him, a little thing like a *Puppy*, of a Darkish Colour; and it shot backwards and forwards between his Legs. He had the courage to use all possible Endeavours of Cutting it with his Ax; but he could not Hit it: the Puppy gave a jump from him, and went, as to him it seem'd into the Ground. Going a little further, there appeared unto him a Black Puppy, somewhat bigger than the first, but as Black as a Cole. Its Motions were quicker than those of his Ax; it flew at his Belly, and away; then at his Throat; so, over his Shoulder one way, and then over his Shoulder another way. His Heart now began to fail him, and he thought the Dog would have tore his Throat out. But he recovered himself, and called upon God in his Distress; and naming the Name of JESUS CHRIST, it vanished away at once. The Deponent spoke not one Word of these Accidents, for fear of affrighting his Wife. But the next Morning *Edmond Eliot*, going into *Martin's* House, this Woman asked him where *Kembal* was? He replied, *At Home, a Bed, for ought he knew*. She returned, *They say, he was frighted last Night*.

Eliot asked, *With what?* She answered, *With Puppies. Eliot* asked, *Where she heard of it, for he had heard nothing of it?* She rejoined, *About the Town.* Altho' *Kembal* had mentioned the Matter to no Creature living.

VIII. *William Brown* testifi'd, That Heaven having blessed him with a most Pious and Prudent Wife, this Wife of his, one day met with *Susanna Martin;* but when she approach'd just unto her, *Martin* vanished out of sight, and left her extreamly affrighted. After which time, the said *Martin* often appear'd unto her, giving her no little trouble; and when she did come, she was visited with Birds, that sorely peck'd and prick'd her; and sometimes, a Bunch, like a Pullet's Egg, would rise in her Throat, ready to choak her, till she cry'd out, *Witch, you shan't choak me!* While this good Woman was in this extremity, the Church appointed a Day of Prayer, on her behalf; whereupon her Trouble ceas'd; she saw not *Martin* as formerly; and the Church, instead of their Fast, gave Thanks for her Deliverance. But a considerable while after, she being Summoned to give in some Evidence at the Court, against this *Martin,* quickly thereupon, this *Martin* came behind her, while she was milking her Cow, and said unto her, *For thy defaming her at Court, I'll make thee the miserablest Creature in the World.* Soon after which, she fell into a strange kind of distemper, and became horribly frantick, and uncapable of any reasonable Action; the Physicians declaring, that her Distemper was præternatural, and that some Devil had certainly bewitched her; and in that condition she now remained.

IX. *Sarah Atkinson* testify'd, That *Susanna Martin* came from *Amesbury* to their House at *Newbury,* in an extraordinary Season, when it was not fit for any to Travel. She came (as she said, unto *Atkinson*) all that long way on Foot. She brag'd and shew'd how dry she was; nor could it be perceived that so much as the Soles of her Shoes were wet. *Atkinson* was amazed at it; and professed, that she should her self have been wet up to the knees, if she had then came so far; but *Martin* reply'd, *She scorn'd to be Drabbled!* It was noted, that this Testimony upon her Trial, cast her in a very singular Confusion.

THE INVISIBILITY OF WITCHES

[From "The Wonders of the Invisible World"]

In all the *Witchcraft* which now Grievously Vexes us, I know not whether anything be more Unaccountable, than the Trick which the Witches have to render themselves, and their Tools *Invisible*. *Witchcraft* seems to be the Skill of Applying the *Plastic Spirit* of the World, unto some unlawful purposes, by means of a Confederacy with *Evil Spirits*. Yet one would wonder how the *Evil Spirits* themselves can do some things; especially at *Invisibilizing* of the Grossest Bodies. I can tell the Name of an Ancient Author, who pretends to show the *way*, how a man may come to walk about *Invisible*, and I can tell the Name of another Ancient Author, who pretends to Explode that way. But I will not speak too plainly Lest I should unawares Poison some of my *Readers*, as the pious *Hemingius* did one of his *Pupils*, when he only by way of Diversion recited a *Spell*, which, they had said, would cure *Agues*. This much I will say; The notion of procuring *Invisibility*, by any *Natural Expedient*, yet known, is, I Believe, a meer PLINYISM; How far it may be obtained by a *Magical Sacrament*, is best known to the Dangerous Knaves that have try'd it. But our *Witches* do seem to have got the knack: and this is one of the Things, that make me think, *Witchcraft* will not be fully understood, until the day when there shall not be one Witch in the World.

There are certain people very *Dogmatical* about these matters; but I'll give them only these three Bones to pick.

First, One of our bewitched people, was cruelly assaulted by a *Spectre*, that, she said, ran at her with a *spindle:* tho' no body else in the Room, could see either the *Spectre* or the *spindle*. At last, in her miseries, giving a snatch at the *Spectre*, she pull'd the *spindle* away, and it was no sooner got into her hand, but the other people then present, beheld, that it was indeed a Real, Proper, Iron *spindle*, belonging they knew to whom; which when they lock'd up very safe, it was nevertheless by *Demons* unaccountably stole away, to do further mischief.

Secondly, Another of our bewitched people, was haunted with a most abusive *Spectre*, which came to her, she said, with a *sheet* about her. After she had undergone a deal of Teaze, from the Annoyance of the *Spectre*, she gave a violent snatch at the sheet, that was upon it; wherefrom she tore a corner, which in her hand immediately became *Visible* to a Roomful of Spectators; a palpable Corner of a Sheet. Her Father, who was now holding her, catch'd that he might keep what his daughter had so strangely siezed, but the unseen *Spectre* had like to have pull'd his hand off, by endeavouring to wrest it from him; however he still held it, and I suppose has it, still to show; it being but a few hours ago, namely about the beginning of this *October*, that this Accident happened; in the family of one *Pitman*, at *Manchester*.

Thirdly, a young man, delaying to procure Testimonials for his Parents, who being under confinement on suspicion of *Witchcraft*, required him to do that service for them, was quickly pursued with odd Inconveniences. But once above the Rest, an Officer going to put his *Brand* on the Horns of some *Cows*, belonging to these people, which tho' he had siez'd for some of their debts, yet he was willing to leave in their possession, for the subsistence of the poor Family; this young man help'd in holding the Cows to be thus branded. The three first *Cows* he held well enough; but when the hot Brand was clap'd upon the Fourth, he *winc'd* and *shrunk* at such a Rate, as that he could hold the Cow no longer. Being afterwards Examined about it, he confessed, that at that very instant when the *Brand* entered the *Cow's Horn*, exactly the like burning *Brand* was clap'd upon his own Thigh; where he has exposed the lasting marks of it, unto such as asked to see them.

Unriddle these Things, — *Et Eris mihi magnus Apollo.*

A TEMPERANCE EXHORTATION OF 1698

[From "The Bostonian Ebenezer" [1]]

And Oh! That the Drinking-Houses in the Town might once come under a laudable *Regulation*. The Town has an *Enormous*

[1] The full title given by the author to this address is "The Bostonian Ebenezer. Some Historical Remarks on the State of Boston, the Chief Town of New-England, and of the English America. With Some Agreeable Methods for Preserving

Number of them; will the *Haunters* of those *Houses* hear the Counsels of Heaven? For *You* that are the *Town-Dwellers*, to be oft, or long in your *Visits* of the *Ordinary*, 'twill certainly expose you to Mischiefs more than ordinary. I have seen certain *Taverns*, where the Pictures of horrible *Devourers* were hang'd out for the *Signs;* and, thought I, 'twere well if such *Signs* were not sometimes too too *Significant:* Alas, Men have their Estates *devoured*, their Names *devoured*, their *Hours devoured*, and their very Souls *devoured*, when they are so besotted, that they are not in their Element, except they be Tipling at such Houses. When once a Man is bewitched with the *Ordinary*, what usually becomes of him? He is a *gone Man;* and when he comes to Die, he'll cry out as many have done, *Ale-Houses are Hell-Houses!* *Ale-Houses are Hell-Houses!* But let the *Owners* of those *Houses* also now hear our Counsels. *Oh! Hearken to me, that God may hearken to you another Day!* It is an *Honest*, and a *Lawful*, tho' it be not a very *Desireable* Employment, that you have undertaken: You may *Glorifie* the Lord Jesus Christ in your Employment if you will, and benefit the Town considerably. There was a very godly Man that was an *Innkeeper*, and a great Minister of God could say to that Man, in 3 *John* 2. *Thy Soul prospereth.* O let it not be said of you, since you are fallen into this Employment, *Thy Soul withereth!* It is thus with too many: Especially, when they that get a *License* perhaps to Sell Drink out of Doors, do stretch their *License* to Sell within Doors. Those *Private Houses*, when once a Professor of the Gospel comes to *Steal* a Living out of them, it commonly precipitates them into abundance of wretchedness and confusion. But I pray God assist you that keep *Ordinaries*, to keep the *Commandments* of God in them. There was an *Inn* at *Bethlehem* where the Lord JESUS CHRIST was to be met withal. Can *Boston* boast of many such? Alas, too ordinarily it may be said, *There is no Room for him in the Inn!* My Friends, let me beg it of you, banish *the unfruitful works of Darkness* from your *Houses*, and then the *Sun of Righteous-*

and Promoting the Good State of That, as well as any other Town in the like Circumstances." The text was 1 Sam. vii, 12; and it was delivered "At Boston Lecture, 7. d. 2. m. 1698." It is included in the "Magnalia," as a sort of appendix to Book I.]

ness will shine upon them. Don't countenance *Drunkenness, Revelling,* and *Mis-spending* of precious Time in your Houses: Let none have the *Snares of Death* laid for them in your Houses. You'll say, *I shall Starve then!* I say, *better Starve than Sin:* But you *shall not.* It is the Word of the Most High, *Trust in the Lord, and do Good, and verily thou shalt be Fed.* And is not *Peace of Conscience,* with a *Little,* better than those *Riches,* that will shortly melt away, and then run like Scalding Metal down the very Bowels of thy Soul?

THE DISCOVERY OF AMERICA

[From the "Magnalia," Book I, Chap. I [1]]

§ 1. It is the Opinion of some, though 'tis *but* an *Opinion, and but* of *some* Learned Men, That when the Sacred Oracles of Heaven assure us, *The Things under the Earth* are some of those, whose *Knees are to bow in the Name of Jesus,* by those *Things* are meant the Inhabitants of *America,* who are *Antipodes* to those of the other *Hemisphere.* I would not Quote any Words of *Lactantius,* tho' there are *some* to Countenance this Interpretation, because of their being so *Ungeographical:* Nor would I go to strengthen the Interpretation by reciting the Words of the *Indians* to the first *White Invaders* of their Territories, *We hear you are come from under the World, to take our World from us.* But granting the *uncertainty* of such an Exposition, I shall yet give the Church of God a certain Account of those *Things,* which in *America* have been Believing and Adoring the glorious *Name* of Jesus; and of that Country in *America,* where those *Things* have been attended with Circumstances most remarkable. I can contentedly allow that *America* (which as the Learned *Nicolas Fuller* Observes, might more justly be called *Columbina*) was altogether unknown to the *Penmen* of the Holy Scriptures, and in the *Ages* when the Scriptures were Penned. I can allow, that those Parts of the Earth, which do not include *America,* are in the inspired Writings of *Luke,* and of *Paul,* stiled, *All the World.* I can allow, that the

[[1] The title of the chapter is "Venisti tandem? *or Discoveries of* AMERICA, *tending to, and ending in, Discoveries of* NEW-ENGLAND."]

Opinion of *Torniellus*, and of *Pagius*, about the Apostles Preaching the Gospel in *America*, has been sufficiently refuted by *Basnagius*. But I am out of the reach of Pope *Zachary's* Excommunication. I can assert the Existence of the *American Antipodes:* And I can Report unto the *European* Churches great Occurrences among these *Americans*. Yet I will Report every one of them with such a Christian and exact Veracity, that no Man shall have cause to use about any one of them, the Words which the great *Austin* (as *great* as he was) used about the Existence of *Antipodes;* it is a Fable, and, *nulla ratione credendum*.

§ 2. If the *Wicked One in whom the whole World lyeth*, were *he*, who like a *Dragon*, keeping a Guard upon the spacious and mighty *Orchards* of *America*, could have such a *Fascination* upon the Thoughts of Mankind, that neither this *Balancing half* of the Globe should be considered in *Europe* till a little more than two Hundred Years ago, nor the *Clue* that might lead unto it, namely, the *Loadstone*, should be known, till a *Neapolitan* stumbled upon it, about an Hundred Years before; yet the overruling *Providence* of the *great God* is to be acknowledged, as well in the *Concealing* of America for so long a time, as in the *Discovering* of it, when the fulness of Time was come for the Discovery: For we may count *America* to have been concealed, while Mankind in the other *Hemisphere* had lost all Acquaintance with it, if we may conclude it had any from the Words of *Diodorus Siculus*, that *Phœnecians* were by great Storms driven off the Coast of Africa, far *Westward*, ἐπὶ πολλὰς ἡμέρας, *for many Days together*, and at last fell in with an Island of prodigious Magnitude: or from the Words of *Plato*, that beyond the Pillars of *Hercules* there was an Island in the *Atlantick* Ocean, ἄμα λιβύης καὶ Ἀσίας μἀζων *larger than* Africa *and* Asia *put together:* Nor should it pass without Remark, that *Three* most memorable things which have born a very great Aspect upon *Humane Affairs*, did near the same time, namely at the Conclusion of the *Fifteenth*, and the beginning of the *Sixteenth Century*, arise unto the World: The First was the *Resurrection of Literature;* the Second was the opening of *America;* the Third was the *Reformation* of *Religion*. But, as probably, the *Devil* seducing the first Inhabitants of *America* into it, therein aimed at the having of them and their

Posterity out of the sound of the *Silver Trumpets* of the *Gospel*,
then to be heard through the *Roman Empire;* if the *Devil* had
any Expectation, that by the Peopling of *America*, he should
utterly deprive any *Europeans* of the Two Benefits, *Literature*
and *Religion*, which dawned upon the miserable World, one just
before, t'other just *after*, the first famed *Navigation* hither, 'tis
to be hop'd he will be disappointed of that Expectation. The
Church of God must no longer be wrapp'd up in *Strabo's* Cloak:
Geography must now find work for a *Christiano-graphy* in Regions
far enough beyond the Bounds wherein the *Church* of God had
thro' all former Ages been circumscribed. Renown'd *Churches*
of Christ must be gathered where the Ancients once Derided
them that look'd for any *Inhabitants*. The Mystery of our Lord's
Garments, made *Four Parts*, by the Soldiers that cast *Lots* for
them, is to be accomplished in the good Sence put upon it by
Austin, who if he had known *America* could not have given a
better *Quadripartita vestis Domini Jesu, quadripartitam figuravit
ejus Ecclesiam, toto scilicet, qui quatuor partibus constat, terrarum
orbe diffusam.*

§ 3. Whatever Truth may be in that Assertion of one who
writes; *If we may credit any Records besides the Scriptures, I
know it might be said and proved well, that this New World was
known, and partly Inhabited by* Britains, *or by* Saxons *from* England, *Three or Four Hundred Years before the* Spaniards *coming
thither;* which Assertion is Demonstrated from the Discourses
between the *Mexicans* and the *Spaniards* at their first Arrival;
and the Popish *Reliques*, as well as *British* Terms and Words,
which the *Spaniards* then found among the *Mexicans*, as well as
from undoubted Passages, not only in other Authors, but in the
British Annals also: Nevertheless, Mankind generally agree to
give unto *Christopher Columbus*, a *Genoese*, the Honour of being
the First *European* that opened a way into these Parts of the World.
It was in the Year 1492. that this famous Man, acted by a most
vehement and wonderful *Impulse*, was carried into the *Northern
Regions* of this vast Hemisphere, which might more justly therefore
have receiv'd its *Name* from *Him*, than from *Americus Vesputius*
a *Florentine*, who in the Year 1497. made a further Detection of the
more *Southern Regions* in this Continent. So a *World*, which

has been one great Article among the *Res deperditae* of *Pancirollus*, is now *found out*, and the Affairs of the *whole World* have been affected by the finding of it. So the *Church* of our Lord Jesus Christ, well compared unto a *Ship*, is now *victoriously* sailing round the *Globe* after Sir *Francis Drake's* renowned Ship, called, *The Victory*, which could boast,

Prima ego velivolis ambivi cursibus orbem.

And yet the Story about *Columbus* himself must be corrected from the Information of *De la Vega*, That one *Sanchez*, a Native of *Helva* in *Spain*, did before him find out these Regions. He tells us, that *Sanchez* using to trade in a small vessel to the *Canaries*, was driven by a furious and tedious Tempest over unto these Western Countries; and at his return he gave to *Colon*, or *Columbus*, an account of what he had seen, but soon after died of a Disease he had got on his dangerous Voyage. However, I shall expect my Reader e're long to grant, that some things done since by Almighty God for the *English* in these Regions, have exceeded all that has hitherto been done for any other Nation: If this *New World* were not found out first by the *English;* yet in those regards that are of all the *greatest*, it seems to be found out more *for* them than any other.

THE LIFE OF MR. RALPH PARTRIDGE

[Chap. XI, Book III, of the "Magnalia"]

When *David* was driven from his Friends into the Wilderness, he made this Pathetical Representation of his Condition, *'Twas as when one doth hunt a Partridge in the Mountains.* Among the many worthy Persons who were persecuted into an *American* Wilderness, for their Fidelity to the Ecclesiastical Kingdom of our true *David*, there was one that bore the *Name*, as well as the *State*, of *an hunted Partridge.* What befel him, was, as *Bede* saith of what was done by *Fœlix, Juxta nominis sui Sacramentum.*

This was Mr. *Ralph Partridge*, who for no Fault but the *Delicacy* of his good *Spirit*, being distress'd by the Ecclesiastical *Setters*, had no Defence, neither of *Beak*, nor *Claw*, but a *Flight* over the Ocean.

The Place where he took Covert, was the Colony of *Plymouth*, and the Town of *Duxbury* in that *Colony*.

This *Partridge* had not only the Innocency of the *Dove*, conspicuous in his blameless and pious Life, which made him very acceptable in his Conversation; but also the Loftiness of an *Eagle*, in the great Soar of his intellectual Abilities. There are some Interpreters, who understanding *Church Officers* by the *living Creatures*, in the Fourth Chapter of the *Apocalypse*, will have the *Teacher* to be intended by the *Eagle* there, for his quick Insight into remote and hidden things. The Church of *Duxbury* had such an *Eagle* in their *Partridge*, when they enjoy'd such a *Teacher*.

By the same *Token*, when the *Platform of Church-Discipline* was to be compos'd, the *Synod* at *Cambridge* appointed three Persons to draw up each of them, *A Model of Church-Government, according to the Word of God*, unto the end, that out of those, the Synod might form what should be found most agreeable; which three Persons were Mr. *Cotton*, and Mr. *Mather*, and Mr. *Partridge*. So that in the Opinion of that Reverend Assembly, this Person did not come far behind the first three, for some of his Accomplishments.

After he had been *Forty Years* a faithful and painful Preacher of the Gospel, rarely, if ever, in all that while interrupted in his Work, by any Bodily Sickness, he dy'd in a good Old Age about the Year 1658.

There was one singular instance of a *weaned Spirit*, whereby he signalized himself unto the Churches of God. That was this: There was a time, when most of the Ministers in the Colony of *Plymouth*, left the Colony, upon the Discouragement which the want of a *competent Maintenance* among the needy and froward Inhabitants, gave unto them. Nevertheless, Mr. *Partridge* was, notwithstanding the *Paucity* and the *Poverty* of his Congregation, so afraid of being any thing that look'd like *a Bird wandring from his Nest*, that he remained with his poor People, till he *took Wing* to become a *Bird of Paradise*, along with the winged *Seraphim* of Heaven.

Epitaphium.

Avolavit! ————

PERSONAL OBSERVATIONS OF A BEWITCHED CHILD

[From the "Magnalia," Book VI, Chap. VII]

It was the Eldest of these Children that fell chiefly under my own Observation: For I took her home to my own Family, partly out of compassion to her Parents, but chiefly, that I might be a critical Eye-Witness of things that would enable me to confute the *Sadducism* of this Debauch'd Age. Here she continu'd well for some Days; applying *her self* to Actions of Industry and Piety: But *Nov.* 20. 1688. she cry'd out, *Ah, they have found me out!* and immediately she fell into her Fits; wherein *we* often observ'd, that she would cough up a Ball as big as a small Egg, into the side of her *Wind pipe*, that would near choak her, till by *Stroaking* and by *Drinking* it was again carry'd *down*.

When I pray'd in the Room, first her Hands were with a *strong*, tho' not *even* Force, clapt upon her Ears: And when her Hands were by our Force pull'd away, she cry'd out, *They make such a Noise, I cannot hear a Word!* She complain'd that *Glover's* Chain was upon her Leg; and assaying to go, her Gate was exactly such as the *chain'd Witch* had before she dy'd. When her *Tortures* pass'd over, still Frolicks would succeed, wherein she *would* continue *Hours*, yea, *Days* together, talking perhaps never *wickedly* but always *wittily* beyond her self: And at certain Provocations her Torments would *renew* upon her, till we had left off to Give them; yet she frequently told us in these Frolicks, *That if she might but steal or be drunk, she should be well immediately.* She told us, *that she must go down to the bottom of our Well*, (and we had much ado to hinder it) *for they said there was Plate there, and they would bring her up safely again.*

We *wonder'd* at this: For she had never heard of any Plate there; and we our *selves*, who had newly bought the House, were ignorant of it: but the *former Owner* of the House just then coming in, told us *There had been Plate for many Years lost at the Bottom of the Well*. Moreover, one singular Passion that frequently attended her, was this:

An *invisible Chain* would be clapt about her, and she in much pain and Fear, cry out when [*They*]¹ began to put it on. Sometimes we could with our Hands knock it off, as it began to be fasten'd: But ordinarily, when it was on, she *would* be pull'd out of her Seat, with such Violence, *towards* the Fire, that it was as much as one or two of us could do to keep her out. Her *Eyes* were not brought to be perpendicular to her Feet, *when* she rose out of her Seat, as the *Mechanism* of an humane Body requires in them that rise; but she was dragg'd *wholly* by other Hands. And if we stamp'd on the Hearth, just between her and the Fire, she scream'd out, *That by jarring the Chain, we hurt her.*

I may add, that [*They*] put an unseen Rope, with a cruel Noose, about her Neck, *whereby* she was choak'd until she was black in the Face: And tho' it was got off before it had kill'd her; yet there were the Red Marks of it, and of a Finger and a Thumb near it, remaining to be seen for some while afterwards. Furthermore, not only upon her own looking into the Bible, but if any one else in the Room did it, *wholly unknown* to her, she would fall into unsufferable Torments.

A *Quaker's Book* being brought her, she could quietly read whole Pages of it; only the Name of GOD and CHRIST, she still skipp'd over, being unable to pronounce it, except sometimes, stammering a Minute or two, or more upon it: And when we urg'd her to tell what the Word was that she miss'd, she would say, *I must not speak it: They say I must not. You know what it is:* 'Tis G, and O, and D. But a Book against *Quakerism* [*They*] would not *allow* her to meddle with. Such Books, as it might have been profitable and edifying for her to read, and especially her Catechisms, if she did but offer to read a Line in them, she would be cast into hideous Convulsions, and be tost about the House like a Foot ball: But Books of Jests being shewn her, she could read them well enough, and have cunning Descants upon them. *Popish Books* [*They*] would not hinder her from reading; but [*They*] would from reading Books against Popery. A Book which pretends to prove *That there are no Witches,* was easily read by her; only the Name *Devils* and *Witches* might not be utter'd. A Book which proves *That there are Witches,* being exhibited unto her, she might not read

[¹ Throughout this selection the brackets are those of the original.]

it: And that Expression in the Story of *Ann Cole*, about running to the Rock, always threw her into sore Confusions.

Divers of these Trials were made by many Witnesses: But I considering that there might be a Snare in it, put a seasonable Stop to this fanciful Business. Only I could not but be amaz'd at one thing: A certain Prayer-Book being brought her, she not only could read it very well, but also did read a large Part of it over, calling it her *Bible*, and putting a more than ordinary Respect upon it. If she were going into her Tortures, at the Tender of this Book, she would recover her self to read it: Only when she came to the Lord's Prayer now and then occurring in that Book, she would have her Eyes put out; so that she must turn over a new Leaf, and then she could read again. Whereas also there are *Scriptures* in that Book, she could read them there: but if any shew'd her the very same Scriptures in the *Bible* it self, she should sooner die than read them: And she was likewise made unable to read the *Psalms* in an ancient Metre, which this Prayer-Book had in the same Volume with it.

Besides these, there was another inexplicable Thing in her Condition. Ever now and then, an Invisible Horse would be brought unto her by those whom she only call'd [*Them,*] and [*Her Company,*] upon the Approach of which, her Eyes wou'd be still clos'd up: For (said she) *They say I am a Tell-tale, and therefore they will not let me see them.* Hereupon she would give a Spring as one mounting an Horse, and setling her self in a riding Posture, she would in her Chair be agitated, as one sometimes Ambling, sometimes Trotting, and sometimes Galloping very furiously. In these Motions we could not *perceive* that she was mov'd by the Stress of her *Feet* upon the Ground, for often she touch'd it not. When she had rode a Minute or two, she would seem to be at a *Rendezvous* with [*Them*] that were [*Her Company,*] and there she would maintain a Discourse with them, asking them many Questions concerning her self [we gave her none of ours] and have Answers from them which indeed none but herself perceiv'd. Then would she return and inform us, *How* [They] *did intend to handle her for a Day or two afterwards,* and some other things that she inquir'd. Her Horse would sometimes throw her with much *Violence;* especially if any one stabb'd or cut the Air under her. But she would briskly mount again, and perform her Fantastick

Journies, mostly in her Chair; but *sometimes* also she would be carry'd from her Chair, out of one Room into another, very odly, in the Postures of a riding Woman. At length, she *pretended*, that her Horse could ride up the Stairs; and unto admiration she rode, (that is, was toss'd as one that rode) up the Stairs. There then stood open the Study of one belonging to the Family: Into which entring, she stood immediately on her *Feet*, and cry'd out, *They are gone! They are gone! They say that they cannot,* —— *God won't let 'em come here!* Adding a Reason for it, which the *Owner* of the Study thought more *Kind* than *True*. And she *presently* and *perfectly* came to her self, so that her whole Discourse and Carriage was alter'd unto the greatest *measure of Sobriety:* and she sate reading of the Bible and other good Books, for a good part of the Afternoon. Her Affairs calling her anon to go down again, the *Dæmons* were in a quarter of a Minute as bad upon her as before; and her *Horse* was *waiting* for her. Some then to see *whether* there had not been a Fallacy in what had *newly* hapned, resolv'd for to have her up unto the Study, where she had been at ease before; but she was then so strangely distorted, that it was an *extream Difficulty* to drag her up stairs. The *Dæmons* would pull her out of the *Peoples* Hands, and make her *heavier* than perhaps *Three* of her self. With incredible Toil. (tho' she kept screaming, *They say I must not go in*) She was pull'd in; *where* she was no sooner got, but she could stand on her *Feet*, and with an alter'd Note, say, *Now I am well.*

She would be faint at first, and say, *She felt something to go out of her!* (the Noises whereof *we* sometimes heard, like those of a *Mouse*), but in a Minute or *two* she could apply her self to *Devotion,* and express her self with *Discretion*, as *well as ever* in her Life.

To satisfie some Strangers, the *Experiment* was divers times with the same Success, *repeated;* until my Lothness to have any thing done like making a Charm of a Room, caus'd me to forbid the Repetition of it. But enough of this. The Ministers of *Boston* and *Charlstown*, kept another Day of *Prayer with Fasting* for *Goodwin's* afflicted Family: After which, the Children had a *Sensible*, but a *Gradual Abatement* of their Sorrows, until *Perfect Ease* was at length restor'd unto them. The young Woman dwelt at my House the rest of the Winter; having by a *vertuous*

Conversation made her self enough *welcome* to the Family.   But e'er long, I thought it convenient for me to entertain my Congregation with a *Sermon* on the *memorable Providences* wherein these Children had been concern'd [*afterwards publish'd.*]   When I had begun to study my Sermon, her *Tormentors* again seiz'd upon her, and manag'd her with a special Design, as was plain, to disturb me in *what* I was then about.

In the worst of her Extravagancies formerly, she was more dutiful to my self than I had reason to expect: But now her *whole Carriage* to me was with a *Sawciness*, which I was not us'd any *where* to be treated *withal.*   She would knock at my Study door, affirming *That some below would be glad to see me*, tho' there was none that ask'd for me: And when I chid her for telling *what* was false, her *Answer* was *Mrs* Mather *is always glad to see you!*   She would call to me with numberless Impertinencies: And when I came *down*, she *would throw* things at me, tho' none of them could ever hurt me: And she would Hector me at a strange rate for something I was doing above, and threaten me with *Mischief* and *Reproach* that should revenge it.   *Few* Tortures now attended her, but such as *were* provok'd.   Her Frolicks were numberless; if we may call them hers.   I *was* in Latin telling some young Gentlemen, That if I should bid her look to God, her Eyes *would* be put out: Upon *which* her Eyes were presently serv'd so.   Perceiving that her Troublers understood *Latin*, some Trials were thereupon made *whether* they understood *Greek* and *Hebrew*, which it seems, they also did; but the *Indian* Languages they did seem not so *well* to understand.

When we *went* unto prayer, the *Dæmons* would *throw* her on the Floor at the Feet of him that pray'd, where she would whistle, and sing, and yell, to *drown* the Voice of the Prayer, and she would fetch *Blows* with her Fist, and Kicks with her Foot, at the Man that Pray'd: But still her Fist and Foot would always recoyl, when they came within an Inch or *two* of him, as if rebounding against a Wall: and then she would beg hard of other People to strike him, which (you may be sure) not being done, she cry'd out, *He has wounded me in the Head.*   But before the Prayer was over, she would be laid for dead, *wholly* senseless, and (unto appearance) breathless, with her Belly swell'd like a Drum; And sometimes with croaking Noises in her. Thus wou'd she lie, most exactly with the Stiffness and Posture of one that had been *two* Days laid out for dead. Once lying thus, as he that was praying, was alluding to the Words of the *Canaanites*, and saying, *Lord, have mercy on a Daughter vex'd with a Devil*, there came a big, but low voice from her, in which the Spectators did not see her Mouth to move, *There's two or three of us.* When Prayer was ended, she would revive in a Minute or two, and continue as frolicksome as before.

COTTON MATHER TO GOVERNOR DUDLEY

Boston, Jan. 20, 1707–8.

Sir,

There have appeared such things in your conduct, that a just concern for the welfare of your Excellency seems to render it necessary, that you should be *faithfully advised* of them. It was not without a design to introduce and exercise this *faithfulness*, that I have in divers letters to your Excellency, *sought out acceptable words*, and acknowledged every thing in the world, that might at all dispose you to give me the hearing. In some of those letters, I have indeed, with the language of the tribe of *Naphtali*, insinuated unto you, what those points were, wherein I earnestly desired that we might observe and confess you *laudable*. And I still imagined that you would at the same time understand my apprehension of there being points, wherein you were too defective. But your Excellency compels me to see that the *schemes of speaking* and *modes of addressing* used among persons of the most polite education, will not answer the expectation I have had of them. You will give me leave to write nothing, but in a style, whereof an ignorant mob, to whom (as well as the *General Assembly*) you think fit to communicate what *fragments* you please of my letters, must be *competent judges*. I must proceed accordingly. And though I may complain of it, that the letters, which I have written formerly to your Excellency, have been improved unto my *damage;* yet I will now venture another, which if it may be for *your service*, I care not, though it be as much for my *detriment* as any of the rest, and exposed as an *appendix* unto them. A letter of mine, the reading whereof to K. William was (as I have heard) of some small service to you in obtaining his royal determination, that you should have his commission for the government, brought upon me an extreme displeasure in the country.   I proposed therein to return good for evil, to conquer evil with good, and retaliate (in my own way) the venoms which you poured upon me, in your last conference with my father, at your leaving *New England.*   And if I never saw after this an expression of your *gratitude,* yet I saw all that I proposed.   However, to hand such a *gross untruth* about the country, as a report (which I hear some of your counsellors do as from you) that at the time of my writing *that letter,* I wrote *another* quite the contrary, to do you a disservice, is but a very mean requital.

When that letter was written, I weakly believed that the *wicked* and *horrid* things done before the *righteous revolution,* had been heartily repented of; and that the rueful business at New York, which many illustrious persons of both houses of parliament often called a *barbarous murder,* and which the king, lords and commons, by an *act of parliament* invited all persons to think so, had been considered with such a repentance, as might save you and your family from any further *storms* of *heaven* for the revenging of it.   I flattered myself with a belief, that you would know no interests but those of a glorious Christ, and of his *people and kingdom, and study what you should render to him* for his wonderful dispensations towards you, in restoring you to your family, with the government of a people, with whom you had been in such evil circumstances.   The whole country were witnesses to some of my poor and plain endeavours, to do the part of a *faithful monitor* unto you, in the *portraiture of a good man,* at your arrival.   Sir, had you then received your government with serious and thankful considerations, perpetually carried on, *how to discharge it as a stewardship for the glorious Lord,* and how to make this an holy and an happy people; and resolution in it to do nothing but what should be *just* and *good;* how honourably, how comfortably would your government have at last expired!   Your late epitaph would have been, *Them that honour me, I will honour.*   And in the mean time, you would not have known the meaning of *a troubled sea.* You might have maintained a very *inoffensive conduct* towards the gentlemen of whom most of all you have stood in fear: or if they had been uneasy, the great God would have accomplished for you the word which the Emperor *Maximilian* wrote upon his tables: whereas now, they are the very persons by whose means most of all *your fear is like to come upon you.* It seems as if the glorious Lord had a controversy with you. He has raised you up very powerful enemies. The best office of love that can be done for you, is, to assist you that your ways *may please* the glorious Lord, and remind you wherein you have *not pleased* him.

Sir, your *snare* has been that thing, the *hatred* whereof is most expressly required of the *ruler*, namely COVETOUSNESS. When a governour shall make his government more an engine to enrich himself, than to *befriend his country*, and shall by the *unhallowed hunger* of riches be prevailed withal to do many wrong, base, dishonourable things; it is a covetousness which will shut *out from the kingdom of heaven;* and sometimes the *loss of a government on earth* also is the punishment of it. Now, Sir, much of this has appeared in your administration; and the disposition *to make haste to be rich* has betrayed you unto things, from which many have wondered, that the *natural goodness*, which they thought was in your *temper*, has not restrained you.

SAMUEL SEWALL

[Samuel Sewall was born in England in 1652, and died in Massachusetts in 1730. His grandparents were residents of America, and his parents had been married in this country, though they lived in England during his early boyhood. He was graduated from Harvard in 1671, and became a resident fellow of the college and for a time keeper of the college library. He studied for the ministry, but finally decided to enter business. During almost all his life he was prominent in public affairs. As one of the Salem witch-judges, he was vigorous in performing what he thought to be his duty. But when, five years later, he had become convinced of his mistake, he caused his famous Bill to be read in the public congregation, while he stood with bowed head in token of penitence. This action, which for a time cost him the friendship of the Mathers and others of his old associates, has done much to heighten the respect with which he has been deservedly held by later generations.

Judge Sewall's voluminous "Diary," which was begun in 1673, when he was still a student at Harvard, and continued until 1729, just before his death, is one of the most readable and valuable writings of the colonial time. It gives a picture of the political and social life of a half century, as it appeared to an alert man of affairs; and it reveals with perfect frankness the personality of the author. Like all works of the kind, it cannot be adequately represented by selections. In the following pages the Diary for January, 1701, contains a sufficient number of consecutive entries to give a slight idea of the whole; and the other selections are detached passages of special interest. Judge Sewall was three times married, and in the intervals of his widowhood conducted several unsuccessful courtships. The propriety of publishing the parts of the "Diary" in which these are recounted may well be questioned, but since they have been made public, a few entries are given regarding the most famous of these unfortunate love affairs. In his lifetime Judge Sewall published only a few pamphlets, including "The Selling of Joseph," said to be the first anti-slavery tract issued in America, and "Phænomena quaedam Apocalyptica ad Aspectum Novi Orbis configurata. Or, some few Lines towards a description of the New Heaven as It makes to those who stand upon the New Earth." This last aims to prove from the more mystical prophecies of the Bible that America may be the seat of the New Jerusalem; and shows something of the minute study of the Scriptures which formed one of the author's chief avocations throughout his life. His "Diary," his "Letter-Book," and some other manuscripts have been published by the Massachusetts Historical Society.

The selections from the "Diary" are from the Collections of the Massachusetts Historical Society, Fifth Series. The passage from "Phænomena quaedam Apocalyptica" is from the second edition, Boston, 1727.]

DISCIPLINE AT HARVARD COLLEGE IN 1674

[From the "Diary"]

Thomas Sargeant was examined by the Corporation: finally, the advice of Mr. Danforth, Mr. Stoughton, Mr. Thatcher, Mr. Mather, (then present) was taken. This was his sentence.

That being convicted of speaking blasphemous words concerning the H. G. he should be therefore publickly whipped before all the Scholars. 2. That he should be suspended as to taking his degree of Bachelour (this sentence read before him twice at the Prts. before the committee, and in the library 1 up before execution). 3. Sit alone by himself in the Hall uncovered at meals, during the pleasure of the President and Fellows, and be in all things obedient, doing what exercise was appointed him by the President, or else be finally expelled the Colledge. The first was presently put in execution in the Library (Mr. Danforth, Jr. being present) before the Scholars. He kneeled down and the instrument Goodman Hely attended the President's word as to the performance of his part of the work. Prayer was had before and after by the President.

JUDGE SEWALL'S PETITION OF PENITENCE

[From the "Diary" for 169⅚]

Copy of the Bill I put up on the Fast day; giving it to Mr. Willard as he pass'd by, and standing up at the reading of it, and bowing when finished; in the Afternoon.

Samuel Sewall, sensible of the reiterated strokes of God upon himself and family; and being sensible, that as to the guilt contracted upon the opening of the late Commission of Oyer and Terminer at Salem (to which the order for this Day relates) he is, upon many accounts, more concerned than any that he knows of, Desires to take the Blame and shame of it, Asking pardon of men, And especially desiring prayers that God, who has an Unlimited Authority, would pardon that sin and all other his sins; personal and Relative: And according to his infinite Benignity, and Sovereignty, Not Visit the sin of him, or of any other, upon himself

or any of his, nor upon the Land: But that He would powerfully defend him against all Temptations to Sin, for the future;
and vouchsafe him the efficacious, saving Conduct of his Word
and Spirit.

THE EVENTS OF A MONTH

[From the "Diary"]

Jany. 1. 1700/1701. Just about Break-a-day Jacob Amsden and 3
other Trumpeters gave a Blast with the Trumpets on the common
near Mr. Alford's [in Margin, — Entrance of the 18th Century].
Then went to the Green Chamber, and sounded there till about
sunrise. Bellman said these verses a little before Break-a-day,
which I printed and gave them. [in Margin — My verses upon
New Century.]

> Once more! our God vouchsafe to shine:
> Correct the Coldness of our Clime.
> Make haste with thy Impartial Light,
> And terminate this long dark night.

> Give the poor Indians Eyes to see
> The Light of Life: and set them free.
> So Men shall God in Christ adore,
> And worship Idols vain, no more.

> So Asia, and Africa,
> Eurôpa, with America;
> All Four, in Consort join'd, shall Sing
> New Songs of Praise to Christ our King.

The Trumpeters cost me five pieces ⅝. Gave to the College-
Library Dr. Owens two last Volumes on the Hebrews. Sent them
by Amsden. When was about to part with Dr. Owen, I look'd, to
read some difficult place; pitch'd on v. 11th of the 8th Chapter —
Know the Lord — I read it over and over one time and another
and could not be satisfied: At last this came in my mind Know the
Lord, *i.e.* Know the Messiah, to whom the word Lord is very
much appropriated &c. *vide locum.* Now my mind was at quiet,
and all seem'd to run smooth. As I hope this is Truth, so I bless

God for this New-years Gift; which I also writt in a spare place, and gave it with the Book to the College.

Satterday, Jany. 4 $\frac{1700}{1701}$. Mrs. Thair is this morn taken with an Apoplexy after she had been up and employ'd a while; was at our pump for water. Dies about six in the Evening.

Between 2 and 3 in the Afternoon Mr. Sergeant, Col. Townsend, and I take the Affidavits of Barth. Green, Jno. Allen and Timo. Green. Present Mr. T. Brattle, Mr. Mico, and Tuthil notified. Mr. Nathl. Oliver, Mr. Hern, Mr. Keeling: Mr. Hirst and my Son. I do not remember any more. Mr. Keeling, upon enquiry, what he call'd for pen and Ink for, whether twas to take notes or no: He own'd it was. Then I said I would also send for one to write, naming Mr. Barnard; so he forebore, and said he would not write.

Jany. 7th. Mrs. Thair is buried: By reason of the Court, Stars were seen before we went; but comfortably Light by remains of the Day. Moon-shine and Snow.

Bearers, Cook, Sewall, Addington, Oakes, Melyen, Maryon, Jno. Buried in the new burying place, close to the Alms-house Ground.

Friday, Jany. 10. $\frac{1700}{1701}$. Mr. John Wait came to me, and earnestly desired me to hasten consummating the Marriage between his Bastian and Jane, Mrs. Thair's Negro. This day I waited upon the Lt. Governour at Dorchester and spent about two hours in looking over and ordering Corporation Bonds, but brought none away with me. I shewed Mr. Green's paper, and asked his Honor's Leave to use his Name. Shew'd it in the morn to Col. Townsend at his own house, and to Mr. Sergeant at his, the night before. I had promised that nothing should be tack'd to their Names, but they should first have a sight of it.

Boston, Jany. 13 $\frac{1700}{1701}$.

Madam, — The inclosed piece of Silver, by its bowing, humble form bespeaks your Favor for a certain young Man in Town. The Name [Real] the Motto [Plus ultra] seem to plead its suitableness for a Present of this Nature. Neither need you to except against the quantity: for you have the Mends in your own hand; And by your generous Acceptance, you may make both it and the Giver Great.

Madam, I am

Your Affect. Friend   S. S.

R

Jany. 14th. Having been certified last night about 10 oclock of the death of my dear Mother at Newbury, Sam. and I set out with John Sewall, the Messenger, for that place. Hired Horses at Charlestown: set out about 10. aclock in a great Fogg. Din'd at Lewis's with Mr. Cushing of Salisbury. Sam and I kept on in Ipswich Rode, John went to accompany Bro. from Salem. About Mr. Hubbard's in Ipswich farms, they overtook us. Sam. and I lodg'd at Crompton's in Ipswich. Bro. and John stood on for Newbury by Moon-shine. Jany. 15th Sam. and I set forward. Brother Northend meets us. Visit Aunt Northend, Mr. Payson. With Bro. and sister we set forward for Newbury: where we find that day appointed for the Funeral: twas a very pleasant Comfortable day.

Bearers, Jno. Kent of the Island, Lt. Cutting Noyes, Deacon William Noyes, Mr. Peter Tappan, Capt. Henry Somersby, Mr. Joseph Woolbridge. I follow'd the Bier single. Then Bro. Sewall and sister Jane, Bro. Short and his wife, Bro. Moodey and his wife, Bro. Northend and his wife, Bro. Tappan and sister Sewall, Sam. and cous. Hannah Tappan. Mr. Payson of Rowley, Mr. Clark, Minister of Excester, were there. Col. Pierce, Major Noyes &c. Cous. John, Richard and Betty Dummer. Went abt. 4. p. m. Nathanl. Bricket taking in hand to fill the Grave, I said, Forbear a little, and suffer me to say That amidst our bereaving sorrows We have the Comfort of beholding this Saint put into the rightfull possession of that Happiness of Living desir'd and dying Lamented. She liv'd commendably Four and Fifty years with her dear Husband, and my dear Father: And she could not well brook the being divided from him at her death; which is the cause of our taking leave of her in this place. She was a true and constant Lover of Gods Word, Worship, and Saints: And she always, with a patient cheerfullness, submitted to the divine Decree of providing Bread for her self and others in the sweat of her Brows. And now her infinitely Gracious and Bountiful Master has promoted her to the Honor of higher Employments, fully and absolutely discharged from all manner of Toil, and Sweat. My honoured and beloved Friends and Neighbours! My dear Mother never thought much of doing the most frequent and homely offices of Love for me; and lavish'd away many Thousands of

Words upon me, before I could return one word in Answer: And therefore I ask and hope that none will be offended that I have now ventured to speak one word in her behalf; when shee her self is become speechless. Made a Motion with my hand for the filling of the Grave. Note, I could hardly speak for passion and Tears. Mr. Tappan pray'd with us in the evening. I lodg'd at sister Gerrishes with Joseph. Bro. and Sam. at Br. Tappans. Jany. 16th. The two Brothers and four sisters being together, we took Leave by singing of the 90th Psalm, from the 8th to the 15th verse inclusively. Mr. Brown the Scholar, was present. Set out abt. 11 for Ipswich, got time enough to hear Mr. Rogers preach the Lecture from Luke 1. 76. about ministerial preparation for Christ. Sung the nine first verses of the 132. Psalm. Mr. Rogers prai'd for the prisoner of death, the Newbury woman who was there in her chains. This is the last Sermon preached in the old Meeting-house. Eat Roost Fowl at Crompton's. Delivered a Letter to the Widow Hale; got very comfortably over the Ferry to Brothers, whether Mr. Hirst quickly came to welcome us and invite us to dine or breakfast next day, which we did, the morning being cold: Visited Madam Bradstreet and Major Brown, and told them of the death of their fellow-passenger. Rec'd me very courteously. Took horse about one p. m. Baited at Lewis's; Stop'd at Govr. Usher's to pay him a visit. He and his Lady being from home, we pass'd on, and got to Charlestown about Sun-set, very comfortably. Found all well at home through the Goodness of God.

Lords-Day, Jany. 29th. $\frac{1700}{1701}$. Ipswich people Meet the first time in their New-Meeting-House, as Deacon Knowlton informs me at Cousin Savages Meeting Jany. 22th.

Jany. 29th $\frac{1700}{1701}$. Sam and I went to Dedham Lecture, and heard Mr. Belchar preach excellently from Mat. 9. 12. Dined at said Belchars. Gave him and some young men with him my New-years verses: He read them and said Amen. Said twas a good Morning's Work.

Jany. 30. Mr. Willard preaches from Eccles. 9. 2. — he that sweareth and he that feareth an Oath. Spoke very closely against the many ways of Swearing amiss. Great Storm.

A NEIGHBORLY ADMONITION

[From the "Diary" for 1701]

Tuesday, June 10th. Having last night heard that Josiah Willard had cut off his hair (a very full head of hair) and put on a Wigg, I went to him this morning. Told his Mother what I came about, and she call'd him. I enquired of him what Extremity had forced him to put off his own hair, and put on a Wigg? He answered, none at all. But said that his Hair was streight, and that it parted behinde. Seem'd to argue that men might as well shave their hair off their head, as off their face. I answered men were men before they had hair on their faces, (half of mankind have never any). God seems to have ordain'd our Hair as a Test, to see whether we can bring our minds to be content to be at his finding: or whether we would be our own Carvers, Lords, and come no more at Him. If disliked our Skin, or Nails; 'tis no thanks to us, that for all that, we cut them not off: Pain and danger restrain us. Your Calling is to teach men self Denial. Twill be displeasing and burdensom to good men: And they that care not what men think of them care not what God thinks of them. Father, Bro. Simon, Mr. Pemberton, Mr. Wigglesworth, Oakes, Noyes (Oliver), Brattle of Cambridge their example. Allow me to be so far a *Censor Morum* for this end of the Town. Pray'd him to read the Tenth Chapter of the Third book of Calvins Institutions. I read it this morning in course, not of choice. Told him that it was condemn'd by a Meeting of Ministers at Northampton in Mr. Stoddards house, when the said Josiah was there. Told him of the Solemnity of the Covenant which he and I had lately enterd into, which put me upon discoursing to him. He seem'd to say would leave off his Wigg when his hair was grown. I spake to his Father of it a day or two after: He thank'd me that had discoursed his Son, and told me that when his hair was grown to cover his ears, he promis'd to leave off his Wigg. If he had known of it, would have forbidden him. His Mother heard him talk of it; but was afraid positively to forbid him; lest he should do it, and so be more faulty.

MEDITATION AND PRAYER

[From the "Diary"]

Febr. 28. 17⅟₁ Midweek: This being my Marriage-day, and having now liv'd in a married Estate Five and Thirty years, notwithstanding my many Sins and Temptations, I spent some time in Meditation and Prayer in the Castle-Chamber. I was much encouraged by reading in Course the 32d. Psalm at family prayer without any foresight of mine. And when I came to pray I was much heartened to ask Forgiveness of God for my multiplied Transgressions, seeing He had directed Peter a sinfull Mortal to forgive 70. times 7. I hope God will forgive and do as the matter may require. While I was thus employ'd Maxwell warned me to Council; but I ventur'd to keep in my Closet; and I understand by the Majr. Genl. they did nothing in Council. Majr. Genl. and his Lady visited us just before the Funeral. Bearers of Mrs. Allen were, Elisha Hutchinson, Saml. Sewall; Giles Dyer, Saml. Checkley; John Cutler, Saml. Phillips: Scarves and Gloves. Whiles I was Spending a little Fewel in privat Devotion I was supply'd with a great Penniworth of Bast by Bastian, and a Load of black Oak by Nathl. Sparhawk.

A LOVE–LETTER AND SOME VISITS OF COURTSHIP

[From the "Diary" for 1720]

[I]

8r. 11th. I writ a few Lines to Madam Winthrop to this purpose: "Madam, These wait on you with Mr. Mayhew's Sermon, and Account of the state of the Indians on Martha's Vinyard. I thank you for your Unmerited Favours of yesterday; and hope to have the Happiness of Waiting on you to-morrow before Eight a-clock after Noon. I pray GOD to keep you, and give you a joyfull entrance upon the Two Hundred and twenty ninth year of Christopher Columbus his Discovery; and take Leave, who am, Madam, your humble Servt.   S. S.

Sent this by Deacon Green, who deliver'd it to Sarah Chickering, her Mistress not being at home.

8r. 12. Give Mr. Whittemore and Willard their Oath to Dr. Mather's Inventory. Visit Mr. Cooper. Go to the Meeting at the Wido Emon's: Mr. Manly pray'd, I read half Mr. Henry's 12th Chapter of the L. Supper. Sung 1., 2, 3, 4, 5, 10, and 12th Verses of the 30th Psalm. Bro. Franklin concluded with Prayer. At Madm. Winthrop's Steps I took leave of Capt Hill, &c.

Mrs. Anne Cotton came to door (twas before 8.) said Madam Winthrop was within, directed me into the little Room, where she was full of work behind a Stand; Mrs. Cotton came in and stood. Madam Winthrop pointed to her to set me a Chair. Madam Winthrop's Countenance was much changed from what 'twas on Monday, look'd dark and lowering. At last, the work, (black stuff or Silk) was taken away, I got my Chair in place, had some Converse, but very Cold and indifferent to what 'twas before. Ask'd her to acquit me of Rudeness if I drew off her Glove. Enquiring the reason, I told her twas great odds between handling a dead Goat, and a living Lady. Got it off. I told her I had one Petition to ask of her, that was, that she would take off the Negative she laid on me the third of October; She readily answer'd she could not, and enlarg'd upon it; She told me of it so soon as she could; could not leave her house, children, neighbours, business. I told her she might do some Good to help and support me. Mentioning Mrs. Gookin, Nath, the widow Weld was spoken of; said I had visited Mrs. Denison. I told her Yes! Afterward I said, If after a first and second Vagary she would Accept of me returning, Her Victorious Kindness and Good Will would be very Obliging. She thank'd me for my Book, (Mr. Mayhew's Sermon), But said not a word of the Letter. When she insisted on the Negative, I pray'd there might be no more Thunder and Lightening, I should not sleep all night. I gave her Dr. Preston, The Church's Marriage and the Church's Carriage, which cost me 6s. at the Sale. The door standing open, Mr. Airs came in, hung up his Hat, and sat down. After awhile, Madam Winthrop moving , he went out. Jno. Eyre look'd in, I said How do ye, or, your servant Mr. Eyre: but heard no word from him. Sarah fill'd a Glass of Wine, she drank to me, I to her, She sent Juno home with me with a good Lantern, I gave her 6d. and bid her thank her Mistress. In some of our Discourse, I told her I had rather go to the Stone-House adjoining to her, than to come to her against her mind. Told her the reason why I came every other night was lest I should drink too deep draughts of Pleasure. She had talk'd of Canary, her Kisses were to me better than the best Canary. Explain'd the expression Concerning Columbus.

[II]

8r. 21 Friday, My Son, the Minister, came to me p.m. by appointment and we pray one for another in the Old Chamber; more especially respecting my Courtship. About 6. a-clock I go to Madam Winthrop's; Sarah told me her Mistress was gon out, but did not tell me whither she went. She presently order'd me a Fire; so I went in, having Dr. Sibb's Bowels with me to read. I read the two first Sermons, still no body came in: at last about 9. a-clock Mr. Jno. Eyre came in; I took the opportunity to say to him as I had done to Mrs. Noyes before, that I hoped my Visiting his Mother would not be disagreeable to him; He answered me with much Respect. When twas after 9. a-clock He of himself said he would go and call her, she was but at one of his Brothers: A while after I heard Madam Winthrop's voice, enquiring somthing about John. After a good while and Clapping the Garden door twice or thrice, she came in. I mention'd somthing of the lateness; she banter'd me, and said I was later. She receiv'd me Courteously. I ask'd when our proceedings should be made publick: She said They were like to be no more publick than they were already. Offer'd me no Wine that I remember. I rose up at 11 a-clock to come away, saying I would put on my Coat, She offer'd not to help me. I pray'd her that Juno might light me home, she open'd the Shutter, and said twas pretty light abroad; Juno was weary and gon to bed. So I came home by Star-light as well as I could. At my first coming in, I gave Sarah five Shillings. I writ Mr. Eyre his name in his Book with the date Octobr. 21, 1720. It cost me 8s. Jehovah jireh! Madam told me she had visited M. Mico, Wendell, and Wm. Clark of the South.

Octobr. 22. Daughter Cooper visited me before my going out of Town, staid till about Sun set. I brought her going near as far as the Orange Tree. Coming back, near Leg's Corner, Little David Jeffries saw me, and looking upon me very lovingly, ask'd me if I was going to see his Grandmother? I said, Not to-night. Gave him a peny, and bid him present my Service to his Grandmother.

Octobr. 24. I went in the Hackny Coach through the Common, stop'd at Madam Winthrop's (had told her I would take my departure from thence). Sarah came to the door with Katee in her Arms: but I did not think to take notice of the Child. Call'd her Mistress. I told her, being encourag'd by David Jeffries loving eyes, and sweet Words, I was come to enquire whether she could find in her heart to leave that House and Neighbourbood, and go and dwell with me at the South-end; I think she said softly, Not yet. I told her It did not ly in my Lands to keep a Coach. If I should, I should be in danger to be brought to keep company with her Neighbour Brooker, (he was a little before sent to prison for Debt). Told her I had an Antipathy against those who would pretend to give themselves; but nothing of their Estate. I would a proportion of my Estate with my self. And I supposed she would do so. As to a Perriwig, My best and greatest Friend, I could not possibly have a greater, began to find me with Hair before I was born, and had continued to do so ever since; and I could not find in my heart to go to another. She commended the book I gave her, Dr. Preston, the Church Marriage; quoted him saying 'twas inconvenient keeping out of a Fashion commonly used. I said the Time and Tide did circumscribe my Visit. She gave me a Dram of Black-Cherry Brandy, and gave me a lump of the Sugar that was in it. She wish'd me a good Journy. I pray'd God to keep her, and came away. Had a very pleasant Journy to Salem.

[III]

Monday, Novr. 7th. My Son pray'd in the Old Chamber. Our time had been taken up by Son and Daughter Cooper's Visit; so that I only read the 130th and 143. Psalm. Twas on the Account of my Courtship. . I went to Mad. Winthrop; found her rocking her little Katee in the Cradle. I excus'd my Coming so late (near Eight). She set me an arm'd Chair and Cusheon; and so the Cradle was between her arm'd Chair and mine. Gave her the remnant of my Almonds; She did not eat of them as before; but laid them away; I said I came to enquire whether she had alter'd her mind since Friday, or remained of the same mind still. She said, Thereabouts. I told her I loved her, and was so fond as to think that she loved me: She said she had a great respect for me. I told her, I had made her an offer, without asking any advice; she had so many to advise with, that twas a hindrance. The Fire was come to one short Brand besides the Block, which Brand was set up in end; at last it fell to pieces, and no Recruit was made: She gave me a Glass of Wine. I think I repeated again that I would go home and bewail my Rashness in making more haste than good Speed. I would endeavour to contain myself, and not go on to sollicit her to do that which she could not Consent to. Took leave of her. As came down the steps she bid me have a Care. Treated me Courteously. Told her she had enter'd the 4th year of her Widowhood. I had given her the News-Letter before: I did not bid her draw off her Glove as sometime I had done. Her Dress was not so clean as somtime it had been. Jehovah jireh!

Midweek, 9r. 9th. Dine at Bro. Stoddard's: were so kind as to enquire of me if they should invite M'm Winthrop; I answer'd No.

SCRIPTURAL PROPHECIES CONCERNING AMERICA

[From "*Phænomena quædam Apocalyptica,*" etc.]

Some judicious and learned Divines have conjectured that *America* is prophesied of in the thirty seventh of *Ezekiel*, under the denomination of a Valley. Certainly, no part of the habitable World, can shew more Bones; or bones more *dry*, than these vast Regions do. Mr. *Downam* thinks that Mr. *Eliot's* taking his Text from thence when he first preached to the *Indians*, has its weight. His Appendix to the Letters from *New-England*, is well worth the reading. The Prophet is said to be carried out in the spirit: and for ought I know, he might be carried beyond the limits of the then known World.

Dan. 11. 45. `And he shall plant the tabernacles of his palace between the seas in the glorious holy Mountain; yet he shall come to his end, and, none shall help him.*

The complexion of this portion of Scripture is such, as constrains me to imagin, that the place designed by the holy Spirit, is no other than *America.* Every word almost has an emphasis carrying in it, to me, the perswasion of this sence. They who remove from one Land to another, there to dwell; that settlement of theirs is call'd a Plantation. Especially, when a Land, before rude and unfurnish'd, is by the New-comers replenished with usefull Arts, Vegetables, Animals. Thus when in the year 1492. *Christopher Columbus* had opened the way, the *Spaniards* planted themselves in the spatious Regions of *America;* and, too much, planted Antichristianisme in the room of Heathenisme.

Tabernacles] So called from the moveableness of their condition, and shortness of their continuance. As Tents, they were lately set up; and, notwithstanding all their Praemunitions, so far as they are *Antichristian*, they shall be taken down before it be long, by the immovable Counsel and Providence of God.

Palace] The Extent, Riches, and Pomp of the *Mexican*, and *Peruvian* Empires are very great: Insomuch that when the Church of *Rome* met with Losses in *Europe*, they pleased themselves with their Gains in the *New-World.* They glory in the many Churches they have planted there; which are, they say, without all mixture of Hereticks. If with Mr. *Nicholas Fuller*, Miscel. sacr. lib. 5. cap. 18. we take this word to signifie *Equile Regium*, Horse-Guards; It will still look upon *America.* The Reputation the *Spaniards* Horses gave them, did much contribute towards their prodigious Conquests. And after above threescore dangerous battels, *Mexico* was at last taken upon *Hippolytus* day; *August* 13, 1521. Since which time, Horses, which were never seen there before, are one of the four Fair Things of that Citie.

Between the Seas] The middle Provinces of the New-World, governed by the Vice-Roys of *Mexico*, and *Peru*, are known to lye between two of the most wide, and famous Seas of the whole World. The *American* Isthmus; respecting its own narrowness, and the bold approaches of the huge Ocean on either side, does command the title of *Non such*. *America* it self, and they who pass thither, are so much concerned with the Sea, that *Peter Martyr* stiled his History *Decads of the Ocean*. And in the general History of *Spain*, part of the King's Title is, *The Islands, and firm Land of the Ocean Sea*. Grimeston, p. 1234.

EBENEZER COOK

[In 1708 there was published in London a pamphlet containing a poem of twenty-one pages with the title "The Sot-Weed Factor: Or, a Voyage to Maryland. A Satyr. In which is describ'd, The Laws, Government, Courts and Constitutions of the Country; and also the Buildings, Feasts, Frolicks, Entertainments and Drunken Humours of the Inhabitants of that Part of *America*. In Burlesque Verse. By Eben. Cook, Gent." Nothing is known of Eben. Cook, Gent. In 1730 there was published in Annapolis a political satire entitled "Sotweed Redivivus: or the Planters Looking-Glass. In Burlesque Verse. Calculated for the Meridian of Maryland. By E. C. Gent." This is in the same metrical form as "The Sot-Weed Factor," and purports to be by the same author; but from the character and quality of the poem it seems rather more probable that some other person adopted this device for the expression of his views. The latest editor of "The Sot-Weed Factor" also ascribes to Ebenezer Cook an elegy published in an Annapolis newspaper in 1728. There seems to be no positive evidence, however, that the author was a permanent resident of Maryland, or indeed that he stayed in the colony longer than the hero of his poem is represented as doing. Nevertheless, "The Sot-Weed Factor" has come to be regarded as one of the more curious bits of early Americana, and can hardly be ignored in a collection like the present. If it be considered as an American production, it shows the greater development of broad humor in the South as compared with New England; and its form, evidently influenced by the school of Butler, illustrates the tendency in the South to follow at a little distance the literary fashions prevailing in England.

The selections are taken from the edition by Bernard C. Steiner, published by the Maryland Historical Society in 1900.]

THE FACTOR'S ADVENTURES

[From "The Sot-Weed Factor"]

I thought it proper to provide,
A Lodging for myself and Guide,
So to our Inn we march'd away,
Which at a little distance lay;
Where all things were in such Confusion,
I thought the World at its conclusion:

A Herd of Planters on the ground,
O'er-whelm'd with Punch, dead drunk we found:
Others were fighting and contending,
Some burnt their Cloaths to save the mending.
A few whose Heads by frequent use,
Could better bare the potent Juice,
Gravely debated State Affairs.
Whilst I most nimbly trip'd up Stairs;
Leaving my Friend discoursing oddly,
And mixing things Prophane and Godly:
Just then beginning to be Drunk,
As from the Company I slunk,
To every Room and Nook I crept,
In hopes I might have somewhere slept;
But all the bedding was possest
By one or other drunken Guest:
But after looking long about,
I found an antient Corn-loft out,
Glad that I might in quiet sleep,
And there my bones unfractur'd keep.
I lay'd me down secure from Fray,
And soundly snoar'd till break of Day;
When waking fresh I sat upright,
And found my Shoes were vanish'd quite;
Hat, Wig, and Stockings, all were fled
From this extended *Indian* Bed:
Vext at the Loss of Goods and Chattel,
I swore I'd give the Rascal battel,
Who had abus'd me in this sort,
And Merchant Stranger made his Sport.
I furiously descended Ladder;
No Hare in *March* was ever madder:
In vain I search'd for my Apparel,
And did with Oast and Servants Quarrel;
For one whose Mind did much aspire
To [1] Mischief, threw them in the Fire;

---

[1] 'Tis the Custom of the Planters, to throw their own, or any other Person's Hat, Wig, Shooes or Stockings in the Fire.

Equipt with neither Hat nor Shooe,
I did my coming hither rue,
And doubtful thought what I should do:
Then looking round, I saw my Friend
Lie naked on a Tables end;
A Sight so dismal to behold,
One wou'd have judg'd him dead and cold;
When wringing of his bloody Nose,
By fighting got we may suppose;
I found him not so fast asleep,
Might give his Friends a cause to weep:
Rise, [1]*Oronooko*, rise, said I,
And from this *Hell* and *Bedlam* fly.
My Guide starts up, and in amaze,
With blood-shot Eyes did round him gaze;
At length with many a sigh and groan,
He went in search of aged Rhoan;
But Rhoan, tho' seldom us'd to faulter,
Had fairly this time slipt his Halter;
And not content all Night to stay,
Ty'd up from Fodder, ran away:
After my Guide to ketch him ran,
And so I lost both Horse and Man;
Which Disappointment, tho' so great,
Did only Mirth and Jests create:
Till one more Civil than the rest,
In Conversation for the best,
Observing that for want of Rhoan,
I should be left to walk alone;
Most readily did me intreat,
To take a Bottle at his Seat;
A Favour at that time so great,
I blest my kind propitious Fate;
And finding soon a fresh supply
Of Cloaths from Stoar-house kept hard by,
I mounted streight on such a Steed,

---

[1] Planters are usually call'd by the Name of *Oronooko*, from their Planting
Oronooko-Tobacco.

Did rather curb, than whipping need;
And straining at the usual rate,
With spur of Punch which lay in Pate,
E'er long we lighted at the Gate:
Where in an antient *Cedar* House,
Dwelt my new Friend, a [1] Cockerouse;
Whose Fabrick,' tho' 'twas built of Wood,
Had many Springs and Winters stood;
When Sturdy Oaks, and lofty Pines
Were level'd with [2] Musmelion Vines,
And Plants eradicated were,
By Hurricanes into the air;
There with good Punch and apple Juice,
We spent our Hours without abuse:
Till Midnight in her sable Vest,
Persuaded Gods and Men to rest;
And with a pleasing kind surprize,
Indulg'd soft Slumbers to my Eyes.
Fierce [3] *Æthon* courser of the Sun
Had half his Race exactly run;
And breath'd on me a fiery Ray,
Darting hot Beams the following Day,
When snug in Blanket white I lay:
But Heat and [4] *Chinces* rais'd the Sinner,
Most opportunely to his Dinner;
Wild Fowl and Fish delicious Meats,
As good as *Neptune's* Doxy eats,
Began our Hospitable Treat;
Fat Venson follow'd in the rear,
And Turkies wild Luxurious Chear:
But what the Feast did most commend,
Was hearty welcom from my Friend.

[1] Cockerouse, is a Man of Quality.
[2] Musmilleon Vines are what we call Muskmilleon Plants.
[3] Æthon is one of the Poetical Horses of the Sun.
[4] Chinces are a sort of vermin like our *Bugs* in *England*.

A BARGAIN WITH A QUAKER

[From "The Sot-Weed Factor"]

I then began to think with Care,
How I might sell my *British* Ware,
That with my Freight I might comply,
Did on my Charter party lie:
To this intent, with Guide before,
I tript it to the Eastern Shoar;
While riding near a Sandy Bay,
I met a *Quaker, Yea* and *Nay;*
A Pious Conscientious Rogue,
As e'er woar Bonnet or a Brogue,
Who neither Swore nor kept his Word,
But cheated in the Fear of God;
And when his Debts he would not pay,
By Light within he ran away.
With this sly Zealot soon I struck
A Bargain for my *English* Truck,
Agreeing for ten thousand weight,
Of *Sot-weed* good and fit for freight,
Broad *Oronooko* bright and sound,
The growth and product of his ground;
In Cask that should contain compleat,
Five hundred of Tobacco neat.
The Contract thus betwixt us made,
Not well acquainted with the Trade,
My Goods I trusted to the Cheat,
Whose crop was then aboard the Fleet;
And going to receive my own,
I found the Bird was newly flown:
Cursing this execrable Slave,
This damn'd pretended Godly Knave;
On due Revenge and Justice bent,
I instantly to Counsel went,
Unto an ambodexter [1] *Quack,*
Who learnedly had got the knack

---

[1] This Fellow was an Apothecary, and turn'd an Attorney at Law.

Of giving Glisters, making Pills,
Of filling Bonds, and forging Wills;
And with a stock of Impudence,
Supply'd his want of Wit and Sense;
With Looks demure, amazing People,
No wiser than a Daw in Steeple;
My Anger flushing in my Face,
I stated the preceeding Case:
And of my Money was so lavish,
That he'd have poyson'd half the Parish,
And hang'd his Father on a Tree,
For such another tempting Fee;
Smiling, said he, the Cause is clear,
I'll manage him you need not fear;
The Case is judg'd, good Sir, but look
In *Galen*, No — in my Lord *Cook*,
I vow to God I was mistook:
I'll take out a Provincial Writ,
And Trounce him for his Knavish Wit;
Upon my Life we'll win the Cause,
With all the ease I cure the *Yaws*:
Resolv'd to plague the holy Brother,
I set one Rogue to catch another;
To try the Cause then fully bent,
Up to *Annapolis* I went,
A City Situate on a Plain,
Where scarce a House will keep out Rain;
The Buildings fram'd with Cyprus rare,
Resembles much our *Southwark* Fair:
But Stranger here will scarcely meet
With Market-place, Exchange, or Street;
And if the Truth I may report,
'Tis not so large as *Tottenham Court.*
St. *Mary's* once was in repute,
Now here the Judges try the Suit,
And Lawyers twice a Year dispute.
As oft the Bench most gravely meet,
Some to get Drunk, and some to eat,

s

A swinging share of Country Treat.
But as for Justice right or wrong,
Not one amongst the numerous throng,
Knows what they mean, or has the Heart,
To give his Verdict on a Stranger's part:
Now Court being call'd by beat of Drum,
The Judges left their Punch and Rum,
When Pettifogger Doctor draws,
His Paper forth, and opens Cause:
And least I should the better get,
Brib'd *Quack* supprest his Knavish Wit.
*   *   *   *   *   *
*   *   *   *   *   *

The Byast Court without delay,
Adjudg'd my Debt in Country Pay;
In[1] Pipe Staves, Corn, or Flesh of Boar,
Rare Cargo for the *English* Shoar:
Raging with Grief, full speed I ran,
To joyn the Fleet at[2] *Kicketan;*
Embarqu'd and waiting for a Wind,
I left this dreadful Curse behind.

May Canniballs transported o'er the Sea
Prey on these Slaves, as they have done on me;
May never Merchant's, trading Sails explore
This Cruel, this Inhospitable Shoar;
But left abandon'd by the World to starve,
May they sustain the Fate they well deserve:
May they turn Savage, or as *Indians* Wild,
From Trade, Converse, and Happiness exil'd;
Recreant to Heaven, may they adore the Sun,
And into Pagan Superstitions run
For Vengeance ripe ——————————————
May Wrath Divine then lay those Regions wast
Where no Man's[3] Faithful, nor a Woman Chast.

[1] There is a Law in this Country, the Plantiff may pay his Debt in Country pay, which consists in the produce of his Plantation.
[2] The homeward bound Fleet meets here.
[3] The Author does not intend by this, any of the *English* Gentlemen resident there.

WILLIAM BYRD

[William Byrd, of Westover, was a type of the wealthy and cultured Virginia gentleman who wrote as an avocation. He was born in Virginia in 1674, and educated in England and on the Continent. Before he returned to America, he studied law at the Middle Temple, and was called to the Bar, and also became a member of the Royal Society. At home he devoted himself to managing the estate which his father had built up, to the performance of many public duties, to the acquiring of a large library, and to the social and intellectual enjoyments available among the aristocracy of Virginia in their best days. One of his public employments was as member of the Commission which in 1728 established the boundary line between Virginia and North Carolina. An elaboration of the journal kept during this survey is the chief of his writings.

Colonel Byrd's writings were not published during his lifetime, but were carefully copied under his direction and bound into a manuscript volume for preservation in his family. The chief papers in this volume are, besides "The History of the Dividing Line," already referred to, "A Journey to the Land of Eden," "A Progress to the Mines," and "An Essay on Bulk Tobacco." The authorship of the last-named essay is questioned by Byrd's latest editor. The other three papers are accounts of expeditions in the less settled parts of the colony. The observations which the author records show his wide interest, which embraced not only matters of practical economic importance, but curiosities in natural history, medicine, etc.; and allusions to his reading are an interesting revelation of the culture of his day. The papers are written in a style that makes even the narration of commonplace facts interesting, and they abound in a wit that, when it avoids the loose conventional jests that were the fashion, is sprightly and genuine.

The chief of the "Westover Manuscripts," as they have been called from the family residence where they were preserved, have been printed in 1841, 1866, and 1901. The following selections are from the latest edition, by John Spencer Bassett.]

THE BEGINNING OF THE SURVEY

[From "The History of the Dividing Line"]

[March] 7. This Morning the Surveyors began to run the Dividing line from the Cedar-Post we had driven into the Sand, allowing near 3 Degrees for the Variation. Without making this

Just allowance, we should not have obeyd his Majesty's order in running a Due West Line. It seems the former Commissioners had not been so exact, which gave our Friends of Carolina but too just an Exception to their Proceedings.

The Line cut Dosier's Island, consisting only of a Flat Sand, with here and there an humble Shrub growing upon it. From thence it crost over a narrow Arm of the Sound into Knot's Island, and there Split a Plantation belonging to William Harding.

The Day being far spent, we encampt in this Man's Pasture, tho' it lay very low, and the Season now inclin'd People to Aguish Distempers. He suffered us to cut Cedar-Branches for our Enclosure, and other Wood for Firing, to correct the moist Air and drive away the Damps. Our Landlady, in the Days of her Youth, it seems, had been a Laundress in the Temple, and talkt over her Adventures in that Station, with as much pleasure as an Old Soldier talks over his Battles and Distempers, and I believe with as many Additions to the Truth.

The Soil is good in many Places of this Island, and the Extent of it pretty large. It lyes in the form of a Wedge: The South End of it is Several Miles over, but towards the North it Sharpens into a Point. It is a Plentiful Place for Stock, by reason of the wide Marshes adjacent to it, and because of its warm Situation. But the Inhabitants pay a little dear for this Convenience, by losing as much Blood in the Summer Season by the infinite Number of Mosquetas, as all their Beef and Pork can recruit in the Winter.

The Sheep are as large as in Lincolnshire, because they are never pincht by cold or Hunger. The whole Island was hitherto reckon'd to lye in Virginia, but now our Line has given the greater Part of it to Carolina. The Principal Freeholder here is Mr. White, who keeps open House for all Travellers, that either Debt or Shipwreck happens to cast in his way.

8. By break of Day we sent away our Largest Periauga, with the Baggage, round the South end of Knot's Island, with Orders to the Men to wait for us in the Mouth of North River. Soon after, we embarkt ourselves on board the smaller Vessel, with Intent, if possible, to find a Passage round the North End of the Island.

We found this Navigation very difficult, by reason of the Continued Shoals, and often stuck fast aground; for tho' the Sound spreads many miles, yet it is in most places extremely Shallow, and requires a Skilful Pilot to Steer even a Canoe safe over it. It was almost as hard to keep our Temper as to keep the Channel, in this provoking Situation. But the most impatient amongst us strokt down their Choler and swallow'd their curses, lest, if they suffer'd them to break out, they might sound like Complaining, which was expressly forbid, as the first Step to Sedition.

At a distance we descry'd Several Islands to the Northward of us, the largest of which goes by the Name of Cedar Island. Our periauga stuck so often that we had a fair chance to be benighted in this wide Water, which must certainly have been our Fate, had we not luckily spied a Canoe that was giving a Fortune-teller a cast from Princess Anne County over to North Carolina. But, as conjurers are Sometimes mistaken, the Man mistrusted we were Officers of Justice in pursuit of a Young Wench he had carry'd off along with him. We gave the Canoe Chase for more than an Hour and when we came up with her, threatend to make them all prisoners unless they would direct us into the right Channel.

By the Pilotage of these People we row'd up an Arm of the Sound, call'd the Back-Bay, till we came to the Head of it. There we were stoppt by a miry Pocoson full half a Mile in Breadth, thro' which we were oblig'd to daggle on foot, plungeing now and then, tho' we pickt our Way, up to the Knees in Mud. At the End of this Charming walk we gain'd the Terra Firma of Princess Anne County. In that Dirty Condition we were afterwards oblig'd to foot it two Miles, as far as John Heath's Plantation, where we expected to meet the Surveyors & the men who waited upon them.

THE GREAT DISMAL SWAMP

[From "The History of the Dividing Line"]

Our Landlord had a tolerable good House and Clean Furniture, and yet we cou'd not be tempted to lodge in it. We chose rather to lye in the open Field, for fear of growing too tender. A clear Sky, spangled with Stars, was our Canopy, which being the last thing we saw before we fell asleep, gave us Magnificent Dreams. The Truth of it is, we took so much pleasure in that natural kind of Lodging, that I think at the foot of the Account Mankind are great Losers by the Luxury of Feather-Beds and warm apartments.

The curiosity of beholding so new and withal so Sweet a Method of encamping, brought one of the Senators of N Carolina to make us a Midnight Visit.   But he was so very Clamorous in his Commendations of it, that the Centinel, not seeing his Quality, either thro' his habit or Behaviour, had like to have treated him roughly.

After excusing the Unseasonableness of his Visit, and letting us know he was a Parliament Man, he swore he was so taken with our Lodging, that he would set Fire to his House as soon as he got Home, and teach his Wife and Children to lie, like us, in the open field.

13. Early this Morning our Chaplain repair'd to us with the Men we had left at Mr. Wilson's.   We had sent for them the Evening before to relieve those who had the Labour Oar from Corotuck-Inlet.   But to our great surprise, they petition'd not to be reliev'd, hoping to gain immortal Reputation by being the first of Mankind that Ventur'd thro' the great Dismal.   But the rest being equally Ambitious of the same Honour, it was but fair to decide their Pretensions by Lot.   After Fortune had declar'd herself, those which she had excluded offer'd Money to the Happy Persons to go in their Stead.   But Hercules would have as soon sold the Glory of cleansing the Augean Stables, which was pretty near the same Sort of Work.

No sooner was the Controversy at an end, but we sent them unfortunate Fellows back to their Quarters, whom Chance had Condemn'd to remain upon Firm Land and Sleep in a whole Skin. In the mean while the Surveyors carry'd the Line 3 Miles, which was no Contemptible day's work, considering how cruelly they were entangled with Bryars and Gall Bushes.   The Leaf of this last Shrub bespeaks it to be of the Alaternus Family.

Our Work ended within a Quarter of a Mile of the Dismal above-mention'd, where the Ground began to be already full of Sunken Holes and Slashes, which had, here and there, some few Reeds growing in them.

Tis hardly credible how little the Bordering inhabitants were acquainted with this mighty Swamp, notwithstanding they had liv'd their whole lives within Smell of it.   Yet, as great Strangers as they were to it, they pretended to be very exact in their Account of its Dimensions, and were positive it could not be above 7 or 8 Miles wide, but knew no more of the Matter than Star-gazers know of the Distance of the Fixt Stars. At the Same time, they were Simple enough to amuse our Men with Idle Stories of the Lyons, Panthers and Alligators, they were like to encounter in that dreadful Place.

In short, we saw plainly there was no Intelligence of this Terra Incognita to be got, but from our own Experience. For that Reason it was resolv'd to make the requisite Dispositions to enter it next Morning. We allotted every one of the Surveyors for this painful Enterprise, with 12 Men to attend them. Fewer than that cou'd not be employ'd in clearing the way, carrying the Chain, marking the Trees, and bearing the necessary Bedding and Provisions. Nor wou'd the Commissioners themselves have Spared their Persons on this Occasion, but for fear of adding to the poor men's Burthen, while they were certain they cou'd add nothing to their Resolution.

We quarter'd with our Friend and Fellow Traveller, William Wilkins, who had been our faithful Pilot to Coratuck, and liv'd about a mile from the Place where the Line ended. Every thing lookt so very clean, and the Furniture so neat, that we were tempted to Lodge within Doors. But the Novelty of being shut up so close quite spoil'd our rest, nor did we breathe so free by abundance, as when we lay in the open Air.

14. Before nine of the Clock this Morning, the Provisions, Bedding and other Necessaries, were made up into Packs for the Men to carry on their Shoulders into the Dismal. They were victuall'd for 8 days at full Allowance, Nobody doubting but that wou'd be abundantly Sufficient to carry them thro' that Inhospitable Place; nor Indeed was it possible for the Poor Fellows to Stagger under more. As it was, their Loads weigh'd from 60 to 70 Pounds, in just Proportion to the Strength of those who were to bear them.

Twou'd have been unconscionable to have Saddled them with Burthens heavier than that, when they were to lugg them thro' a filthy Bogg, which was hardly practicable with no Burthen at all.

Besides this Luggage at their Backs, they were oblig'd to measure the distance, mark the Trees, and clear the way for the Surveyors every Step they went. It was really a Pleasure to see with how much Cheerfulness they undertook, and with how much Spirit they went thro' all this Drudgery. For their Greater Safety, the Commissioners took care to furnish them with Peruvian-Bark, Rhubarb and Hipocoacanah, in case they might happen, in that wet Journey, to be taken with fevers or Fluxes.

Altho' there was no need of Example to inflame Persons already so cheerful, yet to enter the People with better grace, the Author and two more of the Commissioners accompanied them half a Mile into the Dismal. The Skirts of it were thinly Planted with Dwarf Reeds and Gall-Bushes, but when we got into the Dismal itself, we found the Reeds grew there much taller and closer, and, to mend the matter was so interlac'd with bamboe-briars, that there was no scuffling thro' them without the help of Pioneers. At the same time, we found the Ground moist and trembling under our feet like a Quagmire, insomuch that it was an easy Matter to run a Ten-Foot-Pole up to the Head in it, without exerting any uncommon Strength to do it.

Two of the Men, whose Burthens were the least cumbersome, had orders to march before, with their Tomahawks, and clear the way, in order to make an Opening for the Surveyors. By their Assistance we made a Shift to push the Line half a Mile in 3 Hours, and then reacht a small piece of firm Land, about 100 Yards wide, Standing up above the rest like an Island. Here the people were glad to lay down their Loads and take a little refreshment, while the happy man, whose lot it was to carry the Jugg of Rum, began already, like Aesop's Bread-Carriers, to find it grow a good deal lighter.

After reposing about an Hour, the Commissioners recommended Vigour and Constancy to their Fellow-Travellers, by whom they were answer'd with 3 Cheerful Huzzas, in Token of Obedience. This Ceremony was no sooner over but they took up their Burthens and attended the Motion of the Surveyors, who, tho' they workt with all their might, could reach but one Mile farther, the same obstacles still attending them which they had met with in the Morning.

However small this distance may seem to such as are us'd to travel at their Ease, yet our Poor Men, who were oblig'd to work with an unwieldy Load at their Backs, had reason to think it a long way; Especially in a Bogg where they had no firm Footing, but every Step made a deep Impression, which was instantly fill'd with Water. At the same time they were labouring with their Hands to cut down the Reeds, which were Ten-feet high, their Legs were hampered with the Bryars. Besides, the Weather happen'd to be very warm, and the tallness of the Reeds kept off every Friendly Breeze from coming to refresh them. And, indeed, it was a little provoking to hear the Wind whistling among the Branches of the White Cedars, which grew here and there amongst the Reeds, and at the same time not have the Comfort to feel the least Breath of it.

In the mean time the 3 Commissioners return'd out of the Dismal the same way they went in, and, having join'd their Brethren, proceeded that Night as far as Mr. Wilson's.

This worthy Person lives within sight of the Dismal, in the Skirts whereof his Stocks range and Maintain themselves all the Winter, and yet he knew as little of it as he did of Terra Australis Incognita. He told us a Canterbury Tale of a North Briton, whose Curiosity Spurr'd him a long way into this great Desart, as he call'd it, near 20 Years ago, but he having no Compass, nor seeing the Sun for several Days Together, wander'd about till he was almost famisht; but at last he bethought himself of a Secret his Countrymen make use of to Pilot themselves in a Dark day.

He took a fat Louse out of his Collar, and expos'd it to the open day on a Piece of White Paper, which he brought along with him for his Journal. The poor Insect having no Eye-lids, turn'd himself about till he found the Darkest Part of the Heavens, and so made the best of his way towards the North. By this Direction he Steer'd himself Safe out, and gave such a frightful account of the Monsters he saw, and the Distresses he underwent, that no mortall Since has been hardy enough to go upon the like dangerous Discovery.

15. The Surveyors pursued their work with all Diligence, but Still found the Soil of the Dismal so Spongy that the Water ouzed up into every foot-step they took. To their Sorrow, too, they found the Reeds and Bryars more firmly interwoven than they did the day before. But the greatest Grievance was from large Cypresses,

which the Wind had blown down and heap'd upon one another. On the Limbs of most of them grew Sharp Snags, Pointing every way like so many Pikes, that requir'd much Pains and Caution to avoid.

These Trees being Evergreens, and Shooting their Large Tops Very high, are easily overset by every Gust of Wind, because there is no firm Earth to Steddy their Roots. Thus many of them were laid prostrate to the great Encumbrance of the way. Such Variety of Difficulties made the Business go on heavily, insomuch that, from Morning till Night, the Line could advance no further than 1 Mile and 31 Poles. Never was Rum, that cordial of Life, found more necessary than it was in this Dirty Place. It did not only recruit the People's Spirits, now almost Jaded with Fatigue, but serv'd to correct the Badness of the Water, and at the same time to resist the Malignity of the Air. Whenever the Men wanted to drink, which was very often, they had nothing more to do but to make a Hole, and the Water bubbled up in a Moment. But it was far from being either clear or well tasted, and had besides a Physical Effect, from the Tincture it receiv'd from the Roots of the Shrubbs and Trees that grew in the Neighbourhood.

LIFE IN NORTH CAROLINA

[From "The History of the Dividing Line"]

The Pines in this Part of the country are of a different Species from those that grow in Virginia: their bearded Leaves are much longer and their Cones much larger. Each Cell contains a Seed of the Size and Figure of a black-ey'd Pea, which, Shedding in November, is very good Mast for Hogs, and fattens them in a Short time.

The Smallest of these Pines are full of Cones, which are 8 or 9 Inches long, and each affords commonly 60 or 70 Seeds. This Kind of Mast has the Advantage of all other, by being more constant, and less liable to be nippt by the Frost, or Eaten by the Caterpillars. The Trees also abound more with Turpentine, and consequently yield more Tarr, than either the Yellow or the White Pine; And for the same reason make more durable Timber for building. The Inhabitants hereabouts pick up Knots of Light-

wood in Abundance, which they burn into tar, and then carry it to
Norfolk or Nansimond for a Market. The Tar made in this
method is the less Valuable, because it is said to burn the Cordage,
tho' it is full as good for all other uses, as that made in Sweden
and Muscovy.

Surely there is no place in the World where the Inhabitants live
with less Labour than in N Carolina. It approaches nearer to
the Description of Lubberland than any other, by the great felicity
of the Climate, the easiness of raising Provisions, and the Slothful-
ness of the People.

Indian Corn is of so great increase, that a little Pains will Subsist a very large Family with Bread, and then they may have meat
without any pains at all, by the Help of the Low Grounds, and the
great Variety of Mast that grows on the High-land. The Men,
for their Parts, just like the Indians, impose all the Work upon the
poor Women. They make their Wives rise out of their Beds early
in the Morning, at the same time that they lye and Snore, till the
Sun has run one third of his course, and disperst all the unwholesome Damps. Then, after Stretching and Yawning for half an
Hour, they light their Pipes, and, under the Protection of a cloud
of Smoak, venture out into the open Air; tho', if it happens to be
never so little cold, they quickly return Shivering into the Chimney
corner. When the weather is mild, they stand leaning with both
their arms upon the corn-field fence, and gravely consider whether
they had best go and take a Small Heat at the Hough: but generally find reasons to put it off till another time.

Thus they loiter away their Lives, like Solomon's Sluggard,
with their Arms across, and at the Winding up of the Year Scarcely
have Bread to Eat.

To speak the Truth, tis a thorough Aversion to Labor that makes
People file off to N Carolina, where Plenty and a Warm Sun confirm them in their Disposition to Laziness for their whole Lives.

26. Since we were like to be confin'd to this place, till the People
return'd out of the Dismal, twas agreed that our Chaplain might
Safely take a turn to Edenton, to preach the Gospel to the Infidels there, and Christen their Children. He was accompany'd
thither by Mr. Little, One of the Carolina Commissioners, who, to
shew his regard for the Church, offer'd to treat Him on the Road

with a Fricassee of Rum.   They fry'd half a dozen Rashers of very fat Bacon in a Pint of Rum, both which being disht up together, serv'd the Company at once for meat and Drink.

Most of the Rum they get in this Country comes from New England, and is so bad and unwholesome, that it is not improperly call'd "Kill-Devil."   It is distill'd there from forreign molosses, which, if Skilfully manag'd, yields near Gallon for Gallon.   Their molosses comes from the same country, and has the name of "Long Sugar" in Carolina, I suppose from the Ropiness of it, and Serves all the purposes of Sugar, both in their Eating and Drinking.

When they entertain their Friends bountifully, they fail not to set before them a Capacious Bowl of Bombo, so call'd from the Admiral of that name.   This is a Compound of Rum and Water in Equal Parts, made palatable with the said long Sugar.   As good Humour begins to flow, and the Bowl to Ebb, they take care to replenish it with Shear Rum, of which there always is a Reserve under the Table.   But such Generous doings happen only when that Balsam of Life is plenty;   for they have often such Melancholy times, that neither Land-graves nor Cassicks can procure one drop for their Wives, when they ly in, or are troubled with the Colick or Vapours.   Very few in this Country have the Industry to plant Orchards, which, in a Dearth of Rum, might supply them with much better Liquor.

The Truth is, there is one Inconvenience that easily discourages lazy People from making This improvement: very often, in Autumn, when the Apples begin to ripen, they are visited with Numerous Flights of paraqueets, that bite all the fruit to Pieces in a moment, for the sake of the Kernels.   The Havock they make is Sometimes so great, that whole Orchards are laid waste in Spite of all the Noises that can be made, or Mawkins that can be dresst up, to fright 'em away.   These Ravenous Birds visit North Carolina only during the warm Season, and so soon as the Cold begins to come on, retire back towards the Sun.   They rarely Venture so far North as Virginia, except in a very hot Summer, when they visit the most Southern Parts of it.   They are very Beautiful; but like some other pretty Creatures, are apt to be loud and mischievous.

27. Betwixt this and Edenton there are many thuckleberry Slashes, which afford a convenient Harbour for Wolves and Foxes. The first of these wild Beasts is not so large and fierce as they are in other countries more Northerly. He will not attack a Man in the keenest of his Hunger, but run away from him, as from an Animal more mischievous than himself.

The Foxes are much bolder, and will Sometimes not only make a Stand, but likewise assault any one that would balk them of their Prey. The Inhabitants hereabouts take the trouble to dig abundance of Wolf-Pits, so deep and perpendicular, that when a Wolf is once tempted into them, he can no more Scramble out again, than a Husband who has taken the Leap can Scramble out of Matrimony.

Most of the Houses in this Part of the Country are Log-houses, covered with Pine or Cypress Shingles, 3 feet long, and one broad. They are hung upon Laths with Peggs, and their doors too turn upon Wooden Hinges, and have wooden Locks to Secure them, so that the Building is finisht without Nails or other Iron-Work. They also set up their Pales without any Nails at all, and indeed more Securely than those that are nail'd. There are 3 Rails mortised into the Posts, the lowest of which serves as a Sill with a Groove in the Middle, big enough to receive the End of the Pales: the middle Part of the Pale rests against the Inside of the Next Rail, and the Top of it is brought forward to the outside of the uppermost. Such Wreathing of the Pales in and out makes them stand firm, and much harder to unfix than when nail'd in the Ordinary way.

Within 3 or 4 Miles of Edenton, the Soil appears to be a little more fertile, tho' it is much cut with Slashes, which seem all to have a tendency towards the Dismal.

This Town is Situate on the North side of Albemarle Sound, which is there about 5 miles over. A Dirty Slash runs all along the Back of it, which in the Summer is a foul annoyance, and furnishes abundance of that Carolina plague, musquetas. There may be 40 or 50 Houses, most of them Small, and built without Expense. A Citizen here is counted Extravagant, if he has Ambition enough to aspire to a Brick-chimney. Justice herself is but indifferently Lodged, the Court-House having much the Air of a Common Tobacco-House. I believe this is the only Metropolis in the Christian or Mahometan World, where there is neither Church, Chappel, Mosque, Synagogue, or any other Place of Publick Worship of any Sect or Religion whatsoever.

ON THE ALLIGATOR

[From "The History of the Dividing Line"]

In Santee river, as in Several others of Carolina, a Small kind of allegator is frequently seen, which perfumes the Water with a Musky Smell. They Seldom exceed Eight Feet in Length in these parts, whereas, near the Equinoctial, they come up to twelve or Fourteen. And the heat of the Climate don't only make them bigger, but more Fierce and Voracious. They watch the Cattle there when they come to drink and Cool themselves in the River; and because they are not able to drag them into the Deep Water, they make up by Strategem what they want in Force. They Swallow great Stones, the Weight of which being added to their Strength, enables them to tug a Moderate Cow under Water, and as soon as they have drown'd her, they discharge the Stones out of their Maw and then feast upon the Carcass. However, as Fierce and Strong as these Monsters are, the Indians will surprise them Napping as they float upon the Surface, get astride upon their Necks, then whip a short piece of wood like a Truncheon into their Jaws, & holding the Ends with their two hands, hinder them from diving by keeping their mouths open, and when they are almost Spent, they will make to the shoar, where their Riders knock them on the Head and Eat them. This Amphibious Animal is a Smaller kind of Crocodile, having the Same Shape exactly, only the Crocodile of the Nile is twice as long, being when full grown from 20 to Thirty Feet. This Enormous Length is the more to be wonder'd at, because the Crocodile is hatcht from an Egg very little larger than that of a Goose. It has a long Head, which it can open very wide, with very Sharp & Strong teeth. Their Eyes are Small, their Legs Short, with Claws upon their Feet. Their Tail makes half the Length of their Body, and the whole is guarded with hard impenetrable Scales, except the Belly, which is much Softer and Smoother. They keep much upon the Land in the day time, but towards the Evening retire into the Water to avoid the Cold Dews of the Night. They run pretty fast right forward, but are very awkward and Slow in turning, by reason of their unwieldy Length. It is an Error that they have no Tongue, without which they cou'd hardly Swallow their Food; but in eating they move the upper Jaw only, Contrary to all other Animals. The way of catching them in Egypt is, with a Strong Hook fixt to the End of a chain, and baited with a joynt of Pork, which they are very fond of. But a live Hog is generally tyed near, the Cry of which allures them to the Hook. This Account of the Crocodile will agree in most particulars with the Alligator, only the Bigness of the last cannot entitle it to the Name of "Leviathan," which Job gave formerly to the crocodile, and not to the Whale, as some Interpreters wou'd make us believe.

DRAWING A TOOTH

[From "A Journey to the Land of Eden"]

I had an impertinent Tooth in my upper Jaw, that had been loose for some time, and made me chew with great Caution. Particularly I cou'd not grind a Biscuit but with much deliberation and presence of mind. Tooth-Drawers we had none amongst us, nor any of the Instruments they make use of. However, Invention supply'd this want very happily, and I contriv'd to get rid of this troublesome Companion by cutting a Caper. I caused a Twine to be fasten'd round the Root of my Tooth, about a Fathom in Length, and then ty'd the other End to the Snag of a Log that lay upon the ground, in such a Manner that I cou'd just stand upright. Having adjusted my String in this manner, I bent my Knees enough to enable me to spring vigorously off the Ground, as perpendicularly as I cou'd. The force of the Leap drew out the Tooth with so much ease that I felt nothing of it, nor should have believ'd it was come away, unless I had seen it dangling at the End of the String. An Under tooth may be fecht out by standing off the Ground and fastning your String at due distance above you. And having so fixt your Gear, jump off your Standing, and the

weight of your Body, added to the force of the Spring, will poize
out your Tooth with less pain than any Operator upon Earth
cou'd draw it.   This new way of Tooth-drawing, being so silently
and deliberately perform'd, both surprized and delighted all that
were present, who cou'd not guess what I was going about.   I immediately found the benefit of getting rid of this troublesome
Companion, by eating my Supper with more comfort than I had
done during the whole Expedition.

JOHN SECCOMB

[John Seccomb, a Harvard graduate of 1728, long a Congregationalist minister in Massachusetts and Nova Scotia, was the author of "Father Abbey's Will" — a literary curiosity concerning which the most curious fact is its contemporary popularity. It was probably written while Seccomb was a divinity student at Harvard, and was inspired by the death of one Matthew Abdy, a bedmaker and bottlewasher for the college. It was sent to England, and appeared in both the *London Magazine* and the *Gentleman's Magazine* for May, 1732. The poem, as given below, is from the *London Magazine*. The version in the *Gentleman's Magazine* is the same, with a few minor variations, mostly in capitalization. An American reprint of later date, entitled "Father Abbey's Will," is prefixed by an explanatory note dated "December, 1730," and closes with the quatrain: —

> "Thus father Abbey left his spouse,
> As rich as church or college mouse,
> Which is sufficient invitation,
> To serve the college in his station."

In the *London Magazine* for August, 1732, appeared another attempt in the same metre, purporting to be a proposal of marriage from the bedmaker at Yale to "Mistress Abbey." This is also credited to Seccomb.

At first sight it seems hard to account for the publication of this doggerel in the two leading English magazines of the day. Professor Tyler, in his perplexity over this matter, remarks that "It seems to have been widely read in the mother-country as a just specimen of the poetic attainments and of the general literary taste of the Americans." An examination of the position that the poem holds in the magazines tends to throw doubt on this statement. In both it appears anonymously and without any remark as to the nationality of the author. In both it is among other verse effusions, presumably by Englishmen, which are not markedly superior in refinement or wit. Perhaps its popularity must be taken only as a reminder that taste in humor, even more than in other forms of æsthetic expression, has changed since 1730.]

THE LAST WILL OF MR. MATTHEW A——Y OF NEW-ENGLAND

To my dear wife
My joy and life,
I freely now do give her
My whole estate,
With all my plate,
Being just about to leave her.

A tub of soap,
A long cart rope,
A frying pan & kettle,
An ashen pail,
A threshing flail,
An iron wedge and beetle.

Two painted chairs,
Nine warden pears,
A large old dripping platter,
The bed of hay
On which I lay,
An old sauce-pan for butter.

A little mug,
A two-quart jug,
A bottle full of brandy,
A looking-glass
To see your face,
You'll find it very handy.

A musket true
As ever flew,
A pound of shot & wallet,
A leather sash
My calabash,
My powder-horn and bullet.

An old sword blade,
  A garden spade,
A hoe, a rake, a ladder,
  A wooden can,
  A close-stool pan,
A clyster-pipe & bladder.

  A greasy hat,
  My old ram-cat,
A yard and half of linnen,
  A pot of grease,
  A woollen fleece,
In order for your spinning.

  A small-tooth comb,
  An ashen broom,
A candlestick & hatchet,
  A coverlid,
  Strip'd down with red,
A bag of rags to patch it.

  A ragged mat,
  A tub of fat,
A book put out by *Bunyan,*
  Another book
  By *Robin Rook,*
A skain or two of spunyarn.

  An old black muff,
  Some garden stuff,
A quantity of borrage,
  Some devil's weed,
  And burdock seed,
To season well your porridge.

  A chafing dish
  With one salt fish,
If I am not mistaken,

A leg of pork,
A broken fork,
And half a flitch of Bacon.

A spinning wheel,
One peck of meal,
A knife without a handle,
A rusty lamp,
Two quarts of samp,
And half a tallow candle.

My pouch and pipes,
Two oxen tripes,
An oaken dish well carved;
My little dog,
And spotted hog,
With two young pigs just starved.

This is my store,
I have no more,
I heartily do give it.
My years are spun,
My days are done,
And so I think to leave it.

JONATHAN EDWARDS

[Jonathan Edwards was born in 1703, the son of a Connecticut clergyman. He was extremely precocious, and early showed especial interest in philosophy and in natural science. He was graduated from Yale in 1720, and studied divinity. After preaching a few months in New York, and serving as tutor in Yale for two years, he accepted a call to Northampton, Mass. Here he remained for nearly twenty-four years as colleague pastor and pastor, when some differences with his congregation resulted in what was then the very unusual procedure of his dismissal. He then retired to Stockbridge, Mass., as a missionary to the Indians. In 1758 he became president of Princeton College, but died from the small-pox just after he had entered on the duties of his office.

Jonathan Edwards was probably the ablest of the early New England divines, and he illustrates in a peculiar way the influence of the New England intellectual life on character. He possessed fine sensibilities, and if one may judge by much of his prose, he had an artist's sense of form. The awfulness of the logical consequences of his religious faith at first repelled him, but he became reconciled to them by sheer force of intellect and will, and made their inculcation and defence the work of his life. So it came about that the man who perhaps possessed the finest poetic nature in early New England produced no poems, but on the one hand, the greatest philosophical treatise written by an American, and on the other, the most vivid and appalling of the many sermons that pictured eternal torment.

Edwards's greatest work is "A careful and strict Enquiry into the modern prevailing Notions of that Freedom of Will, which is supposed to be essential to Moral Agency, Vertue and Vice, Reward and Punishment, Praise and Blame" — commonly known by the shorter title of "Treatise on the Freedom of the Will." Even those who disagree with his conclusions have generally conceded the great power of original thought shown in this work, and its fairness and clarity of statement. Besides this, he produced a number of other theological writings, including a "Treatise on the Religious Affections," a "Treatise on Original Sin," "The History of Redemption," etc. During his ministry at Northampton he was connected with the beginnings of the revival movement later known as "The Great Awakening," and in consequence he wrote "A Faithful Narrative of the Surprizing Work of God in the Conversion of Many Hundred Souls in Northampton, and the Neighbouring Towns and Villages of New-Hampshire in New-England" (sometimes known as "Narratives of Surprising Conversions"), and "Thoughts on the Revival of Religion in New England in 1740." A considerable number of his own sermons are calculated to stir his hearers by presenting the terrors of future punishment. The most famous, though hardly the most powerful or most representative of these, is entitled "Sinners in the Hands of an Angry God." It must not be inferred, however, that the greater part of Edwards's preaching was of this character. Even these damnatory sermons have a logical structure and a solid basis of thought that makes them far more than blind appeals to feeling. It is unfortunate that the limits of the present work forbid the inclusion of one of the sermons entire, since the wonderful force and clearness of the preacher's method can be seen only by reading a discourse as a whole.

The great bulk of Jonathan Edwards's writings was left in manuscript at the time of his death. Many of his works were first published in Edinburgh, where he was admired as one of the greatest supporters of Calvinism. The first collected edition of his works in America was published in 1809.

The account of religious experiences is from a manuscript found among the author's papers, and printed in Dwight's "Life of Edwards." The selection from the "Faithful Narrative," etc., is from the second edition, London, 1738; that from the "Treatise on the Freedom of the Will" is from the first edition, Boston, 1754. The selection from the Sermons follows the edition of 1844, which, like all the collected editions, modernizes the text.]

EARLY RELIGIOUS EXPERIENCES

[From a private manuscript]

From my childhood up, my mind had been full of objections against the doctrine of God's sovereignty, in choosing whom he would to eternal life, and rejecting whom he pleased; leaving them eternally to perish, and be everlastingly tormented in hell. It used to appear like a horrible doctrine to me. But I remember the time very well, when I seemed to be convinced, and fully satisfied, as to this sovereignty of God, and his justice in thus eternally disposing of men, according to his sovereign pleasure. But never could give an account, how, or by what means, I was thus convinced, not in the least imagining at the time, nor a long time after, that there was any extraordinary influence of God's Spirit in it; but only that now I saw further, and my reason apprehended the justice and reasonableness of it. However, my mind rested in it; and it put an end to all those cavils and objections. And there has been a wonderful alteration in my mind, with respect to the doctrine of God's sovereignty, from that day to this; so that I scarce ever have found so much as the rising of an objection against it, in the most absolute sense, in God shewing mercy to whom he will shew mercy, and hardening whom he will. God's absolute sovereignty and justice, with respect to salvation and damnation, is what my mind seems to rest assured of, as much as of any thing that I see with my eyes; at least it is so at times. But I have often, since that first conviction, had quite another kind of sense of God's sovereignty than I had then. I have often since had not only a conviction, but a *delightful* conviction. The doctrine has very often appeared exceedingly pleasant, bright, and sweet. Absolute sovereignty is what I love to ascribe to God. But my first conviction was not so.

The first instance, that I remember, of that sort of inward, sweet delight in God and divine things, that I have lived much in since, was on reading those words, 1 Tim. i. 17. *Now unto the King eternal, immortal, invisible, the only wise God, be honour and glory for ever and ever, Amen.* As I read the words, there came into my soul, and was as it were diffused through it, a sense of the glory of the Divine Being; a new sense, quite different from any thing I ever experienced before. Never any words of Scripture seemed to me as these words did. I thought with myself, how excellent a Being that was, and how happy I should be, if I might enjoy that God, and be rapt up to him in heaven, and be as it were swallowed up in him for ever! I kept saying, and as it were singing, over these words of scripture to myself; and went to pray to God that I might enjoy him, and prayed in a manner quite different from what I used to do; with a new sort of affection. But it never came into my thought, that there was any thing spiritual, or of a saving nature in this.

From about that time, I began to have a new kind of apprehensions and ideas of Christ, and the work of redemption, and the glorious way of salvation by him. An inward, sweet sense of these things, at times, came into my heart; and my soul was led away in pleasant views and contemplations of them. And my mind was greatly engaged to spend my time in reading and meditating on Christ, on the beauty and excellency of his person, and the lovely way of salvation by free grace in him. I found no books so delightful to me, as those that treated of these subjects. Those words Cant. ii. 1. used to be abundantly with me, *I am the Rose of Sharon, and the Lily of the valleys.* The words seemed to me, sweetly to represent the loveliness and beauty of Jesus Christ. The whole book of Canticles used to be pleasant to me, and I used to be much in reading it, about that time; and found, from time to time, an inward sweetness, that would carry me away, in my contemplations. This I know not how to express otherwise, than by a calm, sweet abstraction of soul from all the concerns of this world; and sometimes a kind of vision, or fixed ideas and imaginations, of being alone in the mountains, or some solitary wilderness, far from all mankind, sweetly conversing with Christ, and wrapt and swallowed up in God. The sense I had of divine things, would often of a sudden kindle up, as it were, a sweet burning in my heart; an ardour of soul, that I know not how to express.

Not long after I first began to experience these things, I gave an account to my father of some things that had passed in my mind. I was pretty much affected by the discourse we had together; and when the discourse was ended, I walked abroad alone, in a solitary place in my father's pasture, for contemplation. And as I was walking there, and looking upon the sky and clouds, there came into my mind so sweet a sense of the glorious *majesty* and *grace* of God, as I know not how to express. — I seemed to see them both in a sweet conjunction; majesty and meekness joined together: it was a sweet, and gentle, and holy majesty; and also a majestic meekness; an awful sweetness; a high, and great, and holy gentleness.

After this my sense of divine things gradually increased, and became more and more lively, and had more of that inward sweetness. The appearance of every thing was altered; there seemed to be, as it were, a calm, sweet, cast, or appearance of divine glory, in almost everything. God's excellency, his wisdom, his purity and love, seemed to appear in every thing; in the sun, moon and stars; in the clouds and blue sky; in the grass, flowers, trees; in the water and all nature; which used greatly to fix my mind. I often used to sit and view the moon for a long time; and in the day, spent much time in viewing the clouds and sky, to behold the sweet glory of God in these things: in the meantime, singing forth, with a low voice, my contemplations of the Creator and Redeemer. And scarce any thing, among all the works of nature, was so sweet to me as thunder and lightening; formerly nothing had been so terrible to me. Before, I used to be uncommonly terrified with thunder, and to be struck with terror when I saw a thunder-storm rising; but now, on the contrary, it rejoiced me. I felt God, if I may so speak, at the first appearance of a thunder storm; and used to take the opportunity, at such times, to fix myself in order to view the clouds, and see the lightnings play, and hear the majestic and awful voice of God's thunder, which oftentimes was exceedingly entertaining, leading me to sweet contemplations of my great and glorious God. While thus engaged, it always seemed natural for me to sing, or chant forth my meditations; or, to speak my thoughts in soliloquies with a singing voice.

ON FUTURE PUNISHMENT

[From "The Future Punishment of the Wicked Unavoidable and Intolerable" [1]]

I come now,

III. To show that as impenitent sinners cannot shun the threatened punishment; so neither can they do any thing to deliver themselves from it, or to relieve themselves under it. This is implied in those words of the text, *Can thine hands be strong?* It is with our hands that we make and accomplish things for ourselves. But the wicked in hell will have no strength of hand to accomplish any thing at all for themselves, or to bring to pass any deliverance, or any degree of relief.

1. They will not be able in that conflict to overcome their enemy, and so to deliver themselves. God, who will then under-

[1] The text of this sermon was Ezekiel xxii. 14. The plan is thus indicated by the author: —

"Doctrine.

"Since God hath undertaken to deal with impenitent sinners, they shall neither shun the threatened misery, nor deliver themselves out of it, nor can they bear it.

"In handling this doctrine, I shall, 1. Show what is implied in God's undertaking to deal with impenitent sinners. 2. That therefore they cannot avoid punishment. 3. That they cannot in any measure deliver themselves from it, or do anything for their own relief under it. 4. That they cannot bear it. 5. I shall answer an inquiry; and then proceed to the use."]

take to deal with them, and will gird himself with might to execute wrath, will be their enemy, and will act the part of an enemy with a witness; and they will have no strength to oppose him. Those who live negligent of their souls under the light of the gospel, act as if they supposed that they should be able hereafter to make their part good with God.   1 Cor. x. 22, "Do we provoke the Lord to jealousy?   Are we stronger than he?"—But they will have no power, no might to resist that omnipotence, which will be engaged against them.

2. They will have no strength in their hands to do any thing to appease God, or in the least to abate the fierceness of his wrath. They will not be able to offer any satisfaction: they will not be able to procure God's pity.   Though they cry, God will not hear them.   They will find no price to offer to God, in order to purchase any favor, or to pay any part of their debt.

3. They will not be able to find any to befriend them, and intercede with God for them.   They had the offer of a mediator often made them in this world; but they will have no offers of such a nature in hell.   None will befriend them.   They will have no friend in HELL; all there will be their enemies.   They will have no friend in heaven: none of the saints or angels will befriend them; or if they should, it would be to no purpose. There will be no creature that will have any power to deliver them, nor will any ever pity them.

4. Nor will they ever be able to make their escape.   They will find no means to break prison and flee.   In hell they will be reserved in chains of darkness forever and ever.   Malefactors have often found means to break prison, and escape the hand of civil justice.   But none ever escaped out of the prison of hell, which is God's prison.   It is a strong prison: it is beyond any finite power, or the united strength of all wicked men and devils, to unlock, or break open the door of that prison.   Christ hath the key of hell; "he shuts and no man opens."

5. Nor will they ever be able to find any thing to relieve them in hell.   They will never find any resting place there; any place of respite; any secret corner, which will be cooler than the rest, where they may have a little respite, a small abatement of the extremity of their torment.   They never will be able to find any

cooling stream or fountain, in any part of that world of torment; no, nor so much as a drop of water to cool their tongues. They will find no company to give them any comfort, or to do them the least good. They will find no place, where they can remain, and rest, and take breath for one minute: for they will be tormented with fire and brimstone; and will have no rest day nor night forever and ever.

Thus impenitent sinners will be able neither to shun the punishment threatened, nor to deliver themselves from it, nor to find any relief under it.

I come now,

IV. To show, that neither will they be able to bear it. Neither will their hands be strong to deliver themselves from it, nor will their hearts be able to endure it. It is common with men, when they meet with calamities in this world, in the first place to endeavor to shun them. But if they find, that they cannot shun them, then after they are come, they endeavor to deliver themselves from them as soon as they can; or at least, to order things so, as to deliver themselves in some degree. But if they find that they can by no means deliver themselves, and see that the case is so that they must bear them; then they set themselves to bear them: they fortify their spirits, and take up a resolution, that they will support themselves under them as well as they can. They clothe themselves with all the resolution and courage they are masters of, to keep their spirits from sinking under their calamities.

But it will be utterly in vain for impenitent sinners to think to do thus with respect to the torments of hell. They will not be able to endure them, or at all to support themselves under them: the torment will be immensely beyond their strength. What will it signify for a worm, which is about to be pressed under the weight of some great rock, to be let fall with its whole weight upon it, to collect its strength, to set itself to bear up the weight of the rock, and to preserve itself from being crushed by it? Much more in vain will it be for a poor damned soul, to endeavor to support itself under the weight of the wrath of Almighty God. What is the strength of man, who is but a worm, to support himself against the power of Jehovah, and against the fierce-

ness of his wrath? What is man's strength, when set to bear
up against the exertions of infinite power? Matt. xxi. 44, "Who-
soever shall fall on this stone shall be broken; but on whomso-
ever it shall fall, it will grind him to powder."

When sinners hear of hell torments, they sometimes think
with themselves: Well, if it shall come to that, that I must go
to hell, I will bear it as well as I can: as if by clothing themselves with resolution and firmness of mind, they would be able
to support themselves in some measure; when, alas! they will
have no resolution, no courage at all. However they shall have
prepared themselves, and collected their strength; yet as soon
as they shall begin to feel that wrath, their hearts will melt and
be as water. However before they may seem to harden their
hearts, in order to prepare themselves to bear, yet the first moment
they feel it, their hearts will become like wax before the furnace.
Their courage and resolution will be all gone in an instant; it
will vanish away like a shadow in the twinkling of an eye. The
stoutest and most sturdy will have no more courage than the
feeblest infant: let a man be an infant, or a giant, it will be all
one. They will not be able to keep alive any courage, any strength,
any comfort, any hope at all.

I come now as was proposed,

V. To answer an inquiry which may naturally be raised concerning these things.

INQUIRY. Some may be ready to say, If this be the case, if
impenitent sinners can neither shun future punishment, nor deliver
themselves from it, nor bear it; then what will become of them?

ANSWER. They will wholly sink down into eternal death.
There will be that sinking of heart, of which we now cannot
conceive. We see how it is with the body when in extreme pain.
The nature of the body will support itself for a considerable time
under very great pain, so as to keep from wholly sinking. There
will be great struggles, lamentable groans and panting, and it
may be convulsions. These are the strugglings of nature to support itself under the extremity of the pain. There is, as it were,
a great lothness in nature to yield to it; it cannot bear wholly to
sink.

But yet sometimes pain of body is so very extreme and exquisite, that the nature of the body cannot support itself under it; however loth it may be to sink, yet it cannot bear the pain; there are a few struggles, and throes, and pantings, and it may be a shriek or two, and then nature yields to the violence of the torments, sinks down, and the body dies. This is the death of the body. So it will be with the soul in hell; it will have no strength or power to deliver itself; and its torment and horror will be so great, so mighty, so vastly disproportioned to its strength, that having no strength in the least to support itself, although it be infinitely contrary to the nature and inclination of the soul utterly to sink; yet it will sink, it will utterly and totally sink, without the least degree of remaining comfort, or strength, or courage, or hope. And though it will never be annihilated, its being and perception will never be abolished; yet such will be the infinite depth of gloominess that it will sink into, that it will be in a state of death, eternal death.

The nature of man desires happiness; it is the nature of the soul to crave and thirst after well-being; and if it be under misery, it eagerly pants after relief; and the greater the misery is, the more eagerly doth it struggle for help. But if all relief be withholden, all strength overborne, all support utterly gone; then it sinks into the darkness of death.

We can conceive but little of the matter; we cannot conceive what that sinking of the soul in such a case is. But to help your conception, imagine yourself to be cast into a fiery oven, all of a glowing heat, or into the midst of a glowing brick-kiln, or of a great furnace, where your pain would be as much greater than that occasioned by accidentally touching a coal of fire, as the heat is greater. Imagine also that your body were to lie there for a quarter of an hour, full of fire, as full within and without as a bright coal of fire, all the while full of quick sense; what horror would you feel at the entrance of such a furnace! And how long would that quarter of an hour seem to you! If it were to be measured by a glass, how long would the glass seem to be running! And after you had endured it for one minute, how overbearing would it be to you to think that you had it to endure the other fourteen!

But what would be the effect on your soul, if you knew you

must lie there enduring that torment to the full for twenty-four hours! And how much greater would be the effect, if you knew you must endure it for a whole year; and how vastly greater still, if you knew you must endure it for a thousand years! O then, how would your heart sink, if you thought, if you knew, that you must bear it forever and ever! That there would be no end! That after millions of millions of ages, your torment would be no nearer to an end, than ever it was; and that you never, never should be delivered.

But your torment in hell will be immensely greater than this illustration represents. How then will the heart of a poor creature sink under it! How utterly inexpressible and inconceivable must the sinking of the soul be in such a case!

This is the death threatened in the law. This is dying in the highest sense of the word. This is to die sensibly; to die and know it; to be sensible of the gloom of death. This is to be undone; this is worthy of the name of destruction. This sinking of the soul under an infinite weight, which it cannot bear, is the gloom of hell. We read in Scripture of the blackness of darkness; this is it, this is the very thing. We read in Scripture of sinners being lost, and of their losing their souls: this is the thing intended; this is to lose the soul: they that are the subjects of this are utterly lost.

THE CONVERSION OF A CHILD

[From "A Narrative of Surprising Conversions"]

But I now proceed to the *other Instance* that I would give an Account of, which is of the *little Child* fore-mentioned. Her Name is *Phebe Bartlet*, Daughter of *William Bartlet*. I shall give the Account as I took it from the mouths of her Parents, whose Veracity none that know them doubt of.

She was born in *March*, in the year 1731. About the latter end of *April*, or beginning of *May*, 1735, she was greatly affected by the talk of her Brother, who had been hopefully converted a little before, at about eleven years of Age, and then seriously talked to her about the great Things of Religion. Her Parents did not know of it at that time, and were not wont, in the Counsels they gave to their Children, particularly to direct themselves to her, by reason of her being so young, and as they supposed not capable of Understanding: but after her Brother had talked to her, they observed her very earnestly to listen to the Advice they gave to the other Children; and she was observed very constantly to retire, several times in a Day, as was concluded, for secret Prayer; and grew more and more engaged in Religion, and was more frequent in her Closet; till at last she was wont to visit it five or six times in a Day: and was so engaged in it, that nothing would at any Time divert her from her stated Closet Exercises. Her Mother often observed and watched her, when such Things occurr'd, as she thought most likely to divert her, either by putting it out of her Thoughts, or otherwise engaging her Inclinations; but never could observe her to fail. She mention'd some very remarkable Instances.

She once of her own accord spake of her Unsuccessfulness, in that she could not find God, or to that purpose. But on *Thursday*, the last Day of *July*, about the middle of the Day, the Child being in the Closet, where it used to retire, its Mother heard it speaking aloud; which was unusual, and never had been observed before: And her Voice seemed to be as of one exceeding importunate and engaged; but her Mother could distinctly hear only these Words, (spoken in her childish Manner, but seemed to be spoken with extraordinary earnestness, and out of Distress of Soul) *Pray* BLESSED LORD *give me Salvation!* I PRAY, BEG *pardon all my Sins!* When the Child had done Prayer, she came out of the Closet, and came and sat down by her Mother, and cried out aloud. Her Mother very earnestly asked her several times, what the matter was, before she would make any Answer; but she continued exceedingly crying, and wreathing her Body to and fro, like one in Anguish of Spirit. Her Mother then asked her, whether she was afraid that God would not give her Salvation. She then answered *yes, I am afraid I shall go to Hell!* Her Mother then endeavoured to quiet her, and told her she *would not have her cry,* she *must be a good Girl, and pray every Day, and* she *hoped God would give her Salvation.* But this did not quiet her at all; but she continued thus earnestly crying and taking on for some time, till at length she suddenly ceased crying, and began to smile, and presently said with a smiling Countenance, *Mother, the Kingdom of Heaven is come to me!* Her Mother was surprised at the sudden Alteration, and at the Speech; and knew not what to make of it, but at first said nothing to her. The Child presently spake again, and said, *there is another come to me, and there is another, there is three;* and being asked what she meant, she answered, *one is, Thy will be done, and there is another, Enjoy him for ever;* by which it seems that when the Child said *there is three come to me,* she meant three Passages of its Catechism that came to her Mind.

After the Child had said this, she retired again into her Closet; and her Mother went over to her Brother's, who was next Neighbour; and when she came back, the Child, being come out of the Closet, meets her Mother with this chearful Speech, *I can find God now!* referring to what she had before complained of that she could not find God. Then the Child spoke again, and said, *I love God!* her Mother asked her, *how well* she loved God, whether she loved God *better than her Father and Mother,* she said *yes.* Then she asked her whether she loved God *better than her little Sister* Rachael. She answered *yes, better than anything!* Then her eldest Sister, referring to her saying she could *find God now,* asked her where she could *find God.* She answered *in Heaven: Why,* said she, *have you been in Heaven?* *No,* said the Child. By this it seems not to have been any Imagination of any thing seen with bodily Eyes, that she called God, when she said I can find God now. Her Mother asked her whether she was *afraid of going to Hell,* and that had made her cry. She answered, *yes, I was; but now I shan't.* Her Mother asked her whether she thought that God had given her Salvation: She answered *yes.* Her Mother asked her, *when.* She answered, *to-day.* She appear'd all that Afternoon exceeding chearful and joyful. One of the Neighbours asked her, how she felt herself? She answer'd, *I feel better than I did.* The Neighbour asked her, what made her feel better: She answered, *God makes me.* That Evening as she lay a-bed, she called one of her little Cousins to her that was present in the Room, as having something to say to him; and when he came, she told him, that *Heaven was better than Earth.* The next day being *Friday,* her Mother asking her

her Catechism, asked her *what God made* her *for:* She answered *to serve him,* and added, *every body should serve God, and get an Interest in Christ.*

The same Day the elder Children, when they came home from School, seemed much affected with the extraordinary Change that seemed to be made in *Phebe:* And her Sister *Abigail* standing by, her Mother took occasion to counsel her, now to improve her Time, to prepare for another World: On which *Phebe* burst out in Tears, and cried out *Poor Nabby!* Her Mother told her she would not have her cry, she hoped that God would give *Nabby* Salvation; but that did not quiet her, but she continued earnestly crying for some time; and when she had in a measure ceased, her Sister *Eunice* being by her, she burst out again, and cried *Poor Eunice!* and cried exceedingly; and when she had almost done, she went into another Room, and there looked upon her Sister *Naomi:* and burst out again, crying *Poor Amy!* Her Mother was greatly affected at such a Behaviour in the Child, and knew not what to say to her. One of the Neighbours coming in a little after, asked her what she had cried for. She seemed at first backward to tell the Reason: her Mother told her she might tell that Person, for he *had given* her *an Apple:* Upon which she said, she *cried because* she *was afraid they would go to Hell.*

At Night a certain Minister, that was occasionally in the Town, was at the House, and talked considerably with her, of the Things of Religion; and after he was gone she sat leaning on the Table, with Tears running out of her Eyes: And being asked what made her cry, she said it was *thinking about God.* The next Day being *Saturday,* she seemed great part of the Day to be in a very affectionate Frame, had four turns of Crying, and seemed to endeavour to curb herself, and hide her Tears, and was very backward to talk of the occasion of it. On the *Sabbath* Day she was asked whether she believed in God; she answered *yes:* And being told that *Christ* was the Son of God, she made ready Answer, and said, *I know it.*

From this Time there has appeared a very remarkable abiding Change in the Child: She has been very strict upon the Sabbath; and seems to long for the Sabbath Day before it comes, and will often in the Week-time be enquiring how long it is to the Sabbath

U

Day, and must have the Days particularly counted over that are between, before she will be contented. And she seems to love God's House, is very eager to go thither: Her Mother once asked her why she had such a Mind to go? whether it was not to see fine Folks? She said *no, it* was *to hear Mr. Edwards preach.* When she is in the place of Worship, she is very far from spending her Time there as Children at her Age usually do, but appears with an Attention that is very extraordinary for such a Child. She also appears very desirous at all Opportunities to go to private religious Meetings; and is very still and attentive at Home, in Prayer-time, and has appeared affected in time of Family-Prayer. She seems to delight much in hearing religious Conversation: When I once was there with some others that were Strangers, and talked to her something of Religion, she seemed more than ordinarily attentive; and when we were gone, she looked out very wistly after us, and said, *I wish they would come again!* Her Mother asked her *why:* Says she, *I love to hear them talk!*

She seems to have very much of the Fear of God before her Eyes, and an extraordinary Dread of Sin against him; of which her Mother mentioned the following remarkable Instance. Sometime in *August,* the last Year, she went with some bigger Children, to get some Plumbs, in a Neighbour's Lot, knowing nothing of any harm in what she did; but when she brought some of the Plumbs into the House, her Mother mildly reproved her, and told her that she *must not get Plumbs without leave, because it was Sin: God* had *commanded* her *not to steal.* The Child seemed greatly surprized, and burst out into Tears, and cried out, *I won't have these Plumbs!* and turning to her Sister *Eunice,* very earnestly said to her, *why did you ask me to go to that Plumb-Tree? I should not have gone if you had not asked me.* The other Children did not seem to be much affected or concerned; but there was no pacifying *Phebe.* Her Mother told her she might go and ask leave, and then it would not be sin for her to eat them; and sent one of the *Children* to that end; and when she returned, her Mother told her that the Owner had given leave, now she might eat them, and it would not be stealing. This still'd her a little while; but presently she broke out again into an exceeding Fit of *Crying:* Her Mother asked her *what* made her *cry again?* *Why* she cried *now, since* they had asked *leave?* *What* it was that troubled her now? And asked her several times very earnestly, before she made any Answer; but at last said, *it was because*, BECAUSE IT WAS SIN. She continued a considerable time crying; and said she would not *go again if Eunice* asked her *an hundred Times;* and she retained her Aversion to that Fruit for a considerable time, under the remembrance of her former Sin.

CONCERNING THE NOTION OF LIBERTY, AND OF MORAL AGENCY

[From the "Treatise on the Freedom of the Will"]

The plain and obvious Meaning of the Words *Freedom* and *Liberty*, in common Speech, is *Power, Opportunity, or Advantage, that any one has, to do as he pleases.* Or in other Words, his being free from Hindrance or Impediment in the Way of doing, or conducting in any Respect, as he wills.[1] And the contrary to Liberty, whatever Name we call that by, is a Person's being hinder'd or unable to conduct as he will, or being necessitated to do otherwise.

If this which I have mentioned be the Meaning of the Word Liberty, in the ordinary Use of Language; as I trust that none that has ever learn'd to talk, and is unprejudiced, will deny; then it will follow, that in Propriety of Speech, neither Liberty, nor it's contrary, can properly be ascribed to any Being or Thing, but that which has such a Faculty, Power or Property, as is called Will. For that which is possessed of no such Thing as *Will*, can't have any *Power* or *Opportunity* of doing *according to it's Will*, nor be necessitated to act *contrary to its Will*, nor be restrained from acting agreeably to it. And therefore to talk of Liberty, or the contrary, as belonging to the *very Will itself*, is not to speak good Sense; if we judge of Sense, and Nonsense, by the original & proper Signification of Words. For the *Will*

---

[1] I say not only *doing*, but *conducting;* because a voluntary forbearing to do, sitting still, keeping Silence &c. are Instances of Persons *Conduct*, about which Liberty is exercised; tho' they are not so properly called *doing*.

it self is not an Agent that *has a Will:* The Power of choosing, it self, has not a Power of chusing. That which has the Power of Volition or Choice is the Man or the Soul, and not the Power of Volition it self. And he that has the Liberty of doing according to his Will, is the Agent or Doer who is possessed of the Will; and not the Will which he is possessed of. We say with Propriety, that a Bird let loose has Power & Liberty to fly; but not that the Bird's Power of flying has a Power & Liberty of flying. To be free is the Property of an Agent, who is possessed of Powers & Faculties, as much as to be cunning, valiant, bountiful, or zealous. But these Qualities are the Properties of Men or Persons; and not the Properties of Properties.

There are two Things that are contrary to this which is called Liberty in common Speech. One is *Constraint;* the same is otherwise called *Force, Compulsion, & Coaction;* which is a Person's being necessitated to do a Thing *contrary* to his Will. The other is *Restraint;* which is his being hindred, and not having Power to do *according* to his Will. But that which has no Will, can't be the Subject of these Things.—I need say the less on this Head, Mr. *Locke* having set the same Thing forth, with so great Clearness, in his *Essay on the human Understanding.*

But one Thing more I would observe concerning what is vulgarly called *Liberty;* namely, that Power & Opportunity for one to do and conduct as he will, or according to his Choice, is all that is meant by it; without taking into the Meaning of the Word, any Thing of the Cause or Original of that Choice; or at all considering how the Person came to have such a Volition; whether it was caused by some external Motive, or internal habitual Bias; whether it was determin'd by some internal antecedent Volition, or whether it happen'd without a Cause; whether it was necessarily connected with something foregoing, or not connected. Let the Person come by his Volition or Choice how he will, yet, if he is able, and there is Nothing in the Way to hinder his pursuing and executing his Will, the Man is fully & perfectly free, according to the primary and common Notion of Freedom.

What has been said may be sufficient to shew what is meant by *Liberty*, according to the common Notions of Mankind, and in the usual & primary Acceptation of the Word: But the Word, as used by *Arminians, Pelagians,* & others, who oppose the *Calvinists,* has an entirely different Signification. — These several Things belong to their Notion of Liberty.

1. That it consists in a *Self-determining* Power in the Will, or a certain Sovereignty the Will has over it self, and it's own Acts, whereby it determines its own Volitions; so as not to be dependent in it's Determinations, on any Cause without it self, nor determined by any Thing prior to it's own Acts. 2. *Indifference* belongs to Liberty in their Notion of it, or that the Mind, previous to the Act of Volition be, *in iquilibrio.* 3. *Contingence* is another Thing that belongs and is essential to it; not in the common Acceptation of the Word, as that has been already explain'd, but as opposed to all *Necessity,* or any fixed & certain Connection with some previous Ground or Reason of its Existence. They suppose the Essence of Liberty so much to consist in these Things, that unless the Will of Man be free in this Sense, he has no real Freedom, how much soever he may be at Liberty to act according to his Will.

A *moral Agent* is a Being that is capable of those Actions that have a moral Quality, and which can properly be denominated good or evil in a moral Sense, vertuous or vicious, commendable or faulty. To moral Agency belongs a *moral Faculty,* or Sense of moral Good & Evil, or of such a Thing as Desert or Worthiness of Praise or Blame, Reward or Punishment; and a Capacity which an Agent has of being influenced in his Actions by moral Inducements or Motives, exhibited to the View of Understanding & Reason, to engage to a Conduct agreable to the moral Faculty.

The Sun is very excellent & beneficial in it's Action and Influence on the Earth, in warming it, and causing it to bring forth it's Fruits; but it is not a moral Agent: It's Action, tho' good, is not vertuous or meritorious. Fire that breaks out in a City, and consumes great Part of it, is very mischievous in its Operation; but is not a moral Agent: what it does is not faulty or sinful, or deserving of any Punishment. The brute Creatures are not moral Agents: the Actions of some of 'em are very profitable & pleasant; others are very hurtful: yet, seeing they have no moral Faculty, or Sense of Desert, and don't act from Choice guided by

Understanding, or with a Capacity of reasoning and reflecting, but only from Instinct, and are not capable of being influenced by moral Inducements, their Actions are not properly sinful or vertuous; nor are they properly the Subjects of any such moral Treatment for what they do, as moral Agents are for their Faults or good Deeds.

THOMAS GODFREY

[Thomas Godfrey's fame rests largely on the fact that he was the author of the first tragedy written and acted in America, but he deserves to be remembered for the intrinsic merit, or at least promise, of some of his performances. He was born in Philadelphia in 1736, and died in North Carolina before reaching the age of twenty-seven. His father, who bore the same name, was a glazier of mathematical proclivities whose memory is preserved in Franklin's "Autobiography." Thomas Godfrey the younger received but a slight education, and was apprenticed to a watchmaker, and afterward engaged in business. Some of his shorter poems were published in the *American Magazine* during his lifetime. The majority are in the heroic couplet, but the author attempted a variety of metres. It is noteworthy that, writing when he did, and of course following Pope and Dryden to a considerable extent, he was influenced by the more musical masters of English verse. The "Assembly of Birds" is a paraphrase of Chaucer's "Parliament of Foules," and "The Court of Fancy" shows indebtedness to the same poet's "Hous of Fame." There are evident echoes of Milton, and hints of the influence of Spenser. Godfrey's tragedy, "The Prince of Parthia," was written shortly before his death, and was performed in Philadelphia in 1767. It is not certain that the author ever saw a play on the stage, and his reading in the dramatists could not have been extensive. "The Prince of Parthia" is a bloody story of ambition, the jealousy of man and woman, and revenge, and is almost ludicrously crude in many ways; but it is interesting as an attempt, unprecedented in America, at one of the higher forms of composition.

The selections are from the only edition of Godfrey's works, which were collected by his friend Nathaniel Evans and published in Philadelphia under the title "Juvenile Poems on Various Subjects, with the Prince of Parthia, a Tragedy," in 1765.]

PASTORAL

[To Dr. J — K —sl — y, jun.]

The young *Alexis* drove his bleating Flock
To the sea's side, where seated on a rock,
That over-look'd the wave, in pensive mood,
He threw his eyes along the azure flood;

His sadn'd brow well anxious care express'd,
And oft the sigh would heave his youthful breast,
His flock neglected rang'd around him wide,
And useless now his pipe hung by his side.

Calm was the sea, the sky appear'd serene,
No angry storms deform'd the pleasing scene;
Hush'd in their caves the ruder winds were laid,
And only gentle western breezes play'd.
Gay beauty round seem'd blooming ev'ry where,
And the bright scene half rob'd him of his care.
When a gay bark with spreading sails display'd,
Appear'd to view, in garlands rich array'd.
Swift o'er the waves with eagle's speed she glides,
And sportive dolphins wanton'd by her sides,
Aloft in air the silken streamers flew,
While the shrill music chear'd the jovial crew.

Oh! thou, from whose blest skill our bodies find
Sweet ease, behold the sickness of the mind:
See, with what force, love sways the youthful heart,
Love, which still triumphs o'er thy heav'nly art.

Alexis thus — the seaman's life how blest!
No anxious thoughts disturb his peaceful breast.
Free as the wind from shore to shore he roves,
Tastes ev'ry sweet, and ev'ry bliss improves.
He wears no haughty beauty's servile chain,
Nor heeds a Delia's frown or cold disdain;
Why was I form'd with such an abject mind,
Slave to a Fair the proudest of her kind?

Then sudden all the heav'ns appear'd o'erspread,
And the loud thunder shook the Ocean's bed,
While streaming lightning dreadful fir'd the sky,
And the rough billows tost their heads on high:
Now to the heav'ns the giddy bark is rear'd,
And as fam'd Argo's rival there appear'd;

And then as sudden from th' amazing height
Sunk midst the watry vales, and shun'd the sight;
While from her shatter'd masts the rude winds bear
Sails, cords and streamers, wildly thro' the air.

    The Shepherd thus, ah! faithless cruel sea,
Thus *Delia* smil'd, and thus she did betray.
Caught by the pleasing views, I left the shore,
And gave my peace to seas untry'd before;
But soon, too soon the pleasing prospects fled,
And swelling waves and tempests did succeed.
Witness, ye groves, and eke, ye pow'rs divine,
How oft she's sworn her faithless heart was mine.
Now, fir'd by female pride, she scorns the truth,
And gives to wealthy *Ageon* her youth.
He's rich in num'rous flocks, scarce knows his store,
My love is all, nor can I boast of more.

    How oft I've led her thro' the shady grove,
While both our souls seem'd join'd in mutual love!
Ah! then the Sirens softness grac'd her tongue,
While quiv'ring on the pleasing sounds I hung,
Such were the sounds which 'woke the slumb'ring shade,
Such were the sounds which rais'd her from the dead!
Such were the sounds of *Amphion's* charming lyre,
And such the music of the heav'nly quire!

    How oft when seated by the chrystal flood,
Pleas'd would we captivate the finny brood!
There in the floating mirror would I trace
Each striking beauty of her angel face,
Her cheek embellish'd with the rosy die,
Her ruby lip, and heav'nly sparkling eye,
'Til some rude wind would o'er the surface pass,
And envious snatch the beauteous mimic face.
How great the change! — and then he starting spy'd
Her body floating on the boist'rous tide.

And by the charmer's side the wild waves bore,
Still link'd in death, *Ageon* to the shore.

But, oh! how fill'd with terror at the sight!
His eyes were veil'd in endless shades of night.
Cold was her breast, quick fleeting life had fled,
And on her faded cheeks the rose lay dead.
Fix'd like a figur'd stone awhile he stood,
And gave the tear with anguish to the flood;
Then frantic clasp'd her midst the briny lave,
And dash'd with anger each intruding wave:
He eager prest her lips, now pale and wet,
But for his warmth a deadly coldness met;
Tho' once with ruby lustre bright they shone,
Their glow was lost, and all their sweetness gone.
Now welcome death, the lovesick Shepherd cry'd,
And fainting on her clay-cold bosom dy'd.

SONG

1

When in *Celia's* heavn'ly Eye
Soft inviting Love I spy,
Tho' you say 'tis all a cheat,
I must clasp the dear deceit.

2

Why should I more knowledge gain,
When it only gives me pain?
If deceiv'd I'm still at rest,
In the sweet Delusion blest.

THE TRIALS OF VIRTUE

[From "The Prince of Parthia" [1]]

ACT IV, SCENE VII.

ARSACES, BARZAPHERNES, AND GOTARZES.

BARZAPHERNES. At length we've forc'd our entrance —
O my lov'd Prince! to see thee thus, indeed,
Melts e'en me to a woman's softness; see
My eyes o'erflow — Are these the ornaments
For Royal hands? rude manacles! oh shameful!
Is this thy room of state, this gloomy goal?
Without attendance, and thy bed the pavement?
But, ah! how diff'rent was our parting last!
When flush'd with vict'ry, reeking from the slaughter,
You saw Arabia's Sons scour o'er the plain
In shameful flight, before your conqu'ring sword;
Then shone you like the God of battle.
　　ARSACES.　　　　　　　　　　Welcome! —
Welcome my loyal friends! *Barzaphernes!*
My good old soldier, to my bosom thus!
Gotarzes, my lov'd Brother! now I'm happy. —
But, say, my soldier, why these threatning arms?
Why am I thus releas'd by force? my Father,
I should have said the King, had he relented,
He'd not have us'd this method to enlarge me.
Alas! I fear, too forward in your love,
You'll brand me with the rebel's hated name.
　　BARZAPHERNES. I am by nature blunt — the soldier's manner.
Unus'd to the soft arts practis'd at courts.

[1 Arsaces, Prince of Parthia, returned from his victory over the Arabians to
find himself hated by his younger brother Vardanes, who was jealous both of
his triumphs in war, and of his success in winning the love of Evanthe. Before
the opening of this scene, Vardanes has persuaded King Artabanus to imprison
Arsaces on a false suspicion, and has then caused the murder of the king, and
taken Evanthe prisoner. These proceedings Vardanes thinks to keep secret until
he has killed Arsaces and usurped the kingdom; but intelligence has been carried
to Barzaphernes, Arsaces's Lieutenant-General, who has hastened to the relief
of the Prince.]

Nor can I move the passions, or disguise
The sorr'wing tale to mitigate the smart.
Then seek it not: I would sound the alarm,
Loud as the trumpet's clangour, in your ears;
Nor will I hail you, as our Parthia's King,
'Til you've full reveng'd your Father's murther.

 ARSACES. Murther? — good heav'n!

 BARZAPHERNES. The tale requires some time;
And opportunity must not be lost;
Your traitor Brother, who usurps your rights,
Must, ere his faction gathers to a head,
Have from his brows his new-born honours torn.

 ARSACES. What, dost thou say, murther'd by *Vardanes?*
Impious parricide! — detested villain! —
Give me a sword, and onward to the charge,
Stop gushing tears, for I will weep in blood,
And sorrow with the groans of dying men. —
Revenge! revenge! — oh! — all my soul's on fire!

 GOTARZES. 'Twas not *Vardanes* struck the fatal blow,
Though, great in pow'r usurp'd, he dares support
The actor, vengeful *Lysias;* to his breast
He clasps, with grateful joy, the bloody villain;
Who soon meant, with ruffian wiles, to cut
You from the earth, and also me.

 ARSACES.   Just heav'ns! —
But, gentle Brother, how didst thou elude
The vigilant, suspicious, tyrant's craft.

 GOTARZES. *Phraates,* by an accident, obtain'd]
The knowledge of the deed, and warn'd by him
I bent my flight toward the camp, to seek
Protection and revenge; but scarce I'd left
The city when I o'ertook the General.

 BARZAPHERNES. 'Ere the sun 'rose I gain'd th' intelligence:
The soldiers when they heard the dreadful tale,
First stood aghast, and motionless with horror.
Then suddenly, inspir'd with noble rage,
Tore up their ensigns, calling on their leaders
To march them to the city instantly.

I, with some trusty few, with speed came forward,
To raise our friends within, and gain your freedom.
Nor hazard longer, by delays, your safety.
Already faithful *Phraates* has gain'd
A num'rous party of the citizens;
With these we mean t'attack the Royal Palace,
Crush the bold tyrant with surprize, while sunk
In false security; and vengeance wreck,
'Ere that he thinks the impious crime be known.
   ARSACES. O! parent being, Ruler of yon heav'n!
Who bade creation spring to order, hear me.
What ever sins are laid upon my soul,
Now let them not prove heavy on this day,
To sink my arm, or violate my cause.
The sacred rights of Kings, my Country's wrongs,
The punishment of fierce impiety,
And a lov'd Father's death, call forth my sword. —

Now on; I feel all calm within my breast,
And ev'ry busy doubt is hush'd to rest;
Smile heav'n propitious on my virtuous cause,
Nor aid the wretch who dares disdain your laws.
END of the FOURTH ACT.

ACT V, SCENE I.

The PALACE.

The Curtain rises, slowly, to soft music, and discovers *Evanthe*
   sleeping on a Sofa; after the music ceases, *Vardanes* enters.

   VARDANES. Now shining Empire standing at the goal,
Beck'ns me forward to increase my speed;
But, yet, *Arsaces* lives, bane to my hopes,
Lysias I'll urge to ease me of his life,
Then give the villain up to punishment.
The shew of justice gains the changeling croud.
Besides, I ne'er will harbour in my bosom
Such serpents, ever ready with their stings —

But now one hour for love and fair *Evanthe* —
Hence with ambition's cares — see, where reclin'd,
In slumbers all her sorrows are dismiss'd,
Sleep seems to heighten ev'ry beauteous feature,
And adds peculiar softness to each grace.
She weeps — in dreams some lively sorrow pains her —
I'll take one kiss — oh! what a balmy sweetness!
Give me another — and another still —
For ever thus I'd dwell upon her lips.
Be still my heart, and calm unruly transports. —
Wake her, with music, from this mimic death.   [Music sounds.]

SONG

Tell me, Phillis, tell me why,
  You appear so wond'rous coy,
When that glow, and sparkling eye,
  Speak you want to taste the joy?
Prithee give this fooling o'er,
Nor torment your lover more.

While youth is warm within our veins,
  And nature tempts us to be gay,
Give to pleasure loose the reins,
  Love and youth fly swift away.
Youth in pleasure should be spent,
Age will come, we'll then repent.

EVANTHE (waking) I come ye lovely shades — Ha! am I here?
Still in the tyrant's palace?   Ye bright pow'rs!
Are all my blessings then but vis'onary?
Methought I was arriv'd on that blest shore
Where happy souls for ever dwell, crown'd with
Immortal bliss; *Arsaces* led me through
The flow'ry groves, while all around me gleam'd
Thousand and thousand shades, who welcom'd me
With pleasing songs of joy — *Vardanes*, ha! —
  VARDANES. Why beams the angry lightning of thine eye

Against thy sighing slave? Is love a crime?
Oh! if to dote, with such excess of passion
As rises e'en to mad extravagance
Is criminal, I then am so, indeed.
    EVANTHE. Away! vile man! —
    VARDANES.   If to pursue thee e'er
With all the humblest offices of love,
If ne'er to know one single thought that does
Not bear thy bright idea, merits scorn —
    EVANTHE. Hence from my sight — nor let me, thus, pollute
Mine eyes, with looking on a wretch like thee,
Thou cause of all my ills; I sicken at
Thy loathsome presence —
    VARDANES.   'Tis not always thus,
Nor dost thou ever meet the sounds of love
With rage and fierce disdain: *Arsaces*, soon,
Could smooth thy brow, and melt thy icy breast.
    EVANTHE. Ha! does it gall thee? Yes, he could, he could;
Oh! when he speaks, such sweetness dwells upon
His accents, all my soul dissolves to love,
And warm desire; such truth and beauty join'd!
His looks are soft and kind, such gentleness
Such virtue swells his bosom! in his eye
Sits majesty, commanding ev'ry heart.
Strait as the pine, the pride of all the grove,
More blooming than the spring, and sweeter far,
Than asphodels or roses infant sweets.
Oh! I could dwell forever on his praise,
Yet think eternity was scarce enough
To tell the mighty theme; here in my breast
His image dwells, but one dear thought of him,
When fancy paints his Person to my eye,
As he was wont in tenderness dissolv'd,
Sighing his vows, or kneeling at my feet,
Wipes off all mem'ry of my wretchedness.
    VARDANES. I know this brav'ry is affected, yet
It gives me joy, to think my rival only
Can in imagination taste thy beauties.

Let him, — 'twill ease him in his solitude,
And gild the horrors of his prison-house,
Till death shall —
    EVANTHE.   Ha! what was that? till death — ye Gods!
Ah, now I feel distress's tort'ring pang —
Thou canst not villain — darst not think his death —
O mis'ry! —
    VARDANES. Naught but your kindness saves him,
Yet bless me, with your love, and he is safe;
But the same frown which kills my growing hopes,
Gives him to death.

JOHN WOOLMAN

[John Woolman, the Quaker, possessed a personal simplicity and a purity of heart that give great charm to his impractically idealistic writings. He was born in Northampton, N. J., in 1720, and passed his boyhood on a farm. During the greater part of his adult life he travelled among the Friends in different parts of America, speaking at their meetings, conversing with them personally, and working with especial vigor against slave-holding, which was then practised by some members of the society. On these trips he supported himself by working at his trade, that of a tailor, and sometimes by acting as a clerk or notary and drawing wills and other papers. In 1772 he went on a visit to the Quakers in England, and died of the smallpox in the city of York soon after his arrival. During his lifetime he published a few tracts, and his "Works" in two parts were issued in Philadelphia after his death. The most important of his writings is his "Journal," which has been many times reprinted. The selections here given are from the edition by J. G. Whittier, published in 1871.]

THE WEARING OF DYED GARMENTS

[From the "Journal"]

The use of hats and garments dyed with a dye hurtful to them, and wearing more clothes in summer than are useful, grew more uneasy to me, believing them to be customs which have not their foundation in pure wisdom. The apprehension of being singular from my beloved friends was a strait upon me, and thus I continued in the use of some things contrary to my judgment.

On the 31st of fifth month, 1761, I was taken ill of a fever, and after it had continued near a week I was in great distress of body. One day there was a cry raised in me that I might understand the cause of my affliction, and improve under it, and my conformity to some customs which I believed were not right was brought to my remembrance. In the continuance of this exercise I felt all the powers in me yield themselves up into the hands of Him who gave me being, and was made thankful that he had taken hold of me by his chastisements. Feeling the necessity of further purifying, there was now no desire in me for health until the design of my correction was answered.   Thus I lay in abasement and brokenness of spirit, and as I felt a sinking down into a calm resignation, so I felt, as in an instant, an inward healing in my nature; and from that time forward I grew better.

Though my mind was thus settled in relation to hurtful dyes, I felt easy to wear my garments heretofore made, and continued to do so about nine months.   Then I thought of getting a hat the natural color of the fur, but the apprehension of being looked upon as one affecting singularity felt uneasy to me.   Here I had occasion to consider that things, though small in themselves, being clearly enjoined by Divine authority, become great things to us; and I trusted that the Lord would support me in the trials that might attend singularity, so long as singularity was only for his sake.   On this account I was under close exercise of mind in the time of our General Spring Meeting, 1762, greatly desiring to be rightly directed; when, being deeply bowed in spirit before the Lord, I was made willing to submit to what I apprehended was required of me, and when I returned home got a hat of the natural color of the fur.

In attending meetings this singularity was a trial to me, and more especially at this time, as white hats were used by some who were fond of following the changeable modes of dress, and as some Friends who knew not from what motives I wore it grew shy of me, I felt my way for a time shut up in the exercise of the ministry. In this condition, my mind being turned toward my Heavenly Father with fervent cries that I might be preserved to walk before him in the meekness of wisdom, my heart was often tender in meetings, and I felt an inward consolation which to me was very precious under these difficulties.

I had several dyed garments fit for use which I believed it best to wear till I had occasion for new ones.   Some Friends were apprehensive that my wearing such a hat savored of an affected singularity; those who spoke with me in a friendly way I generally informed, in a few words, that I believed my wearing it was not in my own will.   I had at times been sensible that a superficial friendship had been dangerous to me; and many Friends being now uneasy with me, I had an inclination to acquaint some with the manner of my being led into these things; yet upon a deeper thought I was for a time most easy to omit it, believing the present dispensation was profitable, and trusting that if I kept my place the Lord in his own time would open the hearts of Friends towards me. I have since had cause to admire his goodness and loving-kindness in leading about and instructing me, and in opening and enlarging my heart in some of our meetings.

A SEA VOYAGE

[From the "Journal"]

Having been some time under a religious concern to prepare for crossing the seas, in order to visit Friends in the northern parts of England, and more particularly in Yorkshire, after consideration I thought it expedient to inform Friends of it at our Monthly Meeting at Burlington, who, having unity with me therein, gave me a certificate. I afterwards communicated the same to our Quarterly Meeting, and they likewise certified their concurrence. Some time after, at the General Spring Meeting of ministers and elders, I thought it my duty to acquaint them with the religious exercise which attended my mind; and they likewise signified their unity therewith by a certificate, dated the 24th of third month, 1772, directed to Friends in Great Britain.

In the fourth month following I thought the time was come for me to make some inquiry for a suitable conveyance; and as my concern was principally towards the northern parts of England, it seemed most proper to go in a vessel bound to Liverpool or Whitehaven. While I was at Philadelphia deliberating on this subject I was informed that my beloved friend Samuel Emlen, junior, intended to go to London, and had taken a passage for himself in the cabin of the ship called the Mary and Elizabeth, of which James Sparks was master, and John Head, of the city of Philadelphia, one of the owners; and feeling a draught in my mind towards the steerage of the same ship, I went first and opened to Samuel the feeling I had concerning it.

My beloved friend wept when I spake to him, and appeared glad that I had thoughts of going in the vessel with him, though my prospect was toward the steerage; and he offering to go with me, we went on board, first into the cabin, — a commodious room, — and then into the steerage, where we sat down on a chest, the sailors being busy about us. The owner of the ship also came and sat down with us. My mind was turned towards Christ, the Heavenly Counsellor, and feeling at this time my own will subjected, my heart was contrite before him. A motion was made by the owner to go and sit in the cabin, as a place more retired; but I felt easy to leave the ship, and, making no agreement as to a passage in her, told the owner if I took a passage in the ship I believed it would be in the steerage; but did not say much as to my exercise in that case.

After I went to my lodgings, and the case was a little known in town, a Friend laid before me the great inconvenience attending a passage in the steerage, which for a time appeared very discouraging to me.

I soon after went to bed, and my mind was under a deep exercise before the Lord, whose helping hand was manifested to me as I slept that night, and his love strengthened my heart. In the morning I went with two Friends on board the vessel again, and after a short time spent therein, I went with Samuel Emlen to the house of the owner, to whom, in the hearing of Samuel only, I opened my exercise in relation to a scruple I felt with regard to a passage in the cabin, in substance as follows: —

"That on the outside of that part of the ship where the cabin was I observed sundry sorts of carved work and imagery; that in the cabin I observed some superfluity of workmanship of several sorts; and that according to the ways of men's reckoning, the sum of money to be paid for a passage in that apartment has some relation to the expense of furnishing it to please the minds of such as give way to a conformity to this world; and that in this, as in other cases, the moneys received from the passengers are calculated to defray the cost of these superfluities, as well as the other expenses of their passage. I therefore felt a scruple with regard to paying my money to be applied to such purposes."

As my mind was now opened, I told the owner that I had, at several times, in my travels, seen great oppressions on this continent, at which my heart had been much affected and brought into a feeling of the state of the sufferers; and having many times been engaged in the fear and love of God to labor with those under whom the oppressed have been borne down and afflicted, I have often perceived that with a view to get riches and to provide estates for children, that they may live conformably to the customs and honors of this world, many are entangled in the spirit of oppression, and the exercise of my soul had been such that I could not find peace in joining in anything which I saw was against that wisdom which is pure.

After this I agreed for a passage in the steerage; and hearing that Joseph White had desired to see me, I went to his house, and next day home, where I tarried two nights. Early the next morning I parted with my family under a sense of the humbling hand of God upon me, and, going to Philadelphia, had an opportunity with several of my beloved friends, who appeared to be concerned for me on account of the unpleasant situation of that part of the vessel in which I was likely to lodge. In these opportunities my mind, through the mercies of the Lord, was kept low in an inward waiting for his help; and Friends having expressed their desire that I might have a more convenient place than the steerage, did not urge it, but appeared disposed to leave me to the Lord.

Having stayed two nights at Philadelphia, I went the next day to Derby Monthly Meeting, where through the strength of Divine love my heart was enlarged towards the youth there present, under which I was helped to labor in some tenderness of spirit. I lodged at William Horn's and afterwards went to Chester, where I met with Samuel Emlen, and we went on board 1st of fifth month, 1772. As I sat alone on the deck I felt a satisfactory evidence that my proceedings were not in my own will, but under the power of the cross of Christ.

Seventh of fifth month. — We have had rough weather mostly since I came on board, and the passengers, James Reynolds, John Till Adams, Sarah Logan and her hired maid, and John Bispham, all sea-sick at times; from which sickness, through the tender mercies of my Heavenly Father, I have been preserved, my afflictions now being of another kind. There appeared an openness in the minds of the master of the ship and in the cabin passengers towards me. We are often together on the deck, and sometimes in the cabin. My mind, through the merciful help of the Lord, hath been preserved in a good degree watchful and quiet, for which I have great cause to be thankful.

As my lodging in the steerage, now near a week, hath afforded me sundry opportunities of seeing, hearing, and feeling with respect to the life and spirit of many poor sailors, an exercise of soul hath attended me in regard to placing out children and youth where they may be likely to be exampled and instructed in the pure fear of the Lord.

Being much among the seamen I have, from a motion of love, taken sundry opportunities with one of them at a time, and have in free conversation labored to turn their minds towards the fear of the Lord.   This day we had a meeting in the cabin, where my heart was contrite under a feeling of Divine love.

I believe a communication with different parts of the world by sea is at times consistent with the will of our Heavenly Father, and to educate some youth in the practice of sailing, I believe may be right; but how lamentable is the present corruption of the world!   How impure are the channels through which trade is conducted!   How great is the danger to which poor lads are exposed when placed on shipboard to learn the art of sailing! Five lads training up for the seas were on board this ship.   Two of them were brought up in our Society, and the other, by name James Naylor, is a member, to whose father James Naylor, mentioned in Sewel's history, appears to have been uncle.   I often feel a tenderness of heart towards these poor lads, and at times look at them as though they were my children according to the flesh.

O that all may take heed and beware of covetousness! O that all may learn of Christ, who was meek and lowly of heart. Then in faithfully following him he will teach us to be content with food and raiment without respect to the customs or honors of this world.   Men thus redeemed will feel a tender concern for their fellow-creatures, and a desire that those in the lowest stations may be assisted and encouraged, and where owners of ships attain to the perfect law of liberty and are doers of the Word, these will be blessed in their deeds.

A ship at sea commonly sails all night, and the seamen take their watches four hours at a time.   Rising to work in the night, it is not commonly pleasant in any case, but in dark rainy nights it is very disagreeable, even though each man were furnished with all conveniences. If, after having been on deck several hours in the night, they come down into the steerage soaking wet, and are so closely stowed that proper convenience for change of garments is not easily come at, but for want of proper room their wet garments are thrown in heaps, and sometimes, through much crowding, are trodden under foot in going to their lodgings and getting out of them, and it is difficult at times for each to find his own. Here are trials for the poor sailors.

Now, as I have been with them in my lodge, my heart hath often yearned for them, and tender desires have been raised in me that all owners and masters of vessels may dwell in the love of God and therein act uprightly, and by seeking less for gain and looking carefully to their ways they may earnestly labor to remove all cause of provocation from the poor seamen, so that they may neither fret nor use excess of strong drink; for, indeed, the poor creatures, in the wet and cold, seem to apply at times to strong drink to supply the want of other convenience. Great reformation is wanting in the world, and the necessity of it among those who do business on great waters hath at this time been abundantly opened before me.

Eighth of fifth month. — This morning the clouds gathered, the wind blew strong from the southeast, and before noon so increased that sailing appeared dangerous. The seamen then bound up some of their sails and took down others, and the storm increasing they put the dead-lights, so called, into the cabin windows and lighted a lamp as at night. The wind now blew vehemently, and the sea wrought to that degree that an awful seriousness prevailed in the cabin, in which I spent, I believe, about seventeen hours, for the cabin passengers had given me frequent invitations, and I thought the poor wet toiling seamen had need of all the room in the crowded steerage. They now ceased from sailing and put the vessel in the posture called lying to.

My mind during this tempest, through the gracious assistance of the Lord, was preserved in a good degree of resignation; and at times I expressed a few words in his love to my shipmates in regard to the all-sufficiency of Him who formed the great deep, and whose care is so extensive that a sparrow falls not without his notice; and thus in a tender frame of mind I spoke to them of the necessity of our yielding in true obedience to the instructions of our Heavenly Father, who sometimes through adversities intendeth our refinement.

About eleven at night I went out on the deck. The sea wrought exceedingly, and the high, foaming waves round about had in some sort the appearance of fire, but did not give much if any light. The sailor at the helm said he lately saw a corposant at the head of the mast. I observed that the master of the ship ordered the carpenter to keep on the deck; and, though he said little, I apprehended his care was that the carpenter with his axe might be in readiness in case of any extremity. Soon after this the vehemency of the wind abated, and before morning they again put the ship under sail.

Tenth of fifth month. — It being the first day of the week and fine weather, we had a meeting in the cabin, at which most of the seamen were present; this meeting was to me a strengthening time. 13th. — As I continue to lodge in the steerage I feel an openness this morning to express something further of the state of my mind in respect to poor lads bound apprentice to learn the art of sailing. As I believe sailing is of use in the world, a labor of soul attends me that the pure counsel of truth may be humbly waited for in this case by all concerned in the business of the seas. A pious father whose mind is exercised for the everlasting welfare of his child may not with a peaceable mind place him out to an employment among a people whose common course of life is manifestly corrupt and profane. Great is the present defect among seafaring men in regard to virtue and piety; and, by reason of an abundant traffic and many ships being used for war, so many people are employed on the sea that the subject of placing lads to this employment appears very weighty.

When I remember the saying of the Most High through his prophet, "This people have I formed for myself; they shall show forth my praise," and think of placing children among such to learn the practice of sailing, the consistency of it with a pious education seems to me like that mentioned by the prophet, "There is no answer from God."

Profane examples are very corrupting and very forcible. And as my mind day after day and night after night hath been affected with a sympathizing tenderness towards poor children who are put to the employment of sailors, I have sometimes had weighty conversation with the sailors in the steerage, who were mostly respectful to me and became more so the longer I was with them. They mostly appeared to take kindly what I said to them; but their minds were so deeply impressed with the almost universal depravity among sailors that the poor creatures in their answers to me have revived in my remembrance that of the degenerate Jews a little before the captivity, as repeated by Jeremiah the prophet, "There is no hope."

BENJAMIN FRANKLIN

[The story of Benjamin Franklin's long and eventful life cannot here be given in detail. He was born in Boston in 1706, and died in Philadelphia in 1790. As a boy he was precocious, and he remained vigorous until his death; so that his active career covered a longer period than the lifetime of most men. He saw the profoundest changes in politics, social life, and scientific thought, and he himself had a part in much that was accomplished in these different lines of activity. He was long an influential editor and publisher at Philadelphia; he served Pennsylvania in various official capacities at home, and as agent in England; he was postmaster-general for the colonies, member of the committee which drafted the Declaration of Independence, Minister to France, member of the Peace Commission, and delegate to the Constitutional Convention; he won international fame for his researches in science; he promoted many plans for civic improvements, and for the founding of educational and benevolent institutions; and in his "Autobiography" he wrote the first American book that is still of wide general interest.

Franklin's strength and versatility were personal qualities which would have been the same anywhere; but it may aid in understanding his character to remember that he was a New Englander who found an opportunity for development in the freer atmosphere of Pennsylvania. The intenser religious faith and the finer idealism of Puritanism he seems never to have had. But he embodied in an unusual degree the shrewdness and practicality of the Puritans. In all that concerned practical matters and getting on in the world he was a typical Yankee. An unfortunate side of his character is seen in many intolerably coarse passages of his writings, and in his "*errata,*" as, in printer's metaphor, he called his breaches of the moral law. These last are to a slight extent redeemed by the frankness with which he confesses them, and regrets them. Neither his life nor his writings were such as to offer the highest inspiration, and yet few writers have had a stronger influence for right living. The secret of this anomaly is that he believed the most practical way to make people good was to teach them to be healthy, wealthy, and wise.

The collected writings of Franklin fill ten large volumes, and treat a great variety of subjects. Most of them are interesting. It is not alone the scientist or the historian who will enjoy reading his accounts of electrical experiments, or his lively political satires. Still, his fame as an author rests mainly on the "Poor Richard Sayings," the "Autobiography," and to a lesser degree on a few of the shorter essays or "Bagatelles." The "Poor Richard Sayings" were proverbs and brief commentaries on life, originally published in "Poor Richard's Almanack," which Franklin edited for many years. Not all these were strictly Franklin's own, but most of those which he borrowed he transformed so as to make them pass current. No other one author has contributed to the language so many familiar aphorisms on practical matters. In 1757 Franklin incorporated many of these sayings in "The Way to Wealth," a portion of which is given below. The "Autobiography" was written in four sections, at intervals from 1771 to just before the author's death. The first part was intended only for the members of the family, but in writing the latter parts Franklin seems to have recognized that they would be published. The charm of the "Autobiography" is due to the naïve frankness of the author, and to the absolute clearness and simplicity of his style. It is one of the few works that interest persons of all ages, and all varieties of taste. The "Bagatelles" were slight essays written while Franklin was in France, and in some cases privately printed in his own house for a small circle of friends. A few of them, such as "The Ephemera," "The Whistle," and the "Dialogue between Franklin and the Gout," were once generally known; but they are less spontaneous than most of the author's work, and to modern readers probably less interesting.

The selections are all from the latest and most accurate collection of Franklin's writings, edited by Albert H. Smyth.]

POOR RICHARD'S ADVICE

[From "The Way to Wealth," the Preface to "Poor Richard Improved," for 1758]

COURTEOUS READER

I have heard that nothing gives an Author so great Pleasure, as to find his Works respectfully quoted by other learned Authors. This Pleasure I have seldom enjoyed; for tho' I have been, if I may say it without Vanity, an *eminent Author* of Almanacks annually now a full Quarter of a Century, my Brother Authors in the same Way, for what Reason I know not, have ever been very sparing in their Applauses, and no other Author has taken the least Notice of me, so that did not my Writings produce me some solid *Pudding*, the great Deficiency of *Praise* would have quite discouraged me.

I concluded at length, that the People were the best Judges of my Merit; for they buy my Works; and besides, in my Rambles, where I am not personally known, I have frequently heard one or other of my Adages repeated, with, *as Poor Richard says*, at the End on't; this gave me some Satisfaction, as it showed not only that my Instructions were regarded, but discovered likewise some Respect for my Authority; and I own, that to encourage the Practice of remembering and repeating those wise Sentences, I have sometimes *quoted myself* with great Gravity.

Judge, then how much I must have been gratified by an Incident I am going to relate to you. I stopt my Horse lately where a great Number of People were collected at a Vendue of Merchant Goods. The Hour of Sale not being come, they were conversing on the Badness of the Times and one of the Company call'd to a plain clean old Man, with white Locks, "Pray, Father Abraham, what think you of the Times? Won't these heavy taxes quite ruin the Country? How shall we be ever able to pay them? What would you advise us to?" Father *Abraham* stood up, and reply'd, "If you'd have my Advice, I'll give it you in short, for *A Word to the Wise is enough*, and *many Words won't fill a Bushel*, as *Poor Richard* says." They join'd in desiring him to speak his Mind, and gathering round him, he proceded as follows;

"Friends," says he, and Neighbours, "the Taxes are indeed very heavy, and if those laid on by the Government were the only Ones we had to pay, we might more easily discharge them; but we have many others, and much more grevious to some of us. We are taxed twice as much by our *Idleness*, three times as much by our *Pride*, and four times as much by our *Folly;* and from these Taxes the Commissioners cannot ease or deliver us by allowing an Abatement. However let us hearken to good Advice, and something may be done for us; *God helps them that help themselves*, as *Poor Richard* says, in his Almanack of 1733.

It would be thought a hard Government that should tax its People one-tenth Part of their *Time*, to be employed in its Service. But *Idleness* taxes many of us much more, if we reckon all that is spent in absolute *Sloth*, or doing of nothing, with that which is spent in idle Employments or Amusements, that amount to nothing. *Sloth*, by bringing on Diseases, absolutely shortens Life. *Sloth, like rust, consumes faster than Labour wears; while the used Key is always bright*, as *Poor Richard* says. *But dost thou love Life, then do not squander Time, for that's the stuff Life is made of,* as *Poor Richard* says. How much more than is necessary do we spend in sleep, forgetting that *The sleeping Fox catches no*

Poultry, and that *There will be sleeping enough in the Grave,* as *Poor Richard* says.

If Time be of all Things the most precious, wasting Time must be, as *Poor Richard* says, *the greatest Prodigality;* since, as he elsewhere tells us, *Lost Time is never found again; and what we call Time enough, always proves little enough:* Let us then up and be doing, and doing to the Purpose; so by Diligence shall we do more with less Perplexity. *Sloth makes all Things difficult, but Industry all easy,* as *Poor Richard* says; and *He that riseth late must trot all Day, and shall scarce overtake his Business at Night;* while *Laziness travels so slowly, that Poverty soon overtakes him,* as we read in *Poor Richard,* who adds, *Drive thy Business, let not that drive thee;* and *Early to Bed, and early to rise, makes a Man healthy, wealthy, and wise.*

So what signifies *wishing* and *hoping* for better Times. We may make these Times better, if we bestir oursleves. *Industry need not wish,* as *Poor Richard* says, *and he that lives upon Hope will die fasting. There are no Gains without Pains; then Help Hands, for I have no Lands,* or if I have, they are smartly taxed. And, as *Poor Richard* likewise observes, *He that hath a Trade hath an Estate; and he that hath a Calling, hath an Office of Profit and Honour;* But then the *Trade* must be worked at, and the *Calling* well followed, or neither the *Estate* nor the *Office* will enable us to pay our Taxes. If we are industrious, we shall never starve; for, as *Poor Richard* says, *At the working Man's House Hunger looks in, but dares not enter.* Nor will the Bailiff or the Constable enter, for *Industry pays Debts, while Despair encreaseth them,* says *Poor Richard.* What though you have found no Treasure, nor has any rich Relation left you a Legacy, *Diligence is the Mother of Good-luck* as *Poor Richard* says, *and God gives all Things to Industry. Then plough deep, while Sluggards sleep, and you shall have Corn to sell and to keep,* says *Poor Dick.* Work while it is called To-day, for you know not how much you may be hindered To-morrow, which makes *Poor Richard* say, *One to-day is worth two To-morrows,* and farther, *Have you somewhat to do To-morrow, do it To-Day.* If you were a Servant, would you not be ashamed that a good Master should catch you idle? ·Are you then your own Master, *be ashamed to catch your-*

self idle, as *Poor Dick* says. When there is so much to be done for yourself, your Family, your Country, and your gracious King, be up by Peep of Day; *Let not the Sun look down and say, Inglorious here he lies.* Handle your Tools without Mittens; remember that *The Cat in Gloves catches no Mice*, as *Poor Richard* says. 'Tis true there is much to be done, and perhaps you are weak-handed, but stick to it steadily; and you will see great Effects, for *Constant Dropping wears away Stones*, and by *Diligence and Patience the Mouse ate in two the Cable*; and *Little Strokes fell great Oaks*, as *Poor Richard* says in his Almanack, the Year I cannot just now remember.

Methinks I hear some of you say, *Must a Man afford himself no Leisure?* I will tell thee, my friend, what *Poor Richard* says, *Employ thy Time well, if thou meanest to gain Leisure; and, since thou art not sure of a Minute, throw not away an Hour.* Leisure is Time for doing something useful; this Leisure the diligent Man will obtain, but the lazy Man never; so that, as *Poor Richard* says *A Life of Leisure and a Life of Laziness are two Things.* Do you imagine that Sloth will afford you more Comfort than Labour? No, for as *Poor Richard* says, *Trouble springs from Idleness, and grevious Toil from needless Ease. Many without Labour, would live by their Wits only, but they break for want of Stock.* Whereas Industry gives Comfort, and Plenty, and Respect: *Fly Pleasures, and they'll follow you. The diligent Spinner has a large Shift; and now I have a Sheep and a Cow, everybody bids me good Morrow;* all which is well said by *Poor Richard*.

But with our Industry, we must likewise be *steady, settled* and *careful*, and oversee our own Affairs *with our own Eyes*, and not trust too much to others; for, as *Poor Richard* says

> *I never saw an oft-removed Tree,*
> *Nor yet an oft-removed Family,*
> *That throve so well as those that settled be.*

And again, *Three Removes is as bad as a Fire;* and again, *Keep thy Shop, and thy Shop will keep thee;* and again, *If you would have your Business done, go; if not, send.* And again,

> *He that by the Plough would thrive,*
> *Himself must either hold or drive.*

And again, *The Eye of a Master will do more work than both his Hands;* and again, *Want of Care does us more Damage than Want of Knowledge;* and again, *Not to oversee Workmen, is to leave them your Purse open.* Trusting too much to others' Care is the Ruin of many; for, as the Almanack says, *In the Affairs of this World, Men are saved, not by Faith, but by the Want of it;* but a Man's own Care is profitable; for, saith *Poor Dick, Learning is to the Studious,* and *Riches to the Careful,* as well as *Power to the Bold,* and *Heaven to the Virtuous,* And farther, *If you would have a faithful Servant, and one that you like, serve yourself.* And again, he adviseth to Circumspection and Care, even in the smallest Matters, because sometimes *A Little Neglect may breed great Mischief;* adding, *for want of a Nail the Shoe was lost; for want of a Shoe the Horse was lost; and for want of a Horse the Rider was lost, being overtaken and slain by the Enemy; all for want of Care about a Horse-shoe Nail.*

IRONICAL ADVICE TO GREAT BRITAIN

[From "Rules by which a Great Empire may be reduced to a small one." Published in the *Gentleman's Magazine*, London, 1773]

An ancient Sage boasted, that, tho' he could not fiddle, he knew how to make a *great city* of a *little one.* The science that I, a modern simpleton, am about to communicate, is the very reverse.

I address myself to all ministers who have the management of extensive dominions, which from their very greatness are become troublesome to govern, because the multiplicity of their affairs leaves no time for *fiddling.*

I. In the first place, gentlemen, you are to consider, that a great empire, like a great cake, is most easily diminished at the edges. Turn your attention, therefore, first to your *remotest* provinces; that, as you get rid of them, the next may follow in order.

II. That the possibility of this separation may always exist, take special care the provinces are never incorporated with the mother country; that they do not enjoy the same common rights, the same privileges in commerce; and that they are governed by *severer laws,* all of *your enacting,* without allowing them any share

in the choice of the legislators.   By carefully making and preserving such distinctions, you will (to keep to my simile of the
cake) act like a wise ginger-bread-baker, who, to facilitate a divi-
sion, cuts his dough half through in those places where, when
baked, he would have it *broken to pieces*.

III.   Those remote provinces have perhaps been acquired,
purchased, or conquered, at the *sole expence* of the settlers, or
their ancestors, without the aid of the mother country.   If this
should happen to increase her *strength*, by their growing numbers,
ready to join in her wars; her *commerce*, by their growing demand
for her manufactures; or her *naval power*, by greater employment
for her ships and seamen, they may probably suppose some merit
in this, and that it entitles them to some favour; you are therefore
to *forget it all, or resent it*, as if they had done you injury.   If they
happen to be zealous whigs, friends of liberty, nurtured in revolution principles, *remember all that* to their prejudice, and resolve
to punish it; for such principles, after a revolution is thoroughly
established, are of *no more use;* they are even *odious* and *abomi-
nable*.

IV.   However peaceably your colonies have submitted to your
government, shewn their affection to your interests, and patiently
borne their grievances; you are to *suppose* them always inclined
to revolt, and treat them accordingly.   Quarter troops among them,
who by their insolence may *provoke* the rising of mobs, and by
their bullets and bayonets *suppress* them.   By this means, like
the husband who uses his wife ill *from suspicion*, you may in time
convert your *suspicions* into *realities*.

V.   Remote provinces must have *Governors* and *Judges*, to represent the Royal Person, and execute everywhere the delegated
parts of his office and authority.   You ministers know, that much
of the strength of government depends on the *opinion* of the people;
and much of that opinion on the *choice of rulers* placed immediately
over them.   If you send them wise and good men for governors,
who study the interest of the colonists, and advance their prosperity,
they will think their King wise and good, and that he wishes the
welfare of his subjects.   If you send them learned and upright
men for Judges, they will think him a lover of justice.   This may
attach your provinces more to his government.   You are therefore

to be careful whom you recommend for those offices. If you can find prodigals, who have ruined their fortunes, broken gamesters or stockjobbers, these may do well as *governors;* for they will probably be rapacious, and provoke the people by their extortions. Wrangling proctors and pettifogging lawyers, too, are not amiss; for they will be forever disputing and quarrelling with their little parliaments. If withal they should be ignorant, wrongheaded, and insolent, so much the better. Attornies' clerks and Newgate solicitors will do for *Chief Justices*, especially if they hold their places *during your pleasure;* and all will contribute to impress those ideas of your government, that are proper for a people *you would wish to renounce it.*

VI. To confirm these impressions, and strike them deeper, whenever the injured come to the capital with complaints of maladministration, oppression, or injustice, punish such suitors with long delay, enormous expence, and a final judgment in favour of the oppressor. This will have an admirable effect every way. The trouble of future complaints will be prevented, and Governors and Judges will be encouraged to farther acts of oppression and injustice; and thence the people may become more disaffected, and at length desperate.

VII. When such Governors have crammed their coffers, and made themselves so odious to the people that they can no longer remain among them, with safety to their persons, *recall and reward* them with pensions. You may make them *baronets* too, if that respectable order should not think fit to resent it. All will contribute to encourage new governors in the same practice, and make the supreme government *detestable.*

VIII. If, when you are engaged in war, your colonies should vie in liberal aids of men and money against the common enemy, upon your simple requisition, and give far beyond their abilities, reflect that a penny taken from them by your power is more honourable to you, than a pound presented by their benevolence; despise therefore their voluntary grants, and resolve to harass them with novel taxes. They will probably complain to your parliaments, that they are taxed by a body in which they have no representative, and that this is contrary to common right. They will petition for redress. Let the Parliaments flout their claims.

Y

reject their petitions, refuse even to suffer the reading of them, and treat the petitioners with the utmost contempt. Nothing can have a better effect in producing the alienation proposed; for though many can forgive injuries, *none ever forgave contempt.*

EARLY TRAINING

[From the "Autobiography"]

My elder brothers were all put apprentices to different trades. I was put to the grammar-school at eight years of age, my father intending to devote me, as the tithe of his sons, to the service of the Church. My early readiness in learning to read (which must have been very early, as I do not remember when I could not read), and the opinion of all his friends that I should certainly make a good scholar, encouraged him in this purpose of his. My uncle Benjamin, too, approved of it, and proposed to give me all his short-hand volumes of sermons, I suppose as a stock to set up with, if I would learn his character. I continued, however, at the grammar-school not quite one year, though in that time I had risen gradually from the middle of the class of that year to be the head of it, and farther was removed into the next class above it, in order to go with that into the third at the end of the year. But my father, in the mean time, from a view of the expense of a college education, which having so large a family he could not well afford, and the mean living many so educated were afterwards able to obtain — reasons that he gave to his friends in my hearing — altered his first intention, took me from the grammar-school, and sent me to a school for writing and arithmetic, kept by a then famous man, Mr. George Brownell, very successful in his profession generally, and that by mild, encouraging methods. Under him I acquired fair writing pretty soon, but I failed in the arithmetic, and made no progress in it. At ten years old I was taken home to assist my father in his business, which was that of a tallow-chandler and sope-boiler; a business he was not bred to, but had assumed on his arrival in New England, and on finding his dying trade would not maintain his family, being in little request. Accordingly, I was employed in cutting wick for the candles, filling the dipping mold and the molds for cast candles, attending the shop, going of errands, etc.

I disliked the trade, and had a strong inclination for the sea, but my father declared against it; however, living near the water, I was much in and about it, learnt early to swim well, and to manage boats; and when in a boat or canoe with other boys, I was commonly allowed to govern, especially in any case of difficulty; and upon other occasions I was generally a leader among the boys, and sometimes led them into scrapes, of which I will mention one instance, as it shows an early projecting public spirit, tho' not then justly conducted.

There was a salt-marsh that bounded part of the mill-pond, on the edge of which, at high water, we used to stand to fish for minnows. By much trampling, we had made it a mere quagmire. My proposal was to build a wharff there fit for us to stand upon, and I showed my comrades a large heap of stones, which were intended for a new house near the marsh, and which would very well suit our purpose. Accordingly, in the evening, when the workmen were gone, I assembled a number of my playfellows, and working with them diligently, like so many emmets, sometimes two or three to a stone, we brought them all away and built our little wharff. The next morning the workmen were surprised at missing the stones, which were found in our wharff. Inquiry was made after the removers; we were discovered and complained of; several of us were corrected by our fathers; and, though I pleaded the usefulness of the work, mine convinced me that nothing was useful which was not honest.

SCHEMES FOR SELF-IMPROVEMENT

[From the "Autobiography"]

About this time I met with an odd volume of the *Spectator*. It was the third. I had never before seen any of them. I bought it, read it over and over, and was much delighted with it. I thought the writing excellent, and wished, if possible, to imitate it. With this view I took some of the papers, and making short hints of the sentiment in each sentence, laid them by a few days, and then, without looking at the book, try'd to compleat the papers again, by expressing each hinted sentiment at length, and as fully as it had been expressed before, in any suitable words that should come to hand. Then I compared my *Spectator* with the original, discovered some of my faults, and corrected them. But I found I wanted a stock of words, or a readiness in recollecting and using them, which I thought I should have acquired before that time if I had gone on making verses; since the continual occasion for words of the same import, but of different length, to suit the measure, or of different sound for the rhyme, would have laid me under a constant necessity of searching for variety, and also have tended to fix that variety in my mind, and make me master of it. Therefore I took some of the tales and turned them into verse; and, after a time, when I had pretty well forgotten the prose, turned them back again. I also sometimes jumbled my collections of hints into confusion, and after some weeks endeavored to reduce them into the best order, before I began to form the full sentences and compleat the paper. This was to teach me method in the arrangement of thoughts. By comparing my work afterwards with the original, I discovered many faults and amended them; but I sometimes had the pleasure of fancying that, in certain particulars of small import, I had been lucky enough to improve the method or the language, and this encouraged me to think I might possibly in time come to be a tolerable English writer, of which I was extreamly ambitious. My time for these exercises and for reading was at night, after work, or before it began in the morning, or on Sundays, when I contrived to be in the printing-house alone, evading as much as I could the common attendance on public worship which my father used to exact of me when I was under his care, and which indeed I still thought a duty, though I could not, as it seemed to me, afford time to practise it.

When about 16 years of age I happened to meet with a book, written by one Tryon, recommending a vegetable diet. I determined to go into it. My brother, being yet unmarried, did not keep house, but boarded himself and his apprentices in another family. My refusing to eat flesh occasioned an inconveniency, and I was frequently chid for my singularity. I made myself acquainted with Tryon's manner of preparing some of his dishes, such as boiling potatoes or rice, making hasty pudding, and a few others, and then proposed to my brother that if he would give me, weekly, half the money he paid for my board, I would board myself. He instantly agreed to it and I presently found that I could save half what he paid me. This was an additional fund for buying books. But I had another advantage in it. My brother and the rest going from the printing-house to their meals, I remained there alone, and, dispatching presently my light repast, which often was no more than a bisket or a slice of bread, a handful of raisins or a tart from the pastry-cook's, and a glass of water, had the rest of the time till their return for study, in which I made the greater progress, from that greater clearness of head and quicker apprehension which usually attend temperance in eating and drinking.

And now it was that, being on some occasion made asham'd of my ignorance in figures, which I had twice failed in learning when at school, I took Cocker's book of Arithmetick, and went through the whole by myself with great ease. I also read Seller's and Shermy's books of Navigation, and became acquainted with the little geometry they contain; but never proceeded far in that science. And I read about this time Locke *on Human Understanding*, and the *Art of Thinking*, by Messrs. du Port Royal.

While I was intent on improving my language, I met with an English grammar (I think it was Greenwood's), at the end of which there were two little sketches of the arts of rhetoric and logic, the latter finishing with a specimen of a dispute in the Socratic method; and soon after I procur'd Xenophon's Memorable Things of Socrates, wherein there are many instances of the same method. I was charm'd with it, adopted it, dropt my abrupt contradiction and positive argumentation, and put on the humble inquirer and doubter. And being then, from reading Shaftesbury and Collins, become a real doubter in many points of our religious doctrine, I found this method safest for myself and very embarrassing to those against whom I used it; therefore I took a delight in it, practis'd it continually, and grew very artful and expert in drawing people, even of superior knowledge, into concessions, the consequences of which they did not foresee, entangling them in difficulties out of which they could not extricate themselves, and so obtaining victories that neither myself nor my cause always deserved. I continu'd this method some few years, but gradually left it, retaining only the habit of expressing myself in terms of modest diffidence; never using, when I advanced anything that may possibly be disputed, the words *certainly, undoubtedly,* or any others that give the air of positiveness to an opinion; but rather say, I conceive or apprehend a thing to be so and so; it appears to me, or *I should think it so or so,* for such and such reasons; or *I imagine it to be so;* or *it is so, if I am not mistaken.* This habit, I believe, has been of great advantage to me when I have had occasion to inculcate my opinions, and persuade men into measures that I have been from time to time engag'd in promoting; and, as the chief ends of conversation are to *inform* or to be *informed,* to *please* or to *persuade,* I wish well-meaning, sensible men would not lessen their power of doing good by a positive, assuming manner, that seldom fails to disgust, tends to create opposition, and to defeat everyone of those purposes for which speech was given to us, to wit, giving or receiving information or pleasure. For, if you would inform, a positive and dogmatical manner in advancing your sentiments may provoke contradiction and prevent a candid attention. If you wish information and improvement from the knowledge of others, and yet at the same time express yourself as firmly fix'd in your present opinions, modest, sensible men, who do not love disputation, will probably leave you undisturbed in the possession of your error. And by such a manner, you can seldom hope to recommend yourself in *pleasing* your hearers, or to persuade those whose concurrence you desire. Pope says, judiciously:

> "*Men should be taught as if you taught them not,*
> *And things unknown propos'd as things forgot;*"

farther recommending to us

> "To speak, tho' sure, with seeming diffidence."

And he might have coupled with this line that which he has coupled with another, I think, less properly,

> " For want of modesty is want of sense."

If you ask, Why less properly? I must repeat the lines,

> " Immodest words admit of no defense,
> For want of modesty is want of sense."

Now, is not *want of sense* (where a man is so unfortunate as to want it) some apology for his *want of modesty?* and would not the lines stand more justly thus?

> "Immodest words admit *but* this defense,
> That want of modesty is want of sense."

This, however, I should submit to better judgments.

FRANKLIN'S ENTRANCE INTO PHILADELPHIA

[From the "Autobiography"]

I have been the more particular in this description of my journey, and shall be so of my first entry into that city, that you may in your mind compare such unlikely beginnings with the figure I have since made there. I was in my working dress, my best clothes being to come round by sea. I was dirty from my journey; my pockets were stuff'd out with shirts and stockings, and I knew no soul nor where to look for lodging. I was fatigued with travelling, rowing, and want of rest. I was very hungry; and my whole stock of cash consisted of a Dutch dollar, and about a shilling in copper. The latter I gave the people of the boat for my passage, who at first refus'd it, on account of my rowing; but I insisted on their taking it. A man being sometimes more generous when he has but a little money than when he has plenty, perhaps thro' fear of being thought to have but little.

Then I walked up the street, gazing about till near the market-house I met a boy with bread. I had made many a meal on bread, and inquiring where he got it, I went immediately to the baker's he directed me to, in Second-street, and ask'd for bisket, intending such as we had in Boston; but they, it seems, were not made in Philadelphia. Then I asked for a three-penny loaf, and. was told they had none such. So not considering or knowing the difference of money, and the greater cheapness nor the names of his bread, I bad him give me three-penny worth of any sort. He gave me, accordingly, three great puffy rolls. I was surpriz'd at the quantity, but took it, and having no room in my pockets, walk'd off with a roll under each arm, and eating the other. Thus I went up Market-street as far as Fourth-street, passing by the door of Mr. Read, my future wife's father; when she, standing at the door, saw me, and thought I made, as I certainly did, a most awkward, ridiculous appearance. Then I turned and went down Chestnut-street and part of Walnut-street, eating my roll all the way, and coming round, found myself again at Market-street wharf, near the boat I came in, to which I went for a draught of the river water; and being filled with one of my rolls, gave the other two to a woman and her child that came down the river in the boat with us, and were waiting to go farther.

Thus refreshed, I walked again up the street, which by this time had many clean-dressed people in it, who were all walking the same way. I joined them, and thereby was led into the great meeting-house of the Quakers near the market. I sat down among them, and after looking round awhile and hearing nothing said, being very drowsy thro' labour and want of rest the preceding night, I fell fast asleep, and continu'd so till the meeting broke up, when one was kind enough to rouse me. This was, therefore, the first house I was in, or slept in, in Philadelphia.

Walking down again toward the river, and looking in the faces of people, I met a young Quaker man, whose countenance I lik'd, and, accosting him, requested he would tell me where a stranger could get lodging. We were then near the sign of the Three Mariners. "Here," says he, "is one place that entertains strangers, but it is not a reputable house; if thee wilt walk with me, I'll show thee a better." He brought me to the Crooked Billet in Water-street. Here I got a dinner; and while I was eating it, several sly questions were asked me, as it seemed to be suspected from my youth and appearance that I might be some runaway.

After dinner, my sleepiness return'd, and being shown to a bed, I lay down without undressing, and slept till six in the evening, was call'd to supper, went to bed again very early, and slept soundly till next morning. Then I made myself as tidy as I could, and went to Andrew Bradford the printer's. I found in the shop the old man his father, whom I had seen at New York, and who, travelling on horseback, had got to Philadelphia before me. He introduc'd me to his son, who receiv'd me civilly, gave me a breakfast, but told me he did not at present want a hand, being lately suppli'd with one; but there was another printer in town, lately set up, one Keimer, who, perhaps, might employ me; if not, I should be welcome to lodge at his house, and he would give me a little work to do now and then till fuller business should offer.

The old gentleman said he would go with me to the new printer; and when we found him, "Neighbor," says Bradford, "I have brought to see you a young man of your business; perhaps you may want such a one." He ask'd me a few questions, put a composing stick in my hand to see how I work'd, and then said he would employ me soon, though he had just then nothing for me to do; and taking old Bradford, whom he had never seen before, to be one of the town's people that had a good will for him, enter'd into a conversation on his present undertaking and prospects; while Bradford, not discovering that he was the other printer's father, on Keimer's saying he expected soon to get the greatest part of the business into his own hands, drew him on by artful questions, and starting little doubts, to explain all his views, what interest he reli'd on, and in what manner he intended to proceed. I, who stood by and heard all, saw immediately that one of them was a crafty old sophister, and the other a mere novice. Bradford left me with Keimer, who was greatly surpris'd when I told him who the old man was.

Keimer's printing-house, I found, consisted of an old shatter'd press, and one small, worn-out font of English, which he was then using himself, composing an Elegy on Aquila Rose, before mentioned, an ingenious young man, of excellent character, much respected in the town, clerk of the Assembly, and a pretty poet. Keimer made verses too, but very indifferently. He could not be said to write them, for his manner was to compose them in the types directly out of his head. So there being no copy, but one pair of cases, and the Elegy likely to require all the letter, no one could help him. I endeavour'd to put his press (which he had not yet us'd, and of which he understood nothing) into order fit to be work'd with; and promising to come and print off his Elegy as soon as he should have got it ready, I return'd to Bradford's, who gave me a little job to do for the present, and there I lodged and dieted. A few days after, Keimer sent for me to print off the Elegy. And now he had got another pair of cases, and a pamphlet to reprint, on which he set me to work.

These two printers I found poorly qualified for their business. Bradford had not been bred to it, and was very illiterate; and Keimer, tho' something of a scholar, was a mere compositor knowing nothing of presswork. He had been one of the French prophets, and could act their enthusiastic agitations. At this time he did not profess any particular religion, but something of all on occasion; was very ignorant of the world, and had, as I afterward found, a good deal of the knave in his composition. He did not like my lodging at Bradford's while I work'd with him. He had a house, indeed, but without furniture, so he could not lodge me; but he got me a lodging at Mr. Read's before mentioned, who was the owner of his house; and my chest and clothes being come by this time, I made rather a more respectable appearance in the eyes of Miss Read than I had done when she first happen'd to see me eating my roll in the street.

PLANS FOR STREET IMPROVEMENTS

[From the " Autobiography "]

Our city, tho' laid out with a beautiful regularity, the streets large, strait, and crossing each other at right angles, had the disgrace of suffering those streets to remain long unpav'd, and in wet weather the wheels of heavy carriages plough'd them into a quagmire, so that it was difficult to cross them; and in dry weather the dust was offensive. I had liv'd near what was call'd the Jersey Market, and saw with pain the inhabitants wading in mud while purchasing their provisions. A strip of ground down the middle of that market was at length pav'd with brick, so that, being once in the market, they had firm footing, but were often over shoes in dirt to get there. By talking and writing on the subject, I was at length instrumental in getting the street pav'd with stone between the market and the brick'd foot-pavement, that was on each side next the houses. This, for some time, gave an easy access to the market dry-shod; but the rest of the street not being pav'd, whenever a carriage came out of the mud upon this pavement, it shook off and left its dirt upon it, and it was soon cover'd with mire, which was not remov'd, the city as yet having no scavengers.

After some inquiry, I found a poor, industrious man, who was willing to undertake keeping the pavement clean, by sweeping it twice a week, carrying off the dirt from before all the neighbours' doors, for the sum of sixpence per month, to be paid by each house. I then wrote and printed a paper setting forth the advantages to the neighbourhood that might be obtain'd by this small expense; the greater ease in keeping our houses clean, so much dirt not being brought in by people's feet; the benefit to the shops by more custom, etc., etc., as buyers could more easily get at them; and by not having, in windy weather, the dust blown in upon their goods, etc., etc. I sent one of these papers to each house, and in a day or two went round to see who would subscribe an agreement to pay these sixpences; it was unanimously sign'd, and for a time well executed. All the inhabitants of the city were delighted with the cleanliness of the pavement that surrounded the market, it being a convenience to all, and this rais'd a general desire to have all the streets paved, and made the people more willing to submit to a tax for that purpose.

After some time I drew a bill for paving the city, and brought it into the Assembly. It was just before I went to England, in 1757, and did not pass till I was gone, and then with an alteration in the mode of assessment, which I thought not for the better, but with an additional provision for lighting as well as paving the streets, which was a great improvement. It was by a private person, the late Mr. John Clifton, his giving a sample of the utility of lamps, by placing one at his door, that the people were first impress'd with the idea of enlighting all the city. The honour of this public benefit has also been ascrib'd to me, but it belongs truly to that gentleman. I did but follow his example, and have only some merit to claim respecting the form of our lamps, as differing from the globe lamps we were at first suppli'd with from London. Those we found inconvenient in these respects: they admitted no air below; the smoke, therefore, did not readily go out above, but circulated in the globe, lodg'd on its inside, and soon obstructed the light they were intended to afford; giving, besides, the daily trouble of wiping them clean; and an accidental stroke on one of them would demolish it and render it totally useless. I therefore suggested the composing them of four flat panes, with a long funnel above to draw up the smoke, and crevices admitting air below, to facilitate the ascent of the smoke; by this means they were kept clean, and did not grow dark in a few hours, as the London lamps do, but continu'd bright till morning, and an accidental stroke would generally break but a single pane, easily repair'd.

I have sometimes wonder'd that the Londoners did not, from the effect holes in the bottom of the globe lamps us'd at Vauxhall have in keeping them clean, learn to have such holes in their street lamps. But, these holes being made for another purpose, viz., to communicate flame more suddenly to the wick by a little flax hanging down thro' them, the other use, of letting in air, seems not to have been thought of; and therefore, after the lamps have been lit a few hours, the streets of London are very poorly illuminated.

THE WHISTLE

[To Madame Brillion]

PASSY, November 10, 1779.

I received my dear friend's two letters, one for Wednesday and one for Saturday. This is again Wednesday. I do not deserve one for to-day, because I have not answered the former. But, indolent as I am, and averse to writing, the fear of having no more of your pleasing epistles, if I do not contribute to the correspondence, obliges me to take up my pen; and as Mr. B. has kindly sent me word, that he sets out to-morrow to see you, instead of spending this Wednesday evening as I have done its namesakes, in your delightful company, I sit down to spend it in thinking of you, in writing to you, and in reading over and over again your letters.

I am charmed with your description of Paradise, and with your plan of living there; and I approve much of your conclusion, that, in the mean time, we should draw all the good we can from this world. In my opinion, we might all draw more good from it than we do, and suffer less evil, if we would take care not to give too much for *whistles*. For to me it seems, that most of the unhappy people we meet with, are become so by neglect of that caution.

You ask what I mean? You love stories, and will excuse my telling one of myself.

When I was a child of seven years old, my friends, on a holiday, filled my pocket with coppers. I went directly to a shop where they sold toys for children; and, being charmed with the sound of a *whistle*, that I met by the way in the hands of another boy, I voluntarily offered and gave all my money for one. I then came home, and went whistling all over the house, much pleased with my *whistle*, but disturbing all the family. My brothers, and sisters, and cousins, understanding the bargain I had made, told me I had given four times as much for it as it was worth; put me in mind what good things I might have bought with the rest of the money; and laughed at me so much for my folly, that I cried with vexation; and the reflection gave me more chagrin than the *whistle* gave me pleasure.

This however was afterwards of use to me, the impression continuing on my mind; so that often, when I was tempted to buy some unnecessary thing, I said to myself, *Don't give too much for the whistle;* and I saved my money.

As I grew up, came into the world, and observed the actions of men, I thought I met with many, very many, who *gave too much for the whistle.*

When I saw one too ambitious of court favour, sacrificing his time in attendance on levees, his repose, his liberty, his virtue, and perhaps his friends, to attain it, I have said to myself, *This man gives too much for his whistle.*

When I saw another fond of popularity, constantly employing himself in political bustles, neglecting his own affairs, and ruining them by that neglect, *He pays, indeed,* said I, *too much for his whistle.*

If I knew a miser, who gave up every kind of comfortable living, all the pleasure of doing good to others, all the esteem of his fellow-citizens, and the joys of benevolent friendship, for the sake of accumulating wealth, *Poor man,* said I, *you pay too much for your whistle.*

When I met with a man of pleasure, sacrificing every laudable improvement of the mind, or of his fortune, to mere corporeal sensations, and ruining his health in their pursuit, *Mistaken man,* said I, *you are providing pain for yourself, instead of pleasure; you give too much for your whistle.*

If I see one fond of appearance, or fine clothes, fine houses, fine furniture, fine equipages, all above his fortune, for which he contracts debts, and ends his career in a prison, *Alas!* say I, *he has paid dear, very dear, for his whistle.*

When I see a beautiful, sweet-tempered girl married to an ill-natured brute of a husband, *what a pity*, say I, *that she should pay so much for a whistle!*

In short, I conceive that great part of the miseries of mankind are brought upon them by the false estimates they have made of the value of things, and by their *giving too much for their whistles.*

Yet I ought to have charity for these unhappy people, when I consider that, with all this wisdom of which I am boasting, there are certain things in the world so tempting, for example, the apples of King John, which happily are not to be bought; for if they were put to sale by auction, I might very easily be led to ruin myself in the purchase, and find that I had once more given too much for the *whistle.*

Adieu, my dear friend, and believe me ever yours very sincerely and with unalterable affection,

B. FRANKLIN.

PATRICK HENRY

[Patrick Henry was one of the most famous of Revolutionary orators, though his reputation to-day rests mostly on tradition, and on confessedly inaccurate reports of a few of his speeches. He was born in Virginia in 1736, and after completing his education, engaged unsuccessfully in business. In 1760 he took up the practice of law, and soon established his reputation as an orator. In 1765 he became a member of the House of Burgesses. Here, according to the well-known anecdote, the awkward and unknown country member introduced outspoken resolutions denouncing the Stamp Act, and stampeded the house in their favor by his speech containing the famous climax: "Cæsar had his Brutus; Charles the First had his Cromwell; and George the Third — may profit by their example." From this time he was active in the public affairs of the colony and the country. He held many official positions, among them member of the continental congress and governor of Virginia; and he declined appointments as secretary of state, chief justice of the United States, and minister to France, which were offered him after the organization of the national government.

Few of Henry's orations have been preserved in authentic form. The traditional version of his most famous speech, delivered in the Virginia convention of 1775, is given partly transposed into the third person, in Wirt's "Life of Patrick Henry." His speeches in the convention of 1788, where he objected to the proposed national constitution as tending to a strongly centralized government, were printed by a shorthand reporter who admitted that his version was verbally inaccurate. Unsatisfactory as these literary remains are, they are sufficient to show the style of the speaker, and they and the traditions that accompanied them had a great influence on later American oratory.

The first selection is based on the report of the 1775 speech in Wirt's "Life of Patrick Henry." The selections from the speech before the convention of 1788 are from the shorthand report already referred to, as given in the "Life, Correspondence and Speeches of Patrick Henry," by William Wirt Henry.]

LIBERTY OR DEATH

[As reported in Wirt's "Life of Patrick Henry" [1]]

Mr. President, it is natural to man to indulge in the illusions of hope. We are apt to shut our eyes against a painful truth — and

[[1] As cited by Wirt, part of this speech is paraphrased with change of person and number. It is here transposed into the obvious form of direct discourse.]

listen to the song of that siren, till she transforms us into beasts. Is this the part of wise men, engaged in a great and arduous struggle for liberty? Are we disposed to be of the number of those, who having eyes, see not, and having ears, hear not, the things which so nearly concern their temporal salvation? For my part, whatever anguish of spirit it may cost, I am willing to know the whole truth; to know the worst, and to provide for it.

I have but one lamp by which my feet are guided, and that is the lamp of experience. I know of no way of judging of the future but by the past. And judging by the past, I wish to know what there has been in the conduct of the British ministry for the last ten years, to justify those hopes with which gentlemen have been pleased to solace themselves and the house? Is it that insidious smile with which our petition has been lately received? Trust it not, sir; it will prove a snare to your feet. Suffer not yourselves to be betrayed with a kiss. Ask yourselves how this gracious reception of our petition comports with those warlike preparations which cover our waters and darken our land. Are fleets and armies necessary to a work of love and reconciliation? Have we shown ourselves so unwilling to be reconciled, that force must be called in to win back our love? Let us not deceive ourselves, sir. These are the implements of war and subjugation — the last arguments to which kings resort. I ask gentlemen, sir, what means this martial array, if its purpose be not to force us to submission? Can gentlemen assign any other possible motive for it? Has Great Britain any enemy in this quarter of the world, to call for all this accumulation of navies and armies? No, sir, she has none. They are meant for us: they can be meant for no other. They are sent over to bind and rivet upon us those chains which the British ministry have been so long forging. And what have we to oppose to them? Shall we try argument? Sir, we have been trying that for the last ten years. Have we any thing new to offer upon the subject. Nothing. We have held the subject up in every light of which it is capable; but it has been all in vain. Shall we resort to entreaty and humble supplication? What terms shall we find, which have not been already exhausted? Let us not, I beseech you, sir, deceive ourselves longer. Sir, we have done every thing that could be done, to avert the storm which is now coming on.

We have petitioned — we have remonstrated — we have supplicated — we have prostrated ourselves before the throne, and have implored its interposition to arrest the tyrannical hands of the ministry and Parliament. Our petitions have been slighted; our remonstrances have produced additional violence and insult; our supplications have been disregarded; and we have been spurned with contempt, from the foot of the throne. In vain, after these things, may we indulge the fond hope of peace and reconciliation. *There is no longer any room for hope.* If we wish to be free — if we mean to preserve inviolate those inestimable privileges for which we have been so long contending — if we mean not basely to abandon the noble struggle in which we have been so long engaged, and which we have pledged ourselves never to abandon, until the glorious object of our contest shall be obtained — we must fight! — I repeat it, sir, we must fight! An appeal to arms and to the God of Hosts, is all that is left us!

They tell us, sir, that we are weak — unable to cope with so formidable an adversary. But when shall we be stronger? Will it be the next week or the next year? Will it be when we are totally disarmed, and when a British guard shall be stationed in every house? Shall we gather strength by irresolution and inaction? Shall we acquire the means of effectual resistance by lying supinely on our backs, and hugging the delusive phantom of hope, until our enemies shall have bound us hand and foot? Sir, we are not weak, if we make a proper use of those means which the God of nature hath placed in our power. Three millions of people armed in the holy cause of liberty, and in such a country as that which we possess, are invincible by any force which our enemy can send against us. Besides, sir, we shall not fight our battles alone. There is a just God who presides over the destinies of nations, and who will raise up friends to fight our battles for us. The battle, sir, is not to the strong alone; it is to the vigilant, the active, the brave. Besides, sir, we have no election. If we were base enough to desire it, it is now too late to retire from the contest. There is no retreat but in submission and slavery! Our chains are forged. Their clanking may be heard on the plains of Boston! The war is inevitable — and let it come!! I repeat it, sir, let it come!!!

z

It is vain, sir, to extenuate the matter. Gentlemen may cry, peace, peace — but there is no peace. The war is actually begun! The next gale that sweeps from the north will bring to our ears the clash of resounding arms! Our brethren are already in the field! Why stand we here idle? What is it that gentlemen wish? What would they have? Is life so dear, or peace so sweet, as to be purchased at the price of chains and slavery? Forbid it, Almighty God! I know not what course others may take; but as for me, give me liberty, or give me death!

AGAINST A CONSOLIDATED GOVERNMENT

[From the shorthand report of the Virginia Convention of 1788]

The honorable gentleman's observations respecting the people's right of being the agents in the formation of this government, are not accurate in my humble conception. The distinction between a national government and a confederacy is not sufficiently discerned. Had the delegates who were sent to Philadelphia a power to propose a consolidated government instead of a confederacy? Were they not deputed by states, and not by the people? The assent of the people in their collective capacity is not necessary to the formation of a federal government. The people have no right to enter into leagues, alliances, or confederations: they are not the proper agents for this purpose: states and sovereign powers are the only proper agents for this kind of government: show me an instance where the people have exercised this business: has it not always gone through the legislatures? I refer you to the treaties with France, Holland, and other nations: how were they made? Were they not made by the states? Are the people therefore in their aggregate capacity, the proper persons to form a confederacy? This, therefore, ought to depend on the consent of the legislatures; the people having never sent delegates to make any proposition of changing the government. Yet I must say, at the same time, that it was made on grounds the most pure, and perhaps I might have been brought to consent to it so far as to the change of government; but there is one thing in it which I never would acquiesce in. I mean the changing it into a consolidated government; which is so abhorrent to my mind.

The honorable gentleman then went on to the figure we ma. with foreign nations; the contemptible one we make in Franc and Holland; which, according to the substance of my notes, he attributes to the present feeble government. An opinion has gone forth, we find, that we are a contemptible people: the time has been when we were thought otherwise. Under this same despised government, we commanded the respect of all Europe: wherefore are we now reckoned otherwise? The American spirit has fled from hence: it has gone to regions, where it has never been expected: it has gone to the people of France in search of a splendid government — a strong energetic government. Shall we imitate the example of those nations who have gone from a simple to a splendid government? Are those nations more worthy of our imitation? What can make an adequate satisfaction to them for the loss they have suffered in attaining such a government — for the loss of their liberty? If we admit this consolidated government, it will be because we like a great splendid one. Some way or other we must be a great and mighty empire; we must have an army, and a navy, and a number of things. When the American spirit was in its youth, the language of America was different: liberty, sir, was then the primary object. We are descended from a people whose government was founded on liberty: our glorious forefathers of Great Britain, made liberty the foundation of every thing. That country is become a great, mighty and splendid nation; not because their government is strong and energetic; but, sir, because liberty is its direct end and foundation. We drew the spirit of liberty from our British ancestors: by that spirit we have triumphed over every difficulty. But now, sir, the American spirit, assisted by the ropes and chains of consolidation, is about to convert this country into a powerful and mighty empire; if you make the citizens of this country agree to become the subjects of one great consolidated empire of America, your government will not have sufficient energy to keep them together: such a government is incompatible with the genius of republicanism. There will be no checks, no real balances, in this government. What can avail your specious, imaginary balances, your rope-dancing, chain-rattling, ridiculous ideal checks and contrivances? But, sir, we are not feared by foreigners; we do not make nations tremble. Would this constitute happiness, or secure liberty? I trust, sir, our political hemisphere will ever direct their operations to the security of those objects.

Consider our situation, sir: go to the poor man, ask him what he does; he will inform you that he enjoys the fruits of his labor, under his own fig-tree, with his wife and children around him, in peace and security. Go to every other member of the society, you will find the same tranquil ease and content; you will find no alarms or disturbances! Why then tell us of dangers to terrify us into an adoption of this new form of government? And yet who knows the dangers that this new system may produce? They are out of the sight of the common people; they cannot foresee latent consequences. I dread the operation of it on the middling and lower classes of people: it is for them I fear the adoption of this system. I fear I tire the patience of the committee, but I beg to be indulged with a few more observations. When I thus profess myself an advocate for the liberty of the people, I shall be told, I am a designing man, that I am to be a great man, that I am to be a demagogue; and many similar illiberal insinuations will be thrown out; but, sir, conscious rectitude outweighs these things with me. I see great jeopardy in this new government. I see none from our present one. I hope some gentleman or other will bring forth, in full array, those dangers, if there be any, that we may see and touch them.

DANGER OF MONARCHY

[From the shorthand report of the Virginia Convention of 1788]

This constitution is said to have beautiful features; but when I come to examine these features, sir, they appear to me horribly frightful: among other deformities it has an awful squinting; it squints toward monarchy; and does not this raise indignation in the breast of every true American? Your president may easily become king: your senate is so imperfectly constructed that your dearest rights may be sacrificed by what may be a small minority; and a very small minority may continue forever unchangeably this government although horridly defective: where are your checks in this government? Your strongholds will be in the hands of your enemies; it is on a supposition that your American governors shall be honest, that all the good qualities of this government are founded: but its defective, and imperfect construction, puts it in their power to perpetrate the worst of mischiefs, should they be bad men: and, sir, would not all the world, from the eastern to the western hemisphere, blame our distracted folly in resting our rights upon the contingency of our rulers being good or bad? Show me that age and country where the rights and liberties of the people were placed on the sole chance of their rulers being good men, without a consequent loss of liberty? I say that the loss of that dearest privilege has ever followed with absolute certainty, every such mad attempt.

If your American chief, be a man of ambition, and abilities, how easy it is for him to render himself absolute! The army is in his hands, and, if he be a man of address, it will be attached to him; and it will be the subject of meditation with him to seize the first auspicious moment to accomplish his design; and, sir, will the American spirit solely relieve you when this happens? I would rather infinitely, and I am sure most of this convention are of the same opinion, have a king, lords, and commons, than a government, so replete with such insupportable evils. If we make a king, we may prescribe the rules by which he shall rule his people, and interpose such checks as shall prevent him from infringing them: but the president in the field at the head of his army can prescribe the terms on which he shall reign master, so far that it will puzzle any American ever to get his neck from under the galling yoke. I cannot with patience think of this idea. If ever he violates the laws, one of two things will happen: he will come at the head of his army to carry everything before him; or, he will give bail, or do what Mr. Chief Justice will order him. If he be guilty, will not the recollection of his crimes teach him to make one bold push for the American throne? Will not the immense difference between being master of everything, and being ignominiously tried and punished, powerfully excite him to make this bold push? But, sir, where is the existing force to punish him? Can he not at the head of his army beat down every opposition? Away with your president, we shall have a king: the army will salute him monarch; your militia will leave you and assist in making him king, and fight against you, and what have you to oppose this force? What will then become of you and your rights? Will not absolute despotism ensue?

THOMAS PAINE

[Thomas Paine, one of the most effective of Revolutionary pamphleteers, was a native of England, where he had a not very successful career as stay-maker and officer in the excise. In 1774, at the age of thirty-seven, he came to Philadelphia, bearing letters from Franklin, whom he had met in England. Though without special literary training or experience, he became editor of a magazine, and soon developed a manner of expression that, while far from correct or elegant, was wonderfully effective. He took an active part in the discussion of public affairs, and in January, 1776, published his pamphlet of "Common Sense," which historians have generally credited as a powerful influence in bringing about the Declaration of Independence. Paine served in the army and in various official positions throughout the war, and at intervals from 1776 to 1783 he wrote the "Crisis," a series of papers which comment on current events and exhort the people to patriotic exertions. At the close of the war his services to the country were enthusiastically recognized by Congress, and by various state legislatures. He then went to Europe, where his "Rights of Man," a reply to Burke's "Reflections on the French Revolution," caused him to be outlawed from England. In France he was made a "citizen" and was chosen a member of the convention. Here he made himself unpopular by his opposition to the execution of the king, and was for a time imprisoned. On his release he attacked Washington for failure to intervene in his behalf, and this, together with his free discussion of religion in "The Age of Reason," made him one of the most unpopular men in America. He died in poverty in New York in 1809, and his sad end was many times "improved" as showing the fate of an infidel.

Paine wrote many other works in America and Europe, but the four mentioned are of chief interest. On the whole "Common Sense" and the "Crisis" are more representative and more creditable than his later writings. No other author of his time is better for the study of the qualities that give a pamphleteer immediate success, and such a study is well worth while because Paine, if not the founder, was the most conspicuous early representative of a school of writing that was long popular in America. He employed a somewhat heightened rhetorical manner, as in the opening lines of the first "Crisis," and he discussed in simple and apparently frank manner matter-of-fact details, as in the references to Washington's retreat in the same paper. He showed what appeared to his partisans as righteous indignation, and to others as prejudice and outbreaks of temper, as in his references to the king and the Tories. It was this lack of respectful dignity that made Paine so violently disliked by his political opponents, and that gave him his undeserved notoriety as a teacher of irreligion. It is not really the radicalism of the views expressed in "The Age of Reason" but an irreverent way of dealing with what most persons feel to be sacred things, that gave the book its bad name.

The selections are from the standard edition of Paine's writings, edited by Moncure D. Conway.]

REASONS FOR INDEPENDENCE

[From "Common Sense"]

I challenge the warmest advocate for reconciliation to show a single advantage that this continent can reap by being connected with Great Britain. I repeat the challenge; not a single advantage is derived. Our corn will fetch its price in any market in Europe, and our imported goods must be paid for buy them where we will.

But the injuries and disadvantages which we sustain by that connection, are without number; and our duty to mankind at large, as well as to ourselves, instruct us to renounce the alliance: because, any submission to, or dependance on, Great Britain, tends directly to involve this Continent in European wars and quarrels, and set us at variance with nations who would otherwise seek our friendship, and against whom we have neither anger nor complaint. As Europe is our market for trade, we ought to form no partial connection with any part of it. It is the true interest of America to steer clear of European contentions, which she never can do, while, by her dependence on Britain, she is made the makeweight in the scale of British politics.

Europe is too thickly planted with kingdoms to be long at peace, and whenever a war breaks out between England and any foreign power, the trade of America goes to ruin, *because of her connection with Britain.* The next war may not turn out like the last, and should it not, the advocates for reconciliation now will be wishing for separation then, because neutrality in that case would be a safer convoy than a man of war. Every thing that is right or reasonable pleads for separation. The blood of the slain, the weeping voice of nature cries, 'TIS TIME TO PART. Even the distance at which the Almighty hath placed England and America is a strong and natural proof that the authority of the one over the other, was never the design of Heaven. The time likewise at which the Continent was discovered, adds weight to the argument, and the manner in which it was peopled, encreases the force of it. The Reformation was preceded by the discovery of America: As if the Almighty graciously meant to open a sanctuary to the persecuted in future years, when home should afford neither friendship nor safety.

The authority of Great Britain over this Continent, is a form of government, which sooner or later must have an end: And a serious mind can draw no true pleasure by looking forward, under the painful and positive conviction that what he calls "the present constitution" is merely temporary. As parents, we can have no joy, knowing that this government is not sufficiently lasting to ensure any thing which we may bequeath to posterity: And by a plain method of argument, as we are running the next generation into debt, we ought to do the work of it, otherwise we use them meanly and pitifully. In order to discover the line of our duty rightly, we should take our children in our hand, and fix our station a few years farther into life; that eminence will present a prospect which a few present fears and prejudices conceal from our sight.

Though I would carefully avoid giving unnecessary offence, yet I am inclined to believe, that all those who espouse the doctrine of reconciliation, may be included within the following descriptions.

Interested men, who are not to be trusted, weak men who *cannot* see, prejudiced men who will not see, and a certain set of moderate men who think better of the European world than it deserves; and this last class, by an ill-judged deliberation, will be the cause of more calamities to this Continent than all the other three.

It is the good fortune of many to live distant from the scene of present sorrow; the evil is not sufficiently brought to their doors to make them feel the precariousness with which all American property is possessed. But let our imaginations transport us a few moments to Boston; that seat of wretchedness will teach us wisdom, and instruct us forever to renounce a power in whom we can have no trust. The inhabitants of that unfortunate city who but a few months ago were in ease and affluence, have now no other alternative than to stay and starve, or turn out to beg.

Endangered by the fire of their friends if they continue within the city, and plundered by the soldiery if they leave it, in their present situation they are prisoners without the hope of redemption, and in a general attack for their relief they would be exposed to the fury of both armies.

Men of passive tempers look somewhat lightly over the offences of Great Britain, and, still hoping for the best, are apt to call out, *Come, come, we shall be friends again for all this.* But examine the passions and feelings of mankind: bring the doctrine of reconciliation to the touchstone of nature, and then tell me whether you can hereafter love, honour, and faithfully serve the power that hath carried fire and sword into your land? If you cannot do all these, then are you only deceiving yourselves, and by your delay bringing ruin upon posterity. Your future connection with Britain, whom you can neither love nor honour, will be forced and unnatural, and being formed only on the plan of present convenience, will in a little time fall into a relapse more wretched than the first. But if you say, you can still pass the violations over, then I ask, hath your house been burnt? Hath your property been destroyed before your face? Are your wife and children destitute of a bed to lie on, or bread to live on? Have you lost a parent or a child by their hands, and yourself the ruined and wretched survivor? If you have not, then are you not a judge of those who have. But if you have, and can still shake hands with the murderers, then are you unworthy the name of husband, father, friend, or lover, and whatever may be your rank or title in life, you have the heart of a coward, and the spirit of a sycophant.

This is not inflaming or exaggerating matters, but trying them by those feelings and affections which nature justifies, and without which we should be incapable of discharging the social duties of life, or enjoying the felicities of it. I mean not to exhibit horror for the purpose of provoking revenge, but to awaken us from fatal and unmanly slumbers, that we may pursue determinately some fixed object. 'Tis not in the power of Britain or of Europe to conquer America, if she doth not conquer herself by delay and timidity. The present winter is worth an age if rightly employed, but if lost or neglected the whole Continent will partake of the misfortune; and there is no punishment which that man doth not deserve, be he who, or what, or where he will, that may be the means of sacrificing a season so precious and useful.

'Tis repugnant to reason, to the universal order of things, to all examples from former ages, to suppose that this Continent can long remain subject to any external power. The most sanguine in Britain doth not think so. The utmost stretch of human wisdom cannot, at this time, compass a plan, short of separation, which can promise the Continent even a year's security. Reconciliation is *now* a fallacious dream. Nature hath deserted the connection, and art cannot supply her place. For, as Milton wisely expresses, "never can true reconcilement grow where wounds of deadly hate have pierced so deep."

Every quiet method for peace hath been ineffectual. Our prayers have been rejected with disdain; and hath tended to convince us that nothing flatters vanity or confirms obstinacy in Kings more than repeated petitioning — and nothing hath contributed more than that very measure to make the Kings of Europe absolute. Witness Denmark and Sweden. Wherefore, since nothing but blows will do, for God's sake let us come to a final separation, and not leave the next generation to be cutting throats under the violated unmeaning names of parent and child.

"THE TIMES THAT TRY MEN'S SOULS"

[From "The Crisis"]

These are the times that try men's souls. The summer soldier and the sunshine patriot will, in this crisis, shrink from the service of their country; but he that stands it *now*, deserves the love and thanks of man and woman. Tyranny, like hell, is not easily conquered; yet we have this consolation with us, that the harder the conflict, the more glorious the triumph. What we obtain too cheap, we esteem too lightly: it is dearness only that gives every thing its value. Heaven knows how to put a proper price upon its goods; and it would be strange indeed if so celestial an article as FREEDOM should not be highly rated. Britain, with an army to enforce her tyranny, has declared that she has a right (*not only to* TAX) but "to BIND *us in* ALL CASES WHATSOEVER," and if being *bound in that manner*, is not slavery, then there is not such a thing as slavery upon earth. Even the expression is impious; for so unlimited a power can belong only to God.

Whether the independence of the continent was declared too soon, or delayed too long, I will not now enter into as an argument; my own simple opinion is, that had it been eight months earlier, it would have been much better. We did not make a proper use of last winter, neither could we, while we were in a dependent state. However, the fault, if it were one, was all our own;[1] we have none to blame but ourselves. But no great deal is lost yet. All that Howe has been doing for this month past, is rather a ravage than a conquest, which the spirit of the Jerseys, a year ago, would have quickly repulsed, and which time and a little resolution will soon recover.

I have as little superstition in me as any man living, but my secret opinion has ever been, and still is, that God Almighty will not give up a people to military destruction, or leave them unsupportedly to perish, who have so earnestly and so repeatedly sought to avoid the calamities of war, by every decent method which wisdom could invent. Neither have I so much of the infidel in me, as to suppose that He has relinquished the government of the world, and given us up to the care of devils; and as I do not, I cannot see on what grounds the king of Britain can look up to heaven for help against us: a common murderer, a highwayman, or a housebreaker, has as good a pretence as he.

'Tis surprising to see how rapidly a panic will sometimes run through a country. All nations and ages have been subject to them: Britain has trembled like an ague at the report of a French fleet of flat bottomed boats; and in the fourteenth century the whole English army, after ravaging the kingdom of France, was driven back like men petrified with fear; and this brave exploit was performed by a few broken forces collected and headed by a woman, Joan of Arc. Would that heaven might inspire some Jersey maid to spirit up her countrymen, and save her fair fellow sufferers

---

[1] The present winter is worth an age, if rightly employed; but, if lost or neglected, the whole continent will partake of the evil; and there is no punishment that man does not deserve, be he who, or what, or where he will, that may be the means of sacrificing a season so precious and useful. [Author's note — a citation from his "Common Sense."]

from ravage and ravishment! Yet panics, in some cases, have their uses; they produce as much good as hurt. Their duration is always short; the mind soon grows through them, and acquires a firmer habit than before. But their peculiar advantage is, that they are the touchstones of sincerity and hypocrisy, and bring things and men to light, which might otherwise have lain forever undiscovered. In fact, they have the same effect on secret traitors, which an imaginary apparition would have upon a private murderer. They sift out the hidden thoughts of man, and hold them up in public to the world. Many a disguised tory has lately shown his head, that shall penitentially solemnize with curses the day on which Howe arrived upon the Delaware.

As I was with the troops at Fort Lee, and marched with them to the edge of Pennsylvania, I am well acquainted with many circumstances, which those who live at a distance know but little or nothing of. Our situation there was exceedingly cramped, the place being a narrow neck of land between the North River and the Hackensack. Our force was inconsiderable, being not one fourth so great as Howe could bring against us. We had no army at hand to have relieved the garrison, had we shut ourselves up and stood on our defence. Our ammunition, light artillery, and the best part of our stores, had been removed, on the apprehension that Howe would endeavor to penetrate the Jerseys, in which case Fort Lee could be of no use to us; for it must occur to every thinking man, whether in the army or not, that these kind of field forts are only for temporary purposes, and last in use no longer than the enemy directs his force against the particular object, which such forts are raised to defend. Such was our situation and condition at fort Lee on the morning of the 20th of November, when an officer arrived with information that the enemy with 200 boats had landed about seven miles above: Major General Green, who commanded the garrison, immediately ordered them under arms, and sent express to General Washington at the town of Hackensack, distant by the way of the ferry = six miles. Our first object was to secure the bridge over the Hackensack, which laid up the river between the enemy and us, about six miles from us, and three from them. General Washington arrived in about three quarters of an hour, and marched at the head of the troops towards the bridge, which place I expected we should have a brush for; however, they did not choose to dispute it with us, and the greatest part of our troops went over the bridge, the rest over the ferry, except some which passed at a mill on a small creek, between the bridge and the ferry, and made their way through some marshy grounds up to the town of Hackensack, and there passed the river. We brought off as much baggage as the wagons could contain, the rest was lost. The simple object was to bring off the garrison, and march them on till they could be strengthened by the Jersey or Pennsylvania militia, so as to be enabled to make a stand. We staid four days at Newark, collected our out-posts with some of the Jersey militia, and marched out twice to meet the enemy, on being informed that they were advancing, though our numbers were greatly inferior to theirs. Howe, in my little opinion, committed a great error in generalship in not throwing a body of forces off from Staten Island through Amboy, by which means he might have seized all our stores at Brunswick, and intercepted our march into Pennsylvania; but if we believe the power of hell to be limited, we must likewise believe that their agents are under some providential controul.

I shall not now attempt to give all the particulars of our retreat to the Delaware; suffice it for the present to say, that both officers and men, though greatly harrassed and fatigued, frequently without rest, covering, or provision, the inevitable consequences of a long retreat, bore it with a manly and martial spirit. All their wishes centered in one, which was, that the country would turn out and help them to drive the enemy back. Voltaire has remarked that King William never appeared to full advantage but in difficulties and in action; the same remark may be made on General Washington, for the character fits him. There is a natural firmness in some minds which cannot be unlocked by trifles, but which, when unlocked, discovers a cabinet of fortitude; and I reckon it among those kind of public blessings, which we do not immediately see, that God hath blessed him with uninterrupted health, and given him a mind that can even flourish upon care.

I shall conclude this paper with some miscellaneous remarks

on the state of our affairs; and shall begin with asking the following question, Why is it that the enemy have left the New-England provinces, and made these middle ones the seat of war? The answer is easy: New-England is not infested with tories, and we are. I have been tender in raising the cry against these men, and used numberless arguments to show them their danger, but it will not do to sacrifice a world either to their folly or their baseness. The period is now arrived, in which either they or we must change our sentiments, or one or both must fall. And what is a tory? Good God! what is he? I should not be afraid to go with a hundred whigs against a thousand tories, were they to attempt to get into arms. Every tory is a coward; for servile, slavish, self-interested fear is the foundation of toryism; and a man under such influence, though he may be cruel, never can be brave.

But, before the line of irrecoverable separation be drawn between us, let us reason the matter together: Your conduct is an invitation to the enemy, yet not one in a thousand of you has heart enough to join him. Howe is as much deceived by you as the American cause is injured by you. He expects you will all take up arms, and flock to his standard, with muskets on your shoulders. Your opinions are of no use to him, unless you support him personally, for 'tis soldiers, and not tories, that he wants.

I once felt all that kind of anger, which a man ought to feel, against the mean principles that are held by the tories: a noted one, who kept a tavern at Amboy, was standing at his door, with as pretty a child in his hand, about eight or nine years old, as ever I saw, and after speaking his mind as freely as he thought was prudent, finished with this unfatherly expression, *"Well! give me peace in my day."* Not a man lives on the continent but fully believes that a separation must some time or other finally take place, and a generous parent should have said, *"If there must be trouble, let it be in my day, that my child may have peace;"* and this single reflection, well applied, is sufficient to awaken every man to duty. Not a place upon earth might be so happy as America. Her situation is remote from all the wrangling world, and she has nothing to do but to trade with them. A man can distinguish himself between temper and principle, and I am as confident, as I am that God governs the world, that America will never be happy till she gets clear of foreign dominion. Wars, without ceasing, will break out till that period arrives, and the continent must in the end be conqueror; for though the flame of liberty may sometimes cease to shine, the coal can never expire.

THOMAS JEFFERSON

[The main facts in the life of Thomas Jefferson are too well known to need more than the briefest restatement here. He was born in Virginia in 1743, received his education at William and Mary College, and studied law. He inherited a considerable estate, which was increased by his marriage, and throughout life he took great interest in agriculture and horticulture, and conducted many experiments in both lines of industry. In 1769 he became a member of the Virginia House of Burgesses, and from this time until the close of his presidential term he was active in public life. Although a relatively young member of the Congress, he was given a place on the committee to prepare a Declaration of Independence, and was chosen by the committee to draft the document. Among the more important offices that he held were governor of Virginia, member of the Peace Commission, Secretary of State, Vice-President, and from 1801 to 1809 President of the United States. From 1809 until his death in 1826 he lived in retirement on his estate at Monticello.

Jefferson's writings, which in the latest edition fill ten volumes, are largely state papers and letters. The "Notes on Virginia," his most ambitious single work, was written in response to inquiries sent out by the French government in 1781, privately printed by the author in Paris in 1784, and published in London in 1787. Since that time it has been, according to Jefferson's latest editor, "perhaps the most frequently reprinted book ever written in the United States south of Mason and Dixon's line." It illustrates Jefferson's wide interest in all scientific and economic matters, his genius for acquiring and managing details, and his fondness for theorizing. The "Autobiography" and the "Anas," both written late in life, give much information regarding the public affairs with which Jefferson was so long concerned. Many of his letters are interesting, and touch a wide variety of topics.

Jefferson's chief characteristics as a writer can be seen in the Declaration of Independence, which it is to be hoped need not be included in a collection like this volume. He had a faculty of making general statements in sounding phrases, and he could marshal details with telling effect. The opening and closing passages of the Declaration, and the catalogue of grievances, respectively illustrate these methods. In judging the Declaration it must in justice be borne in mind that Jefferson was asked to prepare, not an exposition of his personal views, but a document that would be agreed to by all the colonies, and that would be accepted by the general public as a defence of the colonial action. Whatever the defects of the Declaration as a political and literary classic, it can hardly be denied that the author succeeded in accomplishing what he set out to do. The mass of his writings, while many of them show one or the other of the qualities already referred to, are likely to be somewhat disappointing to the reader of to-day.

All the selections here given are from the latest and most complete collection of Jefferson's writings, edited by Paul Leicester Ford. The selection from the "Notes on Virginia" follows the text of the first edition, of 1784. The "Inaugural Address" follows the manuscript draft in Jefferson's autograph, which was possibly intended for reference during the delivery of the address, and which abounds in contractions of words, and oddities of paragraphing, — even parts of sentences being written as separate paragraphs. These peculiarities have not been retained in printing the selection.]

THE FRAMING OF THE DECLARATION

[From the "Autobiography"]

It appearing in the course of these debates [1] that the colonies of N. York, New Jersey, Pennsylvania, Delaware, Maryland, and South Carolina were not yet matured for falling from the parent stem, but that they were fast advancing to that state, it was thought most prudent to wait a while for them, and to postpone the final decision to July 1. but that this might occasion as little delay as possible a committee was appointed to prepare a declaration of independence. The commee were J. Adams, Dr. Franklin, Roger Sherman, Robert R. Livingston & myself. Committees were also appointed at the same time to prepare a plan of confederation for the colonies, and to state the terms proper to be proposed for foreign alliance. The committee for drawing the declaration of Independence desired me to do it. It was accordingly done, and being approved by them, I reported it to the house on Friday the 28th of June when it was read and ordered to lie on the table. On Monday, the 1st of July the house resolved itself into a commee of the whole & resumed the consideration of the original motion made by the delegates of Virginia, which being again debated through the day, was carried in the affirmative by the votes of N. Hampshire, Connecticut, Massachusetts, Rhode Island, N. Jersey, Maryland, Virginia, N. Carolina, & Georgia. S. Carolina and Pennsylvania voted

[1 On a motion of the Virginia delegates declaring the colonies independent of Great Britain.]

against it. Delaware having but two members present, they were divided. The delegates for New York declared they were for it themselves & were assured their constituents were for it, but that their instructions having been drawn near a twelvemonth before, when reconciliation was still the general object, they were enjoined by them to do nothing which should impede that object. They therefore thought themselves not justifiable in voting on either side, and asked leave to withdraw from the question, which was given them. The commee rose & reported their resolution to the house. Mr. Edward Rutledge of S. Carolina then requested the determination might be put off to the next day, as he believed his colleagues, tho' they disapproved of the resolution, would then join in it for the sake of unanimity. The ultimate question whether the house would agree to the resolution of the committee was accordingly postponed to the next day, when it was again moved and S. Carolina concurred in voting for it. In the meantime a third member had come post from the Delaware counties and turned the vote of that colony in favour of the resolution. Members of a different sentiment attending that morning from Pennsylvania also, their vote was changed, so that the whole 12 colonies who were authorized to vote at all, gave their voices for it; and within a few days, the convention of N. York approved of it and thus supplied the void occasioned by the withdrawing of her delegates from the vote.

Congress proceeded the same day to consider the declaration of Independance which had been reported & lain on the table the Friday preceding, and on Monday referred to a commee of the whole. The pusillanimous idea that we had friends in England worth keeping terms with, still haunted the minds of many. For this reason those passages which conveyed censures on the people of England were struck out, lest they should give them offence. The clause too, reprobating the enslaving the inhabitants of Africa, was struck out in complaisance to South Carolina and Georgia, who had never attempted to restrain the importation of slaves, and who on the contrary still wished to continue it. Our northern brethren also I believe felt a little tender under those censures; for tho' their people have very few slaves themselves yet they had been pretty considerable carriers of them to others. The debates having taken up the greater parts of the 2d 3d & 4th days of July were, in the evening of the last, closed the declaration was reported by the commee, agreed to by the house and signed by every member present except Mr. Dickinson.

THE NATURAL BRIDGE

[From the "Notes on Virginia"]

The *Natural bridge*, the most sublime of Nature's works, though not comprehended under the present head, must not be pretermitted. It is on the ascent of a hill, which seems to have been cloven through its length by some great convulsion. The fissure, just at the bridge, is, by some admeasurements, 270 feet deep, by others only 205. It is about 45 feet wide at the bottom and 90 feet at the top; this of course determines the length of the bridge and its height from the water. Its breadth in the middle is about 60 feet, but more at the ends, and the thickness of the mass at the summit of the arch, about 40 feet. A part of this thickness is constituted by a coat of earth, which gives growth to many large trees. The residue, with the hill on both sides, is one solid rock of limestone. The arch approaches the Semielliptical form; but the larger axis of the ellipsis, which would be the cord of the arch, is many times longer than the transverse. Though the sides of this bridge are provided in some parts with a parapet of fixed rocks, yet few men have resolution to walk to them, and look over into the abyss. You involuntarily fall on your hands and feet, creep to the parapet, and peep over it. Looking down from this height about a minute, gave me a violent head ach. If the view from the top be painful and intolerable, that from below is delightful in an equal extreme. It is impossible for the emotions arising from the sublime to be felt beyond what they are here; so beautiful an arch, so elevated, so light, and springing as it were up to heaven, the rapture of the spectator is really indescribable! The fissure continuing narrow, deep, and streight for a considerable distance above and below the bridge, opens a short but very pleasing view of the North mountain on one side, and the Blue ridge on the other, at the distance each of them of about five miles. This bridge is in the county

of Rockbridge, to which it has given name, and affords a public
and commodious passage over a valley which cannot be crossed
elsewhere for a considerable distance. The stream passing under
it is called Cedar Creek. It is a water of James river, and sufficient in the driest seasons to turn a grist mill, though its fountain
is not more than two miles above.

FIRST INAUGURAL ADDRESS

FRIENDS AND FELLOW CITIZENS

Called upon to undertake the duties of the first Executive
office of our country, I avail myself of the presence of that portion
of my fellow citizens which is here assembled to express my
grateful thanks for the favor with which they have been pleased
to look towards me, to declare a sincere consciousness that the
task is above my talents, and that I approach it with those anxious
and awful presentiments, which the greatness of the charge, and
the weakness of my powers so justly inspire. A rising nation
spread over a wide and fruitful land, traversing all the seas with
the rich productions of their industry, engaged in commerce with
nations who feel power and forget right, advancing rapidly to
destinies beyond the reach of mortal eye; when I contemplate
these transcendent objects, and see the honor, the happiness, and
the hopes of this beloved country committed to the issue and the
auspices of this day, I shrink from the contemplation, and humble
myself before the magnitude of the undertaking.

Utterly indeed should I despair, did not the presence of many
whom I here see, remind me, that in the other high authorities
provided by our constitution, I shall find resources of wisdom, of
virtue and of zeal, on which to rely under all difficulties. To you
then, gentlemen, who are charged with the sovereign functions of
legislation, and to those associated with you, I look with encouragement for that guidance and support which may enable us to
steer with safety, the vessel in which we are all embarked amidst
the conflicting elements of a troubled sea.

During the contest of opinion through which we have passed,
the animation of discussions and of exertions, has sometimes
worn an aspect which might impose on strangers unused to think

freely, and to speak and to write what they think. But this being now decided by the voice of the nation, ennounced according to the rules of the constitution, all will of course arrange themselves under the will of the law, and unite in common efforts for the common good. All too will bear in mind the sacred principle that though the will of the Majority is in all cases to prevail, that will, to be rightful, must be reasonable: that the Minority possess their equal rights, which equal laws must protect, and to violate would be oppression.

Let us then, fellow citizens, unite with one heart and one mind; let us restore to social intercourse that harmony and affection, without which Liberty, and even Life itself, are but dreary things. And let us reflect that having banished from our land that religious intolerance under which mankind so long bled and suffered we have yet gained little, if we countenance a political intolerance, as despotic, as wicked and capable of as bitter and bloody persecution. During the throes and convulsions of the antient world, during the agonized spasms of infuriated man, seeking through blood and slaughter his long lost liberty, it was not wonderful that the agitation of the billows should reach even this distant and peaceful shore: that this should be more felt and feared by some, and less by others, and should divide opinions as to measures of safety. But every difference of opinion, is not a difference of principle. We have called, by different names, brethren of the same principle. We are all republicans: we are all federalists. If there be any among us who wish to dissolve this union, or to change its republican form, let them stand undisturbed, as monuments of the safety with which error of opinion may be tolerated where reason is left free to combat it.

I know indeed that some honest men have feared that a republican government cannot be strong; that this government is not strong enough. But would the honest patriot, in the full tide of successful experiment abandon a government which has so far kept us free and firm on the theoretic and visionary fear that this government, the world's best hope may, by possibility, want energy to preserve itself? I trust not. I believe this, on the contrary, the strongest government on earth. I believe it the only one where every man, at the call of the law, would fly to the standard of the law; would meet invasions of public order, as his own personal concern. Some times it is said that man cannot be trusted with the government of himself. — Can he then be trusted with the government of others? Or have we found angels in the form of kings to govern him? — Let History answer this question.

Let us then pursue with courage and confidence our own federal and republican principles, our attachment to Union and Representative government. Kindly separated by nature, and a wide ocean, from the exterminating havoc of one quarter of the globe, Too high-minded to endure the degradations of the others; Possessing a chosen country, with room enough for all descendants to the 1,oooth and 1,oooth generation; Entertaining a due sense of our equal right to the use of our own faculties, to the acquisitions of our own industry, to honor and confidence from our fellow citizens resulting not from birth, but from our actions and their sense of them, enlightened by a benign religion, professed indeed and practiced in various forms, yet all of them inculcating honesty, truth, temperance, gratitude, and the love of man, acknowledging and adoring an over-ruling providence, which by all its dispensations proves that it delights in the happiness of man here, and his greater happiness hereafter: With all these blessings, what more is necessary to make us a happy and a prosperous people? Still one thing more, fellow citizens, a wise and frugal government, which shall restrain men from injuring one another, shall leave them otherwise free to regulate their own pursuits of industry and improvement, and shall not take from the mouth of labor the bread it has earned. This is the sum of good government, and this is necessary to close the circle of our felicities.

About to enter fellow citizens on the exercise of duties, which comprehend everything dear and valuable to you, it is proper you should understand what I deem the essential principles of this government and consequently those which ought to shape it's administration. I will compress them in the narrowest compass they will bear, stating the general principle, but not all its limitations. Equal and exact justice to all men, of whatever state or persuasion, religious or political: Peace, commerce, and honest friendship with all nations, entangling alliances with none: The support of the State governments in all their rights, as the most competent administrators for our domestic concerns, and the surest bulwarks against anti republican tendencies: The preservation of the General government, in it's whole constitutional vigor, as the sheet anchor of our peace at home, and safety abroad. A jealous care of the right of election by the people, a mild and safe corrective of abuses, which are lopped by the sword of revolution, where peaceable remedies are unprovided. Absolute acquiescence in the decisions of the Majority, the vital principle of republics, from which is no appeal but to force, the vital principle and immediate parent of despotism. A well disciplined militia, our best reliance in peace, and for the first moments of war, till regulars may relieve them: The Supremacy of the Civil over the Military authority: Economy in public expense, that labor may be lightly burthened: The honest paiment of our debts and sacred preservation of the public faith: Encouragement of Agriculture, and of Commerce as its handmaid: The diffusion of information, and arraignment of all abuses at the bar of the public reason: Freedom of Religion, freedom of the press, and freedom of Person under the protection of the Habeas corpus: And trial by juries, impartially selected. These principles form the bright constellation which has gone before us, and guided our steps, thro' an age of Revolution and Reformation: The wisdom of our Sages, and blood of our Heroes, have been devoted to their attainment: they should be the Creed of our political faith, the Text of civic instruction, the Touchstone by which to try the services of those we trust; and should we wander from them, in moments of error or alarm, let us hasten to retrace our steps and to regain the road which alone leads to Peace, Liberty and Safety.

I repair then, fellow citizens to the post which you have assigned me. With experience enough in subordinate stations to know the difficulties of this the greatest of all, I have learnt to expect that it will rarely fall to the lot of imperfect man to retire from this station with the reputation and the favor which bring him into it. Without pretensions to that high confidence you reposed in our first and greatest revolutionary character whose pre-eminent services had entitled him to the first place in his country's love, and had destined for him the fairest page in the volume of faithful history, I ask so much confidence only as may give firmness and effect to the legal administration of your affairs. I shall often go wrong thro' defect of judgment: when right, I shall often be thought wrong by those whose positions will not command a view of the whole ground. I ask your indulgence for my own errors, which will never be intentional: and your support against the errors of others who may condemn what they would not if seen in all its parts. The approbation implied by your suffrage, is a great consolation to me for the past; and my future solicitude will be to retain the good opinion of those who have bestowed it in advance, to conciliate that of others, by doing them all the good in my power, and to be instrumental to the happiness and freedom of all. Relying then on the patronage of your good will, I advance with obedience to the work, ready to retire from it whenever you become sensible how much better choice it is in your power to make. And may that infinite power which rules the destinies of the universe lead our councils to what is best, and give them a favorable issue for your peace and prosperity.

ALEXANDER HAMILTON

[Alexander Hamilton was born in the West India Islands in 1757. At the age of thirteen he was performing important duties as clerk in a counting-house; at the age of fifteen he was sent by friends and relatives to New York, where he entered King's College, now Columbia; and at the age of seventeen he wrote "A Full Vindication of the Measures of Congress from the calumnies of their enemies, in answer to a letter under the signature of a Westchester Farmer." This pamphlet and its immediate successor, "The Farmer Refuted," replied so effectively to the powerful loyalist writings of "The Westchester Farmer" that they brought the young college student into general notice, and from this time until his death in 1804, Hamilton was a public man. During the war he served as an officer, and for a considerable time was a member of Washington's staff, and had charge of Washington's official correspondence. Later he was member of Congress, member of the constitutional convention, and Secretary of the Treasury under Washington. His achievements in establishing the financial system of the nation are matters of political history. After he left the cabinet he remained a real and continually active leader of the Federalist party. The duel in which he was fatally wounded by Aaron Burr was the result of political disagreements.

In his political writings, which constitute practically all his works, Hamilton shows a literary style unsurpassed for its purpose by that of any Revolutionary statesman. As might be expected from his age and the circumstances under which he wrote, his earliest pamphlets show a certain speciousness of argument, and an occasional appeal to popular feeling. His later writings are equally notable for clearness of statement and logical accuracy of thought. The greatest work of his pen was "The Federalist." This series of letters to the people of the State of New York was the joint work of Hamilton, Madison, and Jay; but Hamilton originated the plan, and wrote the great majority of the numbers. It was probably the most powerful single influence in securing the adoption of the Federal constitution, and it has since become established as one of our greatest political classics. It is a remarkable tribute to Hamilton's mastery of expression that this work was effective as a popular campaign document in 1788, and is still recognized by the courts and by students of constitutional law as one of the ablest and most exact expositions of the theory of our government. Many of Hamilton's later state papers, especially those dealing with finance, are models of their kind.

The selections here given follow the best edition of Hamilton's works, that prepared by Henry Cabot Lodge. The text of the "Federalist" is that of the original publication.]

THE ISSUE STATED

[From "A Full Vindication"]

The only distinction between freedom and slavery consists in this: In the former state a man is governed by the laws to which he has given his consent, either in person or by his representative; in the latter, he is governed by the will of another. In the one case, his life and property are his own; in the other, they depend upon the pleasure of his master. It is easy to discern which of these two states is preferable. No man in his senses can hesitate in choosing to be free, rather than a slave.

That Americans are entitled to freedom is incontestable on every rational principle. All men have one common original: they participate in one common nature, and consequently have one common right. No reason can be assigned why one man should exercise any power or pre-eminence over his fellow-creatures more than another; unless they have voluntarily vested him with it. Since, then, Americans have not, by any act of theirs, empowered the British Parliament to make laws for them, it follows they can have no just authority to do it.

Besides the clear voice of natural justice in this respect, the fundamental principles of the English constitution are in our favor. It has been repeatedly demonstrated that the idea of legislation or taxation, when the subject is not represented, is inconsistent with *that*. Nor is this all; our charters, the express conditions on which our progenitors relinquished their native countries, and came to settle in this, preclude every claim of ruling and taxing us without our assent.

Every subterfuge that sophistry has been able to invent, to evade or obscure this truth, has been refuted by the most conclusive reasonings; so that we may pronounce it a matter of undeniable certainty, that the pretensions of Parliament are contradictory to the law of nature, subversive of the British constitution, and destructive of the faith of the most solemn compacts.

What, then, is the subject of our controversy with the mother country? It is this: Whether we shall preserve that security to our lives and properties, which the law of nature, the genius of the British constitution, and our charters, afford us; or whether we shall resign them into the hands of the British House of Commons, which is no more privileged to dispose of them than the Great Mogul? What can actuate those men who labor to delude any of us into an opinion that the object of contention between the parent state and the colonies is only three pence duty upon tea? or that the commotions in America originate in a plan, formed by some turbulent men, to erect it into a republican government? The Parliament claims a right to tax us in all cases whatsoever; its late acts are in virtue of that claim. How ridiculous, then, is it to affirm that we are quarrelling for the trifling sum of three pence a pound on tea, when it is evidently the principle against which we contend.

THE FEDERALIST. No. XXIV

To the People of the State of New York:

To the powers proposed to be conferred upon the federal government, in respect to the creation and direction of the national forces, I have met with but one specific objection, which, if I understand it right, is this, — that proper provision has not been made against the existence of standing armies in time of peace; an objection which, I shall now endeavor to show, rests on weak and unsubstantial foundations.

It has indeed been brought forward in the most vague and general form, supported only by bold assertions, without the appearance of argument; without even the sanction of theoretical opinions; in contradiction to the practice of other free nations, and to the general sense of America, as expressed in most of the existing constitutions. The propriety of this remark will appear, the moment it is recollected that the objection under consideration turns upon a supposed necessity of restraining the LEGISLATIVE authority of the nation, in the article of military establishments; a principle unheard of, except in one or two of our State constitutions, and rejected in all the rest.

A stranger to our politics, who was to read our newspapers at the present juncture, without having previously inspected the plan reported by the convention, would be naturally led to one of two conclusions: either that it contained a positive injunction, that standing armies should be kept up in time of peace; or that it vested in the EXECUTIVE the whole power of levying troops, without subjecting his discretion, in any shape, to the control of the legislature.

If he came afterwards to peruse the plan itself, he would be surprised to discover, that neither the one nor the other was the case; that the whole power of raising armies was lodged in the *Legislature,* not in the *Executive;* that this legislature was to be a popular body, consisting of the representatives of the people periodically elected; and that instead of the provision he had supposed in favor of standing armies, there was to be found, in respect to this object, an important qualification even of the legislative discretion, in that clause which forbids the appropriation of money for the support of an army for any longer period than two years — a precaution which, upon a nearer view of it, will appear to be a great and real security against the keeping up of troops without evident necessity.

Disappointed in his first surmise, the person I have supposed would be apt to pursue his conjectures a little further. He would naturally say to himself, it is impossible that all this vehement and pathetic declamation can be without some colorable pretext. It must needs be that this people, so jealous of their liberties, have, in all the preceding models of the constitutions which they have established, inserted the most precise and rigid precautions on this point, the omission of which, in the new plan, has given birth to all this apprehension and clamor.

If, under this impression, he proceeded to pass in review the several State constitutions, how great would be his disappointment to find that *two only* of them[1] contained an interdiction of standing

---

[1] This statement of the matter is taken from the printed collection of State constitutions. Pennsylvania and North Carolina are the two which contain the interdiction in these words: "As standing armies in time of peace are dangerous to liberty, THEY OUGHT NOT to be kept up." This is, in truth, rather a CAUTION than a PROHIBITION. New Hampshire, Massachusetts, Delaware, and Maryland have, in each of their bills of rights, a clause to this effect: "Standing armies are dangerous to liberty, and ought not to be raised or kept up WITHOUT THE CONSENT OF THE LEGISLATURE;" which is a formal admission of the authority of the Legislature. New York has no bills of rights, and her constitution says not a word about the matter. No bills of rights appear annexed to the constitutions of the other States, except the foregoing, and their constitu-

armies in time of peace; that the other eleven had either observed a profound silence on the subject, or had in express terms admitted the right of the Legislature to authorize their existence.

Still, however, he would be persuaded that there must be some plausible foundation for the cry raised on this head. He would never be able to imagine, while any source of information remained unexplored, that it was nothing more than an experiment upon the public credulity, dictated either by a deliberate intention to deceive, or by the overflowings of a zeal too intemperate to be ingenuous. It would probably occur to him, that he would be likely to find the precautions he was in search of in the primitive compact between the States. Here, at length, he would expect to meet with a solution of the enigma. No doubt, he would observe to himself, the existing Confederation must contain the most explicit provisions against military establishments in time of peace; and a departure from this model, in a favorite point, has occasioned the discontent which appears to influence these political champions.

If he should now apply himself to a careful and critical survey of the articles of Confederation, his astonishment would not only be increased, but would acquire a mixture of indignation, at the unexpected discovery, that these articles, instead of containing the prohibition he looked for, and though they had, with jealous circumspection, restricted the authority of the State legislatures in this particular, had not imposed a single restraint on that of the United States. If he happened to be a man of quick sensibility, or ardent temper, he could now no longer refrain from regarding these clamors as the dishonest artifices of a sinister and unprincipled opposition to a plan which ought at least to receive a fair and candid examination from all sincere lovers of their country! How else, he would say, could the authors of them have been tempted to vent such loud censures upon that plan, about a point in which it seems to have conformed itself to the general sense of America as declared in its different forms of

---

tions are equally silent. I am told, however, that one or two States have bills of rights which do not appear in this collection; but that those also recognize the right of the legislative authority in this respect.

— PUBLIUS.

government, and in which it has even superadded a new and powerful guard unknown to any of them? If, on the contrary, he happened to be a man of calm and dispassionate feelings, he would indulge a sigh for the frailty of human nature, and would lament, that in a matter so interesting to the happiness of millions, the true merits of the question should be perplexed and entangled by expedients so unfriendly to an impartial and right determination. Even such a man could hardly forbear remarking, that a conduct of this kind has too much the appearance of an intention to mislead the people by alarming their passions, rather than to convince them by arguments addressed to their understandings.

But however little this objection may be countenanced, even by precedents among ourselves, it may be satisfactory to take a nearer view of its intrinsic merits. From a close examination it will appear that restraints upon the discretion of the legislature in respect to military establishments in time of peace, would be improper to be imposed, and if imposed, from the necessities of society, would be unlikely to be observed.

Though a wide ocean separates the United States from Europe, yet there are various considerations that warn us against an excess of confidence or security. On one side of us, and stretching far into our rear, are growing settlements subject to the dominion of Britain. On the other side, and extending to meet the British settlements, are colonies and establishments subject to the dominion of Spain. This situation and the vicinity of the West India Islands, belonging to these two powers, create between them, in respect to their American possessions and in relation to us, a common interest. The savage tribes on our Western frontier ought to be regarded as our natural enemies, their natural allies, because they have most to fear from us, and most to hope from them. The improvements in the art of navigation have, as to the facility of communication, rendered distant nations, in a great measure, neighbors. Britain and Spain are among the principal maritime powers of Europe. A future concert of views between these nations ought not to be regarded as improbable. The increasing remoteness of consanguinity is every day diminishing the force of the family compact between France and Spain. And politicians have ever with great reason considered the ties of blood as feeble and precarious links of political connection. These circumstances combined, admonish us not to be too sanguine in considering ourselves as entirely out of the reach of danger.

Previous to the Revolution, and ever since the peace, there has been a constant necessity for keeping small garrisons on our Western frontier. No person can doubt that these will continue to be indispensable, if it should only be against the ravages and depredations of the Indians. These garrisons must either be furnished by occasional detachments from the militia, or by permanent corps in the pay of the government. The first is impracticable; and if practicable, would be pernicious. The militia would not long, if at all, submit to be dragged from their occupations and families to perform that most disagreeable duty in times of profound peace. And if they could be prevailed upon or compelled to do it, the increased expense of a frequent rotation of service, and the loss of labor and disconcertion of the industrious pursuits of individuals, would form conclusive objections to the scheme. It would be as burdensome and injurious to the public as ruinous to private citizens. The latter resource of permanent corps in the pay of the government amounts to a standing army in time of peace; a small one, indeed, but not the less real for being small. Here is a simple view of the subject, that shows us at once the impropriety of a constitutional interdiction of such establishments, and the necessity of leaving the matter to the discretion and prudence of the legislature.

In proportion to our increase in strength, it is probable, nay, it may be said certain, that Britain and Spain would augment their military establishments in our neighborhood. If we should not be willing to be exposed, in a naked and defenceless condition, to their insults and encroachments, we should find it expedient to increase our frontier garrisons in some ratio to the force by which our Western settlements might be annoyed. There are, and will be, particular posts, the possession of which will include the command of large districts of territory, and facilitate future invasions of the remainder. It may be added that some of those posts will be keys to the trade with the Indian nations. Can any man think it would be wise to leave such posts in a situation to be at any instant seized by one or the other of two neighboring and formidable powers? To act this part would be to desert all the usual maxims of prudence and policy.

If we mean to be a commercial people, or even to be secure on our Atlantic side, we must endeavor, as soon as possible, to have a navy. To this purpose there must be dock-yards and arsenals; and for the defence of these, fortifications and probably garrisons. When a nation has become so powerful by sea that it can protect its dock-yards by its fleets, this supersedes the necessity of garrisons for that purpose; but where naval establishments are in their infancy, moderate garrisons will, in all likelihood, be found an indispensable security against descents for the destruction of the arsenals and dock-yards, and sometimes of the fleet itself. PUBLIUS.

THE IMPORTANCE OF MAINTAINING PUBLIC CREDIT

[From a report to the House of Representatives, January 14, 1790]

Every breach of the public engagements, whether from choice or necessity, is, in different degrees, hurtful to public credit. When such a necessity does truly exist, the evils of it are only to be palliated by a scrupulous attention, on the part of the Government, to carry the violation no further than the necessity absolutely requires, and to manifest, if the nature of the case admit of it, a sincere disposition to make reparation whenever circumstances shall permit. But, with every possible mitigation, credit must suffer, and numerous mischiefs ensue. It is, therefore, highly important, when an appearance of necessity seems to press upon the public councils, that they should examine well its reality, and be perfectly assured that there is no method of escaping from it, before they yield to its suggestions. For, though it cannot safely be affirmed that occasions have never existed, or may not exist, in which violations of the public faith, in this respect, are inevitable; yet there is great reason to believe that they exist far less frequently than precedents indicate, and are oftenest either pretended, through levity or want of firmness; or supposed, through want of knowledge. Expedients often have been devised

2 B

to effect, consistently with good faith, what has been done in contravention of it.   Those who are most commonly creditors of a nation are, generally speaking, enlightened men; and there are signal examples to warrant a conclusion that, when a candid and fair appeal is made to them, they will understand their true interest too well to refuse their concurrence in such modifications of their claims as any real necessity may demand.

While the observance of that good faith, which is the basis of public credit, is recommended by the strongest inducements of political expediency, it is enforced by considerations of still greater authority.   There are arguments for it which rest on the immutable principles of moral obligation.   And in proportion as the mind is disposed to contemplate, in the order of Providence, an intimate connection between public virtue and public happiness, will be its repugnancy to a violation of those principles.

This reflection derives additional strength from the nature of the debt of the United States.   It was the price of liberty.   The faith of America has been repeatedly pledged for it, and with solemnities that give peculiar force to the obligation.   There is, indeed, reason to regret that it has not hitherto been kept; that the necessities of the war, conspiring with inexperience in the subjects of finance, produced direct infractions; and that the subsequent period has been a continued scene of negative violation or non-compliance.   But a diminution of this regret arises from the reflection, that the last seven years have exhibited an earnest and uniform effort, on the part of the Government of the Union, to retrieve the national credit, by doing justice to the creditors of the nation; and that the embarrassments of a defective Constitution, which defeated this laudable effort, have ceased.

From this evidence of a favorable disposition given by the former Government, the institution of a new one, clothed with powers competent to calling forth the resources of the community, has excited correspondent expectations.   A general belief accordingly prevails, that the credit of the United States will quickly be established on the firm foundation of an effectual provision for the existing debt. The influence which this has had at home is witnessed by the rapid increase that has taken place in the market value of the public securities.   From January to November, they rose thirty-three and a third per cent.; and, from that period to this time, they have risen fifty per cent. more; and the intelligence from abroad announces effects proportionally favorable to our national credit and consequence.

It cannot but merit particular attention, that, among ourselves, the most enlightened friends of good government are those whose expectations are the highest.

To justify and preserve their confidence; to promote the increasing respectability of the American name; to answer the calls of justice; to restore landed property to its due value; to furnish new resources, both to agriculture and commerce; to cement more closely the union of the States; to add to their security against foreign attack; to establish public order on the basis of an upright and liberal policy; — these are the great and invaluable ends to be secured by a proper and adequate provision, at the present period, for the support of public credit.

FRANCIS HOPKINSON

[Francis Hopkinson (1737–1791) illustrates literary tendencies that were naturally rare in the colonial time, and to the student of literary development his writings have an interest disproportionate to their intrinsic merits. He was born in Philadelphia, and after taking a course at the College of Philadelphia, studied law, served for a year as librarian of the Philadelphia library, and spent a year in England. He held many public offices in Pennsylvania and New Jersey, among them member of the Continental Congress, judge of the admiralty, and United States district judge. Though able and active in his profession and in the discharge of his public duties, he had wide interests and many accomplishments. He was a member of scientific and learned societies, a musician and a composer, and an amateur painter. His versatility is shown in the three volumes of miscellaneous writings in prose and verse which he prepared for publication, and which were issued shortly after his death. These include opinions rendered as judge of the admiralty; essays after the Addisonian model; orations on a variety of subjects; satires and burlesques on political topics, on college examinations, on literary fashions, and many other things; scientific papers; and songs written to be set to music by the author. In prose he was perhaps best as a genial humorist. Two of his best-known prose productions are "A Pretty Story" and "The New Roof," political allegories in which he represents respectively the troubles between Great Britain and the colonies, and the proposed federal constitution. His most famous political effort in verse is "The Battle of the Kegs," one of the most popular ballads of the Revolution. Fashions in humor change, and allegory has gone out of favor. To-day "A Pretty Story" may seem less effective than a simple narrative of historical fact, and "The Battle of the Kegs" may appear rather flat; but both appealed to readers of the Revolutionary time. The wit of some of the non-political satires and burlesques may seem fresher, though the subjects of these pieces are mostly of little present interest.

Francis Hopkinson's works are significant as showing that the middle colonies had reached a stage of development where a distinguished lawyer and public man, a signer of the Declaration and a United States judge, could throw off such trifles for his amusement without feeling that they were a waste of time or beneath his dignity. Both Franklin and Byrd sometimes wrote for the pleasure of writing; but Hopkinson is more spontaneous, if less excellent; he relaxes more, and more naturally. The very amateurishness which makes his style inferior to that of either Franklin or Byrd is a sign of the qualities that make him important.

The selections are from the edition before referred to, which was printed in 1792 from manuscripts prepared for the press by the author.]

CONTEMPORARY HISTORY IN ALLEGORY

[From "A Pretty Story" [1]]

CHAP. V

In the mean time the new settlers encreased exceedingly, their dealings at their father's shop became proportionably enlarged, and their partiality for their brethren of the old farm was sincere and manifest. They suffered, indeed, some inconveniences from the *protectors* which had been stationed amongst them, who became very troublesome in their houses. They introduced riot and intemperance into their families, debauched their daughters, and derided the orders they had made for their own good government. Moreover, the old nobleman had, at different times, sent over to them a great number of thieves, murderers, and robbers, who did much mischief by practising those crimes for which they had been banished from the old farm. But they bore those evils with as much patience as could be expected; not chusing to trouble their old father with complaints, unless in cases of important necessity.

Now the steward began to hate the new settlers with exceeding great hatred, and determined to renew his attack upon their peace and happiness. He artfully insinuated to the nobleman and his foolish wife, that it was very mean, and unbecoming their greatness, to receive the contributions of the people of the new farm through the consent of their respective wives: that upon this footing they might some time or other refuse to comply with his requisitions, if they should take into their heads to think them oppressive and unreasonable; and that it was high time they should be compelled to acknowledge his unlimited power and his wife's *omnipotence*, which, if not enforced now, they would soon be able to resist, as they were daily encreasing in numbers and strength.

Another decree was, therefore, prepared and published, directing that the people of the new farm should pay a certain stipend

[[1] In this elaborate political allegory, originally published in 1774, the "old farm" represents England, and the "new farm" America. The "old nobleman" is the king, his "wife" is the parliament, and his "steward" is the ministry. His "sons," the "new settlers," are of course the colonists, and their "wives" are the legislatures of the respective colonies.]

upon particular goods,[1] which they were not allowed to purchase any where but at their father's shop; specifying that this imposition should not be laid as an advance upon the original price of these goods, but should be paid as a tax on their arrival in the new farm; for the express purpose of supporting the dignity of the nobleman's family, and for re-imbursing the expences he pretended to have been at on their account.

This new decree occasioned great uneasiness. The people saw plainly that the steward and their mother-in-law were determined to enslave and ruin them. They again consulted together, and wrote, as before, the most dutiful and persuasive letters to their father — but to no purpose — a deaf ear was turned against all their remonstrances, and their humble requests rejected with contempt.

Finding that this moderate and decent conduct brought them no relief, they had recourse to another expedient: they bound themselves to each other in a solemn engagement,[2] not to deal any more at their father's shop, until this unconstitutional decree should be repealed, which they one and all declared to be a direct violation of the *Great Paper*.

This agreement was so strictly observed, that in a few months the clerks and apprentices in the old gentleman's shop began to raise a terrible outcry. They declared, that their master's trade was declining exceedingly, and that his wife and steward would by their mischievous machinations ruin the whole farm. They sharpened their pens, and attacked the steward, and even the old lady herself, with great severity: insomuch, that it was thought proper to withdraw this attempt also, upon the rights and liberties of the new settlers. One part only of the decree was left still in force, viz. the tax upon *water-gruel*.[3]

Now there were certain men[4] in the old farm, who had obtained an exclusive right of selling *water-gruel*. Vast quantities of this gruel were vended amongst the new settlers, as they were extremely fond of it, and used it universally in their families. They did not, however, trouble themselves much about the tax on *water-gruel;* they were well pleased with the repeal of the

---

[1] Painter's colours, glass, &c.   [2] Non-importation agreement.
[3] Tea.   [4] The India company.

other parts of the decree, and fond as they were of this gruel, they considered it as not absolutely necessary to the comfort of life, and determined to give up the use of it in their families, and so avoid the effects of that part of the decree.

The steward found his designs again frustrated: but was not discouraged by the disappointment. He devised another scheme, so artfully contrived, that he thought himself sure of success. He sent for the persons who had the sole right of vending *water-gruel;* and after reminding them of the obligations they were under to the nobleman and his wife for the exclusive privilege they enjoyed, he requested that they would send sundry waggons laden with gruel to the new farm; promising that the accustomed duty which they paid for their exclusive right should be taken off from all the gruel they should so send amongst the new settlers; and that in case their cargoes should come to any damage, the loss should be made good to them out of his master's coffers.

The gruel-merchants readily consented to this proposal; considering that if their cargoes were sold, their profits would be very great; and if they failed, the steward was to pay the damage. On the other hand, the steward hoped that the new settlers would not be able to resist a temptation, thus thrown in their way, of purchasing their favourite gruel, to which they had been so long accustomed; and if they did use it, subject to the tax aforesaid, he would consider this as a voluntary acknowledgment that the nobleman and his wife had a right to lay upon them what impositions they pleased, and as a resignation of the privileges of the *Great Paper*.

But the new settlers were well aware of this decoy. They saw plainly that the gruel was not sent for their accommodation; and that if they suffered any part of it to be sold amongst them, subject to the tax imposed by the new decree, it would be considered as a willing submission to the assumed omnipotence of their mother-in-law, and a precedent for future unlimited impositions. Some, therefore, would not permit the waggons to be unladen at all; but sent them back untouched to the gruel-merchants; and others suffered them to unload, but would not touch the dangerous commodity; so that it lay neglected about the roads and high-ways till it was quite spoiled. But one of the new settlers, whose name was JACK, either from a keener sense of the injuries intended, or from the necessity of his situation, which was such that he could not send back the gruel, because of a number of mercenaries [1] whom his father had stationed in his house to be a watch over him — he, I say, being almost driven to despair, stove [2] to pieces the casks of gruel which had been sent him, and utterly destroyed the whole cargo.

CHAP. VI

These violent proceedings were soon known at the old farm. Great was the uproar there. The old nobleman fell into a furious passion, declaring that the new settlers meant to throw off all dependence upon him, and rebel against his authority. His wife also tore the padlocks from her lips, and raved and stormed like a Billingsgate, and the steward lost all patience and moderation — swearing most profanely, *that he would leave no stone unturned till he had humbled the settlers of the new farm at his feet, and caused their father to tread upon their necks.* Moreover, the gruel-merchants roared and bellowed for the loss of their gruel; and the clerks and apprentices were in the utmost consternation lest the people of the new farm should again agree to have no dealings with their father's shop.

Vengeance was forthwith prepared, especially against *Jack.* With him they determined to begin; hoping that by making a severe example of him, they should so terrify the other families, that they would all submit to the power of the steward and acknowledge the omnipotence of the *great Madam.*

A very large padlock [3] was sent over to be fastened on *Jack's* great gate; the key of which was given to the old nobleman, who was not to suffer it to be opened until *Jack* had paid for the gruel he had spilt, and resigned all claim to the privileges of the *Great Paper* — nor even then, unless he should think fit. Secondly, a decree was made to new model the regulations and œconomy of *Jack's* family, in such manner that they might in future be more subjected to the will of the steward. And, thirdly, A large gallows was erected before the mansion-house in the old farm, that if any

---

[1] Board of Commissioners.　　[2] Destruction of the tea at Boston.
[3] The Boston Port-bill.

of Jack's children should be suspected of misbehaviour, they should not be convicted or acquitted by the voice of their brethren, according to the purport of the *Great Paper*, but be tied neck and heels, and sent over to be hanged on this gallows.

On hearing of these severities, the people were highly enraged. They were at a loss how to act, or by what means they should avoid the threatened vengeance. But the old lady and the steward persisted. The great padlock was fastened on *Jack's* gate, and the key given to the nobleman as had been determined on; without waiting to know whether *Jack* would pay for the gruel, or allowing him an opportunity to make any apology or defence.

Poor *Jack* was now in a deplorable condition indeed: The great inlet to his farm was entirely shut up; so that he could neither carry out the produce of his land for sale, nor receive from abroad the necessaries for his family.

But this was not all — The old nobleman, along with the padlock aforesaid, had sent an overseer [1] to hector and domineer over *Jack* and his family, and to endeavour to break his spirits by every possible severity; for which purpose, this overseer was attended by a great number of mercenaries, and armed with more than common authorities.

When the overseer first arrived in *Jack's* family, he was received with great respect, because he was the delegate of their aged father. For, notwithstanding all that had past, the people of the new farm loved and revered the old nobleman with true filial affection: and attributed his unkindness entirely to the intrigues of the steward.

But this fair weather did not last long. The new overseer took the first opportunity to show that he had no intention of living in harmony and friendship with the family — Some of *Jack's* domestics had put on their Sunday clothes, and waited on the overseer in the great parlour, to pay him their compliments on his arrival; [2] and to request his assistance in reconciling their father to them, and restoring peace and cordiality between the old and new farms. But he, in a most abrupt and rude manner, stopped them short in the midst of their address; called them a

---

[1] General Gage, made Governor of the province.
[2] Address to General Gage.

parcel of disobedient scoundrels; bid them go about their business; and turning round on his heel, left the room with an air of contempt and disdain.

CHAP. VII

The people of the new farm seeing the importance of their situation, had appointed a grand committee, consisting of some of the most respectable characters from each family, to manage their affairs in this difficult crisis. *Jack*, thus oppressed and insulted, requested the advice [1] of the grand committee as to his conduct. This committee in their answer, sympathized cordially with him in his afflictions — they exhorted him to bear his suffering with fortitude for a time; assuring him, that they looked upon the insults and punishments inflicted on him with the same indignation as if they had been inflicted on themselves; and promised to stand by and support him to the last — They recommended it to him to be firm and steady in the cause of liberty and their just rights, and never to acknowledge the *omnipotence* of their mother-in-law, nor submit to the machinations of their enemy the steward.

In the mean time, lest *Jack's* family should suffer for want of necessaries, his great gate being fast locked, contributions were raised for his relief amongst the other families,[2] and handed to him over the garden wall.

The new overseer still persisted in his hostile behaviour, taking every opportunity to mortify and insult *Jack* and his family — observing that some of the children and domestics held frequent meetings and consultations together, sometimes in the garret, and sometimes in the stable, and understanding that an agreement not to deal with their father's shop, until their grievances should be redressed, was again talked of, he wrote a thundering prohibition,[3] much like a pope's bull, which he caused to be pasted up in every room of the house — In which he declared and protested, that such meetings were treasonable, traitorous, and rebellious, contrary to the dignity of his master, the nobleman, and inconsistent with the duty they owed to his *omnipotent* wife:

---

[1] Boston consults the congress of the states.

[2] Money raised by the states for the relief of the poor of Boston.

[3] Proclamation at Boston forbidding town meetings.

and threatened that if two of the family should be found whispering together, they should be sent over in chains to the old farm, and hanged upon the great gallows before the mansion-house.

These harsh and unconstitutional proceedings of the overseer, so highly irritated *Jack*, and the other families of the new farm, that * * * * * *

Cetera desunt.

THE BATTLE OF THE KEGS

Gallants attend and hear a friend
    Trill forth harmonious ditty,
Strange things I'll tell which late befel
    In Philadelphia city.

'Twas early day, as poets say,
    Just when the sun was rising,
A soldier stood on a log of wood,
    And saw a thing surprising.

As in amaze he stood to gaze,
    The truth can't be denied, sir,
He spied a score of kegs or more
    Come floating down the tide, sir.

A sailor too in jerkin blue,
    This strange appearance viewing,
First damn'd his eyes, in great surprise,
    Then said some mischief's brewing.

These kegs, I'm told, the rebels bold,
    Pack'd up like pickling herring;
And they're come down t'attack the town,
    In this new way of ferrying.

The soldier flew, the sailor too,
    And scar'd almost to death, sir,
Wore out their shoes, to spread the news,
    And ran till out of breath, sir.

Now up and down throughout the town,
　　Most frantic scenes were acted;
And some ran here, and others there,
　　Like men almost distracted.

Some fire cry'd, which some denied,
　　But said the earth had quaked;
And girls and boys, with hideous noise,
　　Ran through the streets half naked.

Sir William he, snug as a flea,
　　Lay all this time a snoring,
Nor dreamed of harm as he lay warm,
　　*　　*　　*　　*　　*

Now in a fright, he starts upright,
　　Awak'd by such a clatter;
He rubs both eyes, and boldly cries,
　　For God's sake, what's the matter?

At his bed-side he then espy'd,
　　Sir Erskine at command, sir,
Upon one foot, he had one boot,
　　And th' other in his hand, sir.

"Arise, arise, sir Erskine cries,
　　"The rebels — more's the pity,
"Without a boat are all afloat,
　　"And rang'd before the city.

"The motley crew, in vessels new,
　　"With Satan for their guide, sir.
"Pack'd up in bags, or wooden kegs,
　　"Come driving down the tide, sir.

"Therefore prepare for bloody war,
　　"These kegs must all be routed,

"Or surely we despised shall be,
"And British courage doubted."

The royal band, now ready stand
    All rang'd in dread array, sir,
With stomach stout to see it out,
    And make a bloody day, sir.

The cannons roar from shore to shore,
    The small arms make a rattle;
Since wars began I'm sure no man
    E'er saw so strange a battle.

The rebel dales, the rebel vales,
    With rebel trees surrounded;
The distant wood, the hills and floods,
    With rebel echoes sounded.

The fish below swam to and fro,
    Attack'd from ev'ry quarter;
Why sure, thought they, the devil's to pay,
    'Mongst folks above the water.

The kegs, 'tis said, tho' strongly made,
    Of rebel staves and hoops, sir,
Could not oppose their powerful foes,
    The conqu'ring British troops, sir.

From morn to night these men of might
    Display'd amazing courage;
And when the sun was fairly down,
    Retir'd to sup their porrage.

An hundred men with each a pen,
    Or more upon my word, sir.
It is most true would be too few,
    Their valour to record, sir.

Such feats did they perform that day,
    Against these wick'd kegs, sir,
That years to come, if they get home,
    They'll make their boasts and brags, sir.

N.B. This ballad was occasioned by a real incident. Certain machines, in the form of kegs, charg'd with gun powder, were sent down the river to annoy the British shipping then at Philadelphia. The danger of these machines being discovered, the British manned the wharfs and shipping, and discharged their small arms and cannons at every thing they saw floating in the river during the ebb tide.

AN EPITAPH FOR AN INFANT

Sleep on, sweet babe! no dreams annoy thy rest,
Thy spirit flew unsullied from thy breast:
Sleep on, sweet innocent! nor shalt thou dread
The passing storm that thunders o'er thy head:
Thro' the bright regions of yon azure sky,
A winged seraph, now she soars on high;
Or, on the bosom of a cloud reclin'd,
She rides triumphant on the rapid wind;
Or from its source pursues the radiant day;
Or on a sun-beam, smoothly glides away;
Or mounts aerial, to her blest abode,
And sings, inspir'd, the praises of her *God:*
Unveiled, thence, to her extensive eye,
Nature, and Nature's Laws, expanded lie:
Death, in one moment, taught this infant more
Than years or ages ever taught before.

SONG VI

O'er the hills far away, at the birth of the morn
I hear the full tone of the sweet sounding horn;
The sportsmen with shoutings all hail the new day
And swift run the hounds o'er the hills far away.

Across the deep valley their course they pursue
And rush thro' the thickets yet silver'd with dew;
Nor hedges nor ditches their speed can delay —
Still sounds the sweet horn o'er hills far away.

SONG VII

I

My gen'rous heart disdains
    The slave of love to be,
I scorn his servile chains,
    And boast my liberty.
        This whining
        And pining
    And wasting with care,
Are not to my taste, be she ever so fair.

II

Shall a girl's capricious frown
Sink my noble spirits down?
Shall a face of white and red
Make me droop my silly head?
Shall I set me down and sigh
For an eye-brow or an eye?
For a braided lock of hair,
Curse my fortune and despair?
    My gen'rous heart disdains, &c.

III

Still uncertain is tomorrow,
Not quite certain is today —
Shall I waste my time in sorrow?
Shall I languish life away?
All because a cruel maid,
Hath not Love with Love repaid.
    My gen'rous heart disdains, &c.

MERCY OTIS WARREN

[Mercy Otis Warren (1728–1814) was one of the most interesting literary women of the Revolutionary time. She was the sister of James Otis and the wife of James Warren, and had an intimate acquaintance with many distinguished patriot families besides the two with which she was thus connected. She carried on an extensive correspondence with notable men and women, and seems to have been consulted, or at least taken into confidence, in many councils regarding political matters. The greater part of her writings are political or have an indirect political bearing. Among her earliest attempts were two satires in dramatic form, "The Adulator" and "The Group." In both these the characters were recognizable as caricatures of contemporaries. Later, she wrote two formal tragedies in blank verse, "The Sack of Rome" and "The Ladies of Castile." These have no direct reference to contemporary events, but both expound the idea of political liberty. These two plays and a few other poems, some of them occasional, make up a volume of "Poems, Dramatic and Miscellaneous," published in 1790. In 1805 she published her "History of the Rise, Progress and Termination of the American Revolution, interspersed with Biographical, Political and Moral Observations." The author's wide acquaintance with political leaders had given her a first-hand knowledge of many facts, and the definiteness of her beliefs and prejudices makes her "observations" interesting if not always profitable.

Mrs. Warren had a tendency to satirize, with the kind of satire that is unrelieved by humor. She was especially famous for her pen pictures of persons that she had known, and she is most interesting when depicting those of whom she does not approve. Some strictures on John Adams near the close of her "History" led to a temporary suspension of friendly relations with that statesman, and to the exchange of some very pointed letters, which have been printed in the Collections of the Massachusetts Historical Society. In both prose and verse Mrs. Warren affected a formal and artificial style. This can be seen in her personal correspondence as well as her writings intended for publication. She signed herself "Philomela" in letters which she addressed to her friend Mrs. Winthrop as "Narcissa," and to her friend Mrs. Adams as "Portia." Even her letters to her children contain artificial poetic talk about "Strephon and Collin," etc. This sort of absurdity was a literary disease prevailing at the time, and while Mrs. Warren was by nature subject to it, and her works may be studied for a knowledge of the symptoms, the importance of her affectation must not be overrated.

The selections follow the first editions of "The Group," the "Poems, Dramatic and Miscellaneous," and the "History," published in Boston in 1775, 1790, and 1805, respectively.]

A LOYALIST DIALOGUE

[From "The Group," Act II, Scene III [1]]

Simple Sappling. Though my paternal Acres are eat up,
My patrimony spent, I've yet an house
My lenient creditors let me improve,
Send up the Troops, 'twill serve them well for Barracks.
I some how think 'twould bear a noble sound,
To have my mansion guarded by the King.

Sylla. Hast thou no sons or blooming daughters there,
To call up all the feelings of a Father,
Least their young minds contaminate by vice,
Caught from such inmates, dangerous and vile,
Devoid of virtue, rectitude, or honour
Save what accords with military fame?
Hast thou no wife who asks thy tender care,
To guard her from Belona's hardy sons?
Who when not toiling in the hostile field
Are faithful vot'ries to the Cyprian Queen.
Or is her soul of such materials made,
Indelicate, and thoughtless of her fame:
So void of either sentiment or sense,
As makes her a companion fit for thee!

Simple Sappling. Silvia's good natur'd, and no doubt will yield,
And take the brawny vet'rans to her board,
When she's assur'd 'twill help her husband's fame.
If she complains or murmurs at the plan,
Let her solicit charity abroad;
Let her go out and seek some pitying friend

[1] The characters in this satiric drama represent well-known British sympa-
thizers. "Sylla" is General Gage; "Brigadier Hateall" is said to be Timothy
Ruggles; "Simple Sappling," Nathaniel Ray Thomas; "Collateralis, a new made
judge," Brown. The stage direction for this scene reads: "*The fragments of
the broken Council appear with trembling servile Gestures, shewing several appli-
cations to the General from the Under-Tools in the distant Counties, begging each a
guard of myrmidons to protect them from the armed multitudes (which the guilty
horrors of their wounded consciences hourly presented to their frightened imaginations) approaching to take speedy vengeance on the Court Parasites, who had fled
for refuge to the Camp, by immediate destruction to their Pimps, Panders and
Sycophants left behind.*"]

2 C

To give her shelter from the wint'ry blast,
Disperse her children round the neighb'ring cots,
And then —— —— —— ——
    Publican. —— —— Then weep thy folly and her own hard fate!
I pity Silvia, I knew the beauteous maid
E'er she descended to become thy wife:
She silent mourns the weakness of her lord,
For she's too virtuous to approve thy deeds.
    Hateall. Pho —— —— what's a woman's tears,
Or all the whinings of that trifling sex?
I never felt one tender thought towards them.
    When young, indeed, I wedded nut brown Kate,
(Blyth bosom Dowager, the jockey's prey)
But all I wish'd was to secure her dower.
I broke her spirits when I'd won her purse;
For which I'll give a recipe most sure
To ev'ry hen peck'd husband round the board;
If crabbed words or surly looks won't tame
The haughty strew [shrew?] nor bend the stubborn mind,
Then the green Hick'ry, or the willow twig,
Will prove a curse for each rebellious dame
Who dare oppose her lord's superior will.
    Sylla. Enough of this, ten thousand harrowing cares
Tear up my peace, and swell my anxious breast.
    I see some mighty victim must appease
An injured nation, tott'ring on the verge
Of wide destruction, made the wanton sport
Of hungry Harpies, gaping for their prey;
Which if by misadventures they should miss,
The disappointed vultures angry fang,
Will sieze the lesser gudgeons of the state,
And sacrifice to mad Alecto's rage;
Lest the tide turning, with a rapid course
The booming torrent rushes o'er their heads,
And sweeps the "cawing cormorants from earth."
    Hateall. Then strike some sudden blow, and if hereafter
Dangers should rise —— then set up for thyself,
And make thy name as famous in Columbia,

As ever Cæsar's was in ancient Gaul.
Who would such distant Provinces subdue,
And then resign them to a foreign lord!
With such an armament at thy command
Why all this cautious prudence?

    Sylla. I only wish to serve my Sov'reign well,
And bring new glory to my master's crown.
Which can't be done by spreading ruin round
This loyal country ——— ——— ———
—— Wro't up to madness by oppression's hand.
How much deceiv'd my royal master is
By those he trusts! — but more of this anon.

    Were it consistent with my former plan,
I'd gladly send my sickly troops abroad
Out from the stench of this infected town,
To breath some air more free from putrefaction;
To brace their nerves against approaching spring,
If my ill stars should destine a campaign,
And call me forth to fight in such a cause.

    To quench the gen'rous spark, the innate love
Of glorious freedom, planted in the breast
Of ev'ry man who boasts a Briton's name,
Until some base born lust of foreign growth
Contaminate his soul, till false ambition,
Or the sordid hope of swelling coffers,
Poison the mind, and brutalize the man.

    Collateralis. I almost wish I never had engag'd
To rob my country of her native rights,
Nor strove to mount on justice solemn bench,
By mean submission cringing for a place.

    How great the pain, and yet how small the *purchase!*
Had I been dumb, or my right hand cut off,
E'er I so servilely had held it up,
Or giv'n my voice abjectly to rescind
The wisest step that mortal man could take
To curb the tallons of tyrannic power,
Out stretch'd rapacious ready to devour
The fair possessions, by our Maker giv'n

Confirm'd by compacts — ratify'd by Heav'n.

Sylla.   Look o'er the annals of our virtuous sires,
And search the story of Britannia's deeds,
From Cæsar's ravages to Hambden's fall;
From the good Hambden down to glorious Wolfe,
Whose soul took wing on Abrahams fatal plain,
Where the young Hero fought Britannia's foes,
And vanquish'd Bourbons dark ferocious hosts,
Till the slaves trembled at a George's name.

'Twas love of freedom drew a Marlborough's sword;
This glorious passion mov'd a Sydney's pen;
And crown'd with Bayes a Harrington and Locke;
'Tis freedom wreathes the Garlands o'er their tombs.

For her how oft have bleeding Heroes fall'n!
With the warm fluid, gushing from their wounds,
Convey'd the purchase to their distant heirs!

And shall I rashly draw my guilty sword,
And dip its hungry hilt in the rich blood
Of the best subjects that a Brunswick boasts,
And for no cause, but that they nobly scorn
To wear the fetters of his venal slaves!

But swift time rolls, and on his rapid wheel
Bears the winged hours, and the circling years.

The cloud cap'd morn, the dark short wintry day,
And the keen blasts of roughned Borea's breath,
Will soon evanish, and approaching spring
Opes with the fate of empires on her wing.   *Exit Sylla.*

THE NECESSARIES OF LIFE

[From a poem "To the Hon. J. Winthrop, Esq. Who, on the American
Determination, in 1774, to suspend all Commerce with Britain, (except
for the real Necessaries of life) requested a poetical List of the Articles
the Ladies might comprise under that Head"]

But if ye doubt, an inventory clear,
Of all she needs, Lamira offers here;
Nor does she fear a rigid Cato's frown,
When she lays by the rich embroider'd gown,

And modestly compounds for just enough —
Perhaps, some dozens of more slighty stuff;
With lawns and lustrings — blond, and mecklin laces,
Fringes and jewels, fans and tweezer cases;
Gay cloaks and hats, of every shape and size,
Scarfs, cardinals, and ribbons of all dyes;
With ruffles stamp'd, and aprons of tambour,
Tippets and handkerchiefs, at least, three score;
With finest muslins that fair India boasts,
And the choice herbage from Chinesan coasts;
(But while the fragrant hyson leaf regales,
Who'll wear the homespun produce of the vales?
For if 'twould save the nation from the curse
Of standing troops; or, name a plague still worse,
Few can this choice delicious draught give up,
Though all Medea's poisons fill the cup.)
Add feathers, furs, rich sattins, and ducapes,
And head dresses in pyramidial shapes;
Side boards of plate, and porcelain profuse,
With fifty ditto's that the ladies use;
If my poor treach'rous memory has miss'd,
Ingenious T——l, shall complete the list.
So weak Lamira, and her wants so few,
Who shall refuse? — they're but the sex's due.

THE BOSTON TEA PARTY

[From the "History of the Rise, Progress and Termination of the American Revolution"]

The storage or detention of a few cargoes of teas is not an object in itself sufficient to justify a detail of several pages; but as the subsequent severities towards the Massachusetts were grounded on what the ministry termed their *refractory behaviour* on this occasion; and as those measures were followed by consequences of the highest magnitude both to Great Britain and the colonies, a particular narration of the transactions of the town of Boston is indispensable. There the sword of civil discord was first drawn, which was not re-sheathed until the emancipation of the thirteen colonies from the yoke of foreign domination was acknowledged by the diplomatic seals of the first powers in Europe. This may apologize, if necessary, for the appearance of locality in the preceding pages, and for its farther continuance in regard to a colony, on which the bitterest cup of ministerial wrath was poured for a time, and where the energies of the human mind were earlier called forth, than in several of the sister states.

Not intimidated by the frowns of greatness, nor allured by the smiles of intrigue, the vigilance of the people was equal to the importance of the event. Though expectation was equally awake in both parties, yet three or four weeks elapsed in a kind of *inertia;* the one side flattered themselves with hopes, that as the ships were suffered to be so long unmolested, with their cargoes entire, the point might yet be obtained; the other thought it possible, that some impression might yet be made on the governor, by the strong voice of the people.

Amidst this suspense a rumour was circulated, that admiral Montague was about to seize the ships, and dispose of their cargoes at public auction, within twenty-four hours. This step would as effectually have secured the duties, as if sold at the shops of the consignees, and was judged to be only a *finesse*, to place them there on their own terms. On this report, convinced of the necessity of preventing so bold an attempt, a vast body of people convened suddenly and repaired to one of the largest and most commodious churches in Boston; where, previous to any other steps, many fruitless messages were sent both to the governor and the consignees, whose timidity had prompted them to a seclusion from the public eye. Yet they continued to refuse any satisfactory answer; and while the assembled multitude were in quiet consultation on the safest mode to prevent the sale and consumption of an herb, *noxious* at least to the political constitution, the debates were interrupted by the entrance of the sheriff with an order from the governor, styling them an illegal assembly, and directing their immediate dispersion.

This authoritative mandate was treated with great contempt, and the sheriff instantly hissed out of the house. A confused murmur ensued, both within and without the walls; but in a few moments all was again quiet, and the leaders of the people returned calmly to the point in question. Yet every expedient seemed fraught with insurmountable difficulties, and evening approaching without any decided resolutions, the meeting was adjourned without day.

Within an hour after this was known abroad, there appeared a great number of persons, clad like the aborigines of the wilderness, with tomahawks in their hands, and clubs on their shoulders, who without the least molestation marched through the streets with silent solemnity, and amidst innumerable spectators, proceeded to the wharves, boarded the ships, demanded the keys, and with much deliberation knocked open the chests, and emptied several thousand weight of the finest teas into the ocean. No opposition was made, though surrounded by the king's ships; all was silence and dismay.

This done, the procession returned through the town in the same order and solemnity as observed in the outset of their attempt. No other disorder took place, and it was observed, the stillest night ensued that Boston had enjoyed for many months. This unexpected event struck the ministerial party with rage and astonishment; while, as it seemed to be an attack upon private property, many who wished well to the public cause could not fully approve of the measure. Yet perhaps the laws of self-preservation might justify the deed, as the exigencies of the times required extraordinary exertions, and every other method had been tried in vain, to avoid this disagreeable alternative. Besides it was alleged, and doubtless it was true, the people were ready to make ample compensation for all damages sustained, whenever the unconstitutional duty should be taken off, and other grievances radically redressed. But there appeared little prospect that any conciliatory advances would soon be made. The officers of government discovered themselves more vindictive than ever: animosities daily increased, and the spirits of the people were irritated to a degree of alienation, even from their tenderest connexions, when they happened to differ in political opinion.

THE CHARACTER OF WASHINGTON

[From the "History of the Rise, Progress and Termination of the American Revolution"]

Mr. Washington was a gentleman of family and fortune, of a polite, but not a learned education; he appeared to possess a coolness of temper, and a degree of moderation and judgment, that qualified him for the elevated station in which he was now placed; with some considerable knowledge of mankind, he supported the reserve of the statesman, with the occasional affability of the courtier. In his character was blended a certain dignity, united with the appearance of good humour; he possessed courage without rashness, patriotism and zeal without acrimony, and retained with universal applause the first military command, until the establishment of independence. Through the various changes of fortune in the subsequent conflict, though the slowness of his movements was censured by some, his character suffered little diminution to the conclusion of a war, that from the extraordinary exigencies of an infant republic, required at times, the caution of Fabius, the energy of Cæsar, and the happy facility of expedient in distress, so remarkable in the military operations of the illustrious Frederick.[1] With the first of these qualities, he was endowed by nature; the second was awakened by necessity; and the third he acquired by experience in the field of glory and danger, which extended his fame through half the globe.

In the late war between England and France, Mr. Washington had been in several military rencounters, and had particularly signalized himself in the unfortunate expedition under general Braddock, in the wilderness on the borders of the Ohio, in the year one thousand seven hundred and fifty-five. His conduct on that occasion raised an *eclat* of his valor and prudence; in consequence of which many young gentlemen from all parts of the continent, allured by the name of major Washington, voluntarily entered the service, proud of being enrolled in the list of officers under one esteemed so gallant a commander.

---

[1] The late king of Prussia, well known for this trait in his character, by all who are acquainted with the history of his reign.

THE CHARACTER OF GENERAL LEE

[From the "History of the Rise, Progress and Termination of the American Revolution"]

No man was better qualified at this early stage of the war, to penetrate the designs, or to face in the field an experienced British veteran, than general Lee. He had been an officer of character and rank in the late war between England and France.[1] Fearless of danger, and fond of glory, he was calculated for the field, without any of the graces that recommend the soldier to the circles of the polite. He was plain in his person even to ugliness, and careless in his manners to a degree of rudeness. He possessed a bold genius and an unconquerable spirit: his voice was rough, his garb ordinary, his deportment morose. A considerable traveller, and well acquainted with most of the European nations, he was frequently agreeable in narration, and judicious and entertaining in observation. Disgusted with the ministerial system, and more so with his sovereign who authorized it, he cherished the American cause from motives of resentment, and a predilection in favor of freedom, more than from a just sense of the rights of mankind.

Without religion or country, principle, or attachment, gold was his deity, and liberty the idol of his fancy: he hoarded the former without taste for its enjoyment, and worshipped the latter as the patroness of licentiousness, rather than the protectress of virtue. He affected to despise the opinion of the world, yet was fond of applause. Ambitious of fame without the dignity to support it, he emulated the heroes of antiquity in the field, while in private life he sunk into the vulgarity of the clown. Congress did wisely to avail themselves of his military experience in the infancy of a confederated army, and still more wisely in placing him in a degree of subordination. He was on the first list of continental officers, and only the generals Washington and Ward were named before him; but though nominally the third in rank, as a soldier he was second to no man. The abilities of general Ward were better

---

[1] He had served with reputation in Portugal, under the command of the count de la Lippe.

adapted to the more quiet disquisitions of the cabinet, that on [than to?] the hostile and dangerous scenes of the field or the camp, both which he soon left and retired to private life, when nothing remained to prevent this singular stranger from taking the command of the armies of the United States, but the life of Washington.

JOHN TRUMBULL

[John Trumbull was perhaps the most representative of the so-called "Hartford Wits," a group of Connecticut men who were associated in literary work during and just after the Revolution. Before the outbreak of serious political trouble the colonists had reached a point where many young men, in college and just out of college, were interesting themselves in what they called *belles lettres*, and attempting writings in prose and verse after the models of the most approved English authors. A little later these men, almost without exception, wrote on political subjects. John Trumbull may be taken as a type of this class. He was born in 1750, of a distinguished Connecticut family. He was remarkably precocious, and, according to a well-known story, passed with credit the examinations for admission to Yale College when but seven years old. Before he actually entered Yale, at the age of thirteen, he had read most of the classic authors studied in that institution, and accordingly had much time for subjects not in the regular curriculum. He was especially interested in English literature, and when later he became a tutor, he worked for the introduction of this study and English composition into the college course. In 1769, while still a student for the Master's degree, he was the chief author of "The Medler," a series of essays modelled on "The Spectator." This was followed by a similar series, "The Correspondent." About the same time he wrote verses plainly reminiscent of Milton, Pope, Goldsmith, and other English poets. In 1772, while a tutor at Yale, he published the first part of "The Progress of Dulness," a Hudibrastic satire in three cantos, in which he ridiculed the existing methods of education, and argued for a college course devoted less exclusively to Latin and Greek. In 1773 he became a student in the law office of John Adams at Boston, and naturally acquired an intense interest in political affairs. In 1774 he published an "Elegy on the Times," and in January, 1776,[1] the first part of "McFingal."

"McFingal," Trumbull's most important work, and the most famous political satire of the Revolution, is a mock-heroic poem in the Hudibrastic metre. Most readers see chiefly the influence of Butler, though Professor Moses Coit Tyler considered that the author's model was the eighteenth-century satirist Churchill. The part of the poem which was published in 1776, and which was an effective political document during the years of conflict, was later divided into two cantos, and supplemented by two more cantos, written in 1782.

After the war Trumbull was associated with other Hartford wits in the

---

[1] The imprint of the first edition is Philadelphia, 1775.

production of satires supporting the Federalists. In 1820 he issued a collected edition of his poetical works, the text of which is, with the omission of a few footnotes, followed in the selections here given. He held various political offices in Connecticut, and in 1825 removed to Detroit, Mich., where he died in 1831.]

INVOCATION TO SLEEP

[From "Ode to Sleep"]

I

Come, gentle Sleep!
Balm of my wounds and softner of my woes,
And lull my weary heart in sweet repose,
And bid my sadden'd soul forget to weep,
　　And close the tearful eye;
　　While dewy eve with solemn sweep,
Hath drawn her fleecy mantle o'er the sky,
　　And chaced afar, adown th' ethereal way,
The din of bustling care and gaudy eye of day.

II

Come, but thy leaden sceptre leave,
　　Thy opiate rod, thy poppies pale,
Dipp'd in the torpid fount of Lethe's stream,
　　That shroud with night each intellectual beam,
And quench th' immortal fire, in deep Oblivion's wave.
　　Yet draw the thick impervious veil
　　O'er all the scenes of tasted woe;
　　Command each cypress shade to flee;
　　Between this toil-worn world and me,
Display thy curtain broad, and hide the realms below.

III

Descend, and graceful in thy hand,
With thee bring thy magic wand,
And thy pencil, taught to glow
In all the hues of Iris' bow.
And call thy bright, aerial train,

Each fairy form and visionary shade,
  That in the Elysian land of dreams,
  The flower-enwoven banks along,
Or bowery maze, that shades the purple streams,
Where gales of fragrance breathe th' enamour'd song,
  In more than mortal charms array'd,
People the airy vales and revel in thy reign.

IV

  But drive afar the haggard crew,
That haunt the guilt-encrimson'd bed,
  Or dim before the frenzied view
Stalk with slow and sullen tread;
  While furies with infernal glare,
Wave their pale torches through the troubled air:
  And deep from Darkness' inmost womb,
Sad groans dispart the icy tomb,
  And bid the sheeted spectre rise,
Mid shrieks and fiery shapes and deadly fantasies.

V

Come and loose the mortal chain,
  That binds to clogs of clay th' ethereal wing;
  And give th' astonish'd soul to rove,
Where never sunbeam stretch'd its wide domain;
  And hail her kindred forms above,
  In fields of uncreated spring,
Aloft where realms of endless glory rise,
And rapture paints in gold the landscape of the skies.

TOM BRAINLESS AT COLLEGE

[From "The Progress of Dulness," Part I]

  Two years thus spent in gathering knowledge,
The lad sets forth t'unlade at college,
While down his sire and priest attend him,
To introduce and recommend him;

Or if detain'd, a letter's sent
Of much apocryphal content,
To set him forth, how dull soever,
As very learn'd and very clever;
A genius of the first emission,
With burning love for erudition;
So studious he'll outwatch the moon
And think the planets set too soon.
He had but little time to fit in;
Examination too must frighten.
Depend upon't he must do well,
He knows much more than he can tell;
Admit him, and in little space
He'll beat his rivals in the race;
His father's incomes are but small,
He comes now, if he come at all.

So said, so done, at college now
He enters well, no matter how;
New scenes awhile his fancy please,
But all must yield to love of ease.
In the same round condemn'd each day,
To study, read, recite and pray;
To make his hours of business double —
He can't endure th' increasing trouble;
And finds at length, as times grow pressing,
All plagues are easier than his lesson.
With sleepy eyes and count'nance heavy,
With much excuse of *non paravi*.[1]
Much absence, *tardes* and *egresses*,
The college-evil on him seizes.
Then ev'ry book, which ought to please,
Stirs up the seeds of dire disease;
Greek spoils his eyes, the print's so fine,
Grown dim with study, or with wine;
Of Tully's latin much afraid,

---

[1] *Non paravi*, I have not prepared for recitation — an excuse commonly given; *tardes* and *egresses* were terms used at college, for coming in late and going out before the conclusion of service.

Each page, he calls the doctor's aid;
While geometry, with lines so crooked,
Sprains all his wits to overlook it.
His sickness puts on every name,
Its cause and uses still the same;
'Tis tooth-ache, cholic, gout or stone,
With phases various as the moon;
But though through all the body spread,
Still makes its cap'tal seat, the head.
In all diseases, 'tis expected,
The weakest parts be most infected.

Kind head-ache hail! thou blest disease,
The friend of idleness and ease;
Who mid the still and dreary bound
Where college walls her sons surround,
In spite of fears, in justice' spite,
Assumest o'er laws dispensing right,
Sett'st from his task the blunderer free,
Excused by dulness and by thee.
Thy vot'ries bid a bold defiance
To all the calls and threats of science,
Slight learning human and divine,
And hear no prayers, and fear no fine.

And yet how oft the studious gain,
The dulness of a letter'd brain;
Despising such low things the while,
As English grammar, phrase and style;
Despising ev'ry nicer art,
That aids the tongue, or mends the heart;
Read ancient authors o'er in vain,
Nor taste one beauty they contain;
Humbly on trust accept the sense,
But deal for words at vast expense;
Search well how every term must vary
From Lexicon to Dictionary;
And plodding on in one dull tone,
Gain ancient tongues and lose their own,
Bid every graceful charm defiance,

And woo the skeleton of science.
   Come ye, who finer arts despise,
And scoff at verse as heathen lies;
In all the pride of dulness rage
At Pope, or Milton's deathless page;
Or stung by truth's deep-searching line,
Rave ev'n at rhymes as low as mine;
Say ye, who boast the name of wise,
Wherein substantial learning lies.
Is it, superb in classic lore,
To speak what Homer spoke before,
To write the language Tully wrote,
The style, the cadence and the note?
Is there a charm in sounds of Greek,
No language else can learn to speak;
That cures distemper'd brains at once,
Like Pliny's rhymes for broken bones?
Is there a spirit found in Latin,
That must evap'rate in translating?
And say are sense and genius bound
To any vehicles of sound?
Can knowledge never reach the brains,
Unless convey'd in ancient strains?
While Homer sets before your eyes
Achilles' rage, Ulysses' lies,
Th' armours of Jove in masquerade,
And Mars entrapp'd by Phœbus' aid;
While Virgil sings, in verses grave,
His lovers meeting in a cave,
His ships turn'd nymphs, in pagan fables,
And how the Trojans eat their tables;
While half this learning but displays
The follies of the former days;
And for our linguists, fairly try them,
A tutor'd parrot might defy them.
   Go to the vulgar — 'tis decreed,
There you must preach and write or plead;
Broach every curious Latin phrase

From Tully down to Lily's days:
All this your hearers have no share in,
Bate but their laughing and their staring.
Interpreters must pass between,
To let them know a word you mean.

   Yet could you reach that lofty tongue
Which Plato wrote and Homer sung;
Or ape the Latin verse and scanning,
Like Vida, Cowley or Buchanan;
Or bear ten phrase-books in your head;
Yet know, these languages are dead,
And nothing, e'er, by death, was seen
Improved in beauty, strength or mien,
Whether the sexton use his spade,
Or sorcerer wake the parted shade.
Think how would Tully stare or smile
At these wan spectres of his style,
Or Horace in his jovial way
Ask what these babblers mean to say.

M'FINGAL'S ACCOMPLISHMENTS

[From "McFingal," Canto I]

No ancient sybil, famed in rhyme,
Saw deeper in the womb of time;
No block in old Dodona's grove
Could ever more orac'lar prove.
Not only saw he all that could be,
But much that never was, nor would be;
Whereby all prophets far outwent he,
Though former days produced a plenty:
For any man with half an eye
What stands before him can espy;
But optics sharp it needs, I ween,
To see what is not to be seen.
As in the days of ancient fame,
Prophets and poets were the same,

2 D

And all the praise that poets gain
Is for the tales they forge and feign:
So gain'd our 'Squire his fame by seeing
Such things, as never would have being;
Whence he for oracles was grown
The very tripod [1] of his town.
Gazettes no sooner rose a lie in,
But strait he fell to prophesying;
Made dreadful slaughter in his course,
O'erthrew provincials, foot and horse,
Brought armies o'er, by sudden pressings,
Of Hanoverians, Swiss and Hessians,
Feasted with blood his Scottish clan,
And hang'd all rebels to a man,
Divided their estates and pelf,
And took a goodly share himself.
All this with spirit energetic,
He did by second-sight prophetic.

Thus stored with intellectual riches,
Skill'd was our 'Squire in making speeches;
Where strength of brains united centers
With strength of lungs surpassing Stentor's. [2]
But as some muskets so contrive it,
As oft to miss the mark they drive at,
And though well aim'd at duck or plover,
Bear wide, and kick their owners over:
So fared our 'Squire, whose reas'ning toil
Would often on himself recoil,
And so much injured more his side,
The stronger arguments he applied;
As old war-elephants, dismay'd,
Trod down the troops they came to aid,
And hurt their own side more in battle,
Than less and ordinary cattle.
Yet at Town-meetings every chief

---

[1] The tripod was a sacred three-legged stool, from which the ancient priests uttered their oracles.
[2] Stentor, the loud-voic'd herald in Homer.

Pinn'd faith on great M'FINGAL'S sleeve;
Which when he lifted, all by rote
Raised sympathetic hands to vote.

M'FINGAL TO THE WHIGS

[From "McFingal," Canto II]

"Your boasted patriotism is scarce,
And country's love is but a farce:
For after all the proofs you bring,
We Tories know there's no such thing.
· Hath not Dalrymple [1] show'd in print,
And Johnson too, there's nothing in't;
Produced you demonstration ample,
From others' and their own example,
That self is still, in either faction,
The only principle of action;
The loadstone, whose attracting tether
Keeps the politic world together:
And spite of all your double dealing,
We all are sure 'tis so, from feeling.
    "Who heeds your babbling of transmitting
Freedom to brats of your begetting,
Or will proceed, as tho' there were a tie,
And obligation to posterity?
We get them, bear them, breed and nurse.
What has posterity done for us,
That we, least they their rights should lose,
Should trust our necks to gripe of noose?
"And who believes you will not run?
Ye're cowards, every mother's son;
And if you offer to deny,

---

[1] This writer undertook to demonstrate, that all the celebrated British patriots were pensioners, in the pay of France. His proof is derived from the letters of the French ambassadors, who, accounting for the monies received from their court, charge so many thousand guineas paid to Hampden, Sidney, and others, as bribes. We are told also that Admiral Russell defeated the French fleet, at a time when he had engaged most solemnly, and received a stipulated sum, to be beaten himself.

We've witnesses to prove it by.
Attend th' opinion first, as referee,
Of your old general, stout Sir Jeffrey; [1]
Who swore that with five thousand foot
He'd rout you all, and in pursuit
Run thro' the land, as easily
As camel thro' a needle's eye.
Did not the mighty Colonel Grant
Against your courage pour his rant,
Affirm your universal failure
In every principle of valour,
And swear no scamperers e'er could match you,
So swift, a bullet scarce could catch you?
And will you not confess, in this
A judge most competent he is;
Well skill'd on running to decide,
As what himself has often tried?
'Twould not methinks be labor lost,
If you'd sit down and count the cost,
And ere you call your Yankies out,
First think what work you've set about.
Have you not roused, his force to try on,
That grim old beast, the British Lion;
And know you not, that at a sup
He's large enough to eat you up?
Have you survey'd his jaws beneath,
Drawn inventories of his teeth,
Or have you weigh'd, in even balance,
His strength and magnitude of talons?
His roar would change your boasts to fear,
As easily, as sour [2] small beer;
And make your feet from dreadful fray,
By native instinct run away.
Britain, depend on't, will take on her
T'assert her dignity and honor,

---

[1] Sir Jeffrey Amherst, Grant, and other officers, who had served in America, were so ignorant, silly, or malicious, as to make such assertions in Parliament.
[2] It is asserted that the roar of a lion will turn small beer sour.

And ere she'd lose your share of pelf,
Destroy your country, and herself.
For has not North declared they fight
To gain substantial rev'nue by't,
Denied he'd ever. deign to treat,
Till on your knees and at his feet?
And feel you not a trifling ague
From Van's '*Delenda est Carthago*'?[1]
For this now Britain has projected,
Think you she has not means t'effect it?
Has she not set at work all engines
To spirit up the native Indians,
Send on your backs the tawny band,
With each an hatchet in his hand,
T'amuse themselves with scalping knives,
And butcher children and your wives;
And paid them for your scalps at sale
More than your heads would fetch by tale;
That she might boast again with vanity,
Her English national humanity?
For now in its primeval sense
This term, *humanity*, comprehends
All things of which, on this side hell,
The *human mind* is capable;
And thus 'tis well, by writers sage,
Applied to Britain and to Gage."

THE COMBAT AT THE LIBERTY POLE

[From "McFingal," Canto III]

M'FINGAL, rising at the word,
Drew forth his old militia-sword;
Thrice cried " King George," as erst in distress,
Knights of romance invoked a mistress;

[1] *Carthage must be annihilated.* There actually existed, a little time before the war, a member of Parliament of the name of *Van*, who in a speech there applied this famous threat of Cato to America, and particularly to Boston, as the place to begin the work of destruction.

And brandishing the blade in air,
Struck terror through th' opposing war.
The Whigs, unsafe within the wind
Of such commotion, shrunk behind.
With whirling steel around address'd,
Fierce through their thickest throng he press'd,
(Who roll'd on either side in arch,
Like Red Sea waves in Israel's march)
And like a meteor rushing through,
Struck on their Pole a vengeful blow.
Around, the Whigs, of clubs and stones
Discharged whole vollies, in platoons,
That o'er in whistling fury fly;
But not a foe dares venture nigh.
And now perhaps with glory crown'd
Our 'Squire had fell'd the pole to ground,
Had not some Pow'r, a whig at heart,
Descended down and took their part; [1]
(Whether 'twere Pallas, Mars or Iris,
'Tis scarce worth while to make inquiries)
Who at the nick of time alarming,
Assumed the solemn form of Chairman,
Address'd a Whig, in every scene
The stoutest wrestler on the green,
And pointed where the spade was found,
Late used to set their pole in ground,
And urged, with equal arms and might,
To dare our 'Squire to single fight.
The Whig thus arm'd, untaught to yield,
Advanced tremendous to the field:
Nor did M'FINGAL shun the foe,
But stood to brave the desp'rate blow;
While all the party gazed, suspended
To see the deadly combat ended;

---

[1] The learned reader will readily observe the allusions in this scene, to the single combats of Paris and Menelaus in Homer, Æneas and the Turnus in Virgil, and Michael and Satan in Milton. [Several footnotes to the rest of this selection, in which the author cites parallel passages from Virgil, Milton, and Juvenal, are omitted.]

And Jove in equal balance weigh'd
The sword against the brandish'd spade,
He weigh'd; but lighter than a dream,
The sword flew up, and kick'd the beam.
Our 'Squire on tiptoe rising fair
Lifts high a noble stroke in air,
Which hung not, but like dreadful engines,
Descended on his foe in vengeance.
But ah! in danger, with dishonor
The sword perfidious fails its owner;
That sword, which oft had stood its ground,
By huge trainbands encircled round;
And on the bench, with blade right loyal,
Had won the day at many a trial,[1]
Of stones and clubs had braved th' alarms,
Shrunk from these new Vulcanian arms,
The spade so temper'd from the sledge,
Nor keen nor solid harm'd its edge,
Now met it, from his arm of might,
Descending with steep force to smite;
The blade snapp'd short — and from his hand,
With rust embrown'd the glittering sand.
Swift turn'd M'FINGAL at the view,
And call'd to aid th' attendant crew,
In vain; the Tories all had run,
When scarce the fight was well begun;
Their setting wigs he saw decreas'd
Far in th' horizon tow'rd the west.
Amazed he view'd the shameful sight,
And saw no refuge, but in flight:
But age unwieldy check'd his pace,
Though fear had wing'd his flying race;
For not a trifling prize at stake;
No less than great M'FINGAL's back.
With legs and arms he work'd his course,
Like rider that outgoes his horse,

---

[1] It was the fashion in New-England at that time, for judges to wear swords on the bench.

And labor'd hard to get away, as
Old Satan struggling on through chaos;
'Till looking back, he spied in rear
The spade-arm'd chief advanced too near:
Then stopp'd and seized a stone, that lay
An ancient landmark near the way;
Nor shall we as old bards have done,
Affirm it weigh'd an hundred ton;   .
But such a stone, as at a shift
A modern might suffice to lift,
Since men, to credit their enigmas,
Are dwindled down to dwarfs and pigmies,
And giants exiled to their cronies
To Brobdignags and Patagonias.
But while our Hero turn'd him round,
And tugg'd to raise it from the ground,
The fatal spade discharged a blow
Tremendous on his rear below:
His bent knee fail'd, and void of strength
Stretch'd on the ground his manly length.
Like ancient oak o'erturn'd, he lay,
Or tower to tempests fall'n a prey,
Or mountain sunk with all his pines,
Or flow'r the plow to dust consigns,
And more things else — but all men know 'em'
If slightly versed in epic poem.
At once the crew, at this dread crisis,
Fall on, and bind him, ere he rises;
And with loud shouts and joyful soul
Conduct him prisoner to the pole.

TIMOTHY DWIGHT

[Timothy Dwight, another of the more famous "Hartford Wits," was the grandson of Jonathan Edwards. He was born in Northampton, Mass., in 1752, and was graduated from Yale College in 1769. He was a tutor in his *Alma Mater* at the same time as Trumbull, with whom he collaborated in literary work. For a year he was chaplain in the Continental army. Afterward he tried farming and teaching, and served a term in the state legislature. In 1783 he became pastor at Greenfield Hill, in Fairfield, Conn., and from 1795 to his death in 1817 he was president of Yale College.

Many writings of President Dwight were published, the majority of them being on religious and theological subjects. Only those most interesting to the student of American literary history can be mentioned here. "Columbia," a song written while he was a chaplain in the army, was for a long time popular. "The Conquest of Canaan," an epic first published in 1785, was said to have been written before 1774, but several references to Revolutionary battles must have been inserted after these events took place, and it is not unlikely that the whole poem was revised just before it was published. In 1794 appeared "Greenfield Hill," a poem in seven parts. It was originally intended that each part should be in the manner of some popular English poet, and although this plan was abandoned, the imitation is obvious in many passages. In 1797 Dwight published a bitter verse satire, "The Triumph of Infidelity." The year after his death five volumes of his sermons were published with the title "Theology explained and defended"; and in 1821 his "Travels in New England and New York" was issued in four volumes. The last-named work is based on notes of all sorts made during the journeys which occupied many of the author's vacations while he was president of Yale.

As a writer of verse, Dwight had command of a small but intense poetic vocabulary, and produced many monotonously sonorous lines in imitation of the eighteenth-century English poets. He was deficient in a sense of humor, and in real poetic insight, and little of his work can truly be called poetry. His satirical and controversial writings are especially unfortunate. The "Travels" shows his credulity, his religious narrowness, and an odd fondness for sensational anecdotes, but it also shows his appreciation of the historic importance of details, and is his most readable, and perhaps his most valuable, work.

The version of "Columbia" here given is from the "Columbian Muse," New York, 1794. The selections from "The Conquest of Canaan," "Greenfield Hill," and the "Travels" are from the first editions of each, published respectively in 1785, 1794, and 1821.]

COLUMBIA

Columbia, Columbia, to glory rise,
The queen of the world, and child of the skies!
Thy genius commands thee; with raptures behold,
While ages on ages thy splendours unfold.
Thy reign is the last, and the noblest of time,
Most fruitful thy soil, most inviting thy clime.
Let the crimes of the east ne'er encrimson thy name,
Be freedom, and science, and virtue, thy fame.

To conquest, and slaughter, let Europe aspire,
Whelm nations in blood, and wrap cities in fire.
Thy heroes the rights of mankind shall defend,
And triumph pursue them, and glory attend.
A world is thy realm: for a world be thy laws,
Enlarg'd as thine empire, and just as thy cause;
On Freedom's broad basis, that empire shall rise,
Extend with the main, and dissolve with the skies.

Fair Science her gates to thy sons shall unbar,
And the east see thy morn hide the beams of her star.
New bards, and new sages, unrival'd shall soar
To fame, unextinguish'd, when time is no more;
To thee, the last refuge of virtue design'd,
Shall fly from all nations the best of mankind;
Here, grateful to heaven, with transport shall bring
Their incense, more fragrant than odours of spring.

Nor less shall thy fair ones to glory ascend,
And Genius and Beauty in harmony blend;
The graces of form shall awake pure desire,
And the charms of the soul ever cherish the fire;
Their sweetness unmingled, their manners refin'd,
And Virtue's bright image, instamp'd on the mind,
With peace, and soft rapture, shall teach life to glow,
And light up a smile in the aspect of woe.

Thy fleets to all nations thy pow'r shall display,
The nations admire, and the ocean obey;
Each shore to thy glory its tribute unfold,
And the east and the south yield their spices and gold.

As the day-spring unbounded, thy splendour shall flow,
And earth's little kingdoms before thee shall bow;
While the ensigns of union, in triumph unfurl'd,
Hush the tumult of war, and give peace to the world.
   Thus, as down a lone valley, with cedars o'erspread,
From war's dread confusion I pensively stray'd —
The gloom from the face of fair heav'n retir'd;
The winds ceas'd to murmur; the thunders expir'd;
Perfumes, as of Eden, flow'd sweetly along,
And a voice, as of angels, enchantingly sung:
"Columbia, Columbia, to glory arise,
The queen of the world, and the child of the skies."

A BATTLE

[From "The Conquest of Canaan," Book III]

   As now the tempest hid the orb of day,
The threatening fronts approach'd, in dark array;
Swift through th' expansion clouds of arrows fly;
Stones shower on stones, and whizz along the sky;
Sing the shrill strings; the hissing darts resound;
From clanging bucklers rattling pebbles bound;
Now here, now there, the warriors fall; amain
Groans murmur; armour sounds; and shouts convulse the plain.
   With deep amaze, the sons of Ai beheld
Their foes, with ardour, tempt the deathful field.
For now, elate, they sought the early fight,
To certain victory march'd with fierce delight;
And fondly hop'd, ere Oran's hosts should come,
To seal devoted Israel's hapless doom.
But vain their hopes; for with firm duty strong,
Undaunted Zimri fir'd the martial throng —
Now, warriors, now — the glowing leader cried —
Shall Israel's arms regain their ravish'd pride;
Ai now shall learn, untaught our force to slight,
What virtue warms us to the generous fight;
That one lost field shall ne'er our race dismay,
Nor shame, nor terror, stain the glorious day.

While thus untroubled thoughts his words confess'd,
All-anxious fears disturb'd his boding breast.
The host he knew distrustful of the sky,
Propense to terror, and prepar'd to fly;
He saw them sad move lingering o'er the plain,
New arm their foes, and double all their train:
And the great Chief a strong injunction gave,
Each post with care to guard, each band to save,
Each opening fair for wise retreat t' imbrace
To tempt no loss, and hazard no disgrace.
But far beyond his thoughts, the sound of war,
The clash of arms, the shouts that rend the air,
Th' inspiring tumults of the dreadful plain,
New strung their nerves, and rous'd their hopes again.
In quick oblivion, flight and fear were lost;
Increasing ardours every bosom toss'd;
Firm-wedg'd, unshaken, rush'd the darkening train;
Spears flew; air murmur'd; corses heap'd the plain;
One flight of twinkling arms, all ether shone;
Earth roar'd one shout confus'd, one mingled groan;
Each host press'd eager; each disdain'd to fly;
And wide confusion blended earth and sky.
    Mean time the storm, along dark mountains driven,
Hung o'er the plain, and wrapp'd the mid-day heaven;
More frequent lightnings blaz'd the skies around,
And peals more dreadful shook the solid ground.
From the black clouds the whirlwinds burst amain,
Scour'd all the groves, and rag'd along the plain;
Beneath, huge shouts the murmuring concave rend,
And drifts of dust in gloomy pomp ascend.
    With boding hearts, the chiefs of Ai survey'd
The sun's pure splendor lost in cloudy shade;
The sun, their god, his smiling face withdrew,
And round the world a fearful darkness flew:
Hence unapprov'd they doom'd the doubtful day,
And scann'd, with careful looks their homeward way:
As thus they backward gaz'd, the driving rain
Rush'd, with impetuous fury, o'er the plain;

Fierce down th' expansion streaming torrents shower'd,
And blood-stain'd brooks along the champain pour'd.
The clash of arms, the long-resounding cries,
Wav'd o'er the world a hoarse, tumultuous noise;
From heaven's huge vault loud-rolling thunders came,
And lightnings blazed unsufferable flame.
Then sad, dishearten'd, from the dreadful fire
Ai's generous leaders bade their host retire.
Reluctant, slow, disdaining base defeat,
From Israel's sons the grisly ranks retreat;
Surpriz'd, fierce Israel see their backward course,
Hang o'er their rear, and press with gathering force;
Intenser shouts ascend; the lightning's flame
Casts o'er the shields a strong alternate gleam;
Loud thunders roll; the fields all quake around:
And the rain rushing roars along the ground.
Then Zimri's piercing voice, with stern commands,
Restrains the fury of his eager bands.
So fierce the thousands burn for raging war,
Even single warriors urge their foes afar;
'Till near the chief, they see the standard rise,
While yet the tempest fills the midway skies,
Then deep-embosom'd in th' obscuring rain,
Their foes untroubled cross the homeward plain.
　　Mean time the winds were pass'd, the storm was o'er,
And streaming torrents ceas'd from heaven to pour;
Strait to the camp, by Zimri's voice compell'd,
The bands slow-moving cross'd the spacious field.
With joy, the chief resolv'd the troubled day,
The fate, and influence of the fierce affray;
Ai, in fierce conflict, fail'd the wreath to gain,
And Israel, dauntless, trod the skirmish'd plain;
He saw the host again to combat won
Their hopes new-kindled, and their terror gone;
Thence his own bosom boding fear dispell'd,
And promis'd triumph on the future field.
　　And now the Youth they pass'd, as, with fond eyes,
He saw the varying fate of combat rise;

To him, deep-pondering, blew the storm in vain,
Scarce heard the peals, or mark'd the battering rain:
'Till Ai, retir'd, the doubtful strife resign'd,
And calm'd the tumults of his anxious mind.
    Then gentler scenes his rapt attention gain'd,
Where God's great hand in clear effulgence reign'd,
The growing beauties of the solemn even,
And all the bright sublimities of heaven.
Above tall western hills, the light of day
Shot far the splendors of his golden ray;
Bright from the storm, with tenfold grace he smil'd,
The tumult soften'd, and the world grew mild.
With pomp transcendant, rob'd in heavenly dies,
Arch'd the clear rainbow round the orient skies;
Its changeless form, its hues of beam divine,
Fair type of truth, and beauty; endless shine,
Around th' expanse, with thousand splendors rare,
Gay clouds sail'd wanton through the kindling air;
From shade to shade, unnumber'd tinctures blend;
Unnumber'd forms of wonderous light extend;
In pride stupendous, glittering walls aspire,
Grac'd with bright domes, and crown'd with towers of fire,
On cliffs cliffs burn; o'er mountains mountains roll:
A burst of glory spreads from pole to pole:
Rapt with the splendor, every songster sings,
Tops the high bough, and claps his glistening wings:
With new-born green, reviving nature blooms,
And sweeter fragrance freshening air perfumes.
    Far south the storm withdrew its troubled reign;
Descending twilight dimm'd the dusky plain;
Black night arose; her curtains hid the ground;
Less roar'd, and less, the thunder's solemn sound;
The bended lightning shot a brighter stream,
Or wrapp'd all heaven in one wide, mantling flame;
By turns, o'er plains, and woods, and mountains, spread
Faint, yellow glimmerings, and a deeper shade.
    From parting clouds, the moon out-breaking shone,
And sate, sole empress, on her silver throne;

In clear, full beauty, round all nature smil'd,
And claim'd o'er heaven, and earth, dominion mild;
With humbler glory, stars her court attend,
And bless'd, and union'd, silent lustre blend.

THE VILLAGE CHURCH AND THE VILLAGE SCHOOL

[From "Greenfield Hill"]

Beside yon church, that beams a modest ray,
With tidy neatness reputably gay,
When, mild and fair, as Eden's seventh-day light,
In silver silence, shines the Sabbath bright,
In neat attire, the village households come,
And learn the path-way to the eternal home.
Hail solemn ordinance! worthy of the SKIES;
Whence thousand richest blessings daily rise;
Peace, order, cleanliness, and manners sweet,
A sober mind, to rule submission meet,
Enlarging knowledge, life from guilt refin'd,
And love to God, and friendship to mankind.
In the clear splendour of thy vernal morn,
New-quicken'd man to light, and life, is born;
The desert of the mind with virtue blooms;
It's flowers unfold, it's fruits exhale perfumes;
Proud guilt dissolves, beneath the searching ray,
And low debasement, trembling, creeps away;
Vice bites the dust; foul Error seeks her den;
And God, descending, dwells anew with men.
Where yonder humbler spire salutes the eye,
It's vane slow turning in the liquid sky,
Where, in light gambols, healthy striplings sport,
Ambitious learning builds her outer court;
A grave preceptor, there, her usher stands,
And rules, without a rod, her little bands.
Some half-grown sprigs of learning grac'd his brow:
Little he knew, though much he wish'd to know,
Inchanted hung o'er Virgil's honey'd lay,
And smil'd, to see desipient Horace play;

Glean'd scraps of Greek; and, curious, trac'd afar,
Through Pope's clear glass, the bright Mæonian star.
Yet oft his students at his wisdom star'd,
For many a student to his side repair'd,
Surpriz'd, they heard him Dilworth's knots untie,
And tell, what lands beyond the Atlantic lie.
  Many his faults; his virtues small, and few;
Some little good he did, or strove to do;
Laborious still, he taught the early mind,
And urg'd to manners meek, and thoughts refin'd;
Truth he impress'd, and every virtue prais'd;
While infant eyes, in wondering silence, gaz'd;
The worth of time would, day by day, unfold,
And tell them, every hour was made of gold.
Brown Industry he lov'd; and oft declar'd
How hardy Sloth, in life's sad evening, far'd.

THE MUTABILITY OF EARTHLY THINGS

[From "Greenfield Hill"]

Ah me! while up the long, long vale of time,
Reflection wanders towards th' eternal vast,
How starts the eye, at many a change sublime,
Unbosom'd dimly by the ages pass'd!
What Mausoleums crowd the mournful waste!
The tombs of empires fallen! and nations gone!
Each, once inscrib'd, in gold, with "AYE TO LAST"
Sate as a queen; proclaim'd the world her own,
And proudly cried, "By me no sorrows shall be known."

Soon fleets the sunbright Form, by man ador'd.
Soon fell the Head of gold, to Time a prey;
The Arms, the Trunk, his cankering tooth devour'd;
And whirlwinds blew the Iron dust away.
Where dwelt imperial Timur? — far astray,
Some lonely-musing pilgrim now enquires:
And, rack'd by storms, and hastening to decay,

Mohammed's Mosque forsees it's final fires;
And Rome's more lordly Temple day by day expires.

As o'er proud Asian realms the traveller winds,
His manly spirit, hush'd by terror, falls;
When some deceased town's lost site he finds,
Where ruin wild his pondering eye appals;
Where silence swims along the moulder'd walls,
And broods upon departed Grandeur's tomb.
Through the lone, hollow aisles sad echo calls,
At each slow step; deep sighs the breathing gloom,
And weeping fields, around, bewail their Empress' doom.

Where o'er an hundred realms, the throne uprose,
The screech-owl nests, the panther builds his home;
Sleep the dull newts, the lazy adders doze,
Where pomp and luxury danc'd the golden room.
Low lies in dust the sky-resembled dome;
Tall grass around the broken column waves;
And brambles climb, and lonely thistles bloom:
The moulder'd arch the weedy streamlet laves,
And low resound, beneath, unnumber'd sunken graves.

Soon fleets the sun-bright Form, by man ador'd;
And soon man's dæmon chiefs from memory fade.
In musty volume, now must be explored,
Where dwelt imperial nations, long decay'd.
The brightest meteors angry clouds invade;
And where the wonders glitter'd, none explain.
Where Carthage, with proud hand, the trident sway'd,
Now mud-wall'd cots sit sullen on the plain,
And wandering, fierce, and wild, sequester'd Arabs reign.

In thee, O Albion! queen of nations, live
Whatever splendours earth's wide realms have known;
In thee proud Persia sees her pomp revive;
And Greece her arts; and Rome her lordly throne:
By every wind, thy Tyrian fleets are blown;

2 E

Supreme, on Fame's dread roll, thy heroes stand;
All ocean's realms thy naval scepter own;
Of bards, of sages, how august thy band!
And one rich Eden blooms around thy garden'd land.

But O how vast thy crimes! Through Heaven's great year,
When few centurial suns have trac'd their way;
When southern Europe, worn by feuds severe;
Weak, doating, fallen, has bow'd to Russian sway;
And setting glory beam'd her farewell ray;
To wastes, perchance, thy brilliant fields shall turn;
In dust, thy temples, towers, and towns decay;
The forest howl, where London's turrets burn;
And all thy garlands deck thy sad, funereal urn.

Some land, scarce glimmering in the light of fame,
Scepter'd with arts, and arms (if I divine)
Some unknown wild, some shore without a name,
In all thy pomp, shall then majestic shine.
As silver-headed Time's slow years decline,
Not ruins only meet th' enquiring eye:
Where round yon mouldering oak vain brambles twine,
The filial stem, already towering high,
Erelong shall stretch his arms, and nod in yonder sky.

PSALM CXXXVII

[From Dwight's revision of Watts's Psalms]

I love thy kingdom, Lord,
The house of thine abode,
The church, our blest Redeemer sav'd
With his own precious blood.

I love thy Church, O God!
Her walls before thee stand,
Dear as the apple of thine eye,
And graven on thy hand.

If e'er to bless thy sons
My voice, or hands, deny,
These hands let useful skill forsake,
This voice in silence die.

If e'er my heart forget
Her welfare, or her wo,
Let every joy this heart forsake,
And every grief o'erflow.

For her my tears shall fall;
For her my prayers ascend;
To her my cares and toils be given,
'Till toils and cares shall end.

Beyond my highest joy
I prize her heavenly ways,
Her sweet communion, solemn vows,
Her hymns of love and praise.

Jesus, thou Friend divine,
Our Saviour and our King,
Thy hand from every snare and foe
Shall great deliverance bring.

Sure as thy truth shall last,
To Zion shall be given
The brightest glories, earth can yield,
And brighter bliss of heaven.

THE ORIGIN OF A NAME

[From the "Travels in New-England and New-York"]

In this township there are two mountains; one of which is named *Mount Cuba*, from a dog which bore that name, and was killed upon it by a bear. The other was named *Mount Sunday*, from the following fact. Seven men, one of them a Mr. Palmer, went into the Eastern part of the township, and, in the language of the country, *were lost;* that is, they became wholly uncertain of the course, which they were to pursue, in order to regain their habitations. Palmer insisted, that it lay in a direction, really Eastward, although he believed it to point Westward. His companions, judging more correctly, determined to take the opposite course. In their progress, they passed over this mountain. The day, on which they ascended it, was the Sabbath; and the mountain has, from this circumstance, derived a name, which it will probably retain, so long as the posterity of the English colonists inhabit this country. The six men, returning home, and not finding Palmer, went again in search of him. In a place, two miles Eastward of the spot where they had left him, they found him engaged in a contest with a bear; which had attacked him the preceding evening, on his way. As the bear was advancing towards him, he was fortunate enough to procure a club; with which he had been able to defend himself, until he made good his retreat to a neighbouring tree. The bear followed him as he ascended the tree; but his club enabled him to keep the animal at bay, until his companions came up, and delivered him from the impending destruction.

I presume you will wonder at my mentioning these trifling incidents. I have mentioned them because they are trifles. The names of mountains, rivers, and other distinguished natural objects, both here and in England, have often seemed to me strange and inexplicable. The little incidents, which I have mentioned, furnish, I suspect, a probable explanation of this enigmatical subject, in a great proportion of cases. Events, sometimes more, and sometimes even less, significant than these, have, I am persuaded, been the origin of a great part of those odd appellations, given to so many of the objects in question. Among the proofs, that this opinion is just, the oddity, and the vulgarity of the appellations, and the speedy oblivion, into which the causes of them have fallen, are, to me, satisfactory. Their oddity proves them to have been derived from incidents, aside from the ordinary course of things: their vulgarity shews them to have been given by persons in humble life; and the fact, that the sources from which they have sprung have been so soon forgotten, evinces their insignificancy.

JOEL BARLOW

[Joel Barlow, the third in the most illustrious trio of "Hartford Wits," seems to have had many of the characteristics of the traditional Yankee. He was born in Connecticut in 1754, and was graduated at Yale College in 1778. Like many other collegians he served in the army during vacations, and is said to have fought at White Plains. After his graduation he studied law, then turned his attention for six weeks to divinity, and at the end of that time became chaplain of a Massachusetts brigade. In the few years immediately after the close of the war he practised law, founded a newspaper, edited a Psalm book for the Congregational Church of Connecticut, and conducted a book-store. Meanwhile he had published, besides his version of the Psalms, "The Prospect of Peace," a poem delivered at the time of his graduation, and "The Vision of Columbus." Both these were afterward utilized in the construction of the "Columbiad." In 1788 Barlow went abroad as agent of a western land company. In England he wrote "Advice to the privileged Orders," in prose, and "The Conspiracy of Kings," in verse. The first-named of these works led to his expulsion from the country, and he went to France, where he took an active part in politics. It was while he was on a political mission in Savoy that he wrote "Hasty Pudding," his mock-heroic tribute to a favorite dish that was unexpectedly set before him. Later he engaged in business in Paris, and served as United States consul to Algiers. His fondness for French ideas in politics and religion made him an object of suspicion in his native state, where Federalism and orthodoxy were dominant. It is said that the Congregational Church of Connecticut discarded his version of the Psalms as the work of an apostate. When in 1805 he returned to America, he took up his residence near Washington. Two years later he published the "Columbiad." In 1811 he was appointed minister to France, and the next year he died in Poland, where he had gone to meet Napoleon.

The "Vision of Columbus," which Barlow published in 1787, is a poem in nine books of heroic couplet. Columbus, despondent in prison, is taken by an angel to a height where he sees all the continent that he has discovered, and its future passes in vision before him. The "Columbiad," which appeared twenty years later, tells the same story at greater length in ten books. Barlow presented the unfortunate spectacle of an author becoming more bombastic and sophomoric as he grew older. By 1807 he had become a devotee of reformed spelling, and had grown fond of pedantic words, many of them of his own coinage. These peculiarities, together with the epic form and title of the new work, the unabashed references to Homer and Virgil in the preface, and the fact that the first edition of the poem was very sumptuous in typography and binding, tended to expose Barlow to ridicule; and the "Columbiad" has ever since been the stock example of an over-ambitious American literary production.

The selections from "The Vision of Columbus" follow the first English edition of 1787. The passage from the "Columbiad" is from the second edition, 1809. The first and second selections show the treatment of the same subject in these two poems. The extract from "The Hasty Pudding" follows the reprint of the first edition (1796) in Duyckinck's "Cyclopædia of American Literature."]

INDEPENDENCE; AND THE COMING OF WAR

[From the "Vision of Columbus"]

Adams, enraged, a broken charter bore,
And lawless acts of ministerial power;
Some injured right in each loose leaf appears,
A king in terrors and a land in tears;
From all the guileful plots the veil he drew,
With eye retortive look'd creation thro',
Oped the wide range of nature's boundless plan,
Traced all the steps of liberty and man;
Crowds rose to vengeance while his accents rung,
And Independence thunder'd from his tongue.

The Hero turn'd. And tow'rd the crowded coast
Rose on the wave a wide-extended host,
They shade the main and spread their sails abroad,
From the wide Laurence to the Georgian flood,
Point their black batteries to the approaching shore,
And bursting flames begin the hideous roar.

Where guardless Falmouth, looking o'er the bay,
Beheld, unmoved, the stormy thunders play,
The fire begins; the shells o'er-arching fly,
And shoot a thousand rainbows thro' the sky;
On Charlestown spires, on Bristol roofs, they light,
Groton and Fairfield kindle from the flight,
Fair Kingston burns, and York's delightful fanes,
And beauteous Norfolk lights the neighbouring plains;
From realm to realm the smoky volumes bend,
Reach round the bays and up the streams extend;

Deep o'er the concave heavy wreaths are roll'd,
And midland towns and distant groves infold.
Thro' the dark curls of smoke the winged fires
Climb in tall pyramids above the spires;
Cinders, high-sailing, kindle heaven around,
And falling structures shake the smouldering ground.
   Now, where the sheeted flames thro' Charlestown roar,
And lashing waves hiss round the burning shore,
Thro' the deep folding fires, a neighbouring height
Thunders o'er all and seems a field of fight.
Like shadowy phantoms in an evening grove,
To the dark strife the closing squadrons move;
They join, they break, they thicken thro' the air,
And blazing batteries burst along the war;
Now, wrapp'd in reddening smoke, now dim in sight,
They sweep the hill or wing the downward flight;
Here, wheel'd and wedg'd, whole ranks together turn,
And the long lightnings from their pieces burn;
There scattering flashes light the scanty train,
And broken squadrons tread the moving plain.
Britons in fresh battalions rise the height,
And, with increasing vollies, give the fight.
Till, smear'd with clouds of dust, and bath'd in gore,
As growing foes their raised artillery pour,
Columbia's hosts move o'er the fields afar,
And save, by slow retreat, the sad remains of war.

INDEPENDENCE; AND THE COMING OF WAR

[From the "Columbiad"]

   Each generous Adams, freedom's favorite pair,
And Hancock rose the tyrant's rage to dare,
Groupt with firm Jefferson, her steadiest hope,
Of modest mien but vast unclouded scope.
Like four strong pillars of her state they stand,
They clear from doubt her brave but wavering band;
Colonial charters in their hands they bore
And lawless acts of ministerial power.

Some injured right in every page appears,
A king in terrors and a land in tears;
From all his guileful plots the veil they drew,
With eye retortive look'd creation thro,
Traced moral nature thro her total plan,
Markt all the steps of liberty and man;
Crowds rose to reason while their accents rung,
And INDEPENDENCE thunder'd from their tongue.

Columbus turn'd; when rolling to the shore
Swells o'er the seas an undulating roar;
Slow, dark, portentious, as the meteors sweep
And curtain black the illimitable deep,
High stalks, from surge to surge, a demon Form
That howls thro heaven and breathes a billowing storm.
His head is hung with clouds; his giant hand
Flings a blue flame far flickering to the land;
His blood-stain'd limbs drip carnage as he strides
And taint with gory grume the staggering tides;
Like two red suns his quivering eyeballs glare,
His mouth disgorges all the stores of war,
Pikes, muskets, mortars, guns and globes of fire
And lighted bombs that fusing trails expire.
Percht on his helmet, two twin sisters rode,
The favorite offspring of the murderous god,
Famine and Pestilence; whom whilom bore
His wife, grim Discord, on Trinacria's shore:
When first their cyclop sons, from Etna's forge,
Fill'd his foul magazine, his gaping gorge:
Then earth convulsive groan'd, high shriek'd the air,
And hell in gratulation call'd him War.

Behind the fiend, swift hovering for the coast,
Hangs o'er the wave Britannia's sail-wing'd host;
They crowd the main, they spread their sheets abroad
From the wide Laurence to the Georgian flood,
Point their black batteries to the peopled shore,
And spouting flames commence the hideous roar.

Where fortless Falmouth, looking o'er her bay,
In terror saw the approaching thunders play,

The fire begins; the shells o'er-arching fly
And shoot a thousand rainbows thro the sky;
On Charlestown spires, on Bedford roofs they light,
Groton and Fairfield kindle from the flight,
Norwalk expands the blaze; o'er Reading hills
High flaming Danbury the welkin fills;
Esopus burns, Newyork's delightful fanes
And sea-nursed Norfolk light the neighboring plains.
From realm to realm the smoky volumes bend,
Reach round the bays and up the streams extend;
Deep o'er the concave heavy wreaths are roll'd,
And midland towns and distant groves infold.
    Thro solid curls of smoke the bursting fires
Climb in tall pyramids above the spires,
Concentring all the winds; whose forces, driven
With equal rage from every point of heaven,
Whirl into conflict, round the scantling pour
The twisting flames and thro the rafters roar,
Suck up the cinders, send them sailing far,
To warn the nations of the raging war,
Bend high the blazing vortex, swell'd and curl'd,
Careering, brightening o'er the lustred world,
Absorb the reddening clouds that round them run,
Lick the pale stars and mock their absent sun:
Seas catch the splendor, kindling skies resound,
And falling structures shake the smoldering ground.
    Crowds of wild fugitives, with frantic tread,
Flit thro the flames that pierce the midnight shade,
Back on the burning domes revert their eyes,
Where some lost friend, some perisht infant lies.
Their maim'd, their sick, their age-enfeebled sires
Have sunk sad victims to the sateless fires;
They greet with one last look their tottering walls,
See the blaze thicken as the ruin falls,
Then o'er the country train their dumb despair
And far behind them leave the dancing glare;
Their own crusht roofs still lend a trembling light,
Point their long shadows and direct their flight.

Till wandering wide they seek some cottage door,
Ask the vile pittance due the vagrant poor;
Or faint and faltering on the devious road,
They sink at last and yield their mortal load.
    But where the sheeted flames thro Charlestown roar,
And lashing waves hiss round the burning shore,
Thro the deep folding fires dread Bunker's height
Thunders o'er all and shows a field of fight.
Like nightly shadows thro a flaming grove,
To the dark fray the closing squadrons move;
They join, they break, they thicken thro the glare,
And blazing batteries burst along the war;
Now wrapt in reddening smoke, now dim in sight,
They rake the hill or wing the downward flight;
Here, wheel'd and wedged, Britannia's veterans turn
And the long lightnings from their muskets burn:
There scattering strive the thin colonial train,
Whose broken platoons still the field maintain;
Till Britain's fresh battalions rise the height
And with increasing vollies give the fight.
When, choked with dust, discolor'd deep in gore
And gall'd on all sides from the ships and shore,
Hesperia's host moves off the field afar
And saves, by slow retreat, the sad remains of war.

HYMN TO PEACE

[From the "Vision of Columbus"]

    Hail sacred Peace, who claim'st thy bright abode
Mid circling saints that grace the throne of God!
Before his arm, around the shapeless earth,
Stretch'd the wide heavens and gave to nature birth;
Ere morning-stars his glowing chambers hung,
Or songs of gladness woke an angel's tongue,
Veil'd in the brightness of the Almighty's mind,
In blest repose thy placid form reclined;
Borne through the heavens with his creating voice,
Thy presence bade the unfolding worlds rejoice,

Gave to seraphic harps their sounding lays,
Their joys to angels, and to men their praise.
  From scencs of blood, these beauteous shores that stain,
From gasping friends that press the sanguine plain,
From fields, long taught in vain thy flight to mourn,
I rise, delightful Power, and greet thy glad return.
Too long the groans of death, and battle's bray,
Have rung discordant through the unpleasing lay:
Let pity's tear its balmy fragrance shed,
O'er heroes' wounds and patriot warriors dead;
Accept, departed shades, these grateful sighs,
Your fond attendants to the approving skies.
  And thou, my earliest friend, my Brother dear,
Thy fall untimely wakes the tender tear.
In youthful sports, in toils, in blood allied,
My kind companion and my hopeful guide,
When Heaven's sad summons, from our infant eyes
Had call'd our last, loved parent to the skies.
Tho' young in arms, and still obscure thy name,
Thy bosom panted for the deeds of fame,
Beneath Montgomery's eye, when, by thy steel,
In northern wilds, the lurking savage fell.
Yet, hapless Youth! when thy great Leader bled,
Thro' the same wound thy parting spirit fled.
  But now the untuneful trump shall grate no more,
Ye silver streams no longer swell with gore;
Bear from your beauteous banks the crimson stain,
With yon retiring navies, to the main.
While other views unfolding on my eyes,
And happier themes bid bolder numbers rise:
Bring, bounteous Peace, in thy celestial throng,
Life to my soul, and rapture to my song;
Give me to trace, with pure unclouded ray,
The arts and virtues that attend thy sway;
To see thy blissful charms, that here descend,
Through distant realms and endless years extend.

A FAVORITE DISH

[From "The Hasty Pudding"]

Dear Hasty Pudding, what unpromised joy
Expands my heart, to meet thee in Savoy!
Doom'd o'er the world through devious paths to roam,
Each clime my country, and each house my home,
My soul is soothed, my cares have found an end,
I greet my long lost, unforgotten friend.
   For thee through Paris, that corrupted town,
How long in vain I wandered up and down,
Where shameless Bacchus, with his drenching hoard,
Cold from his cave usurps the morning board.
London is lost in smoke and steep'd in tea;
No Yankee there can lisp the name of thee;
The uncouth word, a libel on the town,
Would call a proclamation from the crown.
From climes oblique, that fear the sun's full rays,
Chill'd in their fogs, exclude the generous maize:
A grain, whose rich, luxuriant growth requires
Short gentle showers, and bright etherial fires.
   But here, though distant from our native shore,
With mutual glee, we meet and laugh once more,
The same! I know thee by that yellow face,
That strong complexion of true Indian race,
Which time can never change, nor soil impair,
Nor Alpine snows, nor Turkey's morbid air;
For endless years, through every mild domain,
Where grows the maize, there thou art sure to reign.
   But man, more fickle, the bold license claims,
In different realms to give thee different names.
Thee the soft nations round the warm Levant
Polenta call, the French of course *Polente.*
E'en in thy native regions, how I blush
To hear the Pennsylvanians call thee *Mush!*
On Hudson's banks, while men of Belgic spaw
Insult and eat thee by the name *Suppawn.*

All spurious appellations, void of truth;
I've better known thee from my earliest youth,
Thy name is *Hasty-Pudding!* thus my sire
Was wont to greet thee fuming from his fire;
And while he argued in thy just defence
With logic clear, he thus explain'd the sense: —
"In *haste* the boiling cauldron, o'er the blaze,
Receives and cooks the ready powder'd maize;
In *haste* 'tis served, and then in equal *haste*,
With cooling milk, we make the sweet repast.
No carving to be done, no knife to grate
The tender ear, and wound the stony plate;
But the smooth spoon, just fitted to the lip,
And taught with art the yielding mass to dip,
By frequent journeys to the bowl well stored,
Performs the *hasty* honors of the board."
Such is thy name, significant and clear,
A name, a sound to every Yankee dear,
But most to me, whose heart and palate chaste
Preserve my pure hereditary taste.

There are who strive to stamp with disrepute
The luscious food, because it feeds the brute;
In tropes of high-strain'd wit, while gaudy prigs
Compare thy nursling, man, to pamper'd pigs;
With sovereign scorn I treat the vulgar jest,
Nor fear to share thy bounties with the beast.
What though the generous cow gives me to quaff
The milk nutritious: am I then a calf?
Or can the genius of the noisy swine,
Though nursed on pudding, claim a kin to mine?
Sure the sweet song, I fashion to thy praise,
Runs more melodious than the notes they raise.

My song resounding in its grateful glee,
No merit claims: I praise myself in thee.
My father loved thee through his length of days!
For thee his fields were shaded o'er with maize;
From thee what health, what vigor he possess'd,
Ten sturdy freemen from his loins attest;

Thy constellation ruled my natal morn,
And all my bones were made of Indian corn.
Delicious grain! whatever form it take,
To roast or boil, to smother or to bake,
In every dish 'tis welcome still to me,
But most, my *Hasty Pudding*, most in thee.

PHILIP FRENEAU

[While the names of most eighteenth-century American verse-writers have passed into obscurity, if not into oblivion, the fame of Philip Freneau has increased, until he now takes almost unquestioned rank as the most notable American poet before Bryant. He was born in 1752, in New York City. In 1771 he was graduated from Princeton in the same class as James Madison and H. H. Brackenridge. As an undergraduate he made satiric and other rhymes, and collaborated with Brackenridge on a novel; and he was part author of a poem, "The Rising Glory of America," spoken by Brackenridge at commencement. After his graduation he taught school for a time. Early in 1775 he wrote a number of bitter satires on political topics. From the latter part of 1775 to 1778 he was in the West Indies, and it was apparently on his outward voyage that he first felt the charm of the sailor's life. During much of the time from 1778 to 1790 he was on the ocean. In 1780 he was on board a vessel that was captured by the British, and he was imprisoned for some time in the notorious British prison ships in New York harbor. His experiences here form the basis of one of his most vindictive poems. After his release he was for some time master of a vessel engaged in the coasting trade. During all this time he was writing, and contributing to various journals. In 1790 he married, and left the sea to become editor of a paper in New York. The next year he removed to Philadelphia to accept from Jefferson the clerkship for foreign languages in the department of state, and to begin the issue of *The National Gazette*. This paper was violently republican and pro-French, and the Federalists accused Jefferson of retaining Freneau in a government position and inciting him to make unwarranted attacks on other members of the government. It does not appear that these charges were true, but Freneau was foolishly indiscreet, and he was forced to abandon the *Gazette* in 1793. After this he edited other papers for short periods of time, went to sea again, and reprinted some of his writings. He died in 1832.

Freneau was a voluminous writer. The latest collection of his poetical works fills three large volumes, and the editor gives more than a hundred titles of omitted poems. His political satires were popular at a time when feeling was intense, and for many years they were the portion of his writings most readily accessible to students. For this reason he gained the designation, unfortunately perpetuated by his latest editor, of "Poet of the American Revolution." It is really not, however, the political poems that have led to the recent recognition of Freneau's worth. He combined, somewhat strangely, a capacity for the most bitter, violent, and unreasoning hatred,

431

a vivid poetic imagination, and a genuine feeling for nature.   His political pieces are mostly the sort of satire that abounds in invective, and that is unrelieved by humor.   Some of his earlier work, especially "The House of Night," written during his first visit to the West Indies, reveals his powers of imagination;   and some poems of later date, such as "The Wild Honey Suckle" and "The Indian Burying Ground," show an admirable delicacy and lightness of touch.   It is by these, and not by his tirades against the British, that he should be judged.

With the revival of interest in Freneau's work has come, naturally, a tendency to overpraise.   He was not a great, or a highly original, poet.   All his better work shows obvious influences of his English masters, prominent among whom were Milton and Gray.   It is not especially significant that Campbell and Scott each borrowed a good line from his works.   It is notable, however, that in the most troubled time in American history he wrote some poems that were full of quiet idealism, and that he showed the romantic tendency at least as strongly as any of his English contemporaries.

Freneau published collections of his poems in 1786, 1788, 1795, 1809, and 1815, besides many single poems in pamphlets and broadsides.   A collection of "Poems relating to the American Revolution" was edited by Evert A. Duyckinck in 1865.   The selections here given are from the only adequate edition of his poems, that prepared by Professor Fred Lewis Pattee and issued in three volumes at Princeton in 1902-1907.]

A DREAM-PICTURE

[From "The House of Night"]

By some sad means, when Reason holds no sway,
Lonely I rov'd at midnight o'er a plain
Where murmuring streams and mingling rivers flow
Far to their springs, or seek the sea again.

Sweet vernal May! tho' then thy woods in bloom
Flourish'd, yet nought of this could Fancy see,
No wild pinks bless'd the meads, no green the fields,
And naked seem'd to stand each lifeless tree:

Dark was the sky, and not one friendly star
Shone from the zenith or horizon, clear,
Mist sate upon the woods, and darkness rode
In her black chariot, with a wild career.

And from the woods the late resounding note
Issued of the loquacious Whip-poor-will,[1]
Hoarse, howling dogs, and nightly roving wolves
Clamour'd from far off cliffs invisible.

Rude, from the wide extended Chesapeke
I heard the winds the dashing waves assail,
And saw from far, by picturing fancy form'd,
The black ship travelling through the noisy gale.

At last, by chance and guardian fancy led,
I reach'd a noble dome, rais'd fair and high,
And saw the light from upper windows flame,
Presage of mirth and hospitality.

And by that light around the dome appear'd
A mournful garden of autumnal hue,
Its lately pleasing flowers all drooping stood
Amidst high weeds that in rank plenty grew.

The Primrose there, the violet darkly blue,
Daisies and fair Narcissus ceas'd to rise,
Gay spotted pinks their charming bloom withdrew,
And Polyanthus quench'd its thousand dyes.

No pleasant fruit or blossom gaily smil'd,
Nought but unhappy plants or trees were seen,
The yew, the myrtle, and the church-yard elm,
The cypress, with its melancholy green.

There cedars dark, the osier, and the pine,
Shorn Tamarisks, and weeping willows grew,
The poplar tall, the lotos, and the lime,
And pyracantha did her leaves renew.

[1] A bird peculiar to America, of a solitary nature, who never sings but in the night. Her note resembles the name given to her by the country people.

2 F

The poppy there, companion to repose,
Display'd her blossoms that began to fall,
And here the purple amaranthus rose
With mint strong-scented, for the funeral.

And here and there with laurel shrubs between
A tombstone lay, inscrib'd with strains of woe,
And stanzas sad, throughout the dismal green,
Lamented for the dead that slept below.

THE CAPTAIN OF THE HOSPITAL SHIP

[From "The British Prison Ship"]

From this poor vessel, and her sickly crew
An English ruffian all his titles drew,
Captain, esquire, commander, too, in chief,
And hence he gain'd his bread, and hence his beef,
But, sir, you might have search'd creation round
Ere such another miscreant could be found —
Though unprovok'd, an angry face he bore,
We stood astonish'd at the oaths he swore;
He swore, till every prisoner stood aghast,
And thought him Satan in a brimstone blast;
He wish'd us banish'd from the public light,
He wish'd us shrouded in perpetual night!
That were he king, no mercy would he show,
But drive all rebels to the world below;
That if we scoundrels did not scrub the decks
His staff should break our damn'd rebellious necks;
He swore, besides, that if the ship took fire
We too should in the pitchy flames expire;
And meant it so — this tyrant, I engage,
Had lost his breath to gratify his rage. —
If where he walk'd a captive carcase lay,
Still dreadful was the language of the day —
He call'd us dogs, and would have us'd us so,
But vengeance check'd the meditated blow,

The vengeance from our injur'd nation due
To him, and all the base, unmanly crew.

    Such food they sent, to make complete our woes,
It look'd like carrion torn from hungry crows,
Such vermin vile on every joint were seen,
So black, corrupted, mortified, and lean
That once we try'd to move our flinty chief,
And thus address'd him, holding up the beef:

    "See, captain, see! what rotten bones we pick,
"What kills the healthy cannot cure the sick:
"Not dogs on such by Christian men are fed,
"And see, good master, see, what lousy bread!"

    "Your meat or bread (this man of flint replied)
"Is not my care to manage or provide —
"But this, damn'd rebel dogs, I'd have you know,
"That better than you merit we bestow;
"Out of my sight!" — nor more he deign'd to say,
But whisk'd about, and frowning, strode away.

THE CHARACTER OF CORNWALLIS

[From a poem "On the Fall of General Earl Cornwallis"]

A Chieftain join'd with Howe, Burgoyne, and Gage,
Once more, nor this the last, provokes my rage —
Who saw these Nimrods first for conquest burn!
Who has not seen them to the dust return?
This ruffian next, who scour'd our ravag'd fields,
Foe to the human race, Cornwallis yields! —
None e'er before essay'd such desperate crimes,
Alone he stood, arch-butcher of the times,
Rov'd uncontroul'd this wasted country o'er,
Strew'd plains with dead, and bath'd his jaws with gore.

    'Twas thus the wolf, who sought by night his prey,
And plunder'd all he met with on his way,
Stole what he could, and murder'd as he pass'd,
Chanc'd on a trap, and lost his head at last.

    What pen can write, what human tongue can tell
The endless murders of this man of hell!

Nature in him disgrac'd the form divine;
Nature mistook, she meant him for a — swine:
That eye his forehead to her shame adorns;
Blush! nature, blush — bestow him tail and horns! —
By him the orphans mourn — the widow'd dame
Saw ruin spreading in the wasteful flame;
Gash'd o'er with wounds beheld with streaming eye
A son, a brother, or a consort, die! —
Through ruin'd realms bones lie without a tomb,
And souls he sped to their eternal doom,
Who else had liv'd, and seen their toils again
Bless'd by the genius of the rural reign.

But turn your eyes, and see the murderer fall,
Then say — "Cornwallis has atchiev'd it all." —
Yet he preserves the honour and the fame
That vanquish'd heroes only ought to claim —
Is he a hero! — Read, and you will find
Heroes are beings of a different kind: —
Compassion to the worst of men is due,
And mercy heaven's first attribute, 'tis true;
Yet most presume it was too nobly done
To grant mild terms to Satan's first-born son.

Convinc'd we are, no foreign spot on earth
But Britain only, gave this reptile birth,
That white-cliff'd isle, the vengeful dragon's den,
Has sent us monsters where we look'd for men.
When memory paints their horrid deeds anew,
And brings these murdering miscreants to your view,
Then ask the leaders of these bloody bands,
Can they expect compassion at our hands? —

But may this year, the glorious eighty-one,
Conclude successful, as it first begun;
This brilliant year their total downfall see,
And what Cornwallis is, may Clinton be.

TO THE MEMORY OF THE BRAVE AMERICANS UNDER GENERAL GREENE, IN SOUTH CAROLINA, WHO FELL IN THE ACTION OF SEPTEMBER 8, 1781

At Eutaw Springs the valiant died;
　　Their limbs with dust are covered o'er —
Weep on, ye springs, your tearful tide;
　　How many heroes are no more!

If in this wreck of ruin, they
　　Can yet be thought to claim a tear,
O smite your gentle breast, and say
　　The friends of freedom slumber here!

Thou, who shalt trace this bloody plain,
　　If goodness rules thy generous breast,
Sigh for the wasted rural reign;
　　Sigh for the shepherds, sunk to rest!

Stranger, their humble graves adorn;
　　You too may fall, and ask a tear;
'Tis not the beauty of the morn
　　That proves the evening shall be clear. —

They saw their injured country's woe;
　　The flaming town, the wasted field;
Then rushed to meet the insulting foe;
　　They took the spear — but left the shield.

Led by thy conquering genius, Greene,
　　The Britons they compelled to fly;
None distant viewed the fatal plain,
　　None grieved, in such a cause to die —

But, like the Parthian, famed of old,
　　Who, flying, still their arrows threw,
These routed Britons, full as bold,
　　Retreated, and retreating slew.

Now rest in peace, our patriot band;
    Though far from nature's limits thrown,
We trust they find a happier land,
    A brighter sunshine of their own.

TO SIR TOBY, A SUGAR PLANTER IN THE INTERIOR PARTS OF JAMAICA, NEAR THE CITY OF SAN JAGO DE LA VEGA (SPANISH TOWN), 1784

> "*The motions of his spirit are black as night,*
>   *And his affections dark as Erebus.*"
>   — SHAKESPEARE.

If there exists a hell — the case is clear —
Sir Toby's slaves enjoy that portion here:
Here are no blazing brimstone lakes — 'tis true;
But kindled Rum too often burns as blue;
In which some fiend, whom nature must detest,
Steeps Toby's brand, and marks poor Cudjoe's breast.[1]
  Here whips on whips excite perpetual fears,
And mingled howlings vibrate on my ears:
Here nature's plagues abound, to fret and teaze,
Snakes, scorpions, despots, lizards, centipees —
No art, no care escapes the busy lash;
All have their dues — and all are paid in cash —
The eternal driver keeps a steady eye
On a black herd, who would his vengeance fly,
But chained, imprisoned, on a burning soil,
For the mean avarice of a tyrant, toil!
The lengthy cart-whip guards this monster's reign —
And cracks, like pistols, from the fields of cane.
  Ye powers! who formed these wretched tribes, relate,
What had they done, to merit such a fate!
Why were they brought from Eboe's[2] sultry waste,
To see that plenty which they must not taste —
Food, which they cannot buy, and dare not steal;

---

[1] This passage has a reference to the West India custom (sanctioned by law) of branding a newly imported slave on the breast, with a red hot iron, as an evidence of the purchaser's property.

[2] A small negro kingdom near the river Senegal.

Yams and potatoes — many a scanty meal! —
  One, with a gibbet wakes his negro's fears,
One to the windmill nails him by the ears;
One keeps his slave in darkened dens, unfed,
One puts the wretch in pickle ere he's dead:
This, from a tree suspends him by the thumbs,
That, from his table grudges even the crumbs!
  O'er yond' rough hills a tribe of females go,
Each with her gourd, her infant, and her hoe;
Scorched by a sun that has no mercy here,
Driven by a devil, whom men call overseer —
In chains, twelve wretches to their labours haste;
Twice twelve I saw, with iron collars graced! —

  Are such the fruits that spring from vast domains?
Is wealth, thus got, Sir Toby, worth your pains! —
Who would your wealth on terms, like these, possess,
Where all we see is pregnant with distress —
Angola's natives scourged by ruffian hands,
And toil's hard product shipp'd to foreign lands.

  Talk not of blossoms, and your endless spring;
What joy, what smile, can scenes of misery bring? —
Though Nature, here, has every blessing spread,
Poor is the labourer — and how meanly fed! —
  Here Stygian paintings light and shade renew,
Pictures of hell, that Virgil's[1] pencil drew:
Here, surly Charons make their annual trip,
And ghosts arrive in every Guinea ship,
To find what beasts these western isles afford,
Plutonian scourges, and despotic lords: —
  Here, they, of stuff determined to be free,
Must climb the rude cliffs of the Liguanee;[2]
Beyond the clouds, in sculking haste repair,
And hardly safe from brother traitors there.[3]

[1] See Eneid, Book 6th. — and Fénelon's Telemachus, Book 18.
[2] The mountains northward of Kingston.
[3] Alluding to the *Independent* negroes in the blue mountains, who, for a stipulated reward, deliver up every fugitive that falls into their hands, to the English Government.

THE WILD HONEY SUCKLE

Fair flower, that dost so comely grow,
Hid in this silent, dull retreat,
Untouched thy honied blossoms blow,
Unseen thy little branches greet:
  No roving foot shall crush thee here,
  No busy hand provoke a tear.

By Nature's self in white arrayed,
She bade thee shun the vulgar eye,
And planted here the guardian shade,
And sent soft waters murmuring by;
  Thus quietly thy summer goes,
  Thy days declining to repose.

Smit with those charms, that must decay,
I grieve to see your future doom;
They died — nor were those flowers more gay,
The flowers that did in Eden bloom;
  Unpitying frosts, and Autumn's power
  Shall leave no vestige of this flower.

From morning suns and evening dews
At first thy little being came:
If nothing once, you nothing lose,
For when you die you are the same;
  The space between, is but an hour,
  The frail duration of a flower.

THE DEATH SONG OF A CHEROKEE INDIAN

The sun sets in night, and the stars shun the day,
But glory remains when their lights fade away.
Begin, ye tormentors: your threats are in vain
For the son of Alknomock can never complain.

Remember the woods, where in ambush he lay,
And the scalps which he bore from your nation away!
Why do ye delay? — 'till I shrink from my pain?
Know the son of Alknomock can never complain..

Remember the arrows he shot from his bow,
Remember your chiefs by his hatchet laid low,
The flame rises high, you exult in my pain?
Know the son of Alknomock will never complain.

I go to the land where my father is gone:
His ghost shall rejoice in the fame of his son,
Death comes like a friend, he relieves me from pain,
And thy son, O Alknomock, has scorned to complain.

THE INDIAN BURYING GROUND

In spite of all the learned have said,
    I still my old opinion keep;
The posture, that we give the dead,
    Points out the soul's eternal sleep.

Not so the ancients of these lands —
    The Indian, when from life released,
Again is seated with his friends,
    And shares again the joyous feast.[1]

His imaged birds, and painted bowl,
    And venison, for a journey dressed,
Bespeak the nature of the soul,
    Activity, that knows no rest.

His bow, for action ready bent,
    And arrows, with a head of stone,
Can only mean that life is spent,
    And not the old ideas gone.

---

[1] The North American Indians bury their dead in a sitting posture; decorating the corpse with wampum, the images of birds, quadrupeds, &c: And (if that of a warrior) with bows, arrows, tomhawks, and other military weapons.

Thou, stranger, that shalt come this way,
  No fraud upon the dead commit —
Observe the swelling turf, and say
  They do not lie, but here they sit.

Here still a lofty rock remains,
  On which the curious eye may trace
(Now wasted, half, by wearing rains)
  The fancies of a ruder race.

Here still an aged elm aspires,
  Beneath whose far-projecting shade
(And which the shepherd still admires)
  The children of the forest played!

There oft a restless Indian queen
  (Pale Shebah, with her braided hair)
And many a barbarous form is seen
  To chide the man that lingers there.

By midnight moons, o'er moistening dews;
  In habit for the chase arrayed,
The hunter still the deer pursues,
  The hunter and the deer, a shade!

And long shall timorous fancy see
  The painted chief, and pointed spear,
And Reason's self shall bow the knee
  To shadows and delusions here.

TO A DOG

[Occasioned by putting him on shore at the Island of Sapola, for theft]

Since Nature taught you, Tray, to be a thief,
What blame have you, for working at your trade?
What if you stole a handsome round of beef;
Theft, in your code of laws, no crime was made.

The ten commandments you had never read,
Nor did it ever enter in your head:
But art and Nature, careful to conceal,
Disclos'd not even the Eighth — *Thou shalt not steal.*

Then to the green wood, caitiff, haste away:
There take your chance to live — for Truth must say,
We have no right, for theft, to hang up Tray.

ON THE SLEEP OF PLANTS

When suns are set, and stars in view,
Not only man to slumber yields;
But Nature grants this blessing too,
To yonder plants, in yonder fields.

The Summer heats and lengthening days
(To them the same as toil and care)
Thrice welcome make the evening breeze,
That kindly does their strength repair.

At early dawn each plant survey,
And see, revived by Nature's hand,
With youthful vigour, fresh and gay,
Their blossoms blow, their leaves expand.

Yon' garden plant, with weeds o'er-run,
Not void of thought, perceives its hour,
And, watchful of the parting sun,
Throughout the night conceals her flower.

Like us, the slave of cold and heat,
She too enjoys her little span —
With Reason, only less complete
Than that which makes the boast of man.

Thus, moulded from one common clay,
A varied life adorns the plain;
By Nature subject to decay,
By Nature meant to bloom again!

TO MY BOOK

Seven years are now elaps'd, dear rambling volume,
Since, to all knavish wights a foe,
I sent you forth to vex and gall 'em,
Or drive them to the shades below:
With spirit, still, of Democratic proof,
And still despising Shylock's canker'd hoof:
What doom the fates intend, is hard to say,
Whether to live to some far-distant day,
Or sickening in your prime,
In this bard-baiting clime,
Take pet, make wings, say prayers, and flit away.

"Virtue, order, and religion,
"Haste, and seek some other region;
"Your plan is laid, to hunt them down,
"Destroy the mitre, rend the gown,
"And that vile hag, Philosophy, restore" —
Did ever volume plan so much before?

For seven years past, a host of busy foes
Have buzz'd about your nose,
White, black, and grey, by night and day;
Garbling, lying, singing, sighing:
These eastern gales a cloud of insects bring
That fluttering, snivelling, whimpering — on the wing —
And, wafted still as discord's demon guides,
Flock round the flame, that yet shall singe their hides.

Well! let the fates decree whate'er they please:
Whether you're doom'd to drink oblivion's cup,
Or Praise-God Barebones eats you up,
This I can say, you've spread your wings afar,
Hostile to garter, ribbon, crown, and star;
Still on the people's, still on Freedom's side,
With full determin'd aim, to baffle every claim
Of well-born wights, that aim to mount and ride.

TO A CATY-DID[1]

In a branch of willow hid
Sings the evening Caty-did:
From the lofty locust bough
Feeding on a drop of dew,
In her suit of green array'd
Hear her singing in the shade
   Caty-did, Caty-did, Caty-did!

While upon a leaf you tread,
Or repose your little head,
On your sheet of shadows laid,
All the day you nothing said:
Half the night your cheery tongue
Revell'd out its little song,
   Nothing else but Caty-did.

From your lodgings on the leaf
Did you utter joy or grief —?
Did you only mean to say,
I have had my summer's day,
And am passing, soon, away
To the grave of Caty-did: —
   Poor, unhappy Caty-did!

But you would have utter'd more
Had you known of nature's power —
From the world when you retreat,
And a leaf's your winding sheet,
Long before your spirit fled,
Who can tell but nature said,
Live again, my Caty-did!
   Live, and chatter Caty-did.

[1] A well-known insect, when full grown, about two inches in length, and of the exact color of a green leaf. It is of the genus cicada, or grasshopper kind, inhabiting the green foliage of trees and singing such a song as Caty-did in the evening, towards autumn.

Tell me, what did Caty do?
Did she mean to trouble you? —
Why was Caty not forbid
To trouble little Caty-did? —
Wrong, indeed at you to fling,
Hurting no one while you sing
    Caty-did! Caty-did! Caty-did:

Why continue to complain?
Caty tells me, she again
Will not give you plague or pain: —
Caty says you may be hid
Caty will not go to bed
While you sing us Caty-did.
    Caty-did! Cáty-did! Caty-did!

But, while singing, you forgot
To tell us what did Caty not:
Caty-did not think of cold,
Flocks retiring to the fold,
Winter, with his wrinkles old,
Winter, that yourself foretold
    When you gave us Caty-did.

Stay securely in your nest;
Caty now, will do her best,
All she can, to make you blest;
But, you want no human aid —
Nature, when she form'd you, said,
"Independent you are made,
My dear little Caty-did:
Soon yourself must disappear
With the verdure of the year," —
And to go, we know not where,
    With your song of Caty-did.

ON A HONEY BEE DRINKING FROM A GLASS OF WINE AND DROWNED THEREIN

Thou, born to sip the lake or spring,
Or quaff the waters of the stream,
Why hither come on vagrant wing? —
Does Bacchus tempting seem —
Did he, for you, this glass prepare? —
Will I admit you to a share?

Did storms harass or foes perplex,
Did wasps or king-birds bring dismay —
Did wars distress, or labours vex,
Or did you miss your way? —
A better seat you could not take
Than on the margin of this lake.

Welcome! — I hail you to my glass:
All welcome, here, you find;
Here, let the cloud of trouble pass,
Here, be all care resigned. —
This fluid never fails to please,
And drown the griefs of men or bees.

What forced you here, we cannot know,
And you will scarcely tell —
But cheery we would have you go
And bid a glad farewell:
On lighter wings we bid you fly,
Your dart will now all foes defy.

Yet take not, oh! too deep to drink,
And in this ocean die;
Here bigger bees than you might sink,
Even bees full six feet high.
Like Pharoah, then, you would be said
To perish in a sea of red.

Do as you please, your will is mine;
Enjoy it without fear —
And your grave will be this glass of wine,
Your epitaph — a tear —
Go, take your seat in Charon's boat,
We'll tell the hive, you died afloat.

MINOR POEMS OF THE REVOLUTION

[The songs, ballads, and fugitive poems of the Revolution form an interesting collection, though few of them are of especial literary worth. Even the best American national songs produced in the succeeding century are not ranked by impartial critics among the great patriotic poetry of the world; and it is natural that these songs of the Revolution, written when popular taste favored the artificial and the bombastic, should be mediocre in quality. Among the more important classes of poems produced at this time are modifications or parodies of popular songs, rude ballads narrating occurrences of the conflict, and lyrics intended to intensify feeling. Work of all these kinds varied in tone from the most seriously impassioned to broad and often coarse burlesque. An interesting phenomenon was the acceptance by one party of the excessive burlesques of the other, as in the numerous versions of "Yankee Doodle." As the Tories included in their number many of the most cultured men of the country, their songs and occasional poems were often more finished than those of their opponents. The loyalist poetry has, however, been less carefully preserved; and as it was largely in the formal manner preferred by an eighteenth-century gentleman it is somewhat less interesting than the rough and ready verse of the patriots. The selections given below show various forms of this popular poetry. "The Liberty Song," by John Dickinson, resulted from an attempt, on the part of a publicist who had neither the poetic temperament nor skill in versification, to manufacture a patriotic song. "The American Hero," called by its author "A Sapphic Ode," was the work of a scholarly minister and theologian. Loyalist poetry is represented by an anonymous song, "The British Light-Infantry," and a selection from "The Congratulation," by Dr. Jonathan Odell. "The Yankee's Return from Camp" is perhaps the best-known version of the "Yankee Doodle" song. The other anonymous poems illustrate various kinds of popular songs. The ballad of "Nathan Hale" has, in parts, a real poetic quality.

"The British Light-Infantry" is from "The Loyalist Poetry of the Revolution," edited by Winthrop Sargent. The selection from "The Congratulation" is from the same editor's collection, "The Loyal Verses of Joseph Stansbury and Doctor Jonathan Odell." "The Yankee's Return from Camp" follows a broadside issued by Isaiah Thomas in 1813, as reprinted in Duyckinck's "Cyclopædia of American Literature." "The American Hero" is also copied from the last-named source. The other selections are taken from Moore's "Songs and Ballads of the American Revolution."]

2 G   449

THE LIBERTY SONG

[By John Dickinson. 1768]

Come join hand in hand, brave Americans all,
And rouse your bold hearts at fair Liberty's call;
No tyrannous acts, shall suppress your just claim,
Nor stain with dishonor America's name.
   In freedom we're born, and in freedom we'll live;
     Our purses are ready,
     Steady, Friends, steady,
   Not as *slaves*, but as *freemen* our money we'll give.

Our worthy forefathers — let's give them a cheer —
To climates unknown did courageously steer;
Thro' oceans to deserts, for freedom they came,
And, dying, bequeath'd us their freedom and fame.

Their generous bosoms all dangers despis'd,
So highly, so wisely, their birthrights they priz'd;
We'll keep what they gave, we will piously keep,
Nor frustrate their toils on the land or the deep.

The Tree, their own hands had to Liberty rear'd,
They lived to behold growing strong and rever'd;
With transport then cried, — "Now our wishes we gain,
For our children shall gather the fruits of our pain."

How sweet are the labors that freemen endure,
That they shall enjoy all the profit, secure, —
No more such sweet labors Americans know,
If Britons shall reap what Americans sow.

Swarms of placemen and pensioners soon will appear,
Like locusts deforming the charms of the year:
Suns vainly will rise, showers vainly descend,
If we are to drudge for what others shall spend.

Then join hand in hand brave Americans all,
By uniting we stand, by dividing we fall;
In so righteous a cause let us hope to succeed,
For Heaven approves of each generous deed.

All ages shall speak with amaze and applause,
Of the courage we'll show in support of our laws;
To die we can bear, — but to serve we disdain,
For shame is to freemen more dreadful than pain.

This bumper I crown for our sovereign's health,
And this for Britannia's glory and wealth;
That wealth, and that glory immortal may be,
If she is but just, and we are but free.
   In freedom we're born, &c.

VIRGINIA BANISHING TEA

[By a young woman of Virginia. 1774]

Begone, pernicious, baneful tea,
  With all Pandora's ills possessed,
Hyson, no more beguiled by thee
  My noble sons shall be oppressed.

To Britain fly, where gold enslaves,
  And venal men their birth-right sell;
Tell *North* and his bribed clan of knaves,
  Their bloody acts were made in hell.

In Henry's reign those acts began,
  Which sacred rules of justice broke
North now pursues the hellish plan,
  To fix on us his slavish yoke.

But we oppose, and will be free,
  This great good cause we will defend;
Nor bribe, nor Gage, nor North's decree,
  Shall make us "at his feet to bend."

From Anglia's ancient sons we came;
    Those heroes who for freedom fought;
In freedom's cause we'll march; their fame,
    By their example greatly taught.

Our king we love, but North we hate,
    Nor will to him submission own;
If death's our doom, we'll brave our fate,
    But pay allegiance to the throne.

Then rouse, my sons! from slavery free
    Your suffering homes; from God's high wrath;
Gird on your steel; give *liberty*
    To all who follow in our path.

THE PENNSYLVANIA SONG

[1775]

We are the troop that ne'er will stoop
    To wretched slavery,
Nor shall our seed, by our base deed
    Despisèd vassals be;
Freedom we will bequeathe to them,
    Or we will bravely die;
Our greatest foe, ere long shall know,
    How much did Sandwich lie.
        And all the world shall know,
            Americans are free;
        Nor slaves nor cowards we will prove,
            Great Britain soon shall see.

We'll not give up our birthright,
    Our foes shall find us men;
As good as they, in any shape,
    The British troops shall ken.
Huzza! brave boys, we'll beat them
    On any hostile plain;

For freedom, wives, and children dear
    The battle we'll maintain.

What! can those British tyrants think,
    Our fathers cross'd the main,
And savage foes, and dangers met,
    To be enslav'd by them?
If so, they are mistaken,
    For we will rather die;
And since they have become our foes,
    Their forces we defy.
        And all the world shall know,
          Americans are free,
        Nor slaves nor cowards we will prove,
        Great Britain soon shall see.

THE AMERICAN HERO

[By Nathaniel Niles. 1775]

Why should vain mortals tremble at the sight of
Death and destruction in the field of battle,
Where blood and carnage clothe the ground in crimson,
    Sounding with death-groans?

Death will invade us by the means appointed,
And we must all bow to the king of terrors;
Nor am I anxious, if I am prepared,
    What shape he comes in.

Infinite Goodness teaches us submission,
Bids us be quiet under all his dealings;
Never repining, but forever praising
    God, our Creator.

Well may we praise him: all his ways are perfect:
Though a resplendence, infinitely glowing,
Dazzles in glory on the sight of mortals,
    Struck blind by lustre.

Good is Jehovah in bestowing sunshine,
Nor less his goodness in the storm and thunder,
Mercies and judgment both proceed from kindness,
   Infinite kindness.

O, then, exult that God forever reigneth;
Clouds which, around him, hinder our perception,
Bind us the stronger to exalt his name, and
   Shout louder praises.

Then to the wisdom of my Lord and Master
I will commit all that I have or wish for,
Sweetly as babes' sleep will I give my life up,
   When call'd to yield it.

Now, Mars, I dare thee, clad in smoky pillars,
Bursting from bomb-shells, roaring from the cannon,
Rattling in grape-shot like a storm of hailstones,
   Torturing ether.

Up the bleak heavens let the spreading flames rise,
Breaking, like Ætna, through the smoky columns,
Lowering, like Egypt, o'er the falling city,
   Wantonly burned down.[1]

While all their hearts quick palpitate for havoc,
Let slip your blood-hounds, nam'd the British lions;
Dauntless as death stares, nimble as the whirl-wind,
   Dreadful as demons!

Let oceans waft on all your floating castles,
Fraught with destruction, horrible to nature;
Then, with your sails fill'd by a storm of vengeance,
   Bear down to battle.

---

[1] Charlestown, near Boston.

From the dire caverns, made by ghostly miners,
Let the explosion, dreadful as volcanoes,
Heave the broad town, with all its wealth and people,
     Quick to destruction.

Still shall the banner of the King of Heaven
Never advance where I am afraid to follow:
While that precedes me, with an open bosom,
     War, I defy thee.

Fame and dear freedom lure me on to battle,
While a fell despot, grimmer than a death's-head,
Stings me with serpents, fiercer than Medusa's,
     To the encounter.

Life, for my country and the cause of freedom,
Is but a trifle for a worm to part with;
And, if preserved in so great a contest,
     Life is redoubled.

THE YANKEE'S RETURN FROM CAMP

[Cir. 1775]

Father and I went down to camp,
  Along with Captain Gooding,
And there we see the men and boys,
  As thick as hasty pudding.
    Chorus — Yankee Doodle, keep it up,
       Yankee Doodle, dandy,
       Mind the music and the step,
       And with the girls be handy.

And there we see a thousand men,
  As rich as 'Squire David;
And what they wasted every day,
  I wish it could be saved.

The 'lasses they eat every day,
  Would keep an house a winter;
They have as much that, I'll be bound,
  They eat it when they're a mind to.

And there we see a swamping gun,
  Large as a log of maple,
Upon a deuced little cart,
  A load for father's cattle.

And every time they shoot it off,
  It takes a horn of powder,
And makes a noise like father's gun,
  Only a nation louder.

I went as nigh to one myself,
  As Siah's underpinning;
And father went as nigh again,
  I thought the deuce was in him.

Cousin Simon grew so bold,
  I thought he would have cock'd it;
It scar'd me so, I shrink'd it off,
  And hung by father's pocket.

And Captain Davis had a gun,
  He kind of clapt his hand on't,
And stuck a crooked stabbing iron
  Upon the little end on't.

And there I see a pumpkin shell
  As big as mother's bason;
And every time they touch'd it off,
  They scamper'd like the nation.

I see a little barrel too,
  The heads were made of leather,
They knock'd upon't with little clubs,
  And call'd the folks together.

And there was Captain Washington,
  And gentlefolks about him,
They say he's grown so tarnal proud,
  He will not ride without 'em.

He got him on his meeting clothes,
  Upon a slapping stallion,
He set the world along in rows,
  In hundreds and in millions.

The flaming ribbons in his hat,
  They look'd so taring fine ah,
I wanted pockily to get,
  To give to my Jemimah.

I see another snarl of men
  A digging graves, they told me,
So tarnal long, so tarnal deep,
  They 'tended they should hold me.

It scar'd me so, I hook'd it off,
  Nor stop'd, as I remember,
Nor turn'd about, 'till I got home,
  Lock'd up in mother's chamber.

NATHAN HALE

[1776]

The breezes went steadily thro' the tall pines,
  A saying "oh! hu-ush!" a saying "oh! hu-ush!"
As stilly stole by a bold legion of horse,
  For Hale in the bush, for Hale in the bush.

"Keep still!" said the thrush as she nestled her young,
  In a nest by the road; in a nest by the road.
"For the tyrants are near, and with them appear,
  What bodes us no good; what bodes us no good."

The brave captain heard it, and thought of his home,
  In a cot by the brook; in a cot by the brook.
With mother and sister and memories dear,
  He so gaily forsook; he so gaily forsook.

Cooling shades of the night were coming apace,
  The tattoo had beat; the tattoo had beat.
The noble one sprang from his dark lurking place,
  To make his retreat; to make his retreat.

He warily trod on the dry rustling leaves,
  As he pass'd thro' the wood; as he pass'd thro' the wood;
And silently gain'd his rude launch on the shore,
  As she play'd with the flood; as she play'd with the flood.

The guards of the camp, on that dark, dreary night,
  Had a murderous will; had a murderous will.
They took him and bore him afar from the shore,
  To a hut on the hill; to a hut on the hill.

No mother was there, nor a friend who could cheer,
  In that little stone cell; in that little stone cell.
But he trusted in love, from his father above.
  In his heart, all was well; in his heart, all was well.

An ominous owl with his solemn base voice,
  Sat moaning hard by; sat moaning hard by.
"The tyrant's proud minions most gladly rejoice,
  "For he must soon die; for he must soon die."

The brave fellow told them, no thing he restrain'd,
  The cruel gen'ral; the cruel gen'ral.
His errand from camp, of the ends to be gain'd,
  And said that was all; and said that was all.

They took him and bound him and bore him away,
  Down the hill's grassy side; down the hill's grassy side.
'Twas there the base hirelings, in royal array,
  His cause did deride; his cause did deride.

Five minutes were given, short moments, no more,
　For him to repent; for him to repent;
He pray'd for his mother, he ask'd not another,
　To Heaven he went; to Heaven he went.

The faith of a martyr, the tragedy shew'd,
　As he trod the last stage; as he trod the last stage.
And Britons will shudder at gallant Hale's blood,
　As his words do presage, as his words do presage.

"Thou pale king of terrors, thou life's gloomy foe,
　Go frighten the slave, go frighten the slave;
Tell tyrants, to you, their allegiance they owe.
　No fears for the brave; no fears for the brave."

THE BRITISH LIGHT-INFANTRY

[1778]

Hark! hark! the bugle's lofty sound,
Which makes the woods and rocks around
　Repeat the martial strain,
Proclaims the *light-arm'd British troops*
Advance——Behold, rebellion droops;
　She hears the sound with pain.

She sees their glitt'ring arms with fear;
Their nodding plumes approaching near;
　Her gorgon head she hides.
She flees, in vain, to shun such foes,
For *Wayne*, or hapless *Baylor* knows
　How swift their vengeance glides.

The nimble messenger of Jove
On earth alights not from above
　With step so light as theirs:
Hence, have they *feather'd caps*, and *wings*,
And *weapons* which have keener stings
　Than that gay Hermes bears.

A myrtle garland, with the vine,
Venus and Bacchus shall entwine,
    About their brows to place;
As types of love and joy, beneath
The well-earn'd, budding laurel-wreath
    Which shades each hero's face.

D'ESTAING'S DISASTER

[From "The Congratulation," by Dr. Jonathan Odell.   1779]

Joy to great Congress, joy an hundred fold:
The grand cajolers are themselves cajol'd!
In vain has [Franklin's] artifice been tried,
And Louis swell'd with treachery and pride:
Who reigns supreme in heav'n deception spurns,
And on the author's head the mischief turns.
What pains were taken to procure D'Estaing!
His fleet's dispers'd, and Congress may go hang.

Joy to great Congress, joy an hundred fold:
The grand cajolers are themselves cajol'd!
Heav'ns King sends forth the hurricane and strips
Of all their glory the perfidious ships.
His Ministers of Wrath the storm direct;
Nor can the Prince of Air his French protect.
Saint George, Saint David show'd themselves true hearts;
Saint Andrew and Saint Patrick topp'd their parts.
With right Eolian puffs the wind they blew;
Crack went the masts; the sails to shivers flew.
Such honest saints shall never be forgot;
Saint Dennis, and Saint Tammany, go rot.

Joy to great Congress, joy an hundred fold;
The grand cajolers are themselves cajol'd!
Old Satan holds a council in mid-air;
Hear the black Dragon furious rage and swear —

—— Are these the triumphs of my Gallic friends?
How will you ward this blow, my trusty fiends?
What remedy for this unlucky job?
What art shall raise the spirits of the mob?
Fly swift, ye sure supporters of my realm,
Ere this ill-news the rebels overwhelm.
Invent, say any thing to make them mad;
Tell them the King — No, Dev'ls are not so bad;
The dogs of Congress at the King let loose;
But ye, brave Dev'ls, avoid such mean abuse.

Joy to great Congress, joy an hundred fold:
The grand cajolers are themselves cajol'd!
What thinks Sir Washington of this mischance;
Blames he not those, who put their trust in France?
A broken reed comes pat into his mind:
Egypt and France by rushes are defin'd,
Basest of Kingdoms underneath the skies,
Kingdoms that could not profit their allies.
How could the tempest play him such a prank?
Blank is his prospect, and his visage blank:
Why from West-Point his armies has he brought?
Can nought be done? — sore sighs he at the thought.
Back to his mountains Washington may trot:
He take this city — yes, when Ice is hot.

VOLUNTEER BOYS

[By Henry Archer (?). 1780]

Hence with the lover who sighs o'er his wine,
    Cloes and Phillises toasting,
Hence with the slave who will whimper and whine,
    Of ardor and constancy boasting.
        Hence with love's joys,
        Follies and noise,
The toast that I give is the Volunteer Boys.

Nobles and beauties and such common toasts,
    Those who admire may drink, sir;
Fill up the glass to the volunteer hosts,
    Who never from danger will shrink, sir.
        Let mirth appear,
        Every heart cheer,
The toast that I give is the brave volunteer.

Here's to the squire who goes to parade
    Here's to the citizen soldier;
Here's to the merchant who fights for his trade,
    Whom danger increasing makes bolder.
        Let mirth appear,
        Union is here,
The toast that I give is the brave volunteer.

Here's to the lawyer, who, leaving the bar,
    Hastens where honor doth lead, sir,
Changing the gown for the ensigns of war,
    The cause of his country to plead, sir.
        Freedom appears,
        Every heart cheers,
And calls for the health of the law volunteers.

Here's to the soldier, though batter'd in wars,
    And safe to his farm-house retir'd;
When called by his country, ne'er thinks of his scars,
    With ardor to join us inspir'd.
        Bright fame appears,
        Trophies uprear,
To veteran chiefs who became volunteers.

Here's to the farmer who dares to advance
    To harvests of honor with pleasure;
Who with a slave the most skilful in France,
    A sword for his country would measure.

Hence with cold fear,
Heroes rise here;
The ploughman is chang'd to the stout volunteer.

Here's to the peer, first in senate and field,
    Whose actions to titles add grace, sir;
Whose spirit undaunted would never yet yield
    To a foe, to a pension or place, sir.
        Gratitude here,
        Toasts to the peer,
Who adds to his titles, "the brave volunteer."

Thus the bold bands for old Jersey's defence,   .
    The muse hath with rapture review'd, sir;
With our volunteer boys, as our verses commence,
    With our volunteer boys they conclude, sir.
        Discord or noise,
        Ne'er damp our joys,
But health and success to the volunteer boys.

THE DANCE

[1781]

Cornwallis led a country dance,
    The like was never seen, sir,
Much retrograde and much advance,
    And all with General Greene, sir.

They rambled up and rambled down,
    Join'd hands, then off they run, sir,
Our General Greene to Charlestown,
    The earl to Wilmington, sir.

Greene, in the South, then danc'd a set,
    And got a mighty name, sir,
Cornwallis jigg'd with young Fayette,
    But suffer'd in his fame, sir.

Then down he figur'd to the shore,
　　Most like a lordly dancer,
And on his courtly honor swore,
　　He would no more advance, sir.

Quoth he, my guards are weary grown
　　With footing country dances,
They never at St. James's shone,
　　At capers, kicks or prances.

Though men so gallant ne'er were seen,
　　While sauntering on parade, sir,
Or wriggling o'er the park's smooth green,
·　　Or at a masquerade, sir.

Yet are red heels and long-lac'd skirts,
　　For stumps and briars meet, sir?
Or stand they chance with hunting-shirts,
　　Or hardy veteran feet, sir?

Now hous'd in York he challeng'd all,
　　At minuet or all 'amande,
And lessons for a courtly ball,
　　His guards by day and night conn'd.

This challenge known, full soon there came,
　　A set who had the bon ton,
De Grasse and Rochambeau, whose fame
　　Fut brillant pour un long tems.

And Washington, Columbia's son,
　　Whom easy nature taught, sir,
That grace which can't by pains be won,
　　Or Plutus' gold be bought, sir.

Now hand in hand they circle round,
　　This ever-dancing peer, sir;
Their gentle movements, soon confound
　　The earl, as they draw near, sir.

His music soon forgets to play —
  His feet can no more move, sir,
And all his bands now curse the day,
  They jiggèd to our shore, sir.

Now Tories all, what can ye say?
  Come — is not this a griper,
That while your hopes are danc'd away,
  'Tis you must pay the piper.

HUGH HENRY BRACKENRIDGE

[Hugh Henry Brackenridge is notable as the author of the most popular book produced west of the Alleghanies before 1800. He was born in Scotland in 1748, but came to America when a boy. His family were in poor financial circumstances, but, largely through his own exertions, he was graduated from Princeton in 1771. His collaboration with his classmate Freneau in a commencement poem has already been mentioned. After his graduation he taught school, edited a magazine, studied divinity, and served as chaplain in the continental army. During this period he wrote a few popular patriotic poems, and delivered some patriotic sermons that were thought worthy of being published. Before the close of the war he turned to the study of law, and in 1781 he removed to Pittsburg. Here he became active in public affairs, and was perhaps unfortunately prominent in connection with the "Whiskey Insurrection" of 1794. The next year he published a long and elaborate "Vindication" of his conduct in connection with this affair. His most important work was "Modern Chivalry; containing the Adventures of a Captain and Teague O'Regan, his servant." The first part of this picturesque satire appeared in 1796, and the less important second part in 1806. The book is a western Don Quixote, and burlesques with western freedom, and in a manner that shows the western point of view, many political and social customs of the country.

The selections are from the Philadelphia edition of 1804.]

AN ANSWER TO A CHALLENGE

[From "Modern Chivalry"]

On reflection, it seemed advisable to the Captain to write an answer to the card which Colonel or Major Jacko, or whatever his title may have been, had sent him this morning. It was as follows:

Sir,

I have two objections to this duel matter. The one is, lest I should hurt you; and the other is, lest you should hurt me. I do not see any good it would do me to put a bullet through any part of your body. I could make no use of you when dead, for any culinary purpose, as I would a rabbit or a turkey. I am no cannibal to feed on the flesh of men. Why then shoot down a human creature, of which I could make no use? A buffaloe would be better meat. For though your flesh might be delicate and tender; yet it wants that firmness and consistency which takes and retains salt. At any rate it would not be fit for long sea voyages. You might make a good barbecue, it is true, being of the nature of a racoon or an opossum; but people are not in the habit of barbecuing any thing human now. As to your hide, it is not worth the taking off, being little better than that of a year old colt.

It would seem to me a strange thing to shoot at a man that would stand still to be shot at; in as much as I have been heretofore used to shoot at things flying, or running, or jumping. Were you on a tree, now, like a squirrel, endeavouring to hide yourself in the branches, or like a racoon, that after much eying and spying I observe at length in the crotch of a tall oak, with boughs and leaves intervening, so that I could just get a sight of his hinder parts, I should think it pleasurable enough to take a shot at you. But as it is, there is no skill or judgment requisite either to discover or take you down.

As to myself, I do not much like to stand in the way of any thing that is harmful. I am under apprehensions you might hit me. That being the case, I think it most advisable to stay at a distance. If you want to try your pistols, take some object, a tree or a barn door about my dimensions. If you hit that, send me word, and I shall acknowledge that if I had been in the same place, you might also have hit me.

J. F.

TREATING WITH THE INDIANS

[From "Modern Chivalry"]

Not long after this, being at a certain place, the Captain was accosted by a stranger in the following manner: Captain, said he, I have heard of a young man in your service who talks Irish. Now, Sir, my business is that of an Indian treaty-maker; and am on my way with a party of kings, and half-kings to the commissioners, to hold a treaty. My king of the Kickapoos, who was a Welsh blacksmith, took sick by the way, and is dead: I have heard of this lad of yours and could wish to have him a while to supply his place. The treaty will not last longer than a couple of weeks; and as the government will probably allow three or four thousand dollars for the treaty, it will be in our power to make it worth your while, to spare him for that time. Your king of the Kickapoos, said the Captain; what does that mean? Said the stranger, It is just this: you have heard of the Indian nations to the westward, that occasionally make war upon the frontier settlements. It has been a policy of government, to treat with these, and distribute goods. Commissioners are appointed for that purpose. Now you are not to suppose that it is always an easy matter to catch a real chief, and bring him from the woods; or if at some expense one was brought, the goods would go to his use; whereas, it is much more profitable to hire substitutes and make chiefs of our own: And as some unknown gibberish is necessary, to pass for an Indian language, we generally make use of Welch, or Low Dutch, or Irish; or pick up an ingenious fellow here and there, who can imitate a language by sounds of his own, in his mouth, and throat. But we prefer one who can speak a real tongue, and give more for him. We cannot afford you a great deal at this time for the use of your man; because it is not a general treaty where 20,000, or 30,000 dollars are appropriated for the purpose of holding it; but an occasional, or what we call a running treaty, by way of brightening the chain, and holding fast friendship. The commissioners will doubtless be glad to see us, and procure from government an allowance for the treaty. For the more treaties, the more use for commissioners. The business must be kept up, and treaties made if there are none of themselves. My Pianksha, and Choctaw chiefs, are very good fellows; the one of them a Scotch pedlar that talks the Erse; the other has been some time in Canada, and has a little broken Indian, God knows what language; but has been of great service in assisting to teach the rest some Indian custom and manners. I have had the whole of them for a fortnight past under my tuition, teaching them war songs and dances, and to make responses at the treaty. If your man is tractable, I can make him a Kickapoo in about nine days. A breech-clout, and leggins, that I took off the blacksmith that died, I have ready to put on him. He must have part of his head shaved, and painted, with feathers on his crown; but the paint will rub off, and the hair grow in a short time, so that he can go about with you again.

It is a very strange affair, said the Captain. Is it possible that such deception can be practised in a new country. It astonishes me, that the government does not detect such imposition. The government, said the Indian treaty-man, is at a great distance. It knows no more of Indians than a cow does of Greek. The legislature, hears of wars and rumours of wars, and supports the executive in forming treaties. How is it possible for men who live remote from the scene of action, to have adequate ideas of the nature of Indians, or the transactions that are carried on in their behalf? Do you think the one half of those savages that come to treat, are real representatives of the nation? Many of them are not savages at all; but weavers, and pedlars, as I have told you, picked up to make kings and chiefs. I speak of those particularly that come trading down to inland towns, or the metropolis. I would not communicate these mysteries of our trade, were it not that I confide in your good sense, and have occasion for your servant.

It is a mystery of iniquity, said the Captain. Do you suppose that I would countenance such a fraud upon the public? I do not know, said the other; it is a very common thing for men to speculate, nowadays. If you will not, another will. A hundred dollars might as well be in your pocket as another man's. I will give you that for the use of your servant, for a week or two, and say no more about it. It is an idea new to me entirely, said the Captain, that Indian princes, whom I have seen escorted down as such, were no more than trumpery, disguised, as you mention; that such should be introduced to polite assemblies, and have the honour to salute the fair ladies with a kiss, the greatest beauties thinking themselves honoured by having the salu[ta]tion of a sovereign? It is so, said the other; I had a red headed bricklayer once, whom I passed for a Chippawaw; and who has dined with clubs, and sat next the President. He was blind of an eye, and was called blind Sam by the traders. I had given it out that he was a great warrior, and had lost his eye by an arrow, in a contest with a rival nation. These things are now reduced to a system;

and it is so well known to those who are engaged in the traffic, that we think nothing of it.

How the devil, said the Captain, do you get speeches made, and interpret them so as to pass for truth. That is an easy matter, said the other; Indian speeches are nearly all alike. You have only to talk of burying hatche[t]s under large trees, kindling fires, brightening chains; with a demand, at the latter end, of blankets for the backside, and rum to get drunk with.

I much doubt, said the Captain, whether treaties that are carried on in earnest, are of any great use.   Of none at all, said the other; especially as the practice of giving goods prevails; because this is an inducement to a fresh war. This being the case, it can be no harm to make a farce of the whole matter; or rather a profit of it; by such means as I propose to you, and have pursued myself.

After all, said the Captain, I cannot but consider it as a kind of contraband and illicit traffic; and I must be excused from having any hand in it, I shall not betray your secret, but I shall not favour it. It would ill become me, whose object in riding about in this manner, is to give just ideas on subjects, to take part in such ill-gotten gain.

The Indian treaty-man finding it vain to say more, withdrew.

The Captain apprehending that he might not yet drop his designs upon the Irishman, but be tampering with him out of doors, should he come across him, sent for Teague.   For he well knew, that should the Indian treaty-man get the first word of him, the idea of making him a king, would turn his head, and it would be impossible to prevent his going with him.

Teague coming in, said the Captain to him; Teague, I have discovered in you, for some time past, a great spirit of ambition, which is, doubtless, commendable in a young person; and I have checked it only in cases where there was real danger, or apparent mischief.   There is now an opportunity of advancing yourself, not so much in the way of honour as profit. But profit brings honour, and is, indeed, the most substantial support of it.   There has been a man here with me, that carries on a trade with the Indians, and tells me that red-headed scalps are in great demand with them. If you could spare yours, he would give a good price for it. I do not well know what use they make of this article, but so it is, the traders find their account in it. Probably they dress it with the hairy side out, and make tobacco-pouches for the chiefs, when they meet in council. It saves dyeing, and besides, the natural red hair of a man, may, in their estimation, be superior to any colour they can give by art. The taking off the scalp will not give much pain, it is so dextrously done by them with a crooked knife they have for that purpose. The mode of taking off the scalp is this; you lie down upon your back; a warrior puts his feet upon your shoulders, collects your hair in his left hand, and drawing a circle with a knife in his right, makes the incision, and, with a sudden pull, separates it from the head, giving, in the mean time, what is called the scalp yell. The thing is done in such an instant, that the pain is scarcely felt. He offered me an hundred dollars, if I would have it taken off for his use, giving me directions, in the mean time, how to stretch it and dry it on a hoop. I told him, No; it was a perquisite of your own, and you might dispose of it as you thought proper. If you choose to dispose of it, I had no objections; but the bargain should be of your own making, and the price such as should please yourself. I have sent for you, to give you a hint of this chapman, that you may have a knowledge of his wish to possess the property, and ask accordingly. It is probable you may bring him up to a half Johannes more, by holding out a little. But I do not think it would be adviseable to lose the bargain. An hundred dollars for a little hairy flesh, is a great deal. You will trot a long time before you make that with me. He will be with you probably to propose the purchase. You will know when you see him. He is a tall looking man, with leggins on, and has several Indians with him going to a treaty. He talked to me something of making you a king of the Kickapoos, after the scalp is off; but I would not count on that so much; because words are but wind, and promises are easily broken. I would advise you to make sure of the money in the first place, and take chance for the rest.

I have seen among the prints of Hogarth, some such expression of countenance as that of Teague at this instant; who, as soon as he could speak, but with a double brogue on his tongue, began to intimate his disinclination to the traffic. The hair of his scalp itself, in the mean time had risen in opposition to it. Dear master, vid you trow me into ridicule, and the blessed shalvation of my life, and all dat I have in the vorld, to be trown like a dog to de savages, and have my flesh tarn of my head to give to dese vild bastes to make a napsack to carry their parates and tings in, for an hundred dollars or the like. It shall never be said that the hair of the Oregans made mackeseens for a vild Indian to trat upon. I would sooner trow my own head, hair, and all in de fire, dan give it to dese paple to smoke wid, out of deir long pipes.

If this be your determination, said the Captain, it will behove you to keep yourself somewhat close; and while we remain at this public house, avoid any conversation with the chapman or his agents, should they come to tamper with you. For it is not improbable, while they are keeping you in talk, proposing to make you a Kickapoo chief, and the like, they may snatch the scalp off your head, and you not be the wiser for it.

Teague thought the caution good, and resolving to abide by it, retired to the kitchen. The maid at this time, happening to want a log of wood, requested Teague to cut it for her. Taking the ax accordingly, and going out, he was busy chopping, with his head down; while, in the mean time, the Indian treaty-man had returned with one in Indian dress, who was the chief of the Killinoos, or at least passed for such; and whom he brought as having some recruiting talents, and might prevail with Teague to elope, and join the company. I presume, said the Indian treaty-man, you are the waiter of the Captain who lodges here at present. Teague hearing a man speak, and lifting up his head, saw the leggins on the one, and the Indian dress on the other; and with a kind of involuntary effort, threw the ax directly from him at the Killinno. It missed him but about an inch, and fell behind. Teague, in the mean time, raising a shout of desperation, was fixed on the spot, and his locomotive faculties suspended; so that he could neither retreat nor advance, but stood still, like one enchained or enchanted for a moment; the king of the Killinoos, in the mean time, drawing his tomahawk, and preparing for battle.

The Captain, who was reading at a front window, hearing the shout, looked about, and saw what was going on at the wood-pile.

Stop villain, said he, to the king of the Killinoos; you are not to take that scalp yet, however much you may value it. He will not take an hundred dollars for it, nor 500, though you make him king of the Kickapoos, or any thing else. It is no trifling matter to have the ears slit in tatters, and the nose run through with a bodkin, and a goose quill stuck across; so that you may go about your business; you will get no king of the Kickapoos here. Under cover of this address of the Captain, Teague had retired to the kitchen, and ensconced himself behind the rampart of the maid. The Indian treaty-man, and the Killinoo chief, finding the measure hopeless, withdrew, and turned their attention, it is to be supposed, to some other quarter, to find a king of the Kickapoos.

CONTAINING OBSERVATIONS

The captain was certainly to be commended in declining to countenance the imposition of making Teague a Kickapoo chief. Had he been disposed to adventure in a contraband trade of this kind, he might have undertaken it as a principal, and not as furnishing an assistant only. He could have passed Teague for a chief, and himself for an interpreter. He might pretend to have conducted this prince from a very distant nation, and that he had been several moons in travelling, and wanted, the Lord knows how much, goods for his people, that otherwise would come to war. By this means, the Captain would have taken the whole emolument of the treaty, and not have been put off with a small share of the profit which another made by it.

I should like to have seen Teague in an Indian dress, come to treat with the commissioners. It would be necessary for him only to talk Irish, which he might pass for the Shawanese, or other language. The Captain could have interpreted in the usual words on these occasions.

The policy of treating with the Indians is very good; because it takes off a great deal of loose merchandize, that might otherwise lie upon our hands, and cuts away superfluities from the finances of the government; at the same time, as every fresh treaty lays the foundation of a new war, it will serve to check the too rapid growth of the settlements. The extremities of a government, like the arm or ancle of an individual, are the parts at which blood is to be let.

Struck with the good effects of treating with the savages, and that our wise men who conduct affairs, pursue the policy, I have been led to wonder, that the agricultural societies, have not proposed treaties with the wolves and bears that they might not clandestinely invade our sheep and pig folds. This might be done by sending messages to the several ursine and vulpine nations, and calling them to a council-fire, to which four or five hundred wagon load of beef should be sent, and distributed. If it should be said, that this would restrain them no longer from their prey than while they continued to be satiated, the same might be said of the Potawatamies, or other Indian nations; and yet we see that those at the head of our affairs think it prudent to negociate with them.

A bear and wolf treaty might seem an odd thing at first, but we should soon come to be accustomed to it. I should be sorry abuses should prevail, by treaty-making men passing rough water-dogs for bears, or mastiffs for wolves, upon our secretaries at war, or subordinate commissioners; which might be done as in the case of the savages where it is pretended that some tribes had not been at the general treaty, now sends a chief to represent them and get goods.

If our traders go amongst the wolves in consequence of a treaty, I could wish they could check themselves in the introduction of spirituous liquors. A drunk wolf, or bear, would be a dangerous animal. It may be thought that a bear of [or] wolf chief would not get drunk, as it would be setting a bad example to their people; but I have seen Indian kings lying on the earth drunk, and exposing their nakedness, like Noah to Shem, Ham, and Japheth; and if Indians, that are a sort of human creatures, act thus, what might we not expect from a poor brute wolf or bear?

If treaties with the wolves and bears should be found to succeed it might not be amiss to institute them also with the foxes. This is a sagacious animal, and destructive to ducks and other fowls. It would be a great matter to settle a treaty with them, which might be done at the expence of nine or ten thousand dollars laid out in goods.

CHARLES BROCKDEN BROWN

[Charles Brockden Brown is often spoken of as the first American novelist, and sometimes as the first American to devote himself to literature as a profession. He was born in Philadelphia, of Quaker parents, in 1771. After a somewhat desultory schooling, interrupted by poor health, he took up the study of law, but never practised. In his early manhood he came under the influence of Godwin, and this influence is seen both in his social and political philosophy, and in the titles and manner of his novels. His first important writing was "Alcuin," a dialogue on the rights of woman, published in 1797. Between the spring of 1798 and the close of 1801 he published six novels, "Wieland," "Ormond," "Arthur Mervyn," "Edgar Huntley," "Clara Howard," and "Jane Talbot." During the greater part of these three prolific years he was in New York, where he lived and wrote with a group of congenial literary friends. Even while he was turning out novels at the rate of almost two a year he was editing a magazine, and writing fugitive pieces in prose and verse. After his return to Philadelphia in 1801, he edited magazines and wrote political and miscellaneous articles. At the time of his death in 1810 he was engaged on a "General Geography" and a "History of Rome in the Time of the Antonines." This hack work is interesting as showing what an American must do if he would live by his pen in the early years of the century. The only works of Brown that keep his fame alive are the novels already mentioned.

These novels are of considerable intrinsic merit. As has been said, they show the influence of Godwin; and they abound in scenes of terror and mystery such as were the fashion of the time. In plots, and especially in the explanations of horrible and strange occurrences, they are weak. The style, too, is exceedingly loose and faulty. But the author had a genuine appreciation of the way in which mystery and terror affect the human mind, and he knew how to present incidents effectively. Structureless as his novels are, they hold the reader's attention to the end, and they abound in scenes of real power. This is due in part to the fact that the action in each case takes place in America, and that the setting and some of the incidents were based on personal experience and observation. The wild scenery described in "Edgar Huntley" is said to resemble regions near Philadelphia through which Brown wandered as a boy, and the pictures of the yellow fever epidemic in "Ormond" and "Arthur Mervyn" are based on his observations of the plague in New York.

The selections are from the only recent edition of Brown's complete works, published by McKay in 1887.]

A MYSTERIOUS WARNING

[From "Wieland, or the Transformation"]

The state of my mind naturally introduced a train of reflections upon the dangers and cares which inevitably beset a human being. By no violent transition was I led to ponder on the turbulent life and mysterious end of my father. I cherished with the utmost veneration the memory of this man, and every relic connected with his fate was preserved with the most scrupulous care. Among these was to be numbered a manuscript containing memoirs of his own life. The narrative was by no means recommended by its eloquence; but neither did all its value flow from my relationship to the author. Its style had an unaffected and picturesque simplicity. The great variety and circumstantial display of the incidents, together with their intrinsic importance as descriptive of human manners and passions, made it the most useful book in my collection. It was late: but, being sensible of no inclination to sleep, I resolved to betake myself to the perusal of it.

To do this, it was requisite to procure a light. The girl had long since retired to her chamber: it was therefore proper to wait upon myself. A lamp, and the means of lighting it, were only to be found in the kitchen. Thither I resolved forthwith to repair; but the light was of use merely to enable me to read the book. I knew the shelf and the spot where it stood. Whether I took down the book, or prepared the lamp in the first place, appeared to be a matter of no moment. The latter was preferred, and, leaving my seat, I approached the closet in which, as I mentioned formerly, my books and papers were deposited.

Suddenly the remembrance of what had lately passed in this closet occurred. Whether midnight was approaching, or had passed, I knew not. I was, as then, alone and defenceless. The wind was in that direction in which, aided by the deathlike repose of nature, it brought to me the murmur of the waterfall. This was mingled with that solemn and enchanting sound which a breeze produces among the leaves of pines. The words of that mysterious dialogue, their fearful import, and the wild excess to which I was transported by my terrors, filled my imagination anew. My steps faltered, and I stood a moment to recover myself.

I prevailed on myself at length to move towards the closet. I touched the lock, but my fingers were powerless; I was visited afresh by unconquerable apprehensions. A sort of belief darted into my mind that some being was concealed within whose purposes were evil. I began to contend with those fears, when it occurred to me that I might, without impropriety, go for a lamp previously to opening the closet. I receded a few steps; but before I reached the chamber door my thoughts took a new direction. Motion seemed to produce a mechanical influence upon me. I was ashamed of my weakness. Besides, what aid could be afforded me by a lamp?

My fears had pictured to themselves no precise object. It would be difficult to depict in words the ingredients and hues of that phantom which haunted me. A hand invisible and of preternatural strength, lifted by human passions, and selecting my life for its aim, were parts of this terrific image. All places were alike accessible to this foe; or, if his empire were restricted by local bounds, those bounds were utterly inscrutable by me. But had I not been told, by some one in league with this enemy, that every place but the recess in the bank was exempt from danger?

I returned to the closet, and once more put my hand upon the lock. Oh, may my ears lose their sensibility ere they be again assailed by a shriek so terrible! Not merely my understanding was subdued by the sound; it acted on my nerves like an edge of steel. It appeared to cut asunder the fibres of my brain and rack every joint with agony.

The cry, loud and piercing as it was, was nevertheless human. No articulation was ever more distinct. The breath which accompanied it did not fan my hair, yet did every circumstance combine to persuade me that the lips which uttered it touched my very shoulder.

"Hold! Hold!" were the words of this tremendous prohibition, in whose tone the whole soul seemed to be wrapped up, and every energy converted into eagerness and terror.

Shuddering, I dashed myself against the wall, and, by the same involuntary impulse, turned my face backward to examine the mysterious monitor. The moonlight streamed into each window, and every corner of the room was conspicuous, and yet I beheld nothing!

The interval was too brief to be artificially measured, between the utterance of these words and my scrutiny directed to the quarter whence they came. Yet, if a human being had been there, could he fail to have been visible? Which of my senses was the prey of a fatal illusion? The shock which the sound produced was still felt in every part of my frame. The sound, therefore, could not but be a genuine commotion. But that I had heard it was not more true than that the being who uttered it was stationed at my right ear; yet my attendant was invisible.

I cannot describe the state of my thoughts at that moment. Surprise had mastered my faculties. My frame shook, and the vital current was congealed. I was conscious only to the vehemence of my sensations. This condition could not be lasting. Like a tide, which suddenly mounts to an overwhelming height and then gradually subsides, my confusion slowly gave place to order, and my tumults to a calm. I was able to deliberate and move. I resumed my feet, and advanced into the midst of the room. Upward, and behind, and on each side, I threw penetrating glances. I was not satisfied with one examination. He that hitherto refused to be seen might change his purpose, and on the next survey be clearly distinguishable.

Solitude imposes least restraint upon the fancy. Dark is less fertile of images than the feeble lustre of the moon. I was alone, and the walls were checkered by shadowy forms. As the moon passed behind a cloud and emerged, these shadows seemed to be endowed with life, and to move. The apartment was open to the breeze, and the curtain was occasionally blown from its ordinary position. This motion was not unaccompanied with sound. I failed not to snatch a look and to listen when this motion and this sound occurred. My belief that my monitor was posted near was strong, and instantly converted these appearances to tokens of his presence; and yet I could discern nothing.

When my thoughts were at length permitted to revert to the past, the first idea that occurred was the resemblance between the words of the voice which I had just heard and those which had terminated my dream in the summer-house. There are means by which we are able to distinguish a substance from a shadow, a reality from the phantom of a dream. The pit, my brother beckoning me forward, the seizure of my arm, and the voice behind, were surely imaginary. That these incidents were fashioned in my sleep is supported by the same indubitable evidence that compels me to believe myself awake at present; yet the words and the voice were the same. Then, by some inexplicable contrivance, I was aware of the danger, while my actions and sensations were those of one wholly unacquainted with it. Now, was it not equally true that my actions and persuasions were at war? Had not the belief that evil lurked in the closet gained admittance, and had not my actions betokened an unwarrantable security? To obviate the effects of my infatuation, the same means had been used.

In my dream, he that tempted me to my destruction was my brother. Death was ambushed in my path. From what evil was I now rescued? What minister or implement of ill was shut up in this recess? Who was it whose suffocating grasp I was to feel should I dare to enter it? What monstrous conception is this? My brother?

No; protection, and not injury, is his province. Strange and terrible chimera! Yet it would not be suddenly dismissed. It was surely no vulgar agency that gave this form to my fears. He to whom all parts of time are equally present, whom no contingency approaches, was the author of that spell which now seized upon me. Life was dear to me. No consideration was present that enjoined me to relinquish it. Sacred duty combined with every spontaneous sentiment to endear to me my being. Should I not shudder when my being was endangered? But what emotion should possess me when the arm lifted against me was Wieland's?

Ideas exist in our minds that can be accounted for by no established laws. Why did I dream that my brother was my foe? Why but because an omen of my fate was ordained to be communicated? Yet what salutary end did it serve? Did it arm me with caution to elude or fortitude to bear the evils to which I was reserved? My present thoughts were, no doubt, indebted for their hue to the similitude existing between these incidents and those of my dream. Surely it was frenzy that dictated my deed. That a ruffian was hidden in the closet was an idea the genuine tendency of which was to urge me to flight. Such had been the effect formerly produced. Had my mind been simply occupied with this thought at present, no doubt the same impulse would have been experienced; but now it was my brother whom I was irresistibly persuaded to regard as the contriver of that ill of which I had been forewarned. This persuasion did not extenuate my fears or my danger. Why then did I again approach the closet and withdraw the bolt? My resolution was instantly conceived, and executed without faltering.

The door was formed of light materials. The lock, of simple structure, easily forewent its hold. It opened into the room, and commonly moved upon its hinges, after being unfastened, without any effort of mine. This effort, however, was bestowed upon the present occasion. It was my purpose to open it with quickness; but the exertion which I made was ineffectual. It refused to open.

At another time, this circumstance would not have looked with a face of mystery. I should have supposed some casual obstruction and repeated my efforts to surmount it. But now my mind was accessible to no conjecture but one. The door was hindered from opening by human force. Surely, here was a new cause for affright. This was confirmation proper to decide my conduct. Now was all ground of hesitation taken away. What could be supposed but that I deserted the chamber and the house? that I at least endeavoured no longer to withdraw the door?

Have I not said that my actions were dictated by frenzy? My reason had forborne, for a time, to suggest or to sway my resolves. I reiterated my endeavours. I exerted all my force to overcome the obstacle, but in vain. The strength that was exerted to keep it shut was superior to mine.

A casual observer might, perhaps, applaud the audaciousness of this conduct. Whence, but from a habitual defiance of danger, could my perseverance arise? I have already assigned, as distinctly as I am able, the cause of it. The frantic conception that my brother was within, that the resistance made to my design was exerted by him, had rooted itself in my mind. You will compre-

hend the height of this infatuation, when I tell you that, finding all
my exertions vain, I betook myself to exclamations. Surely I was
utterly bereft of understanding.

Now I had arrived at the crisis of my fate. "Oh, hinder not the
door to open," I exclaimed, in a tone that had less of fear than of
grief in it. "I know you well. Come forth, but harm me not.
I beseech you, come forth."

I had taken my hand from the lock, and removed to a small
distance from the door. I had scarcely uttered these words, when
the door swung upon its hinges, and displayed to my view the interior of the closet. Whoever was within was shrouded in darkness. A few seconds passed without interruption of the silence. I
knew not what to expect or to fear. My eyes would not stray from
the recess. Presently, a deep sigh was heard. The quarter from
which it came heightened the eagerness of my gaze. Some one
approached from the farther end. I quickly perceived the out-
lines of a human figure. Its steps were irresolute and slow. I
recoiled as it advanced.

By coming at length within the verge of the room, his form was
clearly distinguishable. I had prefigured to myself a very different personage. The face that presented itself was the last that I
should desire to meet at an hour and in a place like this. My
wonder was stifled by my fears. Assassins had lurked in this
recess. Some divine voice warned me of danger that at this
moment awaited me. I had spurned the intimation, and chal-
lenged my adversary.

I recalled the mysterious countenance and dubious character of
Carwin. What motive but atrocious ones could guide his steps
hither? I was alone. My habit suited the hour, and the place,
and the warmth of the season. All succour was remote. He had
placed himself between me and the door. My frame shook with
the vehemence of my apprehensions.

Yet I was not wholly lost to myself; I vigilantly marked his
demeanour. His looks were grave, but not without perturbation.
What species of inquietude it betrayed the light was not strong
enough to enable me to discover. He stood still; but his eyes
wandered from one object to another. When these powerful
organs were fixed upon me, I shrunk into myself. At length he

21

broke silence. Earnestness, and not embarrassment, was in his tone. He advanced close to me while he spoke:—

"What voice was that which lately addressed you?"

He paused for an answer; but, observing my trepidation, he resumed, with undiminished solemnity, "Be not terrified. Whoever he was, he has done you an important service. I need not ask you if it were the voice of a companion. That sound was beyond the compass of human organs. The knowledge that enabled him to tell you who was in the closet was obtained by incomprehensible means.

"You knew that Carwin was there. Were you not apprized of his intents? The same power could impart the one as well as the other. Yet, knowing these, you persisted. Audacious girl! But perhaps you confided in his guardianship. Your confidence was just. With succour like this at hand you may safely defy me.

"He is my eternal foe; the baffler of my best-concerted schemes. Twice have you been saved by his accursed interposition. But for him I should long ere now have borne away the spoils of your honour."

AN INCIDENT OF THE YELLOW FEVER PANIC IN PHILADELPHIA

[From "Ormond"]

Adjacent to the house occupied by Baxter was an antique brick tenement. It was one of the first erections made by the followers of William Penn. It had the honour to be used as the temporary residence of that venerable person. Its moss-grown pent-house, crumbling walls, and ruinous *porch*, made it an interesting and picturesque object. Notwithstanding its age, it was still tenable.

This house was occupied, during the preceding months, by a Frenchman. His dress and demeanour were respectable. His mode of life was frugal almost to penuriousness, and his only companion was a daughter. The lady seemed not much less than thirty years of age, but was of a small and delicate frame. It was she that performed every household office. She brought water from the pump and provisions from the market. Their house had no visitants, and was almost always closed. Duly, as the morning returned, a venerable figure was seen issuing from his door, dressed in the same style of tarnished splendour and old-fashioned preciseness. At the dinner-hour he as regularly returned. For the rest of the day he was invisible.

The habitations in this quarter are few and scattered. The pestilence soon showed itself here, and the flight of most of the inhabitants augmented its desolateness and dreariness. For some time, Monrose (that was his name) made his usual appearance in the morning. At length the neighbours remarked that he no longer came forth as usual. Baxter had a notion that Frenchmen were exempt from this disease. He was, besides, deeply and rancorously prejudiced against that nation. There will be no difficulty in accounting for this, when it is known that he had been an English grenadier at Dettingen and Minden. It must likewise be added, that he was considerably timid, and had sickness in his own family. Hence it was that the disappearance of Monrose excited in him no inquisitiveness as to the cause. He did not even mention this circumstance to others.

The lady was occasionally seen as usual in the street. There were always remarkable peculiarities in her behaviour. In the midst of grave and disconsolate looks, she never laid aside an air of solemn dignity. She seemed to shrink from the observation of others, and her eyes were always fixed upon the ground. One evening Baxter was passing the pump while she was drawing water. The sadness which her looks betokened, and a suspicion that her father might be sick, had a momentary effect upon his feelings. He stopped and asked how her father was. She paid a polite attention to his question, and said something in French. This, and the embarrassment of her air, convinced him that his words were not understood. He said no more, (what, indeed, could he say?) but passed on.

Two or three days after this, on returning in the evening to his family, his wife expressed her surprise in not having seen Miss Monrose in the street that day. She had not been at the pump, nor had gone, as usual, to market. This information gave him some disquiet; yet he could form no resolution. As to entering the house and offering his aid, if aid were needed, he had too much regard for his own safety, and too little for that of a frog-eating Frenchman, to think seriously of that expedient. His attention was speedily diverted by other objects, and Monrose was, for the present, forgotten.

Baxter's profession was that of a porter. He was thrown out of employment by the present state of things. The solicitude of the guardians of the city was exerted on this occasion, not only in opposing the progress of disease and furnishing provisions to the destitute, but in the preservation of property. For this end the number of nightly watchmen was increased. Baxter entered himself in this service. From nine till twelve o'clock at night it was his province to occupy a certain post.

On this night he attended his post as usual. Twelve o'clock arrived, and he bent his steps homeward. It was necessary to pass by Monrose's door. On approaching this house, the circumstance mentioned by his wife occurred to him. Something like compassion was conjured up in his heart by the figure of the lady, as he recollected to have lately seen it. It was obvious to conclude that sickness was the cause of her seclusion. The same, it might be, had confined her father. If this were true, how deplorable might be their present condition! Without food, without physician or friends, ignorant of the language of the country, and thence unable to communicate their wants or solicit succour, fugitives from their native land, neglected, solitary, and poor.

His heart was softened by these images. He stopped involuntarily when opposite their door. He looked up at the house. The shutters were closed, so that light, if it were within, was invisible. He stepped into the porch, and put his eye to the keyhole. All was darksome and waste. He listened, and imagined that he heard the aspirations of grief. The sound was scarcely articulate, but had an electrical effect upon his feelings. He retired to his home full of mournful reflections.

He was willing to do something for the relief of the sufferers, but nothing could be done that night. Yet succour, if delayed till the morning, might be ineffectual. But how, when the morning came, should he proceed to effectuate his kind intentions? The guardians of the public welfare, at this crisis, were distributed into those who counselled and those who executed. A set of men,

self-appointed to the generous office, employed themselves in
seeking out the destitute or sick, and imparting relief. With
this arrangement Baxter was acquainted. He was resolved to
carry tidings of what he had heard and seen to one of those persons
early the next day.

Baxter, after taking some refreshment, retired to rest. In no
long time, however, he was awakened by his wife, who desired him
to notice a certain glimmering on the ceiling. It seemed the
feeble and flitting ray of a distant and moving light, coming
through the window. It did not proceed from the street, for the
chamber was lighted from the side and not from the front of the
house. A lamp borne by a passenger, or the attendants of a hearse,
could not be discovered in this situation. Besides, in the latter
case it would be accompanied by the sound of the vehicle, and,
probably, by weeping and exclamations of despair. His employment, as the guardian of property, naturally suggested to him the
idea of robbery. He started from his bed, and went to the window.

His house stood at the distance of about fifty paces from that
of Monrose. There was annexed to the latter a small garden or
yard, bounded by a high wooden fence. Baxter's window over-
looked this space. Before he reached the window, the relative
situation of the two habitations occurred to him. A conjecture
was instantly formed that the glimmering proceeded from this
quarter. His eye, therefore, was immediately fixed upon Monrose's back-door. It caught a glimpse of a human figure passing
into the house through this door. The person had a candle in
his hand. This appeared by the light which streamed after him,
and which was perceived, though faintly, through a small window
of the dwelling, after the back-door was closed.

The person disappeared too quickly to allow him to say whether
it was male or female. This scrutiny confirmed rather than weakened the apprehensions that first occurred. He reflected on the
desolate and helpless condition of this family. The father might
be sick; and what opposition could be made by the daughter to
the stratagems or violence of midnight plunderers? This was an
evil which it was his duty, in an extraordinary sense, to obviate.
It is true, the hour of watching was past, and this was not the district assigned to him; but Baxter was, on the whole, of a generous

and intrepid spirit. In the present case, therefore, he did not hesitate long in forming his resolution. He seized a hanger that hung at his bedside, and which had hewn many a Hungarian and French hussar to pieces. With this he descended to the street. He cautiously approached Monrose's house. He listened at the door, but heard nothing. The lower apartment, as he discovered through the keyhole, was deserted and dark. These appearances could not be accounted for. He was, as yet, unwilling to call or to knock. He was solicitous to obtain some information by silent means, and without alarming the persons within, who, if they were robbers, might thus be put upon their guard and enabled to escape. If none but the family were there, they would not understand his signals, and might impute the disturbance to the cause which he was desirous to obviate. What could he do? Must he patiently wait till some incident should happen to regulate his motions?

In this uncertainty, he bethought himself of going round to the back part of the dwelling and watching the door which had been closed. An open space, filled with rubbish and weeds, adjoined the house and garden on one side. Hither he repaired, and, raising his head above the fence, at a point directly opposite the door, waited with considerable impatience for some token or signal by which he might be directed in his choice of measures.

Human life abounds with mysterious appearances. A man perched on a fence at midnight, mute and motionless, and gazing at a dark and dreary dwelling, was an object calculated to rouse curiosity. When the muscular form and rugged visage, scarred and furrowed into something like ferocity, were added, — when the nature of the calamity by which the city was dispeopled was considered, — the motives to plunder, and the insecurity of property, arising from the pressure of new wants on the poor and the flight or disease of the rich, were attended to, — an observer would be apt to admit fearful conjectures.

We know not how long Baxter continued at this post. He remained here, because he could not, as he conceived, change it for a better. Before his patience was exhausted, his attention was called by a noise within the house. It proceeded from the lower room. The sound was that of steps, but this was accompanied with other inexplicable tokens. The kitchen-door at length opened. The figure of Miss Monrose, pale, emaciated, and haggard, presented itself. Within the door stood a candle. It was placed on a chair within sight, and its rays streamed directly against the face of Baxter as it was reared above the top of the fence. This illumination, faint as it was, bestowed a certain air of wildness on features which nature, and the sanguinary habits of a soldier, had previously rendered, in an eminent degree, harsh and stern. He was not aware of the danger of discovery in consequence of this position of the candle. His attention was, for a few seconds, engrossed by the object before him. At length he chanced to notice another object.

At a few yards' distance from the fence, and within it, some one appeared to have been digging. An opening was made in the ground, but it was shallow and irregular. The implement which seemed to have been used was nothing more than a fire-shovel, for one of these he observed lying near the spot. The lady had withdrawn from the door, though without closing it. He had leisure, therefore, to attend to this new circumstance, and to reflect upon the purpose for which this opening might have been designed.

Death is familiar to the apprehensions of a soldier. Baxter had assisted at the hasty interment of thousands, the victims of the sword or of pestilence. Whether it was because this theatre of human calamity was new to him, and death, in order to be viewed with his ancient unconcern, must be accompanied in the ancient manner, with halberds and tents, certain it is that Baxter was irresolute and timid in every thing that respected the yellow fever. The circumstances of the time suggested that this was a grave, to which some victim of this disease was to be consigned. His teeth chattered when he reflected how near he might now be to the source of infection; yet his curiosity retained him at his post.

He fixed his eyes once more upon the door. In a short time the lady again appeared at it. She was in a stooping posture, and appeared to be dragging something along the floor. His blood ran cold at this spectacle. His fear instantly figured to itself a corpse, livid and contagious. Still, he had no power to move. The lady's strength, enfeebled as it was by grief, and perhaps by the absence of nourishment, seemed scarcely adequate to the task which she had assigned herself.

Her burden, whatever it was, was closely wrapped in a sheet. She drew it forward a few paces, then desisted, and seated herself on the ground, apparently to recruit her strength and give vent to the agony of her thoughts in sighs. Her tears were either exhausted or refused to flow, for none were shed by her. Presently she resumed her undertaking. Baxter's horror increased in proportion as she drew nearer to the spot where he stood; and yet it seemed as if some fascination had forbidden him to recede.

At length the burden was drawn to the side of the opening in the earth. Here it seemed as if the mournful task was finished. She threw herself once more upon the earth. Her senses seemed for a time to have forsaken her. She sat buried in reverie, her eyes scarcely open, and fixed upon the ground, and every feature set to the genuine expression of sorrow. Some disorder, occasioned by the circumstance of dragging, now took place in the vestment of what he had rightly predicted to be a dead body. The veil by accident was drawn aside, and exhibited to the startled eye of Baxter the pale and ghastly visage of the unhappy Monrose.

This incident determined him. Every joint in his frame trembled, and he hastily withdrew from the fence. His first motion in doing this produced a noise by which the lady was alarmed; she suddenly threw her eyes upward, and gained a full view of Baxter's extraordinary countenance, just before it disappeared. She manifested her terror by a piercing shriek. Baxter did not stay to mark her subsequent conduct, to confirm or to dissipate her fears, but retired, in confusion, to his own house.

AN ADVENTURE IN THE WILDERNESS

[From "Edgar Huntley"]

I reached the mouth of the cave. Till now I had forgotten that a lamp or a torch might be necessary to direct my subterranean footsteps. I was unwilling to defer the attempt. Light might possibly be requisite, if the cave had no other outlet. Somewhat might present itself within to the eyes, which might forever elude the hands, but I was more inclined to consider it merely as an avenue terminating in an opening on the summit of the steep, or on the opposite side of the ridge. Caution might supply the place of light, or, having explored the cave as far as possible at present, I might hereafter return, better furnished for the scrutiny.

With these determinations, I proceeded. The entrance was low, and compelled me to resort to hands as well as feet. At a few yards from the mouth the light disappeared, and I found myself immersed in the dunnest obscurity. Had I not been persuaded that another had gone before me, I should have relinquished the attempt. I proceeded with the utmost caution, always ascertaining, by outstretched arms, the height and breadth of the cavity before me. In a short time the dimensions expanded on all sides, and permitted me to resume my feet.

I walked upon a smooth and gentle declivity. Presently the wall on one side, and the ceiling, receded beyond my reach. I began to fear that I should be involved in a maze, and should be disabled from returning. To obviate this danger it was requisite to adhere to the nearest wall, and conform to the direction which it should take, without straying through the palpable obscurity. Whether the ceiling was lofty or low, whether the opposite wall of the passage was distant or near, this I deemed no proper opportunity to investigate.

In a short time, my progress was stopped by an abrupt descent. I set down the advancing foot with caution, being aware that I might at the next step encounter a bottomless pit. To the brink of such a one I seemed now to have arrived. I stooped, and stretched my hand forward and downward, but all was vacuity.

Here it was needful to pause. I had reached the brink of a cavity whose depth it was impossible to ascertain. It might be a few inches beyond my reach, or hundreds of feet. By leaping down I might incur no injury, or might plunge into a lake or dash myself to pieces on the points of rocks.

I now saw with new force the propriety of being furnished with a light. The first suggestion was to return upon my footsteps, and resume my undertaking on the morrow. Yet, having advanced thus far, I felt reluctance to recede without accomplishing my purposes. I reflected likewise that Clithero had boldly entered this recess, and had certainly come forth at a different avenue from that at which he entered.

At length it occurred to me that, though I could not go forward, yet I might proceed along the edge of this cavity. This edge would be as safe a guidance, and would serve as well for a clue by which I might return, as the wall which it was now necessary to forsake.

Intense dark is always the parent of fears. Impending injuries cannot in this state be descried, nor shunned, nor repelled. I began to feel some faltering of my courage, and seated myself, for a few minutes, on a stony mass which arose before me. My situation was new. The caverns I had hitherto met with in this desert were chiefly formed of low-browed rocks. They were chambers, more or less spacious, into which twilight was at least admitted; but here it seemed as if I were surrounded by barriers that would forever cut off my return to air and to light.

Presently I resumed my courage and proceeded. My road appeared now to ascend. On one side I seemed still upon the verge of a precipice, and on the other all was empty and waste. I had gone no inconsiderable distance, and persuaded myself that my career would speedily terminate. In a short time, the space on the left hand was again occupied, and I cautiously proceeded between the edge of the gulf and a rugged wall. As the space between them widened I adhered to the wall.

I was not insensible that my path became more intricate and more difficult to retread in proportion as I advanced. I endeavoured to preserve a vivid conception of the way which I had already passed, and to keep the images of the left and right-hand wall, and the gulf, in due succession in my memory.

The path, which had hitherto been considerably smooth, now became rugged and steep. Chilling damps, the secret trepidation which attended me, the length and difficulties of my way, enhanced by the ceaseless caution and the numerous expedients which the utter darkness obliged me to employ, began to overpower my strength. I was frequently compelled to stop and recruit myself by rest. These respites from toil were of use, but they could not enable me to prosecute an endless journey, and to return was scarcely a less arduous task than to proceed.

I looked anxiously forward, in the hope of being comforted by some dim ray, which might assure me that my labours were approaching an end. At last this propitious token appeared, and I issued forth into a kind of chamber, one side of which was open to the air and allowed me to catch a portion of the checkered sky. This spectacle never before excited such exquisite sensations in my bosom. The air, likewise, breathed into the cavern, was unspeakably delicious.

I now found myself on the projecture of a rock. Above and below, the hill-side was nearly perpendicular. Opposite, and at the distance of fifteen or twenty yards, was a similar ascent. At the bottom was a glen, cold, narrow, and obscure. This projecture, which served as a kind of vestibule to the cave, was connected with a ledge, by which, though not without peril and toil, I was conducted to the summit.

This summit was higher than any of those which were interposed between itself and the river. A large part of this chaos of rocks and precipices was subjected, at one view, to the eye. The fertile lawns and vales which lay beyond this, the winding course of the river, and the slopes which rose on its farther side, were parts of this extensive scene. These objects were at any time fitted to inspire rapture. Now my delight was enhanced by the contrast which this lightsome and serene element bore to the glooms from which I had lately emerged. My station, also, was higher, and the limits of my view, consequently, more ample than any which I had hitherto enjoyed.

I advanced to the outer verge of the hill, which I found to overlook a steep no less inaccessible, and a glen equally profound. I changed frequently my station in order to diversify the scenery. At length it became necessary to inquire by what means I should return. I traversed the edge of the hill, but on every side it was equally steep and always too lofty to permit me to leap from it. As I kept along the verge, I perceived that it tended in a circular direction, and brought me back, at last, to the spot from which I had set out. From this inspection, it seemed as if return was impossible by any other way than that through the cavern.

I now turned my attention to the interior space. If you imagine a cylindrical mass, with a cavity dug in the centre, whose edge conforms to the exterior edge; and if you place in this cavity another cylinder, higher than that which surrounds it, but so small as to leave between its sides and those of the cavity a hollow space, you will gain as distinct an image of this hill as words can convey. The summit of the inner rock was rugged and covered with trees of unequal growth. To reach this summit would not render my return easier; but its greater elevation would extend my view, and perhaps furnish a spot from which the whole horizon was conspicuous.

As I had traversed the outer, I now explored the inner, edge of this hill. At length I reached a spot where the chasm, separating the two rocks, was narrower than at any other part. At first view, it seemed as if it were possible to leap over it, but a nearer examination showed me that the passage was impracticable. So far as my eye could estimate it, the breadth was thirty or forty feet. I could scarcely venture to look beneath. The height was dizzy, and the walls, which approached each other at top, receded at the bottom, so as to form the resemblance of an immense hall, lighted from a rift which some convulsion of nature had made in the roof. Where I stood there ascended a perpetual mist, occasioned by a torrent that dashed along the rugged pavement below.

From these objects I willingly turned my eye upon those before and above me, on the opposite ascent. A stream, rushing from above, fell into a cavity, which its own force seemed gradually to have made. The noise and the motion equally attracted my attention. There was a desolate and solitary grandeur in the scene, enhanced by the circumstances in which it was beheld, and by the perils through which I had recently passed, that had never before been witnessed by me.

A sort of sanctity and awe environed it, owing to the consciousness of absolute and utter loneliness. It was probable that human feet had never before gained this recess, that human eyes had never been fixed upon these gushing waters. The aboriginal inhabitants had no motives to lead them into caves like this and ponder on the verge of such a precipice. Their successors were still less likely to have wandered hither. Since the birth of this

continent, I was probably the first who had deviated thus re-
motely from the customary paths of men.

While musing upon these ideas, my eye was fixed upon the
foaming current. At length I looked upon the rocks which confined and embarrassed its course. I admired their fantastic
shapes and endless irregularities. Passing from one to the
other of these, my attention lighted, at length, as if by some
magical transition, on — a human countenance.

Representative Essays on the Theory of Style

Chosen and Arranged

By WILLIAM TENNEY BREWSTER, A.M.

Adjunct Professor of English in Barnard College, Columbia University

Cloth, 12mo, 354 pages, $1.10 net

The essays are chosen to present the art rather than the history of style or the historical view of the theory of style, and they represent as many points of view as is practicable. The volume contains the essays of De Quincey, Newman, Spencer, Lewes (in "The Principles of Success in Literature "), Stevenson, Pater, and Mr. Frederic Harrison, besides some fragments. There is an introduction dealing with the problem of style, and notes and questions for the aid of the student.

Studies in Structure and Style

Based on Seven Modern English Essays

By WILLIAM TENNEY BREWSTER, A.M.

Adjunct Professor of English in Barnard College, Columbia University. With an Introduction by GEORGE R. CARPENTER, *Professor of Rhetoric and English Composition in Columbia University.*

Cloth, 12mo, $1.10 net

The book is intended to supplement the study of the principles of rhetoric by the systematic analysis of several pieces of modern English prose. The treatment of structure is especially full ; general principles are suggested, and the student is guided to carry out the work of analysis for himself. A bibliography of books on style is added.

"The author has used rare discrimination in selecting the essays which he discusses, insisting that they should be of the highest class of modern literature, and that they should serve as models to the student. The analysis of structure and style in this volume is most able, and the book will be found a most valuable one as a text." — *The Boston Daily Advertiser.*

THE MACMILLAN COMPANY

64-66 FIFTH AVENUE, NEW YORK

Theories of Style

With especial reference to Prose Composition. Essays, Excerpts, and Translations arranged and adapted by LANE COOPER, *Ph.D., Assistant Professor of English in Cornell University.*

Cloth, 12mo, xxiii + 460 pages, $1.10

Words and Their Ways
in English Speech

By JAMES BRADSTREET GREENOUGH

Late Professor of Latin in Harvard University

and GEORGE LYMAN KITTREDGE

Professor of English in Harvard University

Cloth, 12mo, x + 431 pages, $1.10 net

" As valuable as a dictionary and as readable as a vivid piece of narrative or descriptive writing. It is indispensable to every student writer." — *Boston Transcript.*

Exercises in Rhetoric and
English Composition

By GEORGE R. CARPENTER

Professor of Rhetoric and English Composition in Harvard University

Cloth, xiii + 222 pages, $1.00 net

"The text represents the substance of teaching which a freshman may fairly be expected to compass, and it is set forth with a clearness and directness and brevity so admirable as to make the volume seem almost the realization of that impossible short method of learning to write which has often been sought for, but never with a nearer approach to being found. . . . We do not hesitate to give unreserved commendation to this little book." — *The Nation.*

THE MACMILLAN COMPANY

64-66 FIFTH AVENUE, NEW YORK

English Poetry

ITS PRINCIPLES AND PROGRESS, WITH REPRE-
SENTATIVE MASTERPIECES AND NOTES.

By CHARLES MILLS GAYLEY, Litt.D., LL.D.,

Professor of the English Language and Literature in the University of California,

and CLEMENT C. YOUNG,

of the Lowell High School, San Francisco, California.

Cloth, 12mo, $1.10 net

A manual for the general reader who takes an interest in the materials and
history of the higher English poetry, and seeks a simple statement of its
principles in relation to life, conduct, and art. The introduction on "The
Principles of Poetry" aims to answer the questions that inevitably arise
when poetry is the subject of discussion, and to give the questioner a grasp
upon the essentials necessary to appreciation and to the formation of an
independent judgment.

"The Introduction on 'The Principles of Poetry' should be an inspiration to both teacher and pupil, and a very definite help in appreciation and
study, especially in the portion that deals with the 'Rhythm of Verse.'
The remarks on the different centuries, in their literary significance and
development, are helpful, and the notes to each poem, lucid and sufficient."
— HARRY S. Ross, Worcester Academy, Worcester, Mass.

For more Advanced Students

A History of English Prosody

From the Twelfth Century to the
Present Day. In three volumes.

By GEORGE SAINTSBURY, M.A. (Oxon.), Hon. LL.D.
(Aberdeen)

Professor of Rhetoric and English Literature in the University of Edinburgh.

VOLUME I. From the Origins to Spenser.

xvii + 428 pages, 8vo, cloth, $2.50 net

VOLUME II. From Shakespeare to Crabbe.

xvi + 583 pages, 8vo, cloth, $3.75 net

"What strikes one is the sensibleness of the book as a whole. Not merely
for enthusiasts on metrics, but for students of literature in general, it is a
good augury toward the probable clearing up of this entire blurred and
cloudy subject to find Omond's mild fairness and Thomson's telling simplicity followed so soon by this all-pervading common sense. . . . The most
extraordinary thing about this volume is that, unintentionally as it would
appear, the author has produced the one English book now existing which is
likely to be of real use to those who wish to perfect themselves in the formal
side of verse composition." — *The Evening Post, New York.*

THE MACMILLAN COMPANY
PUBLISHERS, 64-66 FIFTH AVENUE, NEW YORK

A History of the Eighteenth Century Literature
(1660-1780)

BY EDMUND GOSSE, M.A.

> Clark Lecturer in English Literature at Trinity College, Cambridge.

Cloth, 12mo, $1.00

Contents : — Poetry after the Restoration ; Drama after the Restoration ; Prose after the Restoration ; Pope ; Swift and the Deists ; Defoe and the Essayists ; The Dawn of Naturalism in Poetry ; The Novelists ; Johnson and the Philosophers ; The Poets of the Decadence ; The Prose of the Decadence ; Conclusion, Bibliography, Index.

OSWALD CRAWFORD, in London Academy :

"Mr. Gosse's book is one for the student because of its fulness, its trustworthiness, and its thorough soundness of criticism ; and one for the general reader because of its pleasantness and interest. It is a book, indeed, not easy to put down or to part with."

The English Poets (Selections)

> With Critical Introductions by various writers, and General Introduction by MATTHEW ARNOLD. Edited by THOMAS HUMPHRY WARD, M.A.
>
> *In 4 vols.   Student's Edition. $1.00 each*

Vol. I. Chaucer to Donne. Vol. II. Ben Jonson to Dryden. Vol. III. Addison to Blake. Vol. IV. Wordsworth to Rossetti.

New York Evening Mail :

"The best collection ever made. . . . A nobler library of poetry and criticism is not to be found in the whole range of English literature."

PUBLISHED BY

THE MACMILLAN COMPANY
PUBLISHERS, 64-66 FIFTH AVENUE, NEW YORK

CPSIA information can be obtained at www.ICGtesting.com
Printed in the USA
BVOW040820250412

288598BV00001B/129/P